WOMEN IN THE FAMILY
AND THE ECONOMY

WOMEN IN THE FAMILY AND THE ECONOMY
AN INTERNATIONAL COMPARATIVE SURVEY

Edited by GEORGE KURIAN and RATNA GHOSH

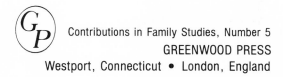

Contributions in Family Studies, Number 5
GREENWOOD PRESS
Westport, Connecticut • London, England

Library of Congress Cataloging in Publication Data
Main entry under title:

Women in the family and the economy.

   (Contributions in family studies; no. 5 ISSN
0147-1023)
   Includes bibliographical references and index.
   1.   Family—Addresses, essays, lectures.
2.   Sex role—Addresses, essays, lectures.
3.   Women—Social conditions—Addresses, essays,
lectures.   4.   Women—Economic conditions—Addresses,
essays, lecutres.   I. Kurian, George.   II. Ghosh,
Ratna.   III.   Series: Contributions in family
studies; no. 5.
HQ518.W57   305.4'2   80-28293
ISBN 0-313-22275-4 (lib. bdg.)

Library of Congress Catalog Card Number: 80-28293
ISBN: 0-313-22275-4
ISSN: 0147-1023

First published in 1981

Greenwood Press
A division of Congressional Information Service, Inc.
88 Post Road West
Westport, Connecticut 06881

Printed in the United States of America

10 9 8 7 6 5 4 3 2 1

Contents

PART II: WOMEN IN THE ECONOMY

Introduction

RATNA GHOSH

This cross-cultural and multi-disciplinary collection of articles on women in family and employment assumes that there are some questions of fundamental importance which can be applied to women across a variety of cultures. Although significant distinctions such as social class, cultural norms and economic structure do exist, the focus of this volume has been rather to explore appropriate indicators and identify similarities and differences relating to the effects of family and employment patterns. The studies are mostly empirical, showing that women everywhere face conflicts of social change in their daily lives. Irrespective of developmental, economic and ideological variations which make life qualitatively different, women around the world face some common problems at home and have some common experiences in employment.

Collectively, the papers in this volume suggest a set of generalizations: that sex-segregation in the work force is a universal phenomenon; that economic strength is related to increased power in the home for women and is therefore related to women's status; but that women's employment means double-work for them; that ideology makes a difference, yet countries with egalitarian philosophies (even socialist ones) have not prevented sex-segregation and overwork for women; that social and structural changes produced by modernization and egalitarian ideologies have not been accompanied by parallel changes in values and attitudes in all aspects.

The effects of modernization, urbanization and industrialization on the position of women have been profound. Yet studies exploring the nature of the interaction of these changes with the status of women have produced contradictory results. Although modernization and urbanization do not result necessarily in sexual equality, several authors have noted a causal relationship between various complex factors related to these phenomena and the emergence of greater power and decision-making roles of women within the family. Studies of industrialization and the impact of increased labor force participation of women on their status have also indicated ambivalent results. Whereas authors have found a strong positive correlation between the economic factor and women's status, male and females are characterized by occupational stratification.

Is biological difference a sufficient explanation for an asymmetrical sexual structure both in the public and private spheres? Not only have men and women been assigned to different spheres of activity but men also have a higher status both at home and in the society at large. Biological differences do not explain status differences. If anything, the female should have a higher status because of her reproductive function. Instead, behavioral differences between the sexes are more reflective of socialization and cultural interpretations of biology. Moreover, men's and women's work are not the same in all societies (Herskovits, 1965; Watson, 1929; Scheinfeld, 1944). In addition, Eleanor Maccoby and Carol Jacklin (1974) point out that there is more variation in performance and capacity within each sex than between sexes. Physiological difference is too simplistic an answer for sexual stratification because it does not explain, for instance, why a higher value is placed on male activities universally than on female work. Women tend to be undervalued and their potentials to be underestimated.

Evidence indicates that prejudice and discrimination have considerable effect on job allocations. Prejudice is the attitude, and discrimination is the overt behavior resulting from covert reactions. Martin (1972:349) points out that they are more than simple social-psychological phenomena because they become incorporated into the social structure and produce unequal rewards. Prejudice and discrimination directed towards women as a group is sexism. In the job market sexism relegates women to the "economic underworld" (Harrington, 1965:26). It operates in two basic ways (Amundsen, 1977:52), first by confining women largely to jobs considered "suitable" to them which also happen to have lower levels of pay and lower prestige. Second, it limits women to the lower positions in the general occupational structure resulting in discrimination not only in matters of pay and rank but also in their being used as a reserve labor force. In the overall range of activities, statistics indicate that women earn half to four-fifths of what men earn. Women's lack of education or training and under-representation in unions does not entirely explain this difference. Myths are perpetuated that women are more emotional than men and therefore cannot make decisions, that they do not like working for other women, that they have greater absenteeism rates—all of which have confining effects on the employment position of women. Marital status for the woman is yet another reason for discrimination, as is the myth that married women represent a temporary work force either because of pregnancies or because of their dependent status. The lesser importance attached to their share of earnings because of the assumed insignificance of their contributions to family income is also used against them. Yet, single women are often thought of as potential candidates for marriage and the stereotypes about married women are projected onto them. So, with regard to marriage in terms of employment women are damned if they do get married and damned if they don't. Several governments have legislated in their Human Rights Codes that marital status questions during offers of employment are discriminatory because civil status has nothing to do with a person's ability to perform a task. The stereotypes regarding married women's lack of enthusiasm and interest in their work and their frequent absences because of family responsibilities (which like other myths have no basis in fact) have nevertheless been reasons for allocating them to less responsible positions and confining them to female employment ghettos. Referred to sometimes as "occupational Balkanization" (Myrdal, 1976:409), this sex-segregation is glaring manifestation of sexism and suggests that not only are women's jobs different but they have lower social esteem and are less valued.

The position of women in the economy has also been analyzed in terms of the caste concept. Myrdal (1944), for example, classifies Negroes as a caste in the United States and draws a parallel with women regarding the disabilities that both groups face. The concept of caste, Andreas (1963:48) points out, best determines how social roles are ascribed rather than achieved, and sex-segregation is a reflection of that. Eichler (1977:53) argues that sexual stratification is more complicated than the rigid vertical ranking of castes because although women are undoubtedly underprivileged in economic, social and political spheres, some women are more privileged than some men. The caste concept appears "too extreme an explanation" (Amundsen, 1971:179), particularly because social class cuts across other barriers.

Theories of social stratification show that women, on their own, have no class status. The class position they obtain (like their names) is derived from their fathers and husbands. But employed women occupy an additional independent status. This is based on criteria such as occupation and education which are used for classifying men, plus the stratifying dimension of sex which has the effect of lowering the woman's independent status. So, the employed woman is double-ranked, but her derived status is always more important than her independent status (Eichler, 1977:59). Two observations can be made about women's position in society. First, because of their derived status women occupy positions in all social classes, but they are under-represented in the upper strata (Eichler, 1977:53; Fogarty, 1971). Second, within each class women occupy a lower position than men because of differences in the power, privilege and prestige of the two groups (Lenski, 1966:74). For employed women this is indicated by their lower average incomes (*Women in the Labour Force*, 1970) and less responsible and prestigious positions (Archibald, 1970). In the case of unemployed women their dependent status makes them occupy lower positions in each stratum.

In his theoretical model of social inequality sociologist Gerhard Lenski (1966) postulates that privilege (status) in society is linked to power. The three sources of power influencing inequality in society, he proposes, are power of property (economic power), power of position and power of force. Applying this paradigm to sexual inequality Blumberg argues that "for women, economic power is the most important influence on their relative equality" with men in their group in terms of basic privileges reflective of their status (1976:19). The difference in status between the sexes and differences in the postions of employed and non-employed women both hinge on economic power. Benston (1969:13) claims that "the roots of the secondary status of women are in fact economic" and points out that women's relationship to the means of production (domestic sphere) is different from that of men's (public sphere). In a society where money determines value, she argues, women's household labor is of less value because it is outside the money economy. Sanday (1973) describes the plight of groups of women who although they did most of the work were treated little better than slaves. So, work in itself does not guarantee power or status. For employed women who do participate in the money economy the lower social value and esteem resulting from sex-segregation in the occupational sphere, as discussed above, and the marginality attributed relegate women's work to lower economic worth.

Several theories of sexual and social stratification, Marxist and non-Marxist, have identified economic power to be most influential for status differences. Based on the economic factor women's power varies from low to high across societies. And, although there appears to be no society where women have any significant power of position or force (Lenski's two other sources of power), Blumberg (1976:20) observes that when women have greater economic power, the power of force tends not to be used against them. Data show a fairly strong inverse relationship between the economic power of women and wife-beating for instance.

Economic power was found to be the strongest influence on the life options (Blumberg, 1974) which affect a person's power to make decisions regarding one's life and a measure of a person's status across societies. Studies in this volume also suggest links between women's economic power and the emergence of egalitarian marital role prescriptions, increased decision-making by wife, decreased fertility, higher aspirations for children. They also discuss the implications of female employment on marital satisfaction, and the human quality of marriage. With new options opening up for women due to industrialization, and control over reproduction because of technological development, women who are striving to take the advantages of economic independence and its correlate of education find that they work longer and harder now than ever before. The right to work does not forfeit the right to leisure. The two-job syndrome analyzed by Myrdal and Klein in *Women's Two Worlds* (1956) implies a continuing dilemma. The consequences of this, indicated by increasing divorce statistics, show that the traditional family structure must change to accommodate new needs. In a cross-cultural examination of women's status, Sanday's (1973) data suggest that the three crucial aspects in any society's survival are reproduction, subsistence and defense. Since women's reproductive role is very significant (while it may limit their role in defense) and women in addition contribute in varying degrees to income and subsistence, it is clear that new ways of dividing labor and providing social services must be developed. Socialization now emphasizes that value of the home role of women to the extent that even when making significant contributions to family income and facing multiple hardships in the process they nevertheless feel guilty about spending time away from home and family.

This is so because rapid changes in the rate of labor force participation have not been accompanied by parallel changes in social values and attitudes. Egalitarian ideologies undoubtedly, have done much to raise the conscious-ness level of men and women to the need for providing options and struc-tures in rectifying the unjustified position of women in society. Because socialist ideology places a major emphasis on economic factors as the explanation of women's oppression considerable structural supports have been built to incorporate women to the work force. Socialist countries have the largest number of women in the work force and in professions. In other countries with egalitarian philosophies such as some Western industrialized countries government supports have encouraged women to work. Studies here point out, for example, that in Israel and France a large percentage of women work and hold high positions in the occupational structure. Yet in all countries, including socialist ones, sex-segregation is still a reality and women still bear the greater burden of home and employment. Even the Family Code of Cuba, which stipulates joint responsibility of spouses in housework, is not enough because legislation on the behavior of sex-roles must be accompanied by education of males and females towards consider-able attitude change in order to be successful.

The ultimate goal of any society is the good life. The means to this end may differ with ideologies and different development and economic condi-tions but the ideal is to maximize eventually the opportunity for the good life for all. Since women constitute half the population they cannot be over-looked nor can a society afford to ignore their potential reserve of working ability. The solution appears to lie in striking an attractive balance between work and leisure, for all. Is it possible to reconcile a woman's employment with a satisfactory home life? After an international analysis of women in careers Fogarty et al. (1971) point out that the life cycles and career patterns of married women are likely to remain different from those of men because of children (p. 44). It is in the interest of the community, they suggest, to redesign career paths and employment practices in working out to the best advantage changes in social and family life of men and women brought about by a married women's employment commitments (pp. 468-469). In examining the family life of highly qualified women, they found that although it takes considerable skill and effort to do so it is possible to adjust a wom-an's high level career with a satisfactory family life and for the husband to be happy in his own career and in the family, and that there is no reason why the dual-career pattern should be detrimental to children (p. 510).

Married or single, women represent a potential reserve of talent and it is in the best interest of society to utilize it. With increasing recognition of human rights, and social justice, the social and cultural barriers to broader and varied roles for women may not be as restrictive in the future as they have been in the past.

Many of the restrictions are in attitudes towards women's work at home and the insignificance attached to the problem of double-work. Women do not ask "to be paid for bringing children into the world", but attitudes such that "maternity not bring (women) more economic prejudice than paternity brings men" are very significant (Québécoises: Equality and Independence, 1978:34). Nor do we advocate that women be paid for their housework (although Statistics Canada estimates Canadian women's housework at $80 billion or 35-40 percent of gross national product). This is not only because many would claim that they labor for love. It is also because to do so would discourage women from their contributions in the labor market and, more significantly, it would perpetuate sexist attitudes in the family by consigning housework and child care to women. Attitude changes concern not only proper roles for males and females but, first, outmoded stereotypes. Finally, the roles of men and women are complementary, not competitive, and the issue of education towards attitude change in the family and in employment, which affects the whole of society, may make a large difference in the daily lives of people.

REFERENCES

Amundsen, Kirsten
  1977 A Second Look at the Silenced Majority. Englewood Cliffs, N.J.: Prentice-Hall, Inc.
  1971 The Silenced Majority, Women and American Democracy. Englewood Cliffs, N.J.: Prentice-Hall, Inc.

Andreas, Carol
  1971 Sex and Caste in America, Englewood Cliffs, N.J.: Prentice Hall, Inc.

Archibald, Kathleen
  1970 Sex and the Public Service. Ottawa: Queen's Printer.

Benston, Margaret
  1969 "The Political Economy of Women's Liberation", Monthly Review 21:4.

Blumberg, Rae Lesser
  1976 "Fairy Tales and Facts: Economy, Family, Fertility, and the Female". In Tinker & Bramsen (eds.), Women and World Development. Overseas Development Council.

1974   "Structural Factors Affecting Women's Status: A Cross Societal Pardigm".
       Paper presented at the International Sociological Association Meeting,
       Toronto, Canada.

Eichler, Margaret
1977   "Women as Personal Dependents". In Marylee Stephenson (ed.), *Women
       in Canada*. Don Mills, Ont.: General Publishing Co. Ltd.

Fogarty, M. P., R. Rapoport, and R. N. Rapoport
1977 Sex, Career and Family. London: George Allen & Unwin Ltd.

Harrington, Michael
1963 The Other America. New York: Macmillan.

Herskovits, Melville J.
1965 Economic Anthropology: The Economic Life of Primitive Peoples. New
     York: W. W. Norton.

Lenski, Gerhard
1966 Power and Privilege: A Theory of Social Stratification. New York: McGraw-
     Hill Book Co.

Maccoby, Eleanor and Carol N. Jacklin
1974 The Psychology of Sex Differences. Stanford, Calif.: Stanford University
     Press.

Martin, W. T. and H. L. Poston
1972   "The Occupational Composition of White Females: Sexism, Racism and
       Occupational Differentiation". Social Forces 50: 349-355.

Myrdal, Alva
1976   "Afterword: New Research Directions". In Lynne B. Iglitzin and Ruth
       Ross (eds), Women in the World: A Comparative Study. Santa Barbara,
       Calif.: Clio Books.

Myrdal, Alva and Viola Klein
1956 Women's Two Roles, Home and Work. London: Routledge & Kegan Paul.

Myrdal, Gunnar
1944   The American Dilemma: The Negro Problem and Modern Democracy. New
       York, London: Harper & Bros.

1978 Quebecoises! Equality and Independence. Bulletin, Special Edition 5: 5,
     Governemente du Québec.

Sanday, Peggy R.
1973   "Toward a Theory of the Status of Women". American Anthropologist
       75: 1682-1700.

Scheinfeld, Amram
   1944 Women and Men. New York: Harcourt, Brace.

Watson, W. T.
   1929 "A New Census and an Old Theory: Division of Labor in the Preliterate
         World". American Journal of Sociology 34 (Jan.): 632–652.

Women's Bureau
   1970 Women in the Labour Force. Ottawa: Queen's Printer.

PART I
WOMEN IN THE FAMILY

WOMEN IN THE FAMILY
Introduction

RATNA GHOSH

In order to obtain a full picture of the situation of women in society it is necessary to analyze the domestic sphere in addition to the public sphere. The traditional division of labor which has confined women to the private and domestic sphere affects the life options of women. But this difference in spheres of action by itself does not create asymetrical relations. Rather, it is the lack of social and economic value placed on a woman's domestic role which, by turning it into a private service, creates a situation of oppression. With modernization, women's contribution in the public sphere and the emergence of egalitarian ideologies are having a considerable impact on women's daily lives and family roles. Although there is a trend towards men and women sharing income, household chores and child care, there is nevertheless an unequal sharing of the burden and fewer hours of leisure time for the working woman. The dilemmas in the complexity of women's roles are far from being solved.

The articles in this section deal with women's position in the family. The studies have been clustered around four themes: women's power within the family, social and cultural barriers faced by women in their lives, the impact of religion on women's roles and attitudes towards feminist ideology.

The power to make significant decisions is considered important in family relations. George H. Conklin has made an empirical study exploring power differences within the household in a district in India. Maximum power for women in this sample was associated with urban place of residence, high education for the wife as well as employment for the wife in the urban setting. Comparing his results with those of Blood and Wolfe in their classic study of power within the American family the author concludes that while "competence" determines who has power in both countries, in the Indian context there are, in addition, cultural variables which correlate highly with decision-making. Moreover, the increase of power for women in India is used for making decisions which emphasize a "business alliance" aspect of marriage in contrast to the individualistic assumption of the Western marriage as a quest for fulfillment.

The rise in female-headed families in some Western nations has been a subject of increasing research. In addition to greater employment opportunities for women in countries such as the United States, Sweden and Britain have government assistance programs which give women the option to survive without male support. While female-headed families in developing societies do not have structural supports, they still exist. Carl Kendall presents an analysis of domestic organization in a rural area of Guatemala and challenges E. A. Hammel and P. Laslett's comparative typology of households because they mask the importance of households where women have the power. Although small in number, the instances in which this phenomenon exists is significant in the total picture of household composition. The author found that female heads of households pursue more varied strategies of domestic organization than their male counterparts.

Parental decision-making has been another area of increasing sociological research. On-Jook Lee Kim and Kyong-Dong Kim take a sex-role modernization approach in explaining the pattern of parental decision-making. Of the indirect measures of modernization used, the mother's education was found to be the most influential factor affecting the role of the mother in child-rearing decisions. Urban residence and the fathers's socio-economic status (SES) were significant only in that they worked indirectly through the mother's education. The mother's employment status was found to be an insignificant factor and had a negative impact, if any, but the authors suggest that this could be because more lower SES mothers were employed.

The next four articles concentrate on ways in which cultural and social barriers affect women in their daily lives and achievements. In her study of South Asian women in Montreal, Ratna Ghosh focuses on both intra- and inter-societal pressures faced by this group because of cultural differences with the dominant culture in a complex society. Integration patterns portray an acceptance by South Asian women of some new patterns of behavior and attitudes relatively easily, others with less enthusiasm and still others with resistance. The roles of religion and social class have been analyzed to account for in-group differences.

While many studies have examined the constraints of different aspects of social structure on women, the impact of male-oriented social planning on the formation of community social systems has been a neglected question. Joan Goldstein discusses the serious omission on the part of planners to respond to the specific needs produced by the changing concept of the role of working and non-working women with regard to their interaction in the home and family. She concludes that the present state of community planning greatly limits the degree of mobility potential for women.

Women's alienation as it relates to birth order is the subject of the next study. Aida K. Tomeh examines this aspect among college women in Lebanon. Evidence shows that no significant differences in alienation are found between first-born and last-born children. Of the three aspects of alienation studied, the trend favors low alienation of the oldest child in the family in terms of powerlessness (i.e. they have higher expectations for control of events), and normlessness (i.e. dislike for socially unapproved behavior). On the dimension meaninglessness (the degree to which events in society are seen as complex) results in birth order do not follow a very consistent pattern. The small differences in birth order show that the conditions in society pervade all orders of birth.

Education has been acknowleged to be a key factor in improving the status of women. The barriers which exist in relation to access to educational opportunities and achievement for women have been much discussed. Recognizing the critical importance of education the Government of India has put special emphasis on large-scale educational programs for women. Yet Muslim women continue to be one of the most backward in terms of education. M. Indu Menon identifies social, structural and institutional factors involving the traditional attitude of the Muslim community in India which hinder the educational progress of the women. The four major factors identified were the insistence on religious education, early marriage, seclusion of women and the absence of socially defined occupational roles for women.

The impact of religion, particularly Islam, on the status of women has also been a subject of discussion. Menon points out that although women in Muslim societies in general are educationally backward, Islam attaches great value to education. Peter C. Dodd notes that scholars have maintained that Islam gives wide scope to women's activities in society and the low status of women in traditional Muslim society represents a diversion from the true religious ideals. Dodd questions the oft-assumed effect of Islam as a major determinant of role and status of women in an Arab society. It was found that a sample of Christian and Muslim youth (controlled for education) held similar patterns of role-expectations regarding appropriate behavior for women. However, substantial differences between norms held by males and females indicate that sex makes an important difference in expectation towards women's emancipation.

George Kurian and Mariam John assess the attitudes of rural women of Christian, Hindu and Muslim communities in a village in India. Four areas of cultural practices are analyzed in relation to four independent variables. Religion was not found to be an influencing factor for attitudes except for the item on marriage rituals. Both the generational and educational variables affected the progressive attitudes of respondents.

The women's liberation movement has been reshaping women's roles in Western countries for some time. The last four articles in this section consider the impact of the feminist ideology on attitudes. The article by Roger Gibbins, J. Rick Ponting and Gladys L. Symons explores to what extent new feminist perspectives have penetrated Canadian consciousness and which groups in particular initiate, support or oppose such ideology. It was found that women's rights are a low priority for Canadians and that public opinion towards the condition of women is mixed because both traditional and feminist positions were evident. Women's demonstration of liberalism was not significantly different from that of men's, and Francophone females were found to be the most liberal of all groups. While social roles, positions and cleavages failed to organize opinion on women's issues, liberalism in this regard was positively related with opinions towards other minority groups.

A comparison of feminist attitudes of a sample of French and American women was undertaken by Ludwig L. Geismar, Benedicte Caupin and Neil DeHaan. The greater feminist egalitarianism of the American women seemingly related to the social significance of the liberation movement in the United States. On the other hand, the authors suggest that the fact that French women constituted a larger percentage of professional and technical workers and held more managerial positions could explain their relative lack of discontent. Still, the French women's educational opportunities were in striking contrast to their career opportunities, and French women continue to hold lower paid and less prestigious positions. The two societies showed similarities in orientation in corresponding levels of education and socio-economic situations. However, egalitarian attitudes and action orientation were not found to be strongly interrelated, so that the action orientation of workers in both societies was similar perhaps because of similarities in work situations. Culture and work situation, the authors propose, mediate between attitudes and advocacy of social action.

Monica Boyd examines the reaction of French Canadian and English Canadian Gallup Poll respondents towards female professionals, married women in the work force, the mother role and male dominance in the family, equal opportunity of women and men, and attitude change due to women's liberation. Women in general were found to be more egalitarian than men. French Canadians tended to be more egalitarian in attitudes toward women in the public sector, but more traditional in their attitudes towards working women and husband dominance. The French emphasis on the mother role, Boyd points out, is significant because it appears to reduce labor force participation of married women in Quebec and may be interpreted as being inconsistent with achieving social and economic equality for women.

The last article in this section is a comparative study by Robert R. Bell of views towards marriage among lower-class Negro women in England, the United States, and Trinidad. The English sample showed a higher positive view towards marriage and showed greater egalitarian attitudes towards rights and obligations of marriage. Analyzing their backgrounds the author concludes that values about sexual behavior in marriage are strongly influenced by social class position.

The sociological and anthropological approaches to cross-cultural studies in this section represent traditional and modern societies. The dramatic changes in women's positions are a universal phenomenon. Social, cultural, historical and economic forces contend against wide and rapid changes in women's lives. But the condition of women affects the condition of all in society. And therefore, changes in roles is the problem and responsibility of both men and women, not of women alone.

Cultural Determinants of Power for Women Within the Family: A Neglected Aspect of Family Research

GEORGE H. CONKLIN*

Culture and Power

When Blood and Wolfe (1960) concluded their classic study of power within the American family, they argued that culture is a poor predictor of the observed patterns of decision-making within the family. Rather, they propose that it is necessary to look for the underlying or more "basic" causes of power differences between husband and wife. In place of cultural factors, Blood and Wolfe suggest that "competence" determines who rules the roost. In the American setting they define farm residence, migration, religion, and age or education of the couple as "cultural" variables. These factors were found to have no predictive effect on family power. The authors put it: "The groups which would be expected to be patriarchal are families now or formerly living on farms, immigrant families, old couples, uneducated couples, and Catholic marriages (because of the Catholic advocacy of the patriarchal ideal). However, none of these expectations is confirmed (Blood and Wolfe 1960:24)."

More practical predictors of who has the actual power of making decisions in the family turn out to be the non-cultural or pragmatic sources of power within a marriage. There are: (1) the occupational status of the husband, since the higher the occupational status of the husband, the more his resources; and (2) age, for as couples approach middle-age, the wife becomes more powerful. Women emerged most powerful in families where the overall resources were lowest. Employment for the wife outside the household increases her resources and thus her power in decision-making, as does higher education for the wife. In short, resource theory states that the spouse which has the best resources to contribute to a marriage ends up with the balance of power within the marriage. For Blood and Wolf resource theory is pragmatic, since it is not cultural attributes or ideal-types which determine who rules the roost, but who in practice can contribute most to the family.

Does Culture Predict ?

When Blood and Wolfe discuss what they call cultural attributes as a source of power within the family, they are addressing themselves to the American family

*Department of Anthropology and Sociology, Sweet Briar College, Sweet Briar, Virginia 24595 U.S.A.

system. But do cultural attributes make a difference in cultures other than urban America where traditional ways of life may be more clearly spelled out? It is possible to argue that this would be the case since the reasons labeled by Blood and Wolfe as the "real" factors in determining conjugal power may be important only in a culture which stresses achievement (Rodman 1972). This paper addresses itself first to the question of explaining power differences within the household between husband and wife in a non-Western setting. It is argued that Blood and Wolfe's work is valuable but incomplete when applied to a non-Western family system.

Secondly, however, this paper will re-examine family theory and culture change. Studies of family systems in non-Western settings have often been guided by the work of Goode (1963) and others who predict that social change such as urbanization, education and industrialization is currently in the process of changing family patterns all over the world. Specifically, Goode predicts that urbanization will lead to an increase in the power of women within the family and that the increase in power will be used to exclude close relatives from the household. In the Indian setting, Kolenda (1967) and Gore (1968) also have stressed that increase of power for women within the household will result in fewer joint households since women will desire a life of their own separate from the relatives. Such theory might best be called the "kinship exclusion theory," because it suggests that desire to set up separate nuclear or isolated households is a cultural value which seems to be spreading around the world through the educational and political system. This paper will also test the kinship exclusion theory, and will offer an alternative explanation for what seems to be happening as education increases in an urban population.

Previous Empirically Based Studies of Power and Culture

Cross-cultural studies of family power have been few, and only the work by Straus (Straus and Winkelman 1969; Foss and Straus 1977; Straus 1975, 1977) has attempted to study power within the household empirically in several different settings in India. Straus asked respondents in India and the United States who had the "final say" about a series of decisions within the family. Straus' results have shown that in the cultural context of India, unlike the United States, cultural variations do count in determining power within the household. For example, "husbands in joint households have more power than husbands living apart from their lineal kin (Straus 1975: 147)." But just as in the United States, "middle class husbands have more power than do working class husbands (Straus 1975: 147)", although age does not seem to matter in determining power within the household. Straus' respondents were children of the couples he was interested in studying, but careful analysis prove that his respondents were highly accurate predictors of family power when couples were later observed playing a game called Simulated Family Activity Measurement or SIMFAM (Straus 1977: 1).

Straus has, therefore, established not only that cultural variations do count in a non-Western setting, but also that Blood and Wolfe's technique of questionnaires on who has the "final say" in decision-making within the family is a good tool for ascertaining differences in family power in a non-Western setting.

While Straus has conducted the only large empirically oriented survey of power within the family in India, there are numerous authors who have speculated on the role of culture in determining power within the joint family system. Most authors seem to follow the lead of Gore (1968) who argues that the emergence of the nuclear family ideal of shared decision-making is most likely to be found in couples who have been in contact with Western education. Western education is thought to be the force in spreading egalitarianism also because learning science would tend to destroy traditional rural organization. Urban residence, concludes Gore, would also serve to bring couples closer together because of greater opportunity to see different ways of life. While Gore has limited empirical support for his findings, Straus' work unfortunately did not include any rural residents, and thus cannot shed light on possible urban-rural differences.

Kolenda has also undertaken a sociological analysis of anthropological writings about the family power in India. Kolenda has developed numerous criteria in her effort to explain why some areas of India seem to have fewer joint households compared to others. In particular, she has argued that various customs support joint household living, and when these customs are present, the power of women will decrease. Any increase in power for women, she finds, will result in increased separations of fathers from sons. Kolenda predicts women will be more powerful if a dowry is not paid, if there is no village exogamy or if there is considerable distance between the residences of the husband and wife's family (Kolenda 1967: 204-205). Although not one of the variables explicitly mentioned, the "modern" family practice whereby a bride and groom have at least been consulted about their marriage should also increase the power of women within the household.

Measuring Power Within the Household in Rural India

The studies by Straus, Gore and Kolenda were familiar to the author when decisions were made about how to measure decision-making power within the family in a rural and urban setting in India, as was Blood and Wolfe's methodology and conclusions about the American family. However, administering a questionnaire to a group of families, many of whom are illiterate, requires that elaborate questions be avoided. Further, items selected for decision-making have to be applicable to all social-strata, not just well-to-do. In order to fulfill these criteria, it was decided to ask each head of household currently living with his wife, "Who has the 'final say' about the following decisions in your family?" For example, each head of household was asked: "Who has the 'final say' about the purchase of the daily ration?" A total of six questions on "final say" were asked (see Table 1). Each of the six questions was also a decision a family in both urban and rural areas would have to face. Each respondent was asked for three alternatives: 1. if the husband alone made the decisions; 2. if it was shared equally between husband and wife; or 3. if the wife alone made the decision. The questions were scored with an 0 if the husband alone made a particular decision,

Table I   MEAN RESPONSES FOR SIX QUESTIONS ON DECISION-MAKING
                                                          WITHIN THE HOUSEHOLD

	Who has the "final" say about:	
	Internal Decision-Making	Mean
1.	Purchase of the daily ration	.58
2.	What kind of a sart to buy	1.18
3.	How much money to save or spend	.48
	External Decision-Making	
4.	Going to visit a festival	.44
5.	If your wife should seek work outside the home	.37
6.	How much education the son should get	.32
	Each question scored as follows:	Score
1.	Husband alone makes the decision or decision made by other person	0
2.	Husband and wife equally share decision	1
3.	Wife alone decides on what to do	2

a 1 if it was shared, and 2 if the wife alone made the decision. The result was
the construction of a "female power scale" (Conklin 1973a). Because the
questions were administered orally, a more elaborate set of responses was not
possible. However, most respondents had little trouble in quickly deciding into
which category to put themselves.

The Survey

The questionnaires containing the six questions of decision-making within the
household were administered to a total of 766 villagers of Dharwar district,
Karnataka State, India, selected at the rate of 1 in 6 from lists of all villagers
drawn up for the purpose. Urban Dharwar was sampled from a list of households compiled for a random sample being given by the Institute of Economic
Research, Dharwar in the spring of 1969. A total of 382 households were interviewed in the city. All interviewing was conducted from February to July of
1969. Only those men who were heads of households and were currently living
with their wives were asked the questions of decision-making. The questionnaire
also contained information about household composition, income, education and
the other factors which might influence decision-making.

Unlike Blood and Wolfe and Straus, however, the responses to the questions
on decision-making were factor analyzed to check for unidimensionality. It was
discovered that the six questions fell into two groups. Questions 1 to 3, relating
to daily decision-making practices internal to the family clustered together; while
questions 4 to 6, with reference to events outside the daily routine, fell into a
second group. For brevity, questions 1 to 3 will be labeled the "internal decision-
making scale"; questions 4 to 6 make up the "external decision-making scale."
Within each scale each question receives equal weight. An individual household
thus has two power scores with a possible low of 0 and a high of 6 on each.

After formal interviewing was completed, the head interviewer returned to several sample households to collect some open-ended statements on how decision-making was accomplished. Each head of household was asked how the purchase of the last sari bought by the family was made. Three examples serve to contrast some of the patterns observed:

1. Case 1310, a man of 44 with 8 living children and over 12 years of formal education reported, "I myself purchase saris for my wife because she does not go to the market. Nor does my wife say a single word about the pattern or colour she wants. Whatever I purchase, she wears."

2. Case 1031, an illiterate coolie who lives with his mother reported, "My wife goes along with my mother and purchases the sari of her choice. It is my mother who decides the price."

3. Case 1332, is that of a professional man who lost his mother when he was only 15. His wife is a teacher. He reported, "My wife is fully in charge of picking clothes for us. She even chooses all my clothes. I do not like to go shopping."

Although the purchase of a sari is often a shared decision (Table 1, item 2), it is also quite clear that a wide variety of patterns exist in how a sari is purchased. Case 1310 and 1332 represent extreme cases, with the remaining example probably coming very close to a middle-class American family. Case 1031 is also a good example of how decision-making often takes place among those living with relatives in a joint household setting. The wife is given a choice of saris, but how much to spend is left to the elder woman of the household.

Measuring the Consequences of Power within the Household

It is possible to establish that there are some households where men dominate the decision-making and others where the women are more powerful. But having established that a variety of patterns exists ignores the question of the possible consequences of decision-making within the family. For example, would a household where the wife was a strong decision-maker spend its money differently from a household where the husband was very powerful? It was therefore decided to go beyond the previous efforts on decision-making within the household by adding questions on possible household expenditures. At the end of the schedule, after all other questions were completed, we asked each respondent, "Let us assume someone gave you Rs. 100 as a gift. How would you spend it?" Following were four forced-choice alternatives. "I would spend the money on:

1. Purchase of a buffalo or improving the house;

2. Purchase of new clothes or improving the house;

3. Paying fees for a son's education or improvement of the house;

4. Improvement of the house or a marriage feast."

Although there are no previous studies to help predict the responses, we hypothesized that in households where women were strong on decision-making men would more often respond that a purchase of interest to the wife would be made. We felt that this would mean: 1. new clothes would be favoured over home repair improvement; 2. that money would go for household needs rather than tuition; 3. that a marriage festival would take preference over the house; and 4. the house would take precedence over the purchase of a buffalo because a buffalo represents a business investment. Irrespective of our original guesses as to how answers might be given, however, was the feeling that differences in household decision-making powers must result in some measurable cousequences either one way or the other. We were, therefore, interested not only in the correlates of possible differences in household decision-making, but also in the consequences of power differences within the household.

Analysis of Results

The results of the survey are presented here using Multiple Classification Analysis. MCA analysis is an extension of analysis of variance, and greatly simplifies the presentation of a complex data series since the mean in a MCA table is adjusted not only for the independent variables but also for significant covariates, if any. This means that when examining a MCA table the results can be easily interpreted since the effect of variables on each other has been corrected for.

Although MCA analysis gives the reader a great deal more information than would the usual regression analysis or one-way analysis of variance, it does have limitations. Specifically, the number of variables it is possible to present is limited to five or fewer, while the number of covariates possible to enter into the calculations is also limited to five. Although ten levels of control is sufficient for analysis of even the most complex effects in the survey presented here, it does mean that it is at times necessary to select for presentation only the largest correlates of each scale. Tables 2 through 7 represent one MCA analysis each.

The Socio-Economic Determinates of Power

Table 2 presents the socio-economic correlates of the internal decision-making scale and Table 3 presents the results for the external decision-making scale. Socio-economic correlates considered were: income, percapita income, a wealth-index scale, how many acres owned, education of the husband, education of the wife, place of residence (rural or urban), and whether the household head migrated to the current place of residence. Husband's occupation status was also entered into the analysis. If a correlate was statistically significant, it is included in the MCA tables. If a correlate is not statistically significant, it still may be reported for comparison purposes. For example, in Table 3 education of husband or of wife is not significant, but education of the husband correlates at a higher level than education of the wife. Education of the husband is, therefore, reported for comparison purposes with the other tables.

Table 2 INFLUENCE OF SOCIO-ECONOMIC VARIABLES ON INTERNAL DECISION-MAKING WITHIN THE HOUSEHOLD: A MULTIPLE CLASSIFICATION ANALYSIS OF MEANS
Grand Mean = 2.25

	N	Unadjusted Deviations	ETA	Adjusted for Independents	BETA
1. Place of Residence*					
Village	592	—.26		—.24	
City	300	.51		.48	
			.20		.19
2. Age of Wife*					
—24	162	—.62		—.62	
25—34	317	—.05		—.06	
35—44	239	.34		.30	
45 up	174	.21		.26	
			.19		.19
3. Education of Wife (years)*					
less than 3	782	—.07		—.06	
4—7 years	104	.43		.32	
8 up	6	2.25		2.33	
			.14		.13
4. Income Per Year (rupees)*					
Below 500	85	—.35		—.05	
500—999	248	.13		.36	
1000—2999	411	—.01		—.04	
3000—5999	108	.01		—.43	
6000 up	40	.00		—.58	
			.07		.15
Multiple r					.310

*Statistically significant at the .001 level.

Table 3   INFLUENCE OF SOCIO-ECONOMIC VARIABLES ON EXTERNAL
                          DECISION-MAKING WITHIN THE HOUSEHOLD: A MULTIPLE
                          CLASSIFICATION ANALYSIS OF MEANS
                          Grand Mean=1.12

	N	Unadjusted Deviations	ETA	Adjusted for Independents	BETA
1. Place of Residence*					
Village	598	—.30		—.31	
City	300	.60		.61	
			.33		.33
2. Age of Household Head***					
—24	16	—.31		—.11	
25—34	190	—.17		—.14	
35—44	274	.00		—.01	
45 on up	418	.09		.08	
			.08		.06
3. Education of Household Head***					
(in years)					
less than 3	613	—.10		.06	
4—7 years	232	.13		—.15	
8 up	53	.57		—.05	
			.13		.07
4. Migration of Household Head**					
Enumerated in Place Born	695	—.12		—.05	
A Migrant	203	.42		.16	
			.17		.07
Multiple r					.35

*statistically significant at the .001 level.

**statistically significant at the .05 level.

***not statistically significant, but shown so reader may ascertain absolute values of deviations for comparison with Table 1.

Where is the patriarchal family located? The best correlate of low female power scores is residence in the village (Tables 2 and 3, item 1). In both scales, rural women have significantly less power than do urban women (see also Conklin 1973a). This relationship is the strongest correlate found, and is at odds with what Blood and Wolfe found for the United States. In Dharwar, farm families are far more conservative than urban families.

In agreement with American families, however, is the finding that age increases the power of the wife (Tables 2 and 3, item 2). This is the norm in India, where as the woman gets older and has children, she is given more power. Although this effect is statistically significant only for internal decision-making, its effect would seem similar for both decision-making scores.

Increased education of husband or wife would seem to result in increased power for the wife (Tables 2 and 3, item 3). Increased education in India does seem to have spread the egalitarian ideal. The results are statistically significant only for internal decision-making, however.

High income, however, correlates with a decrease in the power of the wife in internal decision-making (Table 2, item 4). This finding is in agreement with Blood and Wolfe's results for the United States. The higher the income of a family, the less the wife seems to have to say about decision-making within it. There was no correlate with income on the external decision-making scale.

Migration emerged as a significant correlate of an increase in external decision-making (Table 3, item 4). Migration, even when controlled for urban residence (see adjusted means), still is associated with an increase in the power of the wife. Immigrants are less patriarchal than residents, apparently reflecting the fact that a wife on her own, away from her husband's relatives, is able to bargain for and receive more power than would otherwise be the case. This finding supports the prediction by Kolenda that the longer the distance between the native place of husband and wives, the greater the power for the wife.

In the United States Blood and Wolfe found that if the husband had very high occupational status, then he was more powerful within the family. Because in the sample in Dharwar income correlated so highly with occupational status, occupational status is not reported separately. However, as in the United States, husbands with middle-class or better status were also more powerful than would otherwise be expected. This result is statistically significant for internal decision-making.

The socio-economic correlates of power in Dharwar thus presents a mixed picture, when compared to the patterns discovered by Blood and Wolfe in the United States. Unlike the United States, place of residence is very important in India. Education of the wife, independent of the household's income, increases her power a factor in conformity with Blood and Wolfe's resources theory of power. Migration appears to be a significant correlate of power within the family in India, although it was not for the United States. It would seem, in conclusion, that the factors which emerged as significant in India did not contradict the results for the United States. Rather, there seem to be more factors which correlate with family power in India than in the United States.[1]

Other Determinates of Power

Unlike the United States, in India the joint household is culturally sanctioned. Although it has little effect on external decision-making, living in a joint household decreases the power of the wife on internal decisions (Tables 4 and 5, item 1). This finding confirms the results of Straus in Bombay, as well as virtually all authors who have speculated on the role of the joint household in India. The reader should note that the effect of the joint household is rather slight compared to the larger magnitude of the urban-rural difference.

Items 2, 3 and 4 in Tables 4 and 5 were included in the survey to test Kolenda's summary of the anthropological literature. If the husband and wife are from the same village or city, Kolenda predicted that household power scores would reflect the distance to the wife's natal place. In villages where the wife marries a male within the village, power would be greater for the wife since she has lived there longer and gets support from her kin. The data show it matters little if husband and wife are from the same village or not.

Kolenda also felt that a dowry would influence power scores. Her specific prediction was that a dowry would reduce a woman's power since she had to purchase a husband. Also, dowry is often associated with the prohibition of divorce (Kolenda 1967:179). In Dharwar, however, it is interesting to note that dowry did have an effect on power, but not that predicted. In the Dharwar region the Lingayats believe dowry to be worng, so few men admit to a dowry. Those who do, however, are more likely to be less powerful in decision-maketing. While the correlate for internal decision-making virtually disappears when adjusted for coveriation (chiefly the urban-rural difference), the effect on external decision-making remains even when adjusted. Local residents will argue that a dowry protects a wife since it must be returned if she leaves. This is supported by the data here, at least to the point that it appears that a husband who is faced with returning a dowry seems to have less power over his wife.

The last cultural pattern to be examined is that of consultation with the couple before marriage takes place (Tables 4 and 5, item 4). As with dowry, however, the so-called "modern" practice of consulting with the bride before marriage actually results in a lowering of power for the woman. Why this should be probably rests on the report of one informant who said that men who are naturally dominant insist on seeing the bride first. Those men who let relatives arrange the

---

[1]The reader should note that urban-rural residence is classified by Blood and Wolfe as a "cultural" factor. Please see Table 8 for the complete list. In this and in the following tables, no factor emerged which contradicted the results of Blood and Wolfe for the United States. Rather, many factors not significant in the United States emerged as significant in the cultural context of India.

Table 4   CULTURAL INFLUENCES OF INTERNAL DECISION–MAKING
                                     WITHIN THE HOUSEHOLD: A MULTIPLE-
                                     CLASSIFICATION ANALYSIS OF MEANS
                                                          Grand Mean = 2.25

	N	Unadjusted Deviations	ETA	Adjusted for Independents	BETA	Adjusted for Independents + Covariates[1]	BETA
1. Household Type							
Nuclear	464	.15		.16		.14	
Transitional	224	—.13		—.18		—.06	
Joint	194	—.20		—.18		—.27	
			.09		.10		.09
2. Wife's Native Place***							
Same as spouse	194	—.10		—.08		—.15	
Different	688	.03		.02		.04	
			.03		.02		.05
3. Dowry**							
None	819	—.03		—.03		.00	
Some	63	.44		.43		.05	
			.07		.07		.01
4. Arranged Marriage*							
No consultation	746	.07		.08		.06	
Some consultation	136	—.40		—.42		—.34	
			.10		.10		.08
5. Employment of Wife Outside Household***							
No	710	—.02		—.02		—.04	
Yes	172	.08		.07		.18	
			.02		.02		.05
Multiple r					.16		.32

[1]Covariates: age of wife, place of residence, income of the household, education of the wife of
the household head (See Table 1).
* Statistically significant at the .01 level.
** Statistically significant at the .05 level.
***Not statistically significant, but presented to reader can study magnitude of differences from
    the grand mean.
    Definitions: Nuclear: household made up of couple + any of their unmarried children
                  Transitional: nuclear + any other unmarried relative
                  Joint: Two or more related couples

Table 5

CULTURAL INFLUENCES OF EXTERNAL DECISION-MAKING
WITHIN THE HOUSEHOLD: A MULTIPLE-CLASSIFICATION
ANALYSIS OF MEANS
Grand Mean=1.12

	N	Unadjusted Deviations	ETA	Adjusted for Independents	BETA	Adjusted for Independents+ Covariates[1]	BETA
1. Household Type***							
Nuclear	466	—.01		.01		.01	
Transitional	226	.09		.04		.08	
Joint	194	—.08		—.08		—.12	
			.05		.03		.05
2. Wife's Native Place***							
Same as spouse	195	.09		.09		.04	
Different	691	—.03		—.03		—.01	
			.04		.04		.02
3. Dowry**							
None	823	—.06		—.06		—.04	
Some	63	.81		.76		.50	
			.17		.16		.11
4. Arranged Marriage**							
No consultation	750	.05		.05		.04	
Some consultation	136	—.29		—.25		—.21	
			.09		.08		.07
5. Employment of Wife Outside Household***							
No	712	.04		.03		.01	
Yes	174	—.16		—.12		.03	
			.06		.05		.01
Multiple r					.20		.37

[1]Covariates: place of residence, age of household head, education of household head, migration of household head (See Table II).
**Statistically significant at the .01 level
***Not statistically significant, but presented so reader can study magnitude of differences from the grand mean.
Definitions: Nuclear: household made up of couple+any of their unmarried children
  Transitional: nuclear+any other unmarried relative
  Joint: Two or more related couples

marriage are also those who would be more likely to let their wives have their way more often.   Tradition, it can be concluded, can raise, not just lower, the power of woman within the household.

Employment of the wife outside the hosehold is quite common in India. Women, for example, work in the fields along with their husbands.   In the city, educated wives can be seen working in the post office, governmeet offices, banks and in similar jobs.   Does employment outside the household increase a woman's resources and thus her power?   While the data presented here are not quite significant at the .05 level, the answer is generally yes.   Rural women, engaged in traditional occupations such as harvesting, do not appear to have any increase in power for such work.   Urban wives, however, show an increase in power when gainfully employed outside the household (see Table 4, items 5, adjusted for coveriates).   While the results are not spectacular, it is still possible to conclude that gainful employment for the wife outside the household does increase her resources and thus her power, just as Blood and Wolfe found for the United States.

In summarizing the results of the four highly culture-specific factors which the literature predicted would correlate with power within the household, only one of the four (household composition) behaves as predicted in the literature.   Dowry raises a woman's power, while the modern practice of seeing each other before the wedding lowers a woman's power.   It would seem that the trend in the literature to associate "male dominance" with "tradition" is not supported by the research reported here.   Culture patterns can enhance as well as lower the power of a woman within the household.

Consequences of Power for Women

If increased power for women in decision-making has any important consequences, then perhaps no area would be more likely to show change than decisions on how to spend money.   If given Rs. 100 to spend, would husbands whose wives are powerful spend differently from men who asked no one about family decisions The answer, it seems, is yes.   Few men would use an extra Rs. 100 to buy a buffalo (Tables 6 and 7, item 1), but those who would are more powerful within the family.   It would appear that this effect is especially strong in the urban areas where education is highest.   Using contingency tables, and coding the purchase of a buffalo as 1 and household improvement as 2, gamma works out to be +.24. As with any type of correlational analysis, it is impossible to say without reservation that a rise in power for women causes different purchasing patterns within the family, but it certainly does seem resonable to conclude that it is plausable that a change in the power structure of a family will show up in different values being put on different aspects of family purchasing decisions.   Likewise, a rise in a woman's power is associated with her husband's decision to use extra money to purchase new clothes (Tables 6 and 7, item 2).   When a woman is more powerful, the money is more likely to go for new clothes than it is for household repair or improvement.

Item 3 (Tables 6 and 7), whether to spend 100 rupees for school fees was statistically significant only for the external decision-making measure. The stronger the wife, the more likely is the money to go into the house and not into education. Most men would put the money into school fees, but those who would not are those who have less power in their family.

The last query, whether to spend money on a marriage festival, presents contradictory results. Men whose wives have stronger interest in making decisions on events external to the household would put the money into household improvement, while those with interest in internal decision-making would spend the

Table 6   ECONOMIC CONSEQUENCES OF INTERNAL DECISION-MAKING POWER:
A MULTIPLE-CLASSIFICATION CLASSIFICATION OF MEANS
Grand Mean=2.25

		N	Unadjusted Deviation	ETA	Adjusted for Independents	BETA
1.	Purchase of Buffalo**					
	Yes	222	—.30		—.28	
	Improvement of house	664	.10		.09	
				.10		.09
2.	Purchase of New Clothes*					
	Yes	455	.17		.18	
	Improvement of house	431	—.18		—.19	
				.10		.11
3.	School Fees****					
	Yes	811	.03		.01	
	Improvement of house	75	—.37		—.08	
				.06		.01
4.	Marriage Festival***					
	Yes	841	.03		.03	
	Improvement of house	45	—.60		—.55	
				.08		.07
5.	Place of residence*					
	Village	589	—.25		—.28	
	City	297	.50		.46	
				.20		.18
	Multiple r					.25

*Statistically significant at the .001 level.
**Statistically significant at the .01 level.
***Statistically significant at the .05 level.
****Not statistically significant.

Table 7   ECONOMIC CONSEQUENCES OF EXTERNAL DECISION-MAKING POWER:
                 A MULTIPLE-CLASSIFICATION ANALYSIS OF MEANS
                                                        Grand Mean=1.12

	N	Unadjusted Deviations	ETA	Adjusted for Independents	BETA
1. Purchase of Buffalo*					
Yes	221	—.18		— 18	
Improvement of house	671	.06		.06	
			.08		.08
2. Purchase of New Clothes*					
Yes	457	.14		.13	
Improvement of house	435	—.15		—.14	
			.11		.11
3. School Fees**					
Yes	815	—.01		—.04	
Improvement of house	77	.13		.40	
			.03		.09
4. Marriage Festival*					
Yes	847	—.02		—.02	
Improvement of house	45	.46		.44	
			.08		.08
5. Place of Residence*					
Village	595	—.30		—.31	
City	297	.61		.62	
			.33		.34
Multiple r					.37

*Statistically significant at the .001 level.
**Statistically significant at the .01 level.
***Statistically significant at the .05 level.

money on a marriage festival. It might be possible to speculate as to why this would be. Women with a wider world view would be less interested in spending money on social relations, while those whose power lies in the daily decision-making of running a household would find a marriage feast to be supportive of their interests. But given the lack of previous research of the consequences of different patterns of decision-making, these suggestions must be considered only exploratory at this time.

The initial purpose of including questions on the consequences of decision-making in the survey was not so much to test a specific hypothesis as it was to see if different patterns of decision-making power had measurable consequences. It would seem to be safe to conclude that women would have a definite influence on how money is spent in the family if decision-making were to become more egalitarian and less male-centered than is true at the present time.

Perhaps the most interesting finding, however, is the statistically insignificant correlate between increased power for women and household structure. In the villages, the proportion of joint households is identical to that in the city (Conklin 1973b). Even controlling for demographic availability of kin by examining only those households who have a son age 15 or up, there is no statistically significant difference between household composition in the city or the country. Examining correlates of change at the individual level reveals that just because a man is living apart from his father does not mean that his wife is more powerful. Nor were women who were more powerful in their family less likely to be living in a fraternal brother-brother joint household. In fact, as far as the property aspect of the joint family is concerned, the best correlates of increased cooperation among brothers following the death of the father is higher education of the wives (Conklin 1974). Increased power for women in Dharwar is not associated with increase separation of either property or household.

Discussion

While Blood and Wolfe's study in the United States found few correlates with what they describe as "cultural" variables, it would appear that in the Indian context culture variables do correlate highly with decision-making. However, as in the United States, there is also evidence that what Blood and Wolfe call "competence" is also a factor of importance. A summary of factors associated with power in the family in the United States and in India is presented in Table 8. A total of 13 factors are listed. For the United States, six seem to influence power within

Table 8   CHECKLIST OF SOURCES OF POWER IN MARRIAGE COMPARISON
OF THE UNITED STATES[1] AND INDIA[2]

(+ =more power for wife)

"Cultural Attributes"	United States	India
1. Farm families	no effect	strong —
2. Immigrant (U.S.A.); migrant household (India)	no effect	+
3. Religion: (Catholic-Non-Catholic U.S.A.); (Caste India)	no effect	no effect
4. Age of couple: older wives more powerful	+	+
5. Education: husband higher than wife	—	—
6. Joint household	not applicable	—
7. Village exogamy	not applicable	no effect
8. Giving a dowry for marriage	not applicable	+
9. Prior consultation on marriage	not applicable	—
"Pragmatic Sources of Power"		
10. High occupation status for husband	—	—
11. High income	—	—
12. Wife employed outside the household	+	+
13. Higher education for wife (independent of husband)	+	+

[1]Blood and Wolfe (1960), "Cultural" attributes are those used by Blood and Wolfe.
[2]Present survey.

the household, while in India 11 are significantly related to differences in conjugal power.

The best correlate of power differences in Dharwar is rural or urban residence. Low power scores are associated with rural, uneducated women. Yet in lower income rural families women enjoy greater power than in higher income households, a factor which becomes increasingly clear when education is controlled (see Table 2, item 4). The lowest power scores would, therefore, seem to be in rather well-to-do rural households where the wife is not only poorly educated but is also young and living in a joint household. If her husband has had some consultation in the marriage, she would have less power yet. In India it is usually assumed that competence in ruling the household comes with age, and in both India and the United States older wives gain in power.

Maximum power for women in the family in Dharwar is associated with urban place of residence and with high education for the wife. In addition, if the samples are examined separately, employment for the wife in the urban setting is statistically significant in raising her power. As in the villages, older women of moderate income are more powerful in the household than would be young wives.

In comparing the results for India and the United States, it can be concluded that "competence" is a factor to be dealt with in both cultures (see also Straus 1977: 1). Indeed, there is no reason to believe that in any culture competence does not determine who rules the roost to some degree. The main difference between the United States and India would be that in India there are many more statistically significant correlates of power within the household. Joint household living does seem to lower power for women, but other traditional factors such as dowry seem to raise a woman's ability to make her decision stick. In the United States the urban way of life seems to have penetrated the rural areas of the country. In India, a rural-urban difference remains. In India, both culture and competence are important in determining conjugal power, while in the United States marriage seems less constrained by convention and the couple is more likely to solve their differences based on the comparative resources available to each (see also Straus 1977: 3).

Implications of Social Change in India

In an interesting discussion of social change in modern India, Kapur (1973) has observed that over a ten-year period the educated women she has studied have shown an increasing desire for wealth and comfort, rejecting love and individualism as too fragile a base for marriage :

A greater number of them now want above all, to marry for material possessions and material comforts. Marriage for wealth and comfort is gaining ground among the educated Hindu working woman...They consider marriage to be a give-and-take business alliance in which both husband and wife demand certain benefits in return for other benefits that they think they give. (Kapur 1973:246-247).

Marriage, it seems, is too important to be left to love alone.   Other arrangements are necessary, and cooperation with kin, not their rejection, seem to be one way to increase the "business alliance" side of the equation.

Earlier it was pointed out that the structure-functional view that education leads to exclusion of close kin is what might be called the "kinship exclusion theory" of social change.   Kolenda, it was shown, argues that as women gain in power through use of their kin, etc., that they will use that power to separate households, excluding kin; while Goode (1963) has assumed throughout his description of social change and its effects on family life that social change will break up joint households.   That women in India might use increased power in the household to take what Kapur calls a "business alliance" view of marriage seems to have been unanticipated in nearly all of the literature.   Even Kapur, it should be noted, seems skeptical of her findings, stating that her results seem to indicate trouble her informants have had in adapting to modernization.

Increased power for women in Dharwar seems to be accompanied not by kinship exclusion but by kinship accommodation.   It seems to have escaped the sociological imagination to conceive of rising power for women in a non-Western setting resulting in different consequences than did a similar process in the West. Although it is shown here that many of the same pragmatic factors seem to affect the process of decision-making in both India and the United States, as Straus (1977) has so clearly found, the results of these social processes may turn out to be somewhat different.   Rather than reject kin, the urban wife seems to be using her power to patch up relations among brothers (Conklin 1974). Higher education is correlated with greater tolerance in the family, not less.

In many ways, literature on the family and social change deviates from the remainder of the sociological fields.   In most sociological fields increased education is assumed to result in increased tolerance, while for the family, increased education is assumed to be associated with increased intolerance of joint family life.   The research reported here and to a lesser degree the ten-year survey by Kapur seem to indicate that in the Indian setting, increased power for women in the family decision-making process may well result in women using their power to make decisions which emphasize the "business alliance" aspect of marriage, not the individualistic or Western assumption of marriage as a quest for individual fulfillment.   If this is indeed so, then perhaps it will also be possible to say that for the family also, increased education leads to increased tolerance of kin, not to their rejection for an individualistic path in life.   In India, increased power for women seems correlated with kinship accommodation, not kinship rejection.

REFERENCES

Blood, Robert O. and Donald M. Wolfe
  1960   Husbands and Wives: The Dynamics of Married Living. Glencoe: The Free Press.

Conklin, George H.
  1973a   "Urbanization, Cross-cousin Marriage, and Power for Women: A Sample from Dharwar." Contributions to Indian Sociology: New Series 7:53-63.

1973b   "Emerging Conjugal Role Patterns in a Joint Family System: Correlates of Social Change in Dharwar, India." Journal of Marriage and the Family 35 (November): 742-748.

1974   "The Extended Family as an Independent Factor in Social Change: A Case from India." Journal of Marriage and the Family 36 (November): 798-804.

1976   "The Household in Urban India". Journal of Marriage and the Family 38 (November): 771-779.

Foss, Dennis C. and Murray Straus
1977   "Culture, Crisis and Creativity of Families in Bombay, San Juan and Minneapolis." in Louis Lenero-Otero (ed) Beyond the Nuclear Family Model: Cross Cultural Perspectives. Beverly Hills and London: Sage Publications.

Goode, William J.
1963   World Revolution and Family Patterns. New York: The Free Press.

Gore, M.S.
1968   Urbanization and Family Change. Bombay: Popular Prakashan.

Kapur, Promilla
1973   Love Marriage and Sex. Delhi: Vikas Publishing House.

Kolenda, Pauline
1967   "Regional Differences in Indian Family Structure." In Rober Crane (ed) Regions and Regionalism in South Asian Studies: An Exploratory Study. Durham, N.C.: Monograph Number Five of the Duke University Program on Southern Asia.

Rodman, Hyman
1972   "Marital Power and the Theory of Resources in Cultural Context." Journal of Comparative Family Studies 3 (Spring): 50-70.

Straus, Murray A.
1975   "Husband-wife Interaction in Nuclear and Joint Households." In D. Narain (ed)., Explorations in the Family and Other Essays: Professor K.M. Kapadia Memorial Volume. Bombay: Thacker.

1977   "Exchange and Power in Marriage in Cultural Context: A Multimethod and Multivariate Analysis of Bombay and Minneapolis Families." Paper read at the 1977 meeting of the Association for Asian Studies, New York. Reference to author's reprint ╫SC-20.

Straus, Murray A. and Dorethea Winkelmann
1969   "Social Class, Fertility and Authority in Nuclear and Joint Households in Bombay." Journal of Asian and African Studies 9 (January): 61-74.

2 Female-Headed Households and Domestic Organization in San Isidro, Guatemala: A Test of Hammel and Laslett's Comparative Typology

CARL KENDALL*

Introduction

This paper has a twofold task: (1) to question the validity and utility of the household typology of Hammel and Laslett (Hammel and Laslett 1974) and (2) to present a quantitative and qualitative analysis of domestic organization in rural *Ladino* Guatemala.[1] The treatment of female-headed households in Hammel and Laslett's typology is shown to be inadequate for the description of domestic organization in San Isidro, a *Ladino* town in Eastern Guatemala, and raises the general question of the determination and distribution of authority, decision making, and sexual division of labor implicit in such typologies. This is of particular importance because of the generalizations Laslett has drawn from his analysis of domestic change during the Industrial Revolution and its implications for change in domestic organization in societies undergoing industrialization today.

Mestizo or Ladino social organization, in contrast to its indigenous, counterpart, has not been the subject of a great deal of study by anthropologists in Mesoamerica. Strangely enough, it has served significanty in the generation of hypothesis concerning peasants (Beals 1976:759 ff).

As ethnography, the work falls victim to the complaint voiced by Nutini :
Of all the traditional ethnographic categories, none has been more disregarded than social organization, and it is in this area that the ethnography of Mesoamerica is the poorest. (Nutini, 1967:38).

As comparative sociology, notions such as the folk society, (Redfield 1947) the culture of poverty, (Lewis 1959, 1966) and the open and closed corporate community (Wolf 1955) which have been derived from studies of Indian and *Ladino* or *Mestizo* social organization had a great impact (cf. Wolf and Hansen 1972:72 ff.). While such generalizations would seem to demand a sizable data base and some

*Visiting Professor of Anthropology, Facultad de Ciencias Sociales, Universidad del Valle de Guatemala.
[1]Research was conducted with the support of the Wenner-Gren Foundation for Anthropological Research and the University of Rochester, August 1972, August 1973. The American Philosophical Society provided funds for a return to the fieldsite in August 1975. I wish to thank Dr. Alfredo Mendez-Dominguez for his assistance in reading the article and suggesting modifications.

quantitative treatment of traditional ethnographic categories, Nutini notes that the majority of sources :

> ...are fragmentary (that is, they do not contain information in all the major traditional categories of analysis in marriage and the family) and not infrequently superficial and impressionistic. Statistical and census data are conspicuously absent. In a few cases we are presented with only samples (and one may wonder what prevented the investigator from getting complete censuses, say, of the population or households, especially since they were sometimes dealing with small populations of less than 1,000 individuals and 150 to 200 households); while in the majority of cases there is no quantitative information at all. (Nutini 1967:384).

A number of articles and monographs appeared before and have appeared since Nutini's Article (e.g. Foster 1967; Hinshaw 1975; Mendez-Dominguez 1967; Miller 1964; Paul and Paul 1963; Vogt 1969) that deal with some of these issues. This paper attempts to provide such a description of rural *Ladino* Eastern Guatemala.

The Setting

San Isidro is one of twenty *aldeas* or villages in the *municipio* of Esquipulas. The administrative center (*cabecera*) of the *municipio* is Esquipulas, a city of 9,000 inhabitants and goal of the largest pilgrimage in Central America. Esquipulas is located at latitude 14° 33′ 48″, longitude 89° 21′ 06″ in the far eastern section of Guatemala, bordering on both Honduras and El Salvador. San Isidro was, until 1938, considered part of Honduras. However, an arrangement to straighten the boundaries of Honduras and Guatemala, transferred San Isidro to Guatemala and the *municipio* of Esquipulas. San Isidro is located high on the rim of mountains that separate Guatemala and Honduras at an elevation of 1500-2000 metres, and overlooks the *cabecera* (municipal capital) of Esquipulas some 32 kilometres distant.

The ninety-nine houses that constitute the scattered village of San Isidro are distributed along four main trails that intersect a central undeveloped area where a chapel is located. The chapel and surrounding houses form one of a number of clusters of houses but do not constitute a town center.

Each homestead or premises (Laslett 1972:36 ff.) consists of a single house and auxiliary outbuildings. The house is defined by the presence of hearth and is a residence inhabited by a household. The people of San Isidro do not differentiate between a household and a houseful (cf. Laslett 1972:36 ff.).

The information provided below on domestic organization is based on a complete household census carried out by myself and a local assistant in November 1972. A revisit to San Isidro in 1975 revealed some changes in the census that are noted below, but I believe that the variables to be discussed would be little changed.

Distribution of Population by Sex and Age

San Isidro has a population of 519.   The population is evenly divided by sex :

TABLE 1		DISTRIBUTION OF POPULATION BY SEX
Female	50.87%	(264)
Male	49.13%	(255)
Total	100.00%	(519)

and is relatively young :

TABLE II   DISTRIBUTION OF POPULATION BY AGE

Age Cohort	Frequency	Cumulative Frequency
0—1	8.86%	8.86%
1—5	11.94%	20.80%
6—10	17.14%	37.94%
11—15	12.52%	50.46%
16—20	13.10%	63.56%
21—25	7.12%	70.68%
26—30	5.90%	75.86%
31—35	4.04%	79.72%
36—40	5.20%	84.92%
41—45	4.24%	89.16%
46—50	3.85%	93.01%
51—55	1.92%	94.93%
56—60	2.31%	97.24%
61—65	0.77%	98.01%
66—70	0.96%	98.97%
71—75	0.19%	99.16%
76—80	0.57%	99.73%
81	0.19%	99.92%

It is interesting to note that over half of the population is 15 years of age or younger.

The census that this data represents was conducted in November, a time of relative leisure in San Isidro.   No significant migration to find work is evident. Wage labor on large farms outside of San Isidro is not a significant contribution to the income of most households.

A Methodological Excursus

Although Nutini has demanded quantitative treatment of household variables, quantification is impeded by the confusion of household and family, (cf. Bender 1967; Hammel and Laslett 1974:75) and the profusion of terms such as premises, homestead, houseful and cluster that are used to discuss the domestic correlates of consumption, production, reproduction, socialization and co-residence. In addition, domestic units of analysis are often introduced or defined simply as computational aids in census counting. To use them as elements in the intensive analysis of a single society may be unwarranted (cf. Godelier 1975).

It would seem, then that the need to control, especially for comparative purposes, variables related to domestic organization as well as other areas of social life would necessitate the development of a valid set of definitional criteria and procedures for analysis. As Hammel and Laslett note :

> Because of the importance of the family. and household in all societies and at all historical periods, it is essential to be able to make comparisons between varieties of domestic groups. If we wish to comment on the extent to which the household is affected by social change and especially by the process of modernization, industrialization, social mobilization ... it must be clear what would constitute such change. This means knowing how domestic group structure differs from country to country as well as from period to period.
>
> (Hammel and Laslett 1974:73)

Although Hammel and Laslett have attempted to construct such a set of criteria valid for historical and contemporaneous studies, this paper demonstrates that their criteria fails to account for important sources of variation, and actually overlooks the significance of female-headed households.

To demonstrate this point, we will adopt Hammel and Laslett's criteria and procedures for identifying types of households (Laslett 1972; Hammel and Laslett, 1974). It should be noted that Laslett's concern in these works is clearly historical, and his work *The World We Have Lost* (1971) has had a great impact on the perception of the effect of the industrial revolution on domestic organization. However, in a later work, Hammel and Laslett (1974) were eager to stretch their techniques to the comparative analysis of contemporary domestic organization, a usage for which they are not ideal. Laslett recognizes this difficulty in an earlier discussion (Laslett 1972:32).

Laslett notes :

> "it is impossible, in reality, to follow any particular domestic group throughout its developmental cycle from the evidence of only one listing of inhabitants of the community to which it belonged ... in most cases only somewhat insecure inference is possible as to the point in the cycle reached by any particular domestic group at the time of the listing ... it should be clear that in order to demonstrate conclusively the presence of any form of family household as an ongoing feature of the structure of a community, at county

or a cultural area, many observations would be required over an extended period ... But a collection of such individual listings is a collection of still photographs, and they cannot be used as if they were movie strips. The very drawback to the scheme we have adopted serves to bring out a general limitation on our analytic enterprise. We find ourselves for the most part forced to discuss a process as if it were in fact a state."

(Laslett 1972:33-34)

Although this is clearly a problem for studies relying solely on parish registers or census materials, the contemporary analysis of household organization is not so limited. It may be shown, for example, how household types identified by Laslett and Hammel are related to each other through the developmental cycle, or how the assignment of household headship and the rights and duties entailed by that position affect household organization. This has particular relevance for reconstitution studies (see Wall's comments in Laslett and Wall 1972:xii), Whereas Laslett notes how age and transmission of authority within the household from father to son can modify significantly the categorization of a household, sex of household head is an important criterion that is evidently ignored (cf. Smith 1956). Female-headed households are specifically identified in only one category (3d) in the Laslett-Hammel typology, yet they are found in all 5 categories. San Isidro material will show how the sex of the household head can modify both the distribution of household types (See Table III) and the underlying domestic cycle.

Household Composition

In both a normal and a normative sense, the household is a conjugal family unit composed of husband, wife and unmarried offspring occupying a single house.

Table III represents the distribution of household in San Isidro by Hammel and Laslett types (Hammel and Laslett, 1974:96) :

TABLE III	DISTRIBUTION OF HOUSEHOLDS BY LASLETT-HAMMEL TYPES	
Type 1	Solitaries	2
Type 2	No Family	3
Type 3	Single Family Households	72
Type 4	Extended Family Households	17
Type 5	Multiple Family Hosueholds	5

Type 3, the Single Family Household, is the predominant household in San Isidro. This same type contains the single conjugal family unit (CFU) identified by Hammel and Laslett (1974:92). Households that may be classified as Type 3 households include those that contain a married couple or single person with children, and single widows or widowers with unmarried children in which the widow or widower is still the head of family.[2] The preponderance of

---

[2] The use of widow or widower here is curious, What of women or men who survive mates but not spouses?

Type 3 households in San Isidro is reflected in conventional household parameters as well.

TABLE IV   HOUSEHOLD PARAMETERS

Mean Household Size	5.22
M (E) HS[3]	6.32
Mode	5
Maximum	12
Minimum	1
Standard deviation	2.40

Mean household size for San Isidro differs little from Adam's figures for the department of Chiquimula as a whole in 1950 of 4.9 (Adams 1956:136). The predominance of Type 3 households reflects a pattern of neolocal residence as noted by many authorities (cf. Adams 1956:129; Hunt and Nash 1967:255). This residence pattern is initiated as soon as a child is born to an acknowledged couple.

Construction of a separate house and provision of an independent hearth constitutes the final solemnization of a marriage. Prior to this, husband and wife are a satellite household within, usually, the husband's father's house (cf. Adams 1956:130). The birth of a child, or a formal marriage ceremony will often shortly precede partition. Partition initiates the dispersal stage of the household and is often fraught with the kind of tension in San Isidro that Pitt-Rivers notes in Andalusian households (Pitt-Rivers 1958).

The initiation of the dispersal of the household correlated roughly with the average age of parents for first children. Average age of fathers *(qua pater)* for first child was 26.77 years, for mothers it was 20.98 years. This significant signal point in the life cycle of an individual is somewhat older than anticipated. Parental approval, the various expenses required of a householder, coupled with the long engagement favored by villagers, postpones the creation of new households.

Marriage, as recognized by villagers and researchers exhibits multiple forms : villagers may be church married (*casado por la iglesia*), married by civil authority (*casado civil*) or simply cohabiting (*unidos*). 63.47% of all couples are *casados* and 36.52% are *unidos*, representing a relatively high incidence of formal marriage for this region.

Following marriage, the couple will reside with parents of the groom, the parents of the bride, or neolocally. Preference is expressed for patrilocality for men although residence near the bride's family is an important possibility. This residence will be maintained until a child is born, when separate households are

---

[3](cf. Halpern 1972:409, measure B).

created on new home sites.   The dispersed settlement pattern reflects the village concern for protecting fields and avoiding gossip and envy.

TABLE V   TYPE OF FAMILY AND AGE OF HOUSEHOLD HEAD

Type	Mean Age of Household Head
1. Solitary	68.5 (n=2)
2. No family (e.g., siblings)	55.3 (n=3)
3. Simple family	32.4 (n=72)
4. Extended family	55.3 (n=17)
5. Multiple family	51.8 (n=5)

Changes within the household unit from the moment of inception are predicated on a number of factors, not least of which are the chronological and physiological attributes of the household head.   There is a correspondence between the average age of household head for each Hammel-Laslett household type and the developmental cycle :

In Table V as well, Type 3 households are seen as primary elements of the household system.

The distribution of household type by age reveals the modifications to the simple family household that may occur with the increasing age of the household head and the other members of his family.   Six of the total 17 extended family households (Type 4) involved the addition of a youthful grandchild to an aging couple's household, two other cases involved the maintenance in the household of an elderly parent and godparent.   However, the distribution of household Types 1, 2 and 5 is difficult to explain in terms of the developmental cycle. Although the total number of these households is small, and might be due to truly exceptional events within the life histories of these individuals, a more adequate explanation follows.

An important source of variation appears to be households headed by females. A significant proportion of households in San Isidro are female-headed, although this is not reflected in the Hammel-Laslett types.   16 or 16.2% of total households have female heads of households.   Female-headed households seem viable in San Isidro even though a clear division of labor within productive units by sex is stressed.   More importantly, female-headed households constitute a significant proportion of household Types 1, 2 and 5.

TABLE VI   FEMALE HOUSEHOLDS BY TYPE AND PROPORTION OF CATEGORY

Type		Proportion of Total Female-Headed Households	Proportion of Total Type Category
1.	2	.125	all of Type 1
2.	2	.125	.66 of Type 2
3.	6	.375	.083 of Type 3
4.	4	.25	.23 of Type 4
5.	2	.125	.40 of Type 5

While Type 3 female-headed households constitute the largest number of female-headed households, they constitute only a small proportion of total Type 3 households (see Table VI). An explanation of the position of Type 1,2 and 5 household types in San Isidro depends largely on understanding female-headed households.

TABLE VII   AGE OF HOUSEHOLD HEAD IN FEMALE-HEADED
                                              HOUSEHOLDS BY TYPE

Type	Average Age
1	68.5
2	52.5
3	38.2
4	54.5
5	54.5

Cursory examination of the data in Table VI reveals that female-headed households of Type 3 are underrepresented, and that types 1, 2 and 5 female-headed households constitute a significant proportion of these categories in the community.

An examination of the actual households further substantiates the point. Female-headed households comprise the entire Type 1 category of solitary house-holds. In the two cases reported in Table VI, the women are elderly widows, mothers of large families who still reside in San Isidro. Their houses are near the houses of offspring who assist in cooking and chores, but the women maintain separate households. Their resistance to incorporation stems from a desire for their children's welfare; mothers-in-law being no more popular in Guatemala than popular wisdom would have them in European tradition, and the alternative residential opportunity for the elderly with successful offspring seems to be re-moval to Esquipulas or other nearby towns where "living is easy". Solitary living perhaps represents a strategy of maintaining close family ties without proving burdensome. It is a strategy, however, only tenable for females. Even if the differential mortality of males versus females due to illness and homicide did not account for the absence of solitary male households, males could not maintain their own households because "men can't cook".

2/3 of the Type 2 No Family households are composed of female-headed household.   One involves the household in figure 1.

Figure 1   Single female and adopted godchild

The elderly female who might otherwise be living alone or with a grandchild has taken in a godchild (one of four such cases in San Isidro).   Generally such children assist in chores or carry messages, but many male and female informants contend that houses sound empty and sad without the noise generated by children. Parents regularly send a child to visit solitary females (as this anthropologist's wife quickly discovered) and if regular visiting with grandchildren is not possible, elderly couples or single females may arrange to 'adopt' a grandchild or godchild[4].   The second household is represented in figure 2.

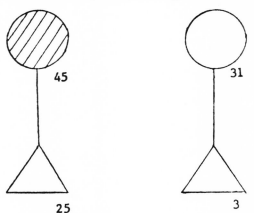

Figure 2   Co-resident females and offspring

[4]Adoption is a separate legal arrangement that must be duly authorized.   The status of a godchild and foster child that is not a blood relative of the adopting parent are different.

Two unrelated females appear to be co-resident in this household, but there is some evidence to suggest that the female head's son is cohabiting with the female border, and therefore, that this household as well as the household in Figure 1 should be classified in some other way. It could be classified as a Type 4, again anomalous, or as two Type 3 households co-resident in the same homestead. The latter is not a serious possibility because of the informal conjugal relationship that might exist and the fact that both females share one hearth. Actually the household represented in Figure 1 is a possibility only for females, since solitary males cannot maintain households. Figure 2 represents the special arrangement single or widowed mothers may have with adult children. The household represented in Figure 2 reflects an uneasy truce between filial and conjugal responsibilities, on the part of the mother and her son, and the need that mothers with small children have for conjugal support.

Type 4 households constitute the second largest type of female-headed households. These female-headed households are successful ventures, even when women are generally proscribed from work in the fields. Some women do plant and harvest, either their own fields or jointly with their husbands, but many with cash incomes hire laborers to plant and harvest and thereby avoid the mild derision of their neighbors. The incorporation of adult children in these households is the strategy these older female household heads utilize (cf. Smith 1963).

2′5 of all Multiple Family Households were female-headed. These households did both contain resident daughters and their off-spring: the conjugal additions in both households were daughters-in-law. Unlike male-headed multiple households such housholds are relatively permanent. More significantly, one of the male-headed multiple households was formed by the addition of a daughter, her children and son-in-law who were in the process of separating. The daughter had moved in with her natal family at the inception of domestic difficulties and the son-in-law visited and provided support. This is another strategy, common in many societies that female-headed simple families may pursue.

The distribution of male-headed household types is represented in Table VIII.

TABLE VIII

Type	Number	Proportion of Male-Headed Category
1. Solitaries	0	0
2. No family	1	.012
3. Simple	66	.7952
4. Extended	13	.1566
5. Multiple	3	.0361

Table VIII expresses most clearly the domestic norm of San Isidro household organization. Although the total number of affected female households is too small to make a powerful argument at this point, it does appear both in a qualitative and quantitative sense that female-headed households must alter the pattern of domestic organization both because of the options available to them in organization, and the needs for support entailed by female headship. A cursory examination of the parameters of total household types, i.e, male and female-headed, does not reveal the units of the domestic cycle, nor the special arrangements necessitated by female headship.

It is unusual that the question of matrilocal stem families, which has generated an enormous literature for decades, should be completely hidden within the Laslett-Hammel typology. Certainly, the question of the economic impact on domestic organization discussed by Laslett in *The World We Have Lost* must consider not only crude changes in total size of domestic groups but also changes to the right-and duty bearing statuses, the etiquette and the effective elements internal to the family itself. Household headship in many societies reflects these changes.

Although the number of female-headed households in San Isidro is small, and the independence of each female-headed household as a unit of production in several cases is difficult to determine, female heads of households do pursue more varied strategies of domestic organization than their male counterparts. In addition, the variation among female-headed households is greater. This variation within female-headed households makes it difficult to delineate a developmental cycle for female-headed domestic groups. Such a cycle must account for 'stem' matrilocal households and solitary female households, which must be part of the total domestic cycle of male and female headed household.

For other families, the conjugal family unit initiates the phase of expansion of the domestic cycle, and although the simple household is usually formed by young spouses, the conjugal family unit may be reinitiated at many points in an individual's life cycle. Widowed, divorced or separated males attempt to remarry as long as they have means for indpendent support; many widowed, separated or divorced females without adult children do remarry. This accounts for the relatively small percentage of Type 3 households among female-headed households.

Extended and multiple families occur in the phase of expansion as children mature and marry and a household's labor force and productive capacity must be adjusted. The late age of first marriages effectively guarantees that an individual will spend most of his life as a member of a Type 3 family. With maturity additional personnel, family or inmates may be added to a household, including in marrying daughters-in-law. Briefly, the family will appear a Type 5 household, but return to Type 4 until all children depart. Finally the family enters a period of replacement. Male and female parents become incorporated in their children's family, or females maintain solitary households.

Although the number of female-headed households in each type is small it does appear that female-headed households significantly modify the total picture of household composition in San Isidro. The Laslett-Hammel typology masks the importance of these households. That the intensive analysis of a single com-

munity should reveal difficulties with Hammel and Laslett's grid is only to re-
assert the primacy of first-hand data and holistic interpretation in the search for
comparative method (cf. Firth 1972:18).

REFERENCES

Adams, R.N.
    1956   *Encuesta sobre la cultura de los ladinos en Guatemala.* Guatemala, Editorial del
            Ministerio de Education Publica.

Beals, R.L.
    1976   Anthropology in Contemporary Mexico. In J. Wilkie *et al.* (eds.). *Contemporary
            Mexico* Berkeley: University of California Press. 753-768.

Bender, D.
    1967   A Refinement of the Concept of Household: Families, Co-residence, and Domestic
            Functions. *American Anthropologist.* 69, 493-504.

Douglas, M.
    1974   Symbolic Orders in the Use of Domestic Space. In P. Ucko *et al.* (eds.). *Man,
            Settlement and Urbanism.* Cambridge (Massachusetts): Schenkman Publishers.
            513-521.

Firth, R.
    1967   *Elements of Social Organization.* Boston: Beacon Press.

Flannery, K.V.
    1976   The Early Mesoamerican House. In K.V. Flannery (ed.). *The Early Mesoamerican
            Village.* New York: Academic Press.

Foster, G.M.
    1967   *Tzintzuntzan: Mexican Peasants in a Changing World.* Boston: Little, Brown and
            Company.

Glick, P.C.
    1947   The Family Cycle. *American Sociological Review.* 12, 164-173.

Godelier, M.
    1975   Modes of Production, Kinship and Demographic Structures, in M. Bloch (ed.)
            Marxist Analyses and Social Anthropology. New York: John Wiley and Sons.

Goody, J.R. (ed.)
    1958   *The Developmental Cycle in Domestic Groups.* Cambridge: University Press.

Halpern, Joel M.
    1972   Town and Countryside in Servia in the Nineteenth Century, Social and Household
            Structure as Reflected in the Census of 1863, *in* Laslett and Walls (eds.) Household
            and Family in Past Time (cited below).

Hammel, E.A. and P. Laslett
    1974   Comparing Household Structure Over Time and Between Cultures. *Comparative
            Studies in Society and History.* 16, 73-109.

Hinshaw, R.E.
    1975   *Panajachel: A Guatemalan Town in Thirty-Year Perspective.* University of Pittsburgh
            Press.

Laslett, P.
    1971   *The World We Have Lost.* 2nd ed. Charles Scribner's Sons.

Laslett, P.
    1972   Introduction: The history of the family, *in* P. Laslett and R. Wall. *Household and
            Family in Past Time.* Cambridge: University Press. 1-89.

Laslett, P. and R. Wall
  1972   *Household and Family in Past Time.* Cambridge: University Press.

Lewis, Oscar
  1959   *Five Families: Mexican Case Studies in the Culture of Poverty.* New York: Basic
          Books.
  1966   *La Vida: A Puerto Rican Family in the Culture of Poverty-San Juan and New York.*
          New York: Random House.

Mendez Dominguez, A.
  1967   *Zaragoza: Laestratificacion social de una comunidad ladino guatemalteca.* Guatemala:
          Tipografia Nacional.

Miller, F.C.
  1964   Tzotzil Domestic Groups. *Journal of the Royal Anthropological Institute.* **94,**
          172-182.

Nutini, H.S.
  1967   A Synoptic Comparison of Mesoamerican Marriage and Family Structure. *South-
          western Journal of Anthropology.* 23, 383-404.
  1968   *San Bernadino Contla.* Pittsburgh: University Press.

Pitt-Rivers, J.
  1958   Ritual Kinship in Spain. *Transactions of the New York Academy of Sciences.*
          11, 423-31.

Redfield, R.
  1947   The Folk Society. *The American Journal of Sociology.* 52. 293-308.

Smith, R.T.
  1956   *The Negro Family in British Guiana.* London: Rouledge & Kegan Paul.
  1963   Culture and Social Structure in the Carribbean: Some Recent Work on Family and
          Kinship Studies. *Comparative Studies in Society and History.* 6, 24-45.

Stern, L.
  1973   Intra-Household Movement in a Ladino Village of Southern Mexico, *Man* (n.s.)
          83, 393-415.

Vogt, E.Z.
  1969   *Zinacantan.* Cambridge, Massachusetts: The Belknap Press.

Wolf, E.R.
  1955   Types of Latin American Peasantry: A Preliminary Discussion. *American Anthropo-
          logists.* 57, 452-471.

Wolf, E.R. and E.C. Hansen
  1972   *The Human Condition in Latin America.* New York: Oxford University Press.

3   A Causal Interpretation of the Effect of Mother's Education and Employment Status on Parental Decision-Making Role Patterns in the Korean Family*

ON-JOOK LEE KIM**
KYONG-DONG KIM***

Parental decision-making behavior has been rather extensively studied in family sociology. The main focus has been on the nature of hierarchical or "power" relationships within the family. Findings of these studies, however, have been inconsistent, leaving room for theoretical reformulation and methodological reconsideration (Safilios-Rothschild, 1970; Buehler et al., 1974).

The major methodological difficulty has been the problem of operationalizing the concept of family power structure in that decision-making behavior in itself may not measure validly the phenomenon so complex as power structure (Wrong, 1968; Safilios-Rothschild, 1970). One way of avoiding this conceptual-operational ambiguity is to consider decision-making behavior simply as a dimension of parental (conjugal) sex role pattern. One parent's relatively active role in certain spheres of family decision may not necessarily measure his/her relative power but simply a degree of role differentiation between the mother and the father.

Despite various attempts at theoretical explanation of differential sex roles reflected in decision-making behavior, not all of the empirical findings have supported any one hypothesis over the other alternatives (Safilios-Rothschild, 1970; Buehler et al., 1974). In fact, little effort has been exerted thus far to employ techniques that may render some meaningful causal interpretation.

This study, therefore, is an attempt to test some of the major theoretical assumptions of the existing schools with the aid of a causal model and thereby to suggest the advantage of sex-role approach to the phenomenon of decision-making behavior in the family.

I. Theoretical Issues

The prevalent and competing "theories" of family power structure or authority relationship are threefold. One of the earliest explanations for the base of

*Our special thanks are due to Professor Edward C. Devereux, Jr. for his critical comments and valuable suggestions on the earlier version of this work from which this particular paper was derived. Also, we are indebted to the following friends for their invaluable assistance in data collection in Korea: Professors Jae.Un Kim, Bom Mo Chung, Sung Jin Lee, and Hwa Jung Kim.
**Duke University
***Seoul National University

family power was offered by Blood and Wolfe (1960) in what has been known as the "resource theory." Their basic argument is that relative resources and competence controlled by each spouse is the most important basis of relative power in the family. Heer (1963), debating this argument, suggested the so-called "theory of exchange". Among other factors, he emphasized the discrepancy between actual and expected return under an alternative to the existing marriage or family as the determining factor.[1] Rodman (1967), noticing very inconsistent empirical findings to-date, proposed a reformulation in his "theory of resources in cultural context." This takes into account the prevalent cultural ideologies about power distribution in the family.

More recently, Centers and his associates (1971) have examined the effects of control of valued resources, personality of spouses, and their relative competence and involvement in family decisions, only to find inconclusiue results. They have, therefore, suggested the possible importance of cultural factors, with Rodman, and role patterning developed in each family in regard to decision-making (1971:277).

Our position is pretty much in line with what Centers and his associates have suggested, but we are in a position to test their ideas. First of all, parental decision-making behavior will be considered as an aspect of sex-role pattering in the family. Secondly, we will test, though indirectly, the effect of socioeconomic conditions and cultural-normative orientations of the society at large on such sex-role patterning within the family. We claim that this is particularly appropriate for explaining changing family sex-role patterns in a society like Korea undergoing a rapid rate of societal transformation accompanying industrialization and urbanization. The basic assumption underlying this view-point is that modernization is affecting the change in sex-role patterns "uniformly in the direction of equalizing the status of woman with that of men" (Seward and Williamson, 1970:19).

In order to examine this assumption, we will use several indirect measures of "modernization," namely, rural-urban residence as an indicator of urbanization, SES as a measure of status mobility instigated by industrialization, and mother's education and labor participation as an indication of her modernizing orientation directly affecting her role in family decision-making. The general research question, then, will be : "what happens to sex-role differentiation between the father and the mother in family decision-making, with the impact of mother's education and occupational involvement in the context of urbanization and upward status mobility ?" More specific hypothetical propositions will be laid out latter.

Rural-Urban Residence : With special reference to conjugal power, Blood and Wolfe (1960) found that the husband in farm families, where a patriarchal tradition would be expected to operate, did not have substantially more power

---

[1] Heer (1963:139) of course suggested five possible bases of family power: external social control, the prior internalization of norms, discrepancy between actual return and return expected under an alternative to the existing marriage or family, relative competence of spouses, and relative involvement.

than in the average family. Heer (1963) suggested that tradition as external control may be weaker in industrial society than in a closely knit rural society. Vermeulen (1970) noted that the father with a traditional family ideology tends to have more power in the Greek family. Even though the actual findings are contradictory, the basic assumption here is that rural families will be more tradition-oriented and urbanization will be a modernizing agent.

The traditional sex role pattern in the Korean family typically was father-dominant or patriarchal and highly differentiated (Kim, 1964; Choi, 1966). But recent studies have indicated substantial departure from this tradition in the direction of equalizing the status of the wife relative to the husband. Furthermore, these studies have concluded that the proportion of families in which both father and mother share family and child-rearing decisions is much higher in urban than in rural families, where father-dominance is still quite strong (Lee, 1960; Koh et al., 1963; Kim, 1969).

Socioeconomic Status : Blood and Wolfe (1960) in their resource theory argued that spouses' familial behavior is greatly influenced and regulated by their relative resources—education, occupation, income and to a lesser extent, social participation. This was based on the evidence provided by Wolfe (1959:108), which supported the assumption that husbands "who are generally successful and prestigeful will have more power and will therefore derive more authority in the home than husbands who are less successful."

Centers and associates (1971) replicated the Blood and Wolfe study and generally confirmed the hypothesis, with some notable exceptions in regard to the effect of education and occupation on family power scores. On the other hand, Safilios-Rothschild (1969) found that wives with college educated husbands reported approximately equal frequencies of egalitarian, husband-dominated, or wife-dominated decisions, and the same pattern was true when they had more education than their husbands. Komarovsky (1967) reported that uneducated and unskilled husbands who earned less money enjoyed more decision-making power than more educated, skilled and higher wage earners.

Contrary or mixed findings are not confined to the United States. Studies in Greece (Safilios-Rothschild, 1967; Vermeulen, 1970) and Yugoslavia (Burin and Zecvic, 1967) reported a significant negative correlation between the father's occupation and education or social status and the extent of his decision-making power. Feldman (1967) found in Ghana that uneducated men and women reported more husband-dominated decision-making than the educated respondents. Other studies in Europe (Safilios-Rothschild, 1970; Michel, 1967) indicated no significant variation in decision-making power by the husband's occupation or education. And a recent five-culture study by Buehler and associates (1974) shows mixed results on the effect of education in family power.

Although findings do not support his argument consistently, Heer (1963:138) earlier offered a different explanation in terms of his exchange theory. Elaborating the possible psychological mechanism involved in the process of decision-making, the alternative to marriage is a crucial factor affecting the degree to which woman is willing to take the risk of endangering the marriage itself by asserting himself too much. Thus, a woman who marries a higher SES man would not exert more power.

Studies from Korea have largely produced results indicating similar tendencies found in Greece and Yugoslavia. That is, parents with higher SES tend to share decisions more frequently than lower SES parents, indicating the declining role of the father (Lee, 1960; Koh et al., 1963; Kim, 1969).

Mother's Education : The same goes for the effect of mother's education, and details of the studies need not be repeated here. According to our formulation, better educated mothers will be found to be more active in family decisions than less educated mothers.

Mother's Employment : Wolfe (1959 : 109) maintained that wives "who are working or have worked outside the home have more power and will derive more authority than wives who have not worked." Some findings have rendered support to this assumption (Blood and Hamblin, 1963; Glueck and Glueck, 1957; Heer, 1958; Hoffman, 1960; Kligler, 1954; Safilios-Rothschild, 1967; Buehler et al., 1974). In the case of Hoffman's study (1960), however, the support appeared in the general sample disappeared in a matched sample. The match was obtained by controlling on husband's occupation, age, and the number of children. Middleton and Putney (1960) found contradicting results to those of Wolfe's while Safilios-Rothschild in her later study (1969) reported that wife's working status did not influence the decision-making pattern. In fact, she noted in her earlier study of the Greek family (1967) that while working wives think they have more say than non-working wives, husbands of working wives do not see any difference. The role of ideology was important in this case.

Again, with these inconsistent results and no clue from Korean family research, we are inclined to believe that mother's employment outside the home would tend to encourage democratic, egalitarian family patterns. As a matter of fact, the traditional Korean families prohibited women from outside involvement including visit to the market or work outside the home. But today's Korean husbands, even in rural areas where we have scanty data, are reported to be more open on this score, not minding their wives' outside activities (Koh et al., 1963), This seems to be a sign of modernization as conceived in our scheme.

II. Data and Instrument

The data were collected in Korea during the summer of 1971. Due to practical limitations, no nationwide representative sample was elicited. But care was used to select three elementary schools in the city roughly representing three echelons of SES and a rural village school about 50 miles away from Seoul, the capital city from which we drew the urban sample.[2] Two sixth grade classes were selected from each school. This was because the larger study of which

---

[2] Sampling was primarily purposive but expert consultation was sought from the Korean Institute for Research in Behavioral Sciences which has not only experience of school children research but contacts with school officials to solicit cooperation.

our survey was an unofficial part used sixth graders.[3] The proportion of boys and girls in each class was roughly 49 to 51. The survey was administered in the classroom in all four schools within a few day's time.

Initially, 740 children answered the questionnaire, but 218 cases had to be dropped because of the absence of one parent from the home due to divorce, death, or lengthy separation. It was considered inappropriate for a study of parental behavior to include families with either parent missing. The use of children's perception as the basis of measuring parental decision-making behavior can be debated. Nevertheless, as will become elear later, we will limit our analysis on the children's perception of parental decision concerning the children's affairs. Furthermore, as Safilios-Rothschild (1970 : 544) has aptly pointed out, decision-making as perceived by the wife, the husband, the children or other family members are most probably very 'significant' variables since it is each person's perceived 'reality' that affects his behavior, the style and quality of interpersonal relationships and, finally, the type of husband-wife and parent-child relationship.

This analysis uses only a small portion of the questionnaire. For parental decision-making behavior, we have used eight items each of which had five-point Likert-type response categories. Four of them dealt with family affairs; for example, decisions about a family picnic, use of family money, seating arrangement at dinner table, and something important which affects the whole family. The other four were on matters related to children; for example, decisions about permission to stay up late or stay overnight at friend's home, about punishment for misbehavior or disobedience, about the purchase of something special and expensive like a bicycle, and about things that children are allowed or not allowed to do.

Each item contained a statement about these matters followed by five response categories ranging from "mostly father decides," through "both parents have say but father's opinion more respected," and "both parents' opinions are equally important," all the way to "mostly mother decides." To construct a scale, each item was assigned a score from 1 to 5 according to the response checked from the alternatives shown above. Using the varimax rotation technique, the eight items were factor analyzed to determine if any of them were measuring the same latent attribute of decision-making. The results are shown in Table 1. Six items stood the test of factor analysis, three of which were on family affairs and the other three on child affairs, all of them obtaining above .60 in factor loadings.

One of the measures derived from this instrument is called the Sex Role Direction (or SR for short hereafter) score, which expresses the relative weight of mothers versus fathers in decision-making. By summing up the three items concerned with decisions in the family affairs in general, we obtain a score which

---

[3] The larger project from which the instrument was adopted for this survey studied sixth graders from all over the world. And this was a project undertaken by the Cornell University Cross-Cultural Studies of Socialization.

TABLE 1   ROTATED FACTOR MATRIX OF EIGHT DECISION-MAKING ITEMS

Item	Factor I	Factor II	Factor III
1. Famil picnic	.072	.629	.326
2. Permission to stay out or stay up late	.772	.019	.108
3. Family money matter	.022	.734	—.278
4. Punishment	.742	.036	—.107
5. Seat arrangement at table	.362	.110	—.657
6. Buying expensive things for child	.392	.129	.662
7. Important family affair	.148	.640	.027
8. Things allowed or not to do	.611	.316	.004
Percent variance	41.77	33.64	24.59

Note : The items in Italics are the ones used for scales.

ranges from 3 to 15, with a midpoint of 9. It should be clear that low scores on this scale indicate the relatively greater weight of the father and higher scores, the increasing importance of the mother, Scores near the scale mid-point of nine indicate that both parents have nearly equal weight in family decisions. A similar scale is obtained by summing the three items concerned with child affairs decision. These two SR scores represent the unilinear, quantitative dependent variables which will be used to test the causal model.

At this point, however, it should be noted that despite the apparently interesting and important comparison that could be made between the two domains of decision-making, i.e., family and child affairs,[4] we had to sacrifice this expedition for the sake of parsimony in view of the kind of involved analysis intended here. In effect, we have performed all the necessary path analyses for both spheres of decision-making. Unfortunately, however, the amount of variance explained by the independent variables was insignificantly small in the case of family affairs SR scores (Appendix A for the completed path model). Therefore, we will confine the analysis to the SR score for child affairs decisions only.

Finally, the independent variables were constructed in the following manner : (1) rural-urban residence in terms of two simple but ordinal categories of rural and urban areas; (2) SES based on a component score of father's education (elementary and below, high school, and college and above) and father's occupation (farm and unskilled blue-collar, skilled blue-collar and white-collar, and

[4] The importance of studying sex role patterns in different dimensions or domains of decision-making has been pointed out by some authors. For example, Wrong (1968:673-674) has aptly put it as follows: "In a stable social relation (where there is recurrent interaction...) a pattern may emerge in which one actor controls the other with respect to particular situations and spheres of conduct—or *scopes*, as they have often been called—while the other actor is regularly dominant in other areas of situated activity (emphasis original)." A comparison of sex role patterns in family and child-rearing affairs domains of decision may have been more interesting but it is spared in this analysis, mainly due to technical problems. But in the larger analysis this has been done extensively.

managerial, professional, and technical), divided into three categories of low, middle and high; (3) mother's education with three categories same as the father's; and (4) mother's employment status with three categories of non-working, part-time employed, and full-time employed.[5]

III. Findings : A Casual Interpretation

On the basis of the theoretical considerations presented above and the measures of variables, we now can proceed with the specific hypotheses and causal interpretation of the effect of mother's education and employment status on SR score in child affairs decisions.

To begin with the separate effect of four independent variables on the dependent variable, SR score for the child affairs domain of decision-making, the following propositions are suggested:

Proposition 1 : "SR score will be higher in urban than in rural families; residence and SR score for child affairs decisions are positively associated."

Proposition 2 : "The higher the level of SES of the family, the higher SR score for child affairs decisions."

Proposition 3 : "The higher the level of mother's education, the higher SR score for child affairs decisions."

Proposition 4 : "The more occupationally involved the mother is, the larger SR score for child affairs decisions."

According to our general research question stated earlier, and on the basis of the above propositions regarding the separate effect of each independent variables we can derive a causal model connecting all the independent variables with the dependent variable. We have assumed that residence and SES are contextual variables representing the degree of urbanization and upward social mobility. Thus, in the causal model, they are considered as exogenous variables. Both of them will be expected to affect the level of mother's education, which in turn will affect the degree of occupational involvement of the mother. The assumed relationships in this flow are all positive. Eventually, then, all these exogenous and endogenous variables are expected to contribute positively to SR score, the dependent variable.

Before we undertake the path analysis, let us examine the four propositions briefly on the basis of the zero-order correlation matrix shown in Table 2. Rural-urban residence, SES, and mother's education are each positively correlated with

---

[5] The frequency distributions for these four independent variables are as follows (N=522, all figures %) :
Rural-urban residence (X_1)...Rural, 16.4%; Urban, 83.6%.
Socioeconomic Status (X_2)...High, 30.4%; Middle, 31.7%; Low, 30.0%; No Response, 7.8%.
Mother's education (X_3)...Elementary and below, 34.6%; High school, 46.7%; College and above, 18.7%.
Mother's employment status (X_4)...Not working, 68.8%; working part-time, 17.0%; working full-time, 14.2%.

SR score at .05 significance level even though the magnitude of coefficients is relatively small. Interestingly, mother's occupational involvement is negatively correlated with SR score and it is statistically significant. Thus propositions 1 through 3 are generally supported but not the fourth proposition. In fact, mother's employment status is negatively associated with all other independent variables as well. The only significant one, of course, is with SES. This is going to require different interpretations but we will put them off until after we complete the path analysis.

TABLE 2   ZERO-ORDER CORRELATION MATRIX OF INDEPENDENT AND
                   DEPENDENT VARIABLES IN THE PATH MODEL (N=522)

	X_1	X_2	X_3	X_4
Residence (X_1)	———			
SES (X_2)	.441**	———		
Mother's education (X_3)	.361**	.605***	———	
Mother's employment (X_4)	—.107*	—.179**	—.073	———
Sex Role Direction (X_5)	.183**	.196**	.195**	.108*

Levels of significance : * .05; ** .01; *** .001; otherwise. not significant.

Because our purpose in the causal analysis is to assess the role of mother's education and occupational involvement in the relationship between residence and SES, and SR score, we will now proceed with specification of a simple recursive model which expresses SR score as a function of contextual variables of residence and SES, and mother's education as the first intervening variable. The equations in this model are:

$$X_3 = b_{31}X_1 + b_{32}X_2 + e_1 \qquad\qquad (1)$$
$$X_5 = b_{51}X_1 + b_{52}X_2 + b_{53}X_3 + e_2 \qquad\qquad (2)$$

where X_1 is residence; X_2 is SES; X_3 is mother's education; X_5 is SR score; and e_1 and e_2 estimated disturbances or the effects of unmeasured variables on the dependent variable in each equation. Figure 1 presents this model.

Note that the interrelationship between residence and SES is simply expressed in zero order correlation and is connected by a curve in Figure 1 instead of a straight line with an arrow. Indeed, they are highly correlated with each other ($r = .441$). And as expected, mother's education is a function of residence and SES with path coefficients of .117 and .554, respectively, with $R^2 = .378$. It is apparent that mother's education is much more significantly influenced by the father's socio-economic status than residence.

Now, as far the entire casual model, however, the amount of variance explained in SR score is meagre 5.7% which is barely significant at .05 level, and path coefficients are fairly small, too. Nevertheless, the direct effect on SR score of residence (beta = .108) is still significant at .05 level and so is that of mother's

Figure 1.   SR Score as a Function of Residence, SES, and Mother's Education

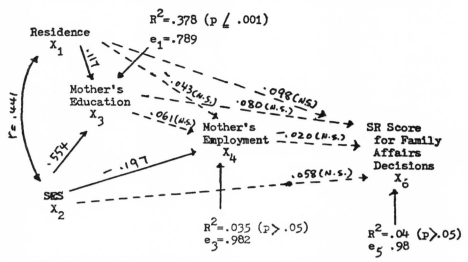

Note :   Insignificant coefficients are indicated by (N.S.) and expressed by dotted line.

education (beta = .104).   In both cases, the indirect effect caused by their correlation with the other two variables in the equation (2) is smaller than the direct effect.   It is SES whose indirect effect (r—beta = .111) is larger than the direct effect (beta = .085 which is insignificant at .05 level) due to its high correlation with residence and especially with mother's education.   At any rate, the role of mother's education is found to be relatively important in mediating between the contextual variables and SR score.   Thus, mother's education may be considered as an influential factor affecting modernization of sex role patterns together with urban residence.

Figure 2 presents a little more elaborate version of the causal model where mother's employment status is specified as an additional intervening endogenous variable.   Here, equation (1) is retained but equation (2) is replaced by equations (3) and (4), as follows:

$$X_4 = b_{41}X_1 + b_{42}X_2 + b_{43}X_3 + e_3 \qquad (3)$$
$$X_5 = b_{51}X_1 + b_{52}X_2 + b_{53}X_3 + b_{54}X_4 + e_4 \qquad (4)$$

Our original assumption was that mother's education, which is affected by residence and SES, influences the degree of mother's occupational involvement which in turn will increase the role of the mother in child-rearing decisions as a modernizing agent.   If this is true,the amount of variance explained in equation (4) should be substantially increased from that of equation (2), by addition of mother's employment as another mediating factor.   Yet, the result shown in Figure 2 indicates only very slight increase in R^2 from .057 to .062.   Again, this is barely significant at .05 level.

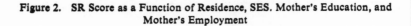

Figure 2.   SR Score as a Function of Residence, SES. Mother's Education, and
Mother's Employment

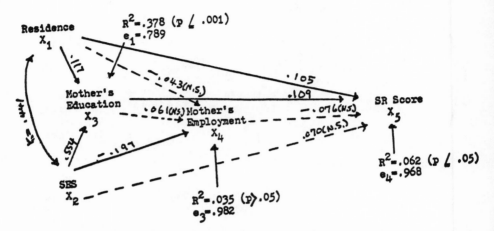

Note :   Insignificant coefficients are indicated by (N.S.) and expressed in broken lines.

How do we interpret this result?   Let us go back to the correlation matrix
presented above.   Mother's employment status was found to be negatively correlated with all other independent and dependent variables, though not all significant.   This is essentially repeated in the causal model shown in Figure 2, except
for its association with mother's education.   One remarkable fact is that the direct effect of SES on mother's occupational involvement (beta = −.197) is greater
than its indirect and direct effects combined (r = −.179).   Of course, the amount
of variance in mother's employment explained by other independent variables is
minimal and insignificant.   And the relative effect of mother's working status on
SR score is insignificant though negative in direction.

It is still residence and mother's education that retain significant relative effect even after mothers' work involvement is introduced in the model.   In fact, the
role of mother's education has increased from equation (2) to equation (4) while
those of residence and SES have been relatively diminished, particularly the latter.
Therefore, one conclusion we ean draw from these observations seems to be that
mother's education as a modernizing agent is the most immediate and relatively
influential factor affecting the role of the mother in child-rearing decisions in the
general context of urbanization which promotes modernization.   Socio-economic
status of the father is not a significant factor in this causal chain except that it
works through mother's education.   And mother's occupational involvement outside the home is not only an insignificant factor but also it has a negative impact
if any.   This negative effect is of course interpreted as a mere reflection of the
fact that more lower-SES mothers tend to work than middle-or upper-SES
mothers.

IV. Discussion

Our main purpose in the study was to provide a causal interpretation of the role of mother's education and occupational involvement in the relationship of rural-urban residence and SES to parental sex role direction in family decision-making, using path analysis. In doing so, we were to test the advantage of a sex role modernization approach to parental decision-making behavior over the other current theories, particularly those of resource and exchange.

The basic reasoning was that urbanization and upward social mobility would improve the level of mother's education and probability of her participation in the labor market. More educated and actively employed mothers would be expected to have greater exposure to modernizing orientations in their role in family decisions in that their role relative to fathers would substantially increase.

According to the resource and exchange theories, this type of causal chain is not easily formulated. For example, to both theories father's SES would increase his relative power in decision-making. In these formulations, however, the effect of mother's education is ambiguous. The resource theory would have to assume that better educated mother should have more say than less educated mother, but it cannot determine how mother's education works relative to father's education if both parents have the same amount of education. According to this reasoning, both families in which both parents have high and low education would tend to be egalitarian in their decision-making behavior. Then, the level of education is reduced to a meaningless variable in itself. Or, take the exchange theory. If the husband's SES including education provides an incentive either to retain or forego the marriage itself on the part of the wife by either refraining from or continuing her aggressive assertion in family decisions, then what exactly is the role of the wife's education? Does it make any difference or is it also wiped out in this argument? Similar arguments can be advanced regarding the role of the mother's employment which involves the role of mother's education in affecting her labor participation.

Perhaps, if these theoretical propositions had been formulated in a more elaborate causal scheme, empirical tests of them might have faired better than they have so far. Note the confusing findings cited earlier. This study in this particular sense alone has provided a beginning of resolving the conflicting results. Moreover, the modernization of sex role approach we propose here reduces the hazard of internal inconsistency within the theoretical argument itself, by pointing the direction of sex role in a consistent fashion.

According to our analysis, it has been firmly established that the level of mother's education is most important in increasing her weight relative to that of the father in decision-making concerning child-rearing matters. Father's SES is only significant by contributing to the role of mother's education, indirectly affecting TR score. The only independent variable with its own direct effect in this chain is the other contextual variable of residence which also contributes to mother's education. The only endogenous variable that has produced contrary results is mother's employment status.

This requires a new interpretation. Our assumption that mother's occupational involvement would increase her relative weight in decision-making is not borne out by the data. Does this, therefore, necessarily mean that our assumption of mother's work outside the home as a modernizing agent is incorrect? By the same token, therefore, is our basic tenet of sex role modernization approach invalidated, as well?

We concede that mother's involvement in the labor market in itself does not constitute modernization. But this can be explained and our modernization of sex role theory can still be advanced. First of all, be reminded of the negative correlations of this variable with all other variables. Second, look at the path eoefficients in Figure 2. More mothers tend to work outside the home in the lower echelon of the society according to our sample. In fact, to some degree there must be relatively more mothers working in rural than in urban area, which is understandable considering the close relationship between residence and SES. The impact of mother's education on her labor participation is ambiguous but not significant anyhow. Thus, what emerges from this picture is that better educated mothers of middle-and upper-SES families in the city tend to be still insulated from active labor participation in the transitional phase of industrialization in a country like Korea, while less educated mothers of lower-SES families even in rural areas may be forced to participate in the labor market out of sheer necessity or the desire to improve their lot even a little bit. This has a dual implication for the role of the mother in family decision-making involving children's affairs. When you are outside working, you are less likely to get actively involved in child-rearing decisions in the first place. And a large proportion of working mothers probably coming from lower SES families and rural families would be less inclined to depart from the traditional mode of father-dominant sex role patterns. On the other hand, the relatively better educated middle-and upper-SES mothers staying home due to the economic and social conditions leaving them out of the labor market might be more inclined to be active in child-rearing matters. After all, they are the ones with more modernized ideas inculcated in them regarding the sex role patterns in the family.

In conclusion, our study has shown at least two things that may be of some importance to family sociology, that is, (1) a sex-role modernization approach can be more useful in explaining the pattern of parental decision-making behavior than some of the existing theories, and (2) a causal interpretation using path analysis technique can shed significant light on some of the theoretically perplexing questions in this area. It should be immoderate and immodest of us if we did not concede that the path model turned out to be far from satisfactory in terms of its size of variance accounted for by the independent variables considered. Further improvement is much desired. But as Duncan has noted, "the contribution of path analysis...does not consist so much in rationalizing calculations of explained variance or in evaluating the 'relative importance' of variables as in making explicit the formulation of assumptions that must precede any such calculations if they are to yield intelligible results" (1970:46).

REFERENCES

Blood, R.O., Jr., and D.M. Wolfe
  1960   Husbands and Wives. New York: Free Press.

Blood, R.O., Jr., and R. L. Hamblin
  1963   "The effect of the wife's employment on the family power structure." Pp. 137-142 in N.W. Bell and E.F. Vogel (eds.), A Modern Introduction to the Family. New York: Free Press.

Buehler, M.H., A.J. Weigart, and D.L. Thomas
  1974   "Correlates of conjugal power: A five culture analysis of adolescent perceptions." Journal of Comparative Family Studies 5 (Spring): 5-16.

Buric, O., and A. Zecevic
  1967   "Family authority, marital satisfaction and the social network in Yugoslavia." Journal of Marriage and the Family 29 (May): 325-336.

Centers, R., B. H. Raven, and A. Rodrigues
  1971   "Conjugal power structure: A re-examination." American Sociological Review 36 (April): 264-277

Choi, Jai-Seuk
  1966   A study of the Korean Family (in Korean). Seoul: Minjung.

Duncan, O. D.
  1970   "Partials, partitions, and paths." Pp. 38-47 in E. F. Borgatta and G. W. Bohrnstedt (eds.), Sociological Methodology. San Francisco: Jossey-Bass.

Feldman, H.
  1967   The Ghanian Family in Transition. Ithaca, NY.: Cornell.

Glueck, S., and E. Gllueck
  1957   "Working mothers and delinquency." Mental Hygiene 41 (July): 327.

Heer D.M.
  1958   "Dominance and the working wife." Social Forces 36:341-347.
  1963   "The measurement and bases of family power: an overview." Marriage and Family Living 25 (May): 133-139.

Hoffman, L.W.
  1960   "Effect of the employment of mothers on parental power relations and division of household tasks." Marriage and Family Living 22 (February): 27-35.

Kim, Kyong-Dong
  1964   "A study of the Confucian values in Korea: content analysis of children's textbooks (in Korean)." Pp. 333-368 in Collection of Papers in Commemoration of Prof. D. Sangbeck Lee on His 60th Birthday. Seoul: Eulyoo.

Kim, On-Jook Lee
  1969   "A study of the family life cycle in urban Korea (in Korean)." Unpublished M.A. thesis. Seoul: Ewha Womans University.

Kligler, D.H.
  1954   "The effects of the employment of married women on husband and wife roles." Unpublished Ph. D. dissertation. New Haven: Yale.

Koh, Whang-Kyung, et al.
  1963   A Study of Korean Rural Family (in Korean). Seoul: Seoul National University Press.

Komarovsky, M.
  1967   Blue Collar Marriage. New York: Random House.

Lee, Hyo-Chai
  1960   "A Sociological study of the households in Seoul (in Korean)," Journal of Korean
            Culture Research Institute 1:9-63.

Michel, A.
  1967   "Comparative data concerning the interaction in French and American Families."
            Journal of Marriage and the Family 29 (May): 337-344.

Middleton, R., and S. W. Putney
  1960   "Dominance in decisions in family: race and class differences." American Journal of
            Sociology 65 (May): 605-609.

Rodman, H.
  1967   "Marital power in France, Greece, Yugoslavia and the United States: a cross-
            national discussion." Journal of Marriage and the Family 29 (May): 320-324.

Safilios-Rothschild, C.
  1967   "A comparison of power structure and marital satisfaction in urban Greek and
            French families." Journal of Marriage and the Family 29 (May): 345-452.
  1969   "Family sociology or wives' family sociology? a cross-cultural examination of decision-
            making." Journal of Marriage and the Family 31 (May): 290-301.
  1970   "The study of family power structure: a review 1960-1969." Journal of Marriage
            and the Family 32 (November): 539-552.

Seward, G.H., and R.C. Williamson
  1970   Sex Role in Changing Society. New York: Random House.

Vermeulen, C.J.J.
  1970   "Families in urban Greece," Unpublished Ph. D. dissertation. Ithaca, N.Y.:
            Cornell.

Wolfe, D.M.
  1959   "Power and authority in the family.". Pp. 99-117 in D. Cartwright (ed.), Studies in
            Social Power. Ann Arbor: University of Michigan.

Wrong. D.H.
  1968   "Some problems in defining social power." American Journal of Sociology 73 (May):
            673-681.

APPENDIX A

SR Score for Family Affairs Decisions as a Function of Residence, SES, Mother's Education, and Mother's Employment

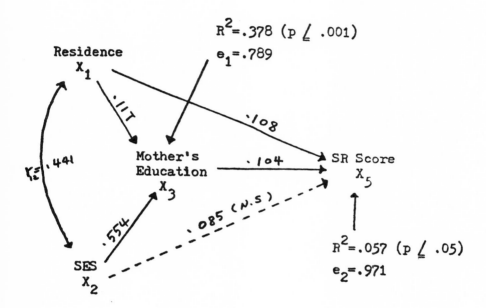

Note : Insignificant coefficients are indicated by (N.S.) and expressed in broken lines

4 Social and Economic Integration of South Asian Women in Montreal, Canada*

South Asian[1] Canadians are a relatively new group but now constitute one of the fastest-growing segments of the Canadian population (Buchignani, 1979:48). While they are still a small group constituting less than 1 percent of the total population, their diversity of values and richness of culture imply a potential contribution to Canadian society.

Canadian society is defined by its government as being bilingual and multicultural. Bilingualism makes English and French[2] the two official languages, and multiculturalism refers to the cultural freedom of all Canadians, confidence in individual identity, respect for others and elimination of discrimination. The British colonial legacy has made the majority of South Asians who go to Canada conversant in English, but they have almost no knowledge of French when they arrive in Canada. Even within the ideal of a cultural mosaic South Asians are often viewed as being culturally too much at variance from other Canadians (Buchignani, 1979:55). Their physical and behavioral differences, and additional differences in personal appearance for women, tend to evoke negative impressions (Naidoo, 1978) for which they find themselves socially isolated. This study of South Asian women and their responses to social and economic aspects of life in a Francophone community in North America was prompted by the dearth of empirical studies on this group of women in Canada, particularly in the French Canadian milieu.

*This research is part of the Minority Education Research Project (MERP) which is funded by the Formation de chercheurs et d'action concertée (FCAC) basic research program of the Quebec Ministry of Education. It is an interuniversity research project located at McGill University's Faculty of Education.

Cette recherche a été entreprise dans le cadre du Projet de Recherche sur l'Education des Minorités (PREM), projet interuniversitaire subventionné par le programme de recherche fondamentale FCAC du Ministére de l'Education du Québec et situé dans la faculté des sciences de l'éducation de l'Université McGill.

[1]The term South Asian is recent. An umbrella term, it refers to a broad category of heterogeneous people originating in the subcontinent of Asia, namely, India, Pakistan, Bangladesh, Sri Lanka and Nepal.

[2]Quebec is a French-speaking province, and its 1977 Language Bill 101 makes French the working language. Quebec is the province in which Montreal is located.

The majority of South Asians are first generation Canadians (except in British Columbia). Their socialization took place in South Asia where the system of beliefs developed during their early years influences their adult lives in Canada. Most of the women went to Canada after they were married, although their husbands may have been in North America longer.

There are significant differences in the socialization patterns of females in South Asia and the Western world. The social and cultural contexts in which their values, attitudes and sex-role ideology are acquired differ. The Western emphasis on the development of individualism is contrary to the South Asian concept of social duty towards family and society. The concept of rights and status is central to women's liberation movements in the West. While there are modernizing trends in South Asia and women are more aware now of access and opportunity, their status consciousness is influenced by the conception of femininity in ancient Indian literature, social and legal treatises which emphasized women's subservience while simultaneously conferring on them esteem and respect—"at once a goddess and a slave" (Basham, 1954:182). The concept of social control of women designed to uphold family honor still pervades social norms, even though industrialization and urbanization have changed considerably the attitudes of women with regard to marriage, employment and personal status. Yet the changes in attitudes remain quite distinct from those of women's liberation in the West, and factors determining women's status in the societies are not the same. Among the currencies by which status is conferred—such as power and love—no one can say which is better, but the opportunity for making decisions on significant matters affecting a person's life has been suggested as a common standard of measurement of freedom and status across societies (Giele, 1977:4).

One aim of this study was to examine the decision-making opportunities with regard to some life options of South Asian women in Canada within the context of the overall issue of the dynamics of acculturation and integration. The basic purpose of the study was to explore the question: How do South Asians view the integration of their women in Canadian society? More specifically, given their educational backgrounds and childhood socialization in South Asia, what are the perceptions of South Asian females and males regarding the behaviors and attitudes of South Asian women towards aspects of social and economic life in Montreal, Canada?

THE STUDY

The data presented here were gathered in the summer of 1979 as part of a larger project. There were two methods of collecting data. First, a structured questionnaire was mailed to 200 husbands and wives of South Asian origin in the metropolitan Montreal region. Subjects were selected on a random basis from a telephone directory of South Asians in Montreal which contained approximately 3,000 names. The 47-item questionnaire consisted of three parts: the first asking for descriptive information of the subject, the second consisting of items on parental background, and the third consisting of items for females regarding their attitudes towards social and economic aspects of life in Canada, with an identical part for males with questions regarding the man's perceptions of women's attitudes. Response to the mailed questionnaire was only 30 percent. Second, the analysis here is based also on thirty in-depth interviews that were carried out during the Fall of 1979. The couples were randomly selected and interviewed in their homes. On the whole, interviewees were very cooperative, and the women seemed especially happy to have an opportunity to verbalize their thoughts.

Description of the sample

Respondents exhibited heterogeneity in most respects. They belonged to various linguistic, regional and religious groups in India. There were respondents from Pakistan and Bangladesh but none from Sri Lanka and Nepal. Of the religions represented 46 percent were Hindus, 46 percent were Muslims, 4 percent were Christians and 4 percent were Sikhs. Most had gone to Canada from cities in India, Pakistan and Bagladesh, some from East Africa (Uganda). The majority were Canadian citizens (75 percent) although more women than men had kept their immigrant status even when they had been in Canada for more than three years.[3]

The majority of the men had been in Canada between 10 and 15 years; the majority of the women had been there less than 10 years, indicating that many of the men had gone back to South Asia to get married. The majority of males and females were in their thirties.

The population distribution of the study sample showed that the socioeconomic backgrounds were of two categories. The larger group was of the middle and upper middle classes in India, Pakistan, Bangladesh and Uganda and were professionals in Canada. A smaller percentage was from the lower middle class. The latter had either left Bangladesh and Uganda as refugees, or had gone via England and were factory workers, mechanics, welders and could be viewed as members of Canada's working class. Educational background of respondents and their parents was taken as the defining factor for class. Due to Canadian immigration policy most South Asians emigrating to Canada between 1965 and 1967 and between 1968 and 1972 were educated professionals (Paul, 1975). Since the Ugandan crisis in 1972, and with recent changes in immigration policy, which though restrictive, indicate a shift in the composition of South Asian immigrants to skilled workers.

[3]An immigrant can apply for Canadian citizenship after three years of residence in Canada.

The educational backgrounds of the respondents and their parents were in two groups. In the larger middle class group all the males had a university education, the females had either a post secondary education or a first degree (some had more). The parents of both males and females in this group showed the fathers as having a post secondary and university education, all the mothers as having some schooling (a few had university degrees). In the working class group, the males either had a high school education or post secondary training. The females also had either an elementary or high school education. Their parents showed fathers' education as ranging from no formal education to high school. The majority of mothers had no formal education, very few had an elementary education.

The majority of the parents were living in their home countries. A few widowed mothers were in Montreal with the respondents (18 percent).

FINDINGS

The following findings are based on the woman's stated view of herself and the husband's stated perceptions on how his wife views herself.

Social Integration

Middle class respondents tended to view the woman's education as the expected thing to do. Women in both classes considered their education to be an asset to being a good wife and mother. Few considered education as a means to economic independence.

Maintenance of cultural identity while adjusting to the demands of cultural life in Canada is an important concern. In terms of overall cultural values and attitudes the majority would like to retain some of its own and adopt some Canadian ones. With the exception of one man's perception of his wife, no one indicated willingness to adopt completely the values and attitudes of Canadian society. Only a few women showed a preference for retaining all their cultural values (9 percent).

The attempt to adjust to a practical problem is evident from ideas towards dress. All respondents said that the women wear both native dress (sarees and salwar kameez) and Western outfits. The majority of the women kept their long hair (60 percent). A few had worn their hair short in their home countries, and the few who cut their hair after they went to Canada said they did so for convenience (16 percent).

Questions on integration in terms of day-to-day eating habits indicated that the few who were vegetarians cooked their native foods. The majority (80 percent) were non-vegetarian and experimented with Western cuisine. Without exception, all Muslim women did not eat pork even when their husbands did. A few women had remained vegetarians. Most non-vegetarian Hindu women and all men in that category ate beef.

Items on freedom and mobility indicated that an overwhelming majority felt freer in Canada than in their home countries. A small number felt as free, and others who felt less free did so because of the lack of domestic help and transportation. The majority did not drive a car. Those who drove did so to go shopping, and they made up part of the small percentage of women who did their grocery shopping on their own. The majority did their grocery shopping with their husbands.

Making friends in a new and unfamiliar environment is not easy. While most women had friends outside their own linguistic groups, about half of them indicated a preference for mixing with members of their own regional group. Relatively few women made friends among their neighbors. An important means of making friends was through their husbands.

Respondents in this sample tended to show a preference for their own cultural activities. Most of them celebrated their religious festivals and participated in native cultural functions. A lot of them saw Hindi or Bengali movies, many of them saw English movies also. None went to French movies. Very few went to English or French theater, Western ballets and dance performances, and Western music concerts. A few went to Oriental dance performances. Most respondents rarely or never went to restaurants; a small number said they went often.

An important area of adjustment is in child-rearing. The task of raising children in South Asia is often shared by several people in the extended family or by domestic help. Most of the families interviewed had either one or two children; some had three; only one had four. Respondents were asked who had the main responsibility of raising children. Both husbands and wives considered child-raising a shared responsibility, although few shared it equally. Some women thought of child-raising as the husband's overall responsibility, but the day-to-day chores related to child-rearing were believed to belong primarily in the wife's domain. The majority of the couples sent their children to English schools and a very few to French immersion classes in English schools. The language spoken at home generally tended to be the mother tongue, and many spoke English as well. Some women could not speak English at all, and very few knew French. Without exception all parents wanted their children to visit their country of origin. With regard to existing or expected conflicts with their children, all Muslim women either had or conceived of problems in food choice. Of the total sample very few perceived of career choice, ways of dress or choice of friends as conflict areas. However, 75 percent considered dating, particularly among girls, as a matter of great concern. As one male respondent put it: "Clinging to old values creates the conflicts which seem to exist in all families of South Asian origin where teenaged children are present."

With regard to the sensitive issue of socializing with the opposite sex, data revealed a definite difference in standard for females. Asked if, when saying hello or goodbye, a Westerner of the opposite sex were to give a kiss, female responses and male perceptions were consistent. Very few women would not mind at all if she or her husband were kissed goodbye. Most would prefer a handshake for both. Several women indicated that they would not mind if their husbands were kissed, but they did not want to be kissed. The males who did not mind being kissed did mind their wives saying goodbye or hello with more than a handshake.

The group of questions relating to marriage indicated that 80 percent of the people interviewed had had arranged marriages in which they had little or no say. But they considered the most desirable arrangement to be one in which the couple and the parents made the choice together. Input from parents was important largely because of parents' experience, maturity and wisdom, because their help and support could then be expected in case of marital problems, and also because it was considered good to keep everyone happy. Most respondents would like their children to choose their spouses but with their help and guidance. None wanted to make the entire decision to choose the spouse for their children, and only 20 percent would leave the decision on the children. There was an overall approval of marriages with other linguistic groups from South Asia for their children, but fewer people approved of inter-religious marriages, and very few approved of inter-racial marriages. All Muslim women preferred their own religious group. Of the 25 percent who did not mind inter-racial marriages all approved of their children marrying whites, but the majority disapproved of their children marrying blacks.

Marriage is still considered by 50 percent of those interviewed to be for life no matter what marital problems occur. In case of problems 20 percent thought marriage counselling was a good idea and 30 percent thought it was better to part after unsuccessful attempts at reconciliation. Only about 50 percent had some knowledge of services available with regard to marriage counselling, separation and divorce, and legal aid.

Civic and political participation of this group was restricted and narrow. With the exception of a few who took French courses, participation in interest courses, women's groups, school committees, neighborhood associations and recreation centers was negligible. Stated reasons for not participating were lack of time and interest, lack of knowledge about organizations, inability to speak either English or French (25 percent) and not wanting to go alone (10 percent). Over 50 percent were active in their linguistic community clubs. More wives indicated an interest in politics (50 percent) than their husbands perceived their wives as having (25 percent). Information on politics was gathered through television and newspapers. The only means of participation in this area, if at all, was voting in elections (25 percent from women's responses, 4 percent according to husband's perceptions).

Decision-making

In the area of decision-making, respondents indicated that issues such as size of family, joining the labor force and type of school for children were determined by the husband and wife together. Decisions regarding type of dress, hair length and style were made by all the women, and the husbands agreed with them (4 percent said they did not care whether or not their husbands agreed). Food preparation was influenced by husband's as well as children's preferences. Husbands always consulted their wives on major purchases.

Economic Integration

In terms of adaptation to economic structure, around 60 percent of the South Asian women sampled worked outside the home even when they had not worked in their home countries. Employment was usually for extra income and in very few cases because the woman wanted to work for self-fulfillment. Fifty percent of the women had tried to improve their skills in Canada either by taking job-related courses or learning French and English. Only 50 percent of those who worked felt that they had jobs that suited their qualifications. Among those who did not work, some could not find suitable jobs, and some intended to work when their children grew up. Working women had membership in unions only when mandatory, but 99 percent were neither active nor interested in union activity.

Open-ended responses indicated that a large percentage perceived racism and sexism as discriminating factors in the Canadian job market. "It is difficult to express my feelings, but we are not treated as equals", wrote one female respondent. Examples offered were lack of Canadian experience, under-employment, lack of information and resources for finding employment. They were perceived as allowing themselves to be discriminated against because they were often not aware of their rights. Opportunities for women were seen to be few; for South Asian women they were fewer.

While some women felt it was difficult for them to assert themselves to obtain jobs "as immigrants belonging to a different race", most women commented about the opportunities available for making money. One group considered the ease with which jobs were available despite lack of qualifications (e.g. factory work) to be a tremendous opportunity, whereas others felt that only low paying jobs were easily available. The better opportunities for career and qualifications were not availed of without considerable effort.

Analysis

Integration into society is a personal and individual process, and the respondents in this study show great variability in this respect. Although the sample was heterogeneous in many respects, a common cultural heritage and history is shared by the majority of the people of South Asia. Cultural differences with Western society are significant. It is only since 1947 that their independent governments have made different impacts on the status of women. Nevertheless, emphasis on sexual modesty and seclusion of women is influenced to a greater or lesser degree by religious (Jahan, 1975; Smock, 1977; Lindenbaum, 1974), and class affiliations. It is these two factors—religion and class—rather than linguistic or regional differences, which influence variations in perceptions towards social and economic life within this sample. The fact that the sample was small makes it difficult for us to draw definitive conclusions from this study. Nevertheless, significant patterns and trends emerge. The analysis made here is in terms of (1) South Asian women in Canadian society as a whole and (2) differences in response within the South Asian community itself because of religious and class variations.

1. The general patterns of response to the social and economic environment are made either by holding on to value systems and behavioral patterns developed in South Asia or, alternatively, by adopting new patterns which are deemed to be advantageous and therefore acquired to meet their new needs in a new environment. Within a multicultural society effective participation in the larger community requires only certain degrees of integration so that assimilation is controlled and ethnic minorities can retain their cultural identity. But discrepancies between the policy and ideal society on the one hand, and experiences of resistance and hostility towards cultural differences on the other create an ambivalence. Racial difference in Canada is defined not only in biological, but also in cultural terms (Buchignani, 1979:66). As a visible minority, South Asians have been victims of racial discrimination (Buchignani, 1979; Frideres, 1978; Naidoo, 1978; Berry, 1977; Ubale, 1977; Richmond, 1977) and South Asian women have, in addition, faced prejudicial attitudes for differences in personal appearance, food, language and values (Buchignani, 1979:54; Naidoo, 1978:244).

Data revealed that South Asian women's integration into social and economic life in Montreal follows patterns of interaction which are partly Canadian and partly responsive to traditional values. This supports previous studies of acculturation of South Asians in Canada: one on women which portrayed a complementary interaction between traditional and contemporary roles in life (Naidoo, 1978:231), and another study which found the socialization patterns of children of families from India in Canada to be a creative adjustment of Canadian practices and traditional sentiments (Kurian and Ghosh, 1978:30). The French factor in Montreal causes additional problems. Although

Montreal is a large cosmopolitan center and the impact of the emphasis on French is rather recent, South Asians going to other parts of Canada generally have one less hurdle to deal with—many of them already know English. Lack of knowledge of French makes fewer jobs available to them. Yet the majority continue to send their children to English schools because that is where they started. A trend seems to be developing towards sending younger children to French immersion in English schools and for a small number of women to taking French courses. This could be viewed as an excellent opportunity to learn an important language. Anglophone and Francophone perceptions of South Asians as an ethnic group have been found to be similar. A national survey on how respondents perceived Canadian ethnic groups relative to themselves conducted in 1977 by Berry et al. (p. 96) indicated that Angloceltic respondents put East-Indian Canadians 23rd on a scale of 27, whereas French-Canadians put them as 24th.

Integration patterns emerging from this study portray an acceptance by South Asian women of some new patterns of behavior and attitudes relatively easily (dress); others with less enthusiasm (food, children's choice of career, jobs, inter-religious marriages for their children, selection of spouse by children); and still others with resistance (dating, male/female relationships, inter-racial marriages, political and cultural participation, union activity).

Perhaps the greatest cultural differences are in values and attitudes affecting relationships between males and females. Dating of children, particularly girls, and the whole question of marriage and choice of spouse is a sensitive area and one affected by perceptions of female chastity and honor in South Asia. Compromise is indicated by willingness to allow selection of spouse by children and expecting to have some parental input. Dating problems are likely in the future, to be tackled with innovativeness as the children grow up, through control by enforcing time limits, for example. Inter-racial marriage is another problematic area, and changes on this issue are indicated by some acceptance of whites, but not yet of blacks. The sanctity of marriage is very important and defensiveness in this area was exhibited by a general reluctance to acknowledge awareness of services relating to marriage counselling and divorce, as if such knowledge is an indication of marital problems.

The idea of male protectiveness is prevalent in most societies, but in South Asia it is more emphasized. The adult woman's contacts with other Canadian males, her lack of mobility (many do not drive cars although their families own cars), lack of independent participation in cultural and social activities (e.g. membership in linguistic group clubs but not neighborhood associations) may indicate an underlying need for protection by males.

Areas of acceptance and change occur where negative consequences are perceived as resulting from continuing tradtional patterns, e.g. Western outfits are worn not only to combat extreme weather conditions but also to appear less visible, thus minimizing social contrast effects. Areas of cultural retention are those where negative effects are not perceived. Women work but do not participate in union activity. The saree is still considered feminine and beautiful and worn on special occasions; some women continue to wear their hair long. Observance of religious festivals, social and cultural ethnic activities continue while participation in the broader Canadian activities is very limited.

Decisions regarding major life options (Giele, 1977:4) of South Asian women in this sample may be analyzed as follows:

a. Political Expression: Generally minimal, any expressed interest has a middle class bias. There is a strong consciousness of racial, and even sexual, discrimination in Canadian society.

b. Work and Mobility: A large number of women feel socially isolated. Lack of access to transportation and absence of a large social network indicate the possibility of alienation and emotional problems such as loneliness, yet more women feel free here—free from family interference and control. Greater potential for independence exists and "for those who can let their hair down the opportunities are limitless", wrote one male respondent. Labor force participants tend to occupy lower level jobs either because they lack specialization, or because initial entry into the economic structure is difficult for racist reasons such as lack of Canadian experience or difficulties in having qualifications evaluated, or because as dependents, they take whatever jobs they get.

c. Family Formation, Duration and Size: The majority of women have been subjected to control in their choice of marriage partners, as were the men. Women, however, participate in decisions regarding family size. Whereas legally women have the right to divorce, South Asian women largely view marriage as a life-long commitment regardless of problems.

d. Education: All women have some education and a number of them have had considerable opportunities in this regard, although they did not tend to reach the same levels as their husbands.

e. Health and Sexual Control: Data indicate preference for some control over children's choice of marriage partners. There is apprehension about girls dating. There is a tendency for greater control and restrictions for females in male-female relationships.

f. Cultural Expression: Women, more than men, show evidence of being custodians of religious and cultural convictions in terms of food, dress and language, religious and cultural participation.

2. Differences within the South Asian group:

a. Religion: Historically Hindu and Islamic concepts of women's chastity and family honor influenced each other, but women's traditional status persisted in Muslim society because as a comprehensive code of life, Islam governs all aspects of society. In this sample religion influenced differences in food habits and choice of marriage partners. None of the Muslim women irrespective of class, ate pork, and all of them either experienced or expected conflicts on this issue with their children. All of them considered inter-religious marriages as undesirable even if they did not object to their children marrying from other linguistic groups. Among non-vegetarian Hindus more women than men had remained vegetarians. For Hindu, Christian and Sikh respondents religion was not an important factor in children's marriages.

b. Social Class: In South Asia as in all developing countries, significant class differences in women's lifestyles cut across religious and ethnic lines. The urban middle class woman has leisure time and the opportunity to pursue a career, not because of status position vis-à-vis men but because of help from working class women employed to do the housework and to look after the children. Both the area of female seclusion and domestic life pose a contrasting situation in Canada. Class distinctions, even among South Asians, cannot be viewed in the same context as in the Indian subcontinent because lower class people cannot, for financial and other reasons, emigrate to Canada. And even for the lower middle class South Asians who have recently started to emigrate, there is a definite rise in living standard in terms of consumer goods. Class distinctions become less evident where domestic help is not easily available (compensated to an extent by household gadgets), and when the need to establish themselves economically often leads middle class South Asians to experience status demotion in terms of considerable downward occupational mobility[4] (Buchignani, 1979:60). Nevertheless, certain influences of class due to higher educational background, such as facility in English and differences in work atmosphere and social milieu subject individuals to varying degrees of positive or negative, overt or subtle experiences in terms of integration. Distinct class differences exist on how women view their education, the types of jobs they will take up, the opportunities taken for increasing education and skills, kinds of activities they participate in, their mobility (none of the working class women drive cars or expressed interest in doing so) and the breadth of life experiences and variety of people they come in contact with.

Conclusion

While this generation of South Asian women has integrated with varying degrees to life in Montreal, the next generation will see more fundamental changes. And while their behavior will more closely approximate the majority culture, their acceptance by dominant groups remains uncertain and this ambiguity may lead to severe personal crises (Hacker, 1951:68). Yet change

[4]Studies show South Asian immigrants achieve economic security comparatively quickly (3 years in Canada, 1974:15).

is inevitable, perhaps desirable, but a total break with traditions would leave the next generation with no cultural moorings. All respondents in this sample show a conscious desire to maintain cultural identity. Successful integration will depend on increased interaction, communication and understanding, with the onus on both the larger community to accept and appreciate, and the ethnic minority to creatively change and retain.

REFERENCES

Basham, A. L.
   1954   The Wonder That Was India. New York: Grove Press.

Berry, John, et al.
   1977   Multiculturalism and Ethnic Attitudes in Canada. Ottawa: Minister of Supply and Services.

Buchignani, N. L.
   1979   "South Asian Canadians and the ethnic mosaic." Canadian Ethnic Studies 11: 1: 48-67.

Canada, Department of Manpower and Immigration.
   1974   Three Years in Canada. Ottawa: Information Canada.

Desai, N.
   1957   Woman in Modern India. Bombay: Vora & Co. Publishers Private Ltd.

Frideres, J.
   1978   "British Canadian attitudes toward minority ethnic groups in Canada." Ethnicity 5: 20-32.

Giele, J. Z.
   1977   "Comparative perspectives on women." In Giele and Smock (eds.), Women: Roles and Status in Eight Countries. Toronto: John Wiley & Sons.

Hacker, H. M.
   1951   "Women as a minority group." Social Forces 30: 60-69.

Hate, C. A.
   1930   "The social position of Hindu women." Ph.D. thesis, Bombay: University School of Economics and Sociology.

Jahan, R.
   1975   "Women in Bangladesh." In Rohrlich-Leavitt (ed.), Women Cross-Culturally: Change and Challenge. Chicago: Mouton Publishers.

Kapur, P.
   1970   Marriage and the Working Woman in India. Delhi: Vikas Publications.

Kurian, G. and R. Ghosh.
  1978   "Changing authority within the context of socialization in Indian families."
          Social Science 53: 1: 24-32.

Lindenbaum, S.
  1974   The Social and Economic Status of Women in Bangladesh. Dacca: Ford
          Foundation.

Naidoo, J. C.
  1978   New perspectives on South Asian women in Canada. 18th Interdisci-
          plinary Seminar, Waterloo, Presentation.

Papanek. H.
  1975   "Women in South and Southeast Asia: issues and research." Signs 1: 1: 193-214.

Richmond, A.
  1974   Aspects of the Absorption and Adaptation of Immigrants. Ottawa:
          Department of Manpower and Immigration.

Smock, Audrey.
  1977   "Bangladesh: A struggle with tradition and poverty." In Janet Giele &
          Audrey Smock (eds.), Women: Roles and Status in Eight Countries. Toronto:
          John Wiley & Sons.

Ubale, B.
  1977   Equal Opportunity and Public Policy. A Report Submitted to the Attor-
          ney General of Ontario by the South Asian Canadian Community, Ottawa.

5 Planning for Women in the New Towns: New Concepts and Dated Roles*

JOAN GOLDSTEIN**

Introduction

"Little Boxes on the hillside, Little Boxes all the same."   (Reynolds, 1962)

Malvina Reynolds' humorous folk song, "Little Boxes," served as comment on the apparent uniformity and conformity associated with suburban housing and life style. This may have been the phenomenon planners referred to as, "homogeneity," but it presupposed a degree of sameness about what people required in their housing and their community. And it may well have been an assumption with little foundation in real research, that people, and women in particular, either do not know what they want, or will want what we, the planners will give them.

It is the intent of this paper to examine the concept of New Towns in the light of the changing concept of the role of women, their interaction with the home, family and work force; and further, to question the overall impact of male-oriented social planning on the formation of community social systems.

The Approach

The research is primarily focused on the New Towns of England and the United States for two reasons: one, that they appear most similar in their concept of the role of women; and second, that the research, such as it is, was most available on the subject from these two countries.

The three basic issues are: the role of women in marriage, (single women, although greater numbers exist via divorce, widowhood, and extended single life, are given little or no consideration in the vision of planners); the role of women in child care, (and, more recently, the role of men in child care); and the place of women in the work force. These are the vital points in the changing status of women and should be directly related to planning of community facilities and transportation systems as well as housing configurations.

Moreover, although social scientists have pointed to the industrial society as the causal factor in separating and further distancing the place of residence from the place of work, (Galbraith, 1971; Gans, 1968), these social analysts have tended to

*Revised version of a paper presented at the Annual meeting of the American Sociological Association, San Francisco, August, 1975.
**Department of Sociology, Graduate Center, CUNY, New York, U.S.A.

overlook the impact this environmental separation would have upon the second sex, upon women in and out of the work force and upon family roles and organization as a result. The geographical separation of the sexes was accomplished in suburban and New Town communities as an unintended consequence of the industrial society which further separated the work place from the residential community. This splintering of work and residence was already in process in urban communities prior to suburban growth patterns, but the distances in urban communities were more social than geographic.

Separation of the Sexes

The extended family, suggests Young and Willmott (1957) was the woman's trade union organized by women for women. Since their study of East London families in the late 1950's, a historical perspective on family and community interaction in the 1960's and early 1970's suggests that what has been in transition is the concept of family, and the role of women in and out of the home.

In their study of *Family and Kinship in East London,* Young and Willmott quote an earlier study (1896 to be exact) on a neighboring borough of working class families:

"Being a prisoner to child bearing, the wife could not easily mend her finances for herself by going out to work."

(Young and Willmott, 1957:4)

In this statement, we have the complex of problems related specifically to the status of women in the 19th, and to some extent, 20th centuries: Financial dependence based on continuous child-bearing and caring. It was on this point that the separation of the sexes relegated parenthood to women, and work to men. But for men, the "bar in the pub was as much a part of their living space as the room in their home, with one exception—that one was more or less reserved for members of their own sex, while the other was not" (Young and Willmott, 1957:8). Separate roles created separate worlds, and the institution of the British "mum" evolved. In Young and Willmott's definition, the status of "mum" was a high and powerful one amongst working class families because she could intervene in the lives of her children. The British "mum" continued to select and arrange the method of childbirth for her children's pregnancies even though the Welfare state was then providing full pre-natal and midwifery services. It was particularly significant when working class young couples began moving to the estates, the New Towns, and leaving behind the always available and helping, "mum." This break in the kinship pattern was presumably the cause of problems for couples moving to the New Towns. But what had really happended in the "institution of the mum" was that the woman had filled the parenting role almost exclusively, while the man had simply worked, albeit in a frustrating and unrewarding job. This sharp demarkation in sex roles gave the woman a more intense and involved participation in the lives of her children and grandchildren. She was merely filling the parenting vacumn left by the man whose primary participation in the family was as the breadwinner.

But by the 1960's Gavron notes, (1966), this was already in a state of change. In her study of *The Captive Wife*, Gavron states that Young and Willmott's study of East London dealt with families during the middle 1950's and did not account for social changes which would affect the younger generation. She suggests that the attitudes and expectations of the younger couples were more readily affected by the following conditions:

1. Full employment, particularly of adolescent labor.
2. Increased employment of married women.
3. Rise of the Welfare State in which state midwifery replaces "mum."
4. Increased employment meant increased wealth. Homes could be pleasanter and the man would have greater incentive to spend his leisure time at home.

Gavron contends that the younger couples preferred their independence from the "mum" generation when they had the financial ability to do so. In most cases, this required wives as well as husbands to participate in the work force.

The relationship between marriage roles and work participation is an interesting one. Gavron points out that, "the great increase in employment of married women could be expected to have an effect on family relationships as many wives would now be released from complete financial dependence on their husbands" (Gavron, 1966:xi). And despite the cliche that the women's movement is a middle class movement, Gavron points out that during this century, social, economic and technological changes have had a revolutionary effect on the status of women in this country, particularly working class women (Gavron, 1966:xi). To make this point, she cites Titmuss' observation on the social revolution of women:

"...the development of personal, legal, and political liberties of half the population of this country within the span of less than eighty years stands as one of the supreme examples of consciously developed social change."

(Gavron, 1966:3)

It is the World Wars, both I and II which create periods when the most rigid divisions between what constituted male activity and what constituted female were broken down. The changes in the structure and pattern of family life were directly the result of key demographic changes which had revolutionized the life of women, from one of constant child-bearing, ill health, and early loss of youth, to a life in which ten years at most are devoted to the care and production of small children. However, we cannot assume that this transition eclipsed older, more established systems of kinship and sex roles. Patterns of socialization and kinship roles do not modify on demand simply because the succeeding generation no longer requires the system. There is still a widespread network of extended families in East London and remnants of old systems survive in pockets of the past.

In summary then, since economic functions were taken out of the family, the sphere of men became separate from the sphere of women. Men became the breadwinners whose main role was in the economic sphere while women took care of the household. In connection with her role in the household as "mum," she developed this "trade union" which provided the structure for fulfilling her role. But as the state increases its function in the welfare of the family, it also displaces the function of "mum." This has implications for the structure of the family, and for the placement and planning of communities.

Changing the Role of Family: Woman as Person

If the extended family evolved to provide protection from poverty and economic depression, the modern family is expected to give much more recognition to the individual than was the case in the past. Suzanne Keller, in her essay on the Future Role of Women has argued that the "changes in the role of women will not therefore, occur in a social vacuum, but will be nourished by developments in the wider society—in work, family, community and leisure" (Keller, 1973). What she suggests is that we design the physical environment properly to encourage different patterns of social and family life—some of these anti-natalistic in their impact. All of these shifts imply changes in family, household and work patterns.

To what extent have the New Towns, the planned communities responded to the present and future role of women? Do we know what it is that women want or need? How has this been reflected in the social planning, the landscape planning, the community structure of any of the New Towns?

FINDINGS

Non-Working Women in the New Towns

In *The Levittowners* study, Gans attempts to measure the level and character of "boredom" in the community. "About a third of the women and more than half of the men are never bored and only a few women are constantly so," he comments. Further on he notes that:

> "...about a third of the bored women attributed it to the menstrual period, poor health, or a periodic bad mood. But two other reasons are mentioned more often: housework and being struck" (Gans, 1967:228).

In addition, he mentions that there is a lack of shopping facilities and centers where women could go as a change of activity. And then, further on, Gans attempts to measure the degree of loneliness in the Levittown community and finds it primarily familial, that is, the longing for continued social contact with extended family members, and again, it is women who exhibit this problem more than men.

One solution Gans suggests would be through community-wide nursery schools and day care centers; but he does not adequately explain their lack of existence other than to suggest that it is well-educated women who use them, those whom Gans believes suffer least from being "stuck."

> "If nursery schools were attached to the public school system, they (mothers) would be less reluctant to use them, but they would still need to find activities of enough significance of justify leaving their children in someone's care" (Gans, 1967:228).

According to Gans, women could only feel comfortable leaving their pre-school children for a few hours if they had activities sufficiently important to warrent this non-mothering behavior. Significantly, the women Gans is describing did not show an interest in community activities as they were structured in Levittown; however, he adds, they would respond favorably to work opportunities. And of those opportunities he notes the narrow and limited choices: "However, jobs for women, except as teachers, are as rare in Levittown as in other suburbs. Still, many unfilled community posts exist" (Gans, 1967:228).

The community posts Gans is referring to fall under the category of non-professional, such as teacher aide or nurses aide. For those women above that educational or professional level, such positions do not represent a challenge or a source of stimulation. He makes note of the situation; but Gans does not conclude that the planners had ignored or omitted the basic needs of those community members "stuck" within the confines of the community: the non-working wife, (and, co-incidentally, the teen-ager).

The second and more serious problem is social isolation (Gans, 1967:228). The lack of adequate public transportation to the city accounts to some extent for this concern. Once again, we note the social isolation of women from a source of change and stimulation. The men will commute to work and thereby supplement their social and environmental stimulation; and the women will be left to a community with lack of day care facilities, or at least inadequate day care facilities, non-existent job possibilities, and lack of sufficient public transportation to permit easy travel to an urban center, which was, in this case, Philadelphia.

Although Gans notes these problems, he moves on to the impact of these conditions on marital relations, and suggests that professional counselling services could be developed for such communities. What he does not concern himself with, is the serious omission by planners to respond to the specific needs of women, and in this case, the non-working woman. The working woman will be discussed at a later point.

In an earlier work on Columbia, Maryland, once again Gans writes that social isolation, most prevalent among women, could provide problems for Columbia residents, (Gans, 1968:185), and notes as well the feeling of being "stuck" amongst women and teenagers. Low density and lack of public transportation are also identified as key factors in increasing the social isolation and boredom.

Women planners have begun to express raised consciousness on the subject. Abu-Lughod, trained in both urban planning and sociology, noted with indignation a recent conference of prominent urban planners in which the four-day work week was enthusiastically explored:

"It would permit even more complete separation of work from residence!...A man could go into the city to work, spend three nights there, and then return to his family out in the country...It was designed for men only. Married females with children were presumably to remain on rural 'breeding farms.' The status of single women was indeterminant; perhaps they were to be kept in the city for those other three nights? Sex roles were to be totally differentiated..." (Abu-Lughod, 1974:38).

The ill-defined malaise characterized as "boredom and loneliness" in non-working women was labeled a problem only when it led to marital difficulties. The condition of women's life style was not itself a consideration. But what of working women in planned communities? Does participation in the work force correct the problems of isolation and restricted mobility noted for the non-working women?

Women and Work in the New Towns

While American new communities were controlled by the private market, and often had to attract industry after residential units were built and occupied, (Burchell, 1972), British New Towns were publicly developed and could not emerge without an economic base. As a result of public planning, the British New Towns were located with some proximity to an industry, though even this economic base was not sufficient to employ the residents entirely. Nevertheless the proportion of women in the labor force has been growing in England, and is reflected in the New Towns closest to London; though the percentage does not out-distance that of London. Thomas (1969) measures the labor activity by the journeys to work by men and women in 1951, 61 and 66. He demonstrates that women have increased their local journeys from 57.8 per cent in 1951 to 72.3 per cent in 1966. Thomas differentiates crossing journeys to surrounding London as a sort of commuter pattern; and local journeys as part-time work, and visiting and shopping expeditions. By comparison, men have slightly decreased their crossing journeys, while women have markedly increased their local journeys. This is explained as the increase of part-time work and local jobs for women because men still hold on to the transportation (family car) and women may choose to stay closer to schools and children.

In a startling comment with respect to the role of women, Thomas asserts that the self-containment of New Towns is made possible by the restricted roles relegated to women.

> "The fact that New Towns have become self-contained has little to do with journeys to work by men. They have become self-contained partly because the women who live or work in the New Towns seem to have become less mobile, and partly because the number of women who live or work in the new towns have been growing much faster than the corresponding number of men" (Thomas, 1969:399).

The number of women in the work force has increased heavily since 1951 (from 15.4 thousands in 1951 to 73.3 thousands in 1966) but the positions appear to the locally based and primarily junior or low level positions. Although increasing numbers of women in the New Towns have been entering the work force, this does not necessarily deal with problems of public transportation to urban areas or to the need for effective day care or child care facilities. Women in the London New Towns may be holding two positions, part-time or full time worker and full time housekeeper, a duo role with even greater restrictions than the non-working woman.

Improving the life style of women as well as men should be the goal of planning for New Towns. At the moment it remains as the title of this paper suggests: New Concepts and dated roles.

Discussion and Conclusions

The three basic issues which affect the lives of both working and non-working women in New Town communities are: proximity to high density (cosmopolitan, urban) areas; adequate public transportation to these areas, and child care arrangements. The notion of self-contained, controlled density communities may be arrived at by the sacrifice of women's mobility potential. A self-contained community must be analyzed from the point of view of those who live within such an arrangement. Though changing a new community into a city, in part, runs counter to the concept of New Towns, what cities contain, such as universities to further educational development; greater choice of jobs and careers; variety and stimulation of interests and activities, may be what women need to fulfill their lives beyond the early phase of marriage and motherhood.

The mistake was to assume that women never change, nor the condition of their lives, nor their goals. It is not a simple alternative that some women stay at home and want to stay at home and will always want to stay at home—or the reverse. The New Towns concept does not seem to deal with the question of change, either in an economic, chronological, or life cycle context. It presents a fixed point in time, a time for young marriages with young children—or old marriages with older persons, as in the case of the leisure village communities. So far, New Town planners have not dealt with the life span concept, and they have not considered women at any point along the continum.

What has been in transition is the concept of the family, and the role of women in and out of the home. As noted in Gan's study on *The Levittowners*, some of the women studied wanted to go "back" to the earlier style of the women's trade union, while others wanted to go "forward" to the new pattern of working and having the state take care of their children. For both of these groups there is a degree of conflict and anomie; and the situation to which both types are responding is characterized by isolation, boredom and loneliness. The reason for this, as the study suggests, is that women are in a transition period between the institution of "mum," and some alternative for it.

Concurrently, the state of community planning, which to a significant extent structures the mobility potential of women, demonstrates minimal awareness of their needs. The New Towns were selected for study specifically because they were to be the product of new concepts in community planning. Clearly, there is strong interaction between community structure and the degree of mobility potential for women. As such, future research should focus on this interactive relationship so that community may more accurately reflect rather than restrict the role choice of women.

REFERENCES

Abbott, Sidney
    1972   "New Hope for New Towns," Design and Environment 3 (Spring): 28-36.

Abu-Lughod, Janet L.
    1974   "Designing a City for All," in Planning, Women & Change, ed., Hapgood and
            Gertels, Planning Advisory Service, 301 (April): 37-42.

Allen, Irving Lewis (ed.)
    1977   New Towns and the Suburban Dream. Port Washington, N.Y.: Kennikat Press.

Burchell, Robert
    1972   New Communities American Style. Rutgers University Center for Urban Policy
            Research.

Fava, Sylvia
    1977   "The Pop Sociology of Suburbs and New Towns," In Allen, I.L. (ed.) New Towns
            and the Suburban Dream: 106-118. Port Washington, N.Y.: Kennikat Press.

Galbraith, Kenneth
    1971   The New Industrial State. Boston: Houghton Mifflin.

Gans, Herbert J.
    1967   The Levittowners: Ways of Life and Politics in a New Suburban Community. New
            York: Albert A. Knopf, Inc.
    1968   People and Plans: Essays on Urban Problems and Solutions. New York: Basic
            Books.
    1972   "How to Succeed in Integrating New Towns," Design and Environment 3 (Winter):
            28-52.

Gavron, Hannah
    1966   The Captive Wife. London: Routledge & Kegan Paul.

Howard, Phillip
    1972   "Reston Revisited," Design & Environment 3 (Spring): 23-27.

Keller, Suzanne
    1973   "The Future Role of Women," Annals of the American Academy of Social and
            Political Science. (July): 2-10.

Lopata, Helena Znaniecki
    1971   Occupation: Housewife. New York: Oxford University Press.

Stein, C.S.
    1957   Towards New Towns for America. Cambridge, Mass.: M.I.T. Press.

Temple, Charlotte
    1974   "Planning and the Married Woman with Children—A New Towns Perspective," in
            Planning, Women and Change, ed., Hapgood and Gertels, Planning Advisory Service,
            301 (April): 43-49.

Thomas, Ray
    1969   London New Towns: A Study of Self Contained and Balanced Communities, 35,
            Broadsheet 510, Planning. (April): 399-0.

Young, Michael and Peter Willmott
    1957   Family and Kinship in East London. London: Routledge & Kegan Paul, Ltd.

6 Birth Order and Alienation Among College Women in Lebanon*

AIDA K. TOMEH**

This study stems basically from a number of previous findings which suggest that attitudinally and behaviorally first born children are traditionally oriented while last borns are peer oriented (Kammeyer, 1966, 1967a; Tomeh, 1969, 1970, 1971, 1972, 1976; MacArthur, 1956; Bradley, 1968; Palmer, 1966; Bragg and Allen, 1970; Singer, 1971; Lasko, 1954; Rosen, 1964; Harris and Howard, 1968). This particular patterning of findings made it of interest to pursue further the empirical relationship between birth order and alienation. Another reason is that such a study could extend our knoledge on birth order as a family structure variable and alienation as a social psychological phenomenon in a different social structure. Indeed, research material on other cultures is far from complete. This paper, therefore, may provide a cross-cultural perspective.

Although the family holds a prime position in sociology as a basic social institution, structural features of the family such as birth order, sibling order, or family size have been somewhat neglected. Only recently three have been signs of increasing interest in sibling position by sociologists (Bossard and Ball, 1956; Brim, 1958; Elder and Bouserman, 1963; Rosen, 1961; Rossi, 1965; Kammeyer, 1966, 1967a, 1967b; Tomeh, 1969, 1970, 1971, 1972, 1976). However, psychologists, especially those interested in child development have widely recognized the importance of birth order in the family (Altus, 1966; Warren, 1966; Heilbrun Jr. and Fromme, 1965; Stroup and Hunter, 1965; Sutton-Smith et al., 1964; Connors, 1963; Sampson, 1962; Gerard, 1961; Radloff, 1961; Roe, 1953; Schachter, 1959; Sears, 1950).[1] The concern with birth order in this study may provide some insight on the influence of structural vairables in the family, though birth order is only an indicator of some other variable factors.

On similar grounds, most of the empirical research on alienation seems to be limited to the analysis of American samples and similar research on other

*The author is indebted to Beirut University College for granting permission to conduct the larger study of which this is only a part. Special gratitude is due to the students without whom the study would not have been possible.

Paper presented at the National Council on Family Relations Annual Meetings, October 20-23, 1976, New York, New York.

**Aida K. Tomeh, Ph.D. Professor, Department of Sociology, Bowling Green State University, Bowling Green, Ohio 43403.

[1]Extensive review of the literature on ordinal position appears in psychological and child development periodicals and books since the 1920's and even prior to that date.

cultures is not readily available with the exception of a few studies (Almond and Verba, 1963; Seeman, 1966, 1967; Tomeh, 1974). This existing gap in our knowledge stimulated the interest in the concept of alienation.

Previous literature directly or indirectly related to the subject matter of this paper is practically non-existent. Thus the interpretive link between birth order and alienation is based on theoretical explanations as well as other relevant empirical findings.

The primary concern of this study is to examine the extent to which alienation varies with birth order. While a number of explanations can be advanced to explain the differential by birth order,[2] the theoretical interpretation which is advanced here is based on different socialization patterns of children in different ordinal positions. What is implied in this argument is that childrearing practices, sibling relationships, family conditions (social isolation, social involvement, cultural origin, attitudes of parents, etc.) as well as the role of society in which the family lives are factors which influence birth order effects. The principal assumption of this frame of reference is that children in different ordinal positions are subject to different patterns of interaction and as adults have different social learning experiences (Sears, 1950:398; Warren, 1966:38-39).

To illustrate in part, it has been noted that parents consider the birth and presence of the first born in the family to be a significant event. An awareness of this position of importance is transmitted to the child along with a sense of responsibility to the kin group. Parents also have more time and energy to devote to the process of socializing the first born child and require more of her/him. As a result, the first born child tends to build views that are similar to her/his parents especially in the absence of generational peers to mediate between the adult world and that of the child's. In the presence of siblings, it is usually the first born who is expected to be a role model for younger brothers and sisters—another responsibility which cannot be easily dismantled. This often noted characteristic of the interaction pattern between the first born child and other members of the family has been used to account for the adult and traditional orientation of the first born. The same interactional pattern and learning experience may also reduce the level of alienation among first born children.

As for later children the most outstanding features of the interactive processes which influence their behaviors and attitudes are in some respects mirror images of the oldest children. More specifically, parents tend to attach less importance to the birth of having the later child than they did to the first one. Parents also tend to be more relaxed, less anxious, and less conservative with later born children (Sears, Maccoby, and Levin, 1957). Consequently, the pressure on the last born is less demanding in maintaining family obligations. The relative permissiveness

---

[2]For example, other explanations of the differential by birth order are physiological and economic. Warren (1966:38-39) has a brief discussion of the physiological interpretation. Altus (1966:45) cites one instance in which economic factors are used to explain why first-born sons attend college more than later born sons, Adler uses a personality explanation (Ansbacher and Ansbacher, 1956, for Adler's views on birth order)'.

on the part of the parents may encourage secondary contacts (Tomeh, 1976). It is also possible that the last child perceives the oldest sibling as a source of anxiety since it is the first child who enters school, graduates, gets a job, etc. Thus, competing with an older sibling for a superior position or for parental attention may cause some stress for the last born. Under these conditions, younger children turn to peers to find their models (Tomeh, 1970). It is this interactive situation which has been used to explain, by and large, the peer orientation and the other direction of the last born. The same set of factors may contribute to the greater alienation of the last born.

Although the above described differential interactive processes within the family are important, societal conditions cannot be ignored. In this respect, the Middle Eastern society traditionally has been characterized by its religious moral system, strong family ties and bonds, approved cultural authoritarianism and paternalism, closely guarded sex and a deep sense of in-group loyalties. However, this way of life is being slowly and gradually challenged by the development of modern scientific inventions, higher education, mass communication, and the decline in social and geographical isolation (Armstrong and Hirabayashi, 1956; Hirabayashi and El Khatib, 1958; Hirabayashi and Ishaq, 1958; Lerner, 1958; Melikian and Prothro, 1957). As a result, the old order is becoming no longer tenable and there appears to be a rapid awakening to the realization that men and women must take part in the building of the new society. With this change there seems to be often a discrepancy between verbal acceptance and emotional accept-ance for which no coordinated system of interpersonal relations has developed. Thus a man may prefer an educated wife, yet failing to see its accompaniments of greater independence for the woman and a more demanding relationship than the previous situation (Gillespie and Allport, 1955; Camilleri, 1967 on role conflict for women).

Further, the transition from parental arrangement to one of individual choice, and from social segregation to an intermingling of the sexes is likely to create role conflict. The people of the Middle East are just beginning, however, to realize the impact of this change and are therefore facing the necessity of thinking through the implications of modern life for their traditional, religious and moral world views. The dilemma is how to find a way of integrating reason and production with meaning and spirit. In spite of the current evolutionary pro-cess of change in attitudes and values (Tomeh, 1968, 1970), this overall pattern which characterizes the Middle Eastern society is likely to have social psychologi-cal effects upon its members (Tomeh, 1974). The family as related to the rest of society is affected by those conditions and the problem for research then is to de-termine some of the social-psychological characteristics in terms of alienation that differ by birth order status. In other words, the effects of being in a certain place in the family hierarchy may be influenced by the social environment in which it exists.

It is reasoned here that societal conditions may have less of an impact on the first born than the last born child in view of the differences in socialization patterns described earlier as well as the tendency on the part of the first born to be traditionally oriented both attitudinally and behaviorally (Tomeh, 1969, 1971, 1972, 1976; MacArthur, 1956; Lasko, 1954; Rosen, 1964; Harris and Howard, 1968; Singer, 1971; Palmer, 1966; Bragg and Allen, 1970; and Kammeyer, 1966). This disposition on the part of first born children may provide a cushioning support against the alienative effects generated by a changing ʃsociety. In contrast, the peer orientation of last born children and their characteristic exposure to outside influences (Tomeh, 1970), 1976; Hall and Barger, 1964; MacArthur, 1956) are attributes that are closely linked to the larger society—a system which itself is in the process of rapid social change. The consequence of this situation in terms of alienation may be somewhat greater on this group of children. Although friendship groups and the mass media are viewed as intermediate structures in society that provide the individual with support, they may not be as effective as the familial group.

It must be emphasized, however, that since familial and societal conditions are subject to change, there is nothing fixed or inevitable about the effect of being born into a certain place in the family; that is to say, birth order effects change as those conditions change. This is particularly true in the case of societies which are in a stage of rapid social change such as the Middle East. For example, it may well be that with the changing conditions of the Middle Eastern society, the generational gap may be widening considerably whereby the younger generation possibly finds the attitudes and values of their parents outdated. In this context, the differential by birth order may not be too pronounced or perhaps the traditional oriented sibling may feel an increasing sense of alienation in contrast to the peer oriented sibling.

A cautionary comment must be made regarding the theoretical interpretations presented above; namely that for the most part, characterizations of family interaction, the processes of differential socialization and the effects of a changing society that have been advanced as significant influences on the behavior and attitudes of children by order of birth are not definitive in terms of empirical evidence, but they are propositions that come from the literature on birth order.

It must also be noted at the outset, that in the view of the transitional and changing nature of the Middle Eastern society, *sharp* differences in levels of alienation among various sibling patterns are not very likely. The impact of social change may dilute rather than increase the effect of birth order. Variable conditions such as college status, religious preference, size of hometown, country of origin, size of family, socio-economic status, which may influence birth order and the level of alienation will be discussed.

Measurement of Variables

Following Seeman's (1959) conceptual scheme, alienation in this research is viewed as multidimensional, which under certain conditions can be related, but for

purposes of analysis and conceptual clarity should not be treated as a single attitude.[3] Three aspects of alienation are investigated:

1. Powerlessness measures the extent to which an individual feels that he
    himself can control the outcome of events that concern her/him on the
    level of the larger social system (Seeman, 1963) for a discussion on its
    use and development). The conceptualization of powerlessness is based
    on social learning theory of Rotter (1954) who argues that behavior is a
    function of values and expectations which people tend to develop inclu-
    ding a sense of control or lack of it. The specific content of the items
    which compose the powerlessness scale deal with one's perceived expecta-
    tion of control on issues of concern related to war, peace, world opinion
    of one's country, government decisions, inflation and other political
    and economic events. Thus, powerlessness implies a trust in fate and
    lack of mastery over outcomes either by oneself or by others like oneself,
    whereas a low degree of powerlessness is the expectation of intended and
    purposive control (Neal and Retting, 1963). The following are illustra-
    tive items.

    Wars between countries seem inevitable despite efforts of men to pre-
    vent them.

    The average person can have very little influence on government
    decisions.

    People like me can change the outcome of world events if we make
    ourselves heard (reversed scoring).

    More and more, I feel helpless in the face of what's happening in
    the world today.

2. Normlessness refers to the expectancy for socially unapproved behavior
    required to achieve given goals. The items are limited to moral judg-
    ments in business and the government in one's own society in terms of
    the extent to which ethical codes are violated in order to achieve socially
    approved objectives. In this respect a high degree of normlessness
    implies lack of adherence to moral judgments and the acceptance of
    socially unapproved means (Neal and Retting, 1963; Merton, 1957:128).
    The following items are examples:

    In order to be elected to public office a candidate must make promi-
    ses he does not intend to keep.

    Knowing the right people is more important than ability in getting
    a government job.

[3]The correlation coefficients between the alienation subscales used in this study are relatively low.
The largest obtained correlation is between normlessness and powerlessness (r=.26 significant at
the .05 level) and the lowest correlation is between normlessness and meaninglessness (r=.04 not
significant at the .05 level). Thus, while it is feasible to consider the subscales as part of the
same general concept, there appears to be enough independence among the different scales to
warrant treating them as separate variables.

In getting a good job, it is necessary to exaggerate one's abilities or personal qualifications for the job.

3. Meaninglessness refers to the degree to which events in the larger society are perceived as extremely complex, unclear, and intricate. Accordingly, persons who experience high meaninglessness view the social order as incoherent and their minimal standards for clarity in decision-making and problem-solving are not met. On the other extreme, low meaninglessness implies a sense of understanding events in society at large in terms of their order and predictability. In this study, however, meaninglessness is used in the context of the college institution relative to unsatisfaction with college work and instruction. The following is a sample of the items used in the scale:

I feel that what I am learning now in college will be useful to me later on (reversed scoring).

In general I feel I am sufficiently challenged and motivated by my instructors (reversed scoring).

I feel I am advised adequately by my instructors and told enough about how I am coming along in my course work (reversed scoring).

The response pattern to the items in each of the above three scales uses a four-point format: strongly agree, agree, disagree, strongly disagree, ranked from "1" to "4" respectively; "1" designates high alienation and "4" designates low alienation. For every respondent a total score is obtained for all the items in each scale. The total score distributions of each scale was divided into "high" and "low" alienation at the median.[4]

Sample

The data presented here were gathered in the winter of 1965 as part of a larger project. The sample for this investigation consisted of 523 young women college students between 18 and 23 years of age enrolled full time in a university college in Lebanon. Each of these students received a mailed questionnaire. Questionnaires were successfully completed and returned by approximately 83 percent of the total sample, yielding an N of 434 (the remaining 89 non-returns were "refusals").[5]

---

[4]The reliability of the alienation measures tested by the test-retest technique shows a reproducibility coefficient of .86 for the powerlessness scale, .90 for the normlessness scale, and .89 for the meaninglessness scale. The coefficient of scalability (Menzel, 1953) for the respective scales in that order is .52, .53, and .48. These results suggest high reliability. Similar alienation measures based on American samples have been repeatedly used, showing a reliability ranging between .73 and .84 or higher (Dean, 1961:756).

[5]The analysis of the non-respondent sample (17 percent) showed the same population distribution as the regular sample. Since the response rate was high and the population composition of the respondence and non-respondents was similar, one might safely conclude that differences in results might be very negligible.

The population distribution of the study sample showed that slightly over one-third of the students were freshmen, one-fourth were sophomores; their fathers were predominantly of higher socioeconomic status of Lebanese or Jordanian origin, about one-half of them came from large cities and were Christian, and the rest came from small cities and were Christian, and the rest came from small cities and were Moslem. The population of this university college perhaps falls in the upper range of the educational institutions in the Middle East. Although not enrolling proportionate numbers of college-going students from various social strata, diversity within the college as shown above is sufficient to perform a partial test of the effect of population characteristics upon the relationship between birth order and alienation.

FINDINGS

Powerlessness

When levels of powerlessness by birth order[6] are compared, no significant differences appear, though the trend is in the direction expected. Fifty-two percent of the first born children perceive low powerlessness as compared to 46 percent of the last borns.[7] In otherwords, oldest children indicate that they feel slightly more in control over their own lives.

Table 1 shows the relationship between birth order and powerlessness when demographic characteristics are controlled. Accordingly, when college status is considered, last and first born children report approximately a similar rate in the degree of powerlessness during the freshman year. However, first born sophomores appear to be slightly more powerless than youngest siblings of the same college level. The expected birth order differential is in the direction predicted for upperclass women. These results suggest that college experience has a different effect on the attitudes of different orders of birth resulting from various influences on campus (Newcomb, 1950; Kammeyer, 1966).

It is further noticed that for first born children an advance in college status is likely to decrease their level of powerlessness; for inbetween children, powerlessness increases during the sophomore year, drops during the last two years of college but does not reach the low powerlessness score of the freshman year. The high level of powerlessness during their sophomore year may be a function of being in an intermediate position in the birth order hierarchy as well as in college status, both of which seem to interfere in the degree of perceived powerlessness. Beyond the sophomore level, however, college life is likely to provide a sense of effectiveness and a deeper trust in the predictability of others. As for last borns, it seems that a sense of trust and control is at its highest level during the sophomore year.

---

[6] First born girls and only children are combined in this analysis because of the limited number of cases in the latter category (2 percent).

[7] The chi-square of independence is applied throughout the analysis. In the tables that follow, the X^2 and probability values are presented and the pattern of relationships is clearly shown by the percentage distributions. Kandall tau C is used as a measure of the degree of association.

When religion is controlled (Table 1) the expected differential by birth order is somewhat in the direction predicted for the Christian group, whereas no differences appear in the other religious denomination. It is noticed further, that first and last born Moslem girls are slightly more in control of their lives than their Christian counterparts. It may be that Moslem girls perceive greater mastery of events in order to increase their social mobility in society and maintain control of the social system as a majority group. On the other hand, Christians in the Middle East have historically not been the forerunners of the social, political, or economic institutions in society; as a result their perceived expectation of control on issues related to the obove concerns is likely to be low. In any event, the differences between the two religious groups are not wide.

TABLE 1   BIRTH ORDER AND POWERLESSNESS BY DEMOGRAPHIC CHARACTERISTICS

	College Status (percent)								
	Freshman			Sophomore			Upperclass women		
Powerlessness	First	In-between	Last	First	In-between	Last	First	In-between	Last
Low	45	61	42	52	37	57	60	52	43
High	55	39	58	48	63	43	40	48	57
Number of cases	(51)	(72)	(31)	(31)	(49)	(30)	(37)	(89)	(35)
	$X^2=4.63, df=2, P>.25, C=.02$			$X^2=3.45, df=2, P>.05, C=.04$			$X^2=1.99, df=2, P>.05, C=.12$		

	Religious Affiliation (percent)					
	Christian			Moslem		
Powerlessness	First	In-between	Last	First	In-between	Last
Low	49	51	44	53	52	50
High	51	49	56	47	48	50
Number of cases	(67)	(88)	(66)	(51)	(124)	(34)
	$X^2=.81, df=2, C=.05, P>.05$			$X^2=.08. df=2, P>.05, C=02$		

	Size of Hometown (percent)								
	15,000 or less			15,000 to 99,000			100,000 or more		
Powerlessness	First	In-between	Last	First	In-between	Last	First	In-between	Last
Low	56	71	52	50	45	41	51	47	46
High	44	29	48	50	55	59	49	53	54
Number of cases	(31)	(49)	(21)	(24)	(56)	(27)	(65)	(108)	(52)
	$X^2=3.36, df=2, P>.05, C=.02$			$X^2=.44, df=2, P>.05, C=.07$			$X^2=.30, df=2. P>.05, C=.04$		

(Contd.)

Table 1 (*Cantd.*)

	Nationality of Father (percent)								
	Lebanese			Jordanian			Other Middle Eastern		
Powerlessness	First	In-between	Last	First	In-between	Last	First	In-between	Last
Low	48	51	45	44	48	22	54	51	68
High	52	49	55	56	52	78	46	49	32
Number of cases	(48)	(96)	(53)	(27)	(50)	(18)	(24)	(51)	(19)
	$X^2=.47, df=2,$ $P>.05, C=.02$			$X^2=3.69. df=2,$ $P>.05, C=.13$			$X^2=1.72, df=2,$ $P>.05, C=.09$		

	Size of Nuclear Family (percent)					
	Small: Five or less children			Large: Six or more children		
Powerlessness	First	In-between	Last	First	In-between	Last
Low	49	46	51	65	53	42
High	51	54	49	35	47	58
Number of cases	(37)	(48)	(49)	(40)	(110)	(24)
	$X^2=.26, df=2,$ $P>.05, C=.03$			$X^2=3.49, df=2,$ $P>.05, C=.14$		

Further analysis of the same table shows that for residents of middle and large sized cities, there is a tendency on the part of first born children to be more in control of their environment as compared to youngest siblings. The differential by birth order is largest for those who come from middle sized cities (9 per cent), though the difference is not significant. It is also noted that for each ordinal rank, the level of powerlessness increases with an increase in size of hometown. Those brought up in the confines of a small city are generally complacent and secure, feel no discontent, and have no interest in change. At the same time, they are aware of who is doing what, how, and when. This situation permits members of such a community to feel in control of the environment. As the size of the city increases, the members find that their traditions no longer form a dependable guide to behavior and perceive their environment as unpredictable, uncertain, and beyond one's own control, especially in view of the rapid social changes which tend to characterize large cities.

When nationality of father is considered, the differential by birth order is least visible among Lebanese children, most evident among Jordanians, and reversed for the other Middle Easterners—Iraqis, Syrians, Egyptians, Saudi Arabians, North Africans, and those from the Arab Peninsula. For the latter nationality group, first and last born children appear to be more in control of their own lives than the Lebanese or the Jordanians. Last born Jordanians report the highest level of powerlessness, while last born other Middle Easterners appear to be least powerless. It is interesting to note that a previous study showed high club membership for the same sibling position of these two nationality groups (Tomeh, 1976). For the former group, high club membership is associated with high powerlessness, whereas for the latter group, high club membership is related to low powerlessness. According to mass theorists, voluntary groups including clubs, act as mechanisms to reduce alienation (Kornhauser, 1959). Results here show that the above argument applies only to last born other Middle Easterners. The generality of the mediation hypothesis is thus in question.

In any event, nationality of father appears to be an intervening variable in the relationship between birth order and powerlessness possibly in terms of the conditions surrounding it, i.e., environmental opportunities, life style of parents, extra familial contacts, etc., the exact impact of which is hard to determine at this point.

Findings on size of family[8] (Table 1) show that in the small family the level of powerlessness is almost the same for the different orders of birth. In the large family, however, the expected differential is as predicted, though not significant. It is further noticed that first and inbetween children of a large family perceive lower levels of powerlessness than their counterparts in the small family, whereas the reverse is true for last born children. Studies on American samples show that the different alienation dimensions separately and in combination under certain circumstances differentiate family size (Rainwater, 1965; Groat and Neal, 1967, 1973; Neal and Groat, 1970) in that high alienation is significantly associated with a large family. Only the results on the last born support American studies, thus suggesting that birth order is an important consideration. It may be that the youngest child in the small family perceives more parental attention than the youngest in the large family. It is in the small family that parents afford an opportunity to devote more of their time and effort to children than would be possible in a large family. In such a situation the frequency and emotional intensity of interaction between the parent and especially the youngest child is likely to be high, whereas in the large family it is dispersed. Possibly the greater involvement, care, affection, and expectations perceived by the youngest child in the small family may explain the increased level of control.

As for the first born in the large family who exhibits the highest control of all siblings, one needs to understand the family values of the Middle Eastern society where the first child becomes the parent model and is expected to carry the responsibility of acting as an alternative love object, especially when there are several children in the family who actually look at the oldest child as a parent. In view of this important and influential function of the first birth order position, the greater feeling of control perceived by the eldest child in the large

---

[8]Family size was divided into two categories at the Median, thus the obtained division in family size of "five children or less" designating small family size, and "six or more children" designating large family size. The frequency distribution of cases in one, two, or three children per family was extremely small to warrant such a category for purposes of analysis. Note that the traditional values and customs of the Middle Eastern culture tend to sustain a high birth rate.

family may not be so surprising. We need to know more about the differences in the patterns of interaction between child and parent in families of different sizes.

Further controls like socioeconomic status[9] show (Table 2) that the level of alienation in terms of powerlessness is almost the same for different orders of birth who are socialized by parents of a low educational level and a low white-collar status. However, first born children of fathers with a high school education report the highest level of powerlessness as compared to later born siblings of the same socioeconomic group, while first and inbetween children of high educational and occupational groups show a greater amount of control over their destiny than younger siblings. This in part suggests that for older children, when the objective criteria for achieving high socioeconomic status are most favorable, the expectation of one's life helps predict who will actually be upward mobile. Interestingly enough, youngest children of a high socioeconomic background are not benefiting from this situation since they appear to have a high level of powerlessness. It is possible that by the time the last born child comes along, parents would have exhausted their economic resources to provide equitable opportunities. Of course, in the lower economic levels, resources are limited for all children and the feasibility of providing some children with fringe benefits over others is slight.

TABLE 2   BIRTH ORDER AND POWERLESSNESS BY SOCIO-ECONOMIC STATUS

| | Education of Father (percent) | | | | | | | | |
| | Elementary | | | High School | | | College | | |
Powerlessness	First	In-between	Last	First	In-between	Last	First	In-between	Last
Low	50	51	48	38	48	53	57	56	34
High	50	49	52	62	52	47	43	44	66
Number of cases	(20)	(51)	(27)	(24)	(57)	(32)	(76)	(92)	(38)
	$X^2=.06, df=2,$ $P>.05, C=.02$			$X^2=1.37, df=2,$ $P>.05, C=.11$			$X^2=6.20, df=2,$ $P>.05, C=.14$		

| | Occupation of Father (percent) | | | | | |
| | Low White-Collar | | | High White-Collar | | |
Powerlessness	First	In-between	Last	First	In-between	Last
Low	51	48	53	52	57	40
High	49	52	47	48	43	60
Number of cases	(47)	(115)	(47)	(73)	(98)	(53)
	$X^2=.43, df=2,$ $P>.05, C=.02$			$X^2=4.25, df=2,$ $P>.05, C=.08$		

[9] "High white-collar" includes professionals and allied, managers of large businesses, officials; "Low white-collar" refers to managers of small businesses, land owners, proprietors, clerical and kindred workers, craftsmen, technicians. The absense of a blue-collar category is due to the fact that Middle Eastern university students represent a relatively high socioeconomic stratum in the Middle Eastern society.

Moreover, several studies have shown that some child training practices vary with social class. It has been reported, for example, that middle class parents are more accepting and accessible to the child than parents in the lower class (Bronfenbrenner, 1958; Clausen and Williams, 1968; Kohn, 1959). Other studies show that there is greater emphasis on independent mastery in early childhood for the middle class than the lower class child. On the average, parents in the higher social strata tend to train their children earlier in independent mastery than those in the lower strata (Rosen, 1956, 1964). Possibly this may be due to the emphasis on success and achievement in the middle class subculture. Our results give partial support to the above findings in that the degree of perceived control increases at the high socio-economic levels for first and inbetween children, but it decreases for last born children. It must be remembered that first born children tend to be trained early in mastering their environment. In part, this is related to their being the only object of parental attention and expectations; their parents also tend to overestimate their ability, especially in the absence of other sibling models against which their performance can be compared. Youngest children also receive training in independent control but the effects of this training may be cancelled by the excessive indulgence which youngest children tend to receive, not only from their parents but also from other relatives. Thus an overindulged child may simply not internalize the expectations of her/his parents and consequently end up with low perceptions of control. Of course, as social class becomes high, the last born child enjoys an added luxury which in turn may account for increased powerlessness.

Normlessness

Similar results are repeated when birth order is related to normlesness, in that first born children perceive slightly less normlessness than last borns (a difference of 7 percent).

An examination of Table 3 shows that when college status is controlled, first born children become more normless as they advance in college; inbetween children experience a sharp increase in normlessness during their sophomore year and a slight decrease in the last two years of college; last borns also perceive high normlessness in the sophomore year, but as they reach the junior and senior level an adherence to approved ethical codes is observed. What these orders of birth have in common is that they all become most susceptible to feelings of normlessness during the sophomore year. This particular year seems to be crucial in the moral judgement that students make. However, a higher college level has a different effect on the level of normlessness of each ordinal rank. It is interesting to note that with the exception of intermediate children, the findings on normlessness and college status are in reverse of those on powerlessness. This suggests that while the two dimensions of alienation are independent of each other, they are related in other cases.

Within each college level, first borns are more likely to adhere to moral norms than last born girls, except at the junior and senior level where their normlessness rates become equal. It may be that the pressure of graduating and becoming successful necessitates striving by any means available to make ends meet. This kind of situation possibly leads to the relative similarity in the degree of normlessness of all orders of birth.

TABLE 3   BIRTH ORDER AND NORMLESSNESS BY DEMOGRAPHIC
                                                                CHARACTERISTICS

| | College Status (percent) | | | | | | | | |
| | Freshmen | | | Sophomore | | | Upperclass women | | |
Normlessness	First	In-between	Last	First	In-between	Last	First	In-between	Last
Low	51	58	39	42	35	30	43	39	43
High	49	42	61	58	65	70	57	61	57
Number of cases	(51)	(72)	(31)	(31)	(49)	(30)	(37)	(89)	(35)
	$X^2=3.37, df=2,$ $P>.05, C=.06$			$X^2=.97, df=2,$ $P>.05, C=.10$			$X^2=.23, df=2,$ $P>.05, C=.01$		

| | Religious Affiliation (percent) | | | | | |
| | Christian | | | Moslem | | |
Normlessness	First	In-between	Last	First	In-between	Last
Low	43	47	33	49	44	50
High	57	53	67	51	56	50
Number of cases	(67)	(88)	(66)	(51)	(124)	(34)
	$X^2=2.83, df=2,$ $P>.05, C=.08$			$X^2=.71, df=2,$ $P>.05, C=.01$		

| | Size of Hometown (percent) | | | | | | | | |
| | 15,000 or Less | | | 15,000 to 99,000 | | | 100,000 or more | | |
Normlessness	First	In-between	Last	First	In-between	Last	First	In-between	Last
Low	42	53	43	58	39	37	43	44	38
High	58	47	57	42	61	63	57	56	62
Number of cases	(31)	(49)	(21)	(24)	(56)	(27)	(65)	(108)	(52)
	$X^2=1.17, df=2,$ $P>.05, C=.03$			$X^2=3.01, df=2,$ $P>.05, C=.15$			$X^2=5.20, df=2,$ $P>.05, C=.03$		

(Contd.)

Table 3 (cont.)

	Nationality of Father (percent)								
	Lebanese			Jordanian			Other Middle Eastern		
Normlessness	First	In-between	Last	First	In-between	Last	First	In-between	Last
Low	42	44	40	48	44	28	38	43	53
High	58	56	60	52	56	72	62	57	47
Number of cases	(48)	(96)	(53)	(27)	(50)	(18)	(24)	(51)	(19)
	$X^2=.24, df=2,$ $P>.05, C=.02$			$X^2=1.99, df=2,$ $P>.05, C=.13$			$X^2=3.97, df=2,$ $P>.05, C=.27$		

	Size of Nuclear Family (percent)					
	Small: Five or less Children			Large: Six or more children		
Normlessness	First	In-between	Last	First	In-between	Last
Low	35	46	47	65	44	33
High	65	54	53	35	56	67
Number of cases	(37)	(48)	(49)	(40)	(110)	(24)
	$X^2=1.39, df=2,$ $P>.05, C=.10$			$X^2=7.22, df=2,$ $P>.05, C=.20$		

When the effect of religion is considered (Table 3), the birth order differential is in the direction predicted for Christian girls only. First and last born Moslem girls report a similar rate of normlessness. It appears that the strict religious training of Islam which includes a set of moral codes, is applied with full pressure, thus cancelling the effect of birth order. It is further observed that first and especially last born Moslem girls adhere to moral norms more than their Christian counterparts. These results may reflect the minority status of Christians in the social structure, a condition which is likely to impede equal representation and participation in the social system. Perhaps the denial of participation in procedural matters related to government and business (as the items on the normlessness scale indicate) tends to influence Christian respondents to accept socially unapproved means in this area. The struggle appears to be much harder for the last born Christian who has to make it in the system by any available means. In general, Christians as compared to Moslems, are not only more powerless but more normless for most orders of birth.

When size of hometown is analyzed, it seems that in the small city, first and last borns perceive a similar level of normlessness. Like powerlessness, the birth order differential by normlessness is most distinct for those from middle sized cities. In the large city, first borns are slightly more likely to adhere to normative codes than their youngest siblings. It is rather clear that the middle sized city appears to generate different effects that affect orders of birth differently. It can be argued, for example, that middle sized cities are in normative conflict due to the clash between the traditional values of the small town and the modern urban values of the large city (Smelser, 1964). Those caught in between two sets of a value system are in an ambiguous situation which, in turn, contributes to normlessness. It is the last born child who seems to be most affected by such conditions, whereas the first born has possibly managed to have a buffer zone that guards against deterioration of the moral order. The above argument is further supported by the fact that the level of normlessness for later born children increases with an increase in size of city.

When nationality of father is considered, the pattern in the level of normlessness by birth order is similar to powerlessness. That is to say, no differences appear among the Lebanese, sharp differences among the Jordanians, and a reversal of the birth order differential among other Middle Easterners. Moreover, while intermediate children of each nationality group perceive the same degree of normlessness, some differences appear among the other siblings. First born Jordanians abide most to normative standards followed by the Labanese and other Middle Easterners of the same birth order group. Among the last borns, the Jordanians show the highest level of normlessness, then the Lebanese, and other Middle Easterners in that order. Again, the high club membership of last born Jordanians (Tomeh, 1976) is not associated with less alienation in the normlessness sense.

In the context of family size, the results of birth order and normlessness are similar to powerlessness. The first born in the large family perceives less normlessness than the last born child, whereas in the small family the reverse is true. It is also noticed that first and inbetween children of large families exceed the level of their counterparts in the small family in terms of abiding to normative standards. Thus studies which have shown high alienation among large families have perhaps generalized too freely when birth order and cultural background appear to make a difference in the relation between family size and alienation.

The findings on socioecononomic status (Table 4) are in some cases similar to those on powerlessness. It is observed, first of all, that for each educational and occupational level, first borns, and for the most part in between children, adhere to normative standards more than youngest siblings, though the differentials are not significant. The largest difference is noted in the high white-collar group (10 percent). These results can perhaps be explained in terms of the high expectation that parents have for first born children who in turn may internalize the standards of conduct expected of them. In this respect the last born child is provided with a realistic standard against which her/his performance may be evaluated. As a result, youngest children may adopt behavioral and attitudinal patterns different from those of oldest siblings to prevent themselves from being evaluated unfavorably. This strategy tends to generate loss of commonly held standards and low predictability in the behavior of the youngest child. At the same time, alienation may also stem from frustration of ambitions (Germani,

1966; Meier, 1959; Wilensky, 1966) especially when the youngest child is unable to measure up to the level of the oldest sibling.

TABLE 4   BIRTH ORDER AND NORMLESSNESS BY SOCIO-ECONOMIC STATUS

| | Education of Father (percent) | | | | | | | | |
| | Elementary | | | High School | | | College | | |
Normlessness	First	In-between	Last	First	In-between	Last	First	In-between	Last
Low	45	43	37	46	46	38	46	45	40
High	55	57	63	54	54	62	54	55	60
Number of cases	(20)	(51)	(27)	(24)	(67)	(32)	(76)	(92)	(38)
	$X^2=.37, df=2,$ $p>.05, C=.06$			$X^2=.72, df=2,$ $p>.05, C=.07$			$X^2=.45, df=2,$ $p>.05, C=.05$		

| | Occupation of Father (percent) | | | | | |
| | Low White-Collar | | | High White-Collar | | |
Normlessness	First	In-between	Last	First	In-between	Last
Low	51	46	47	42	44	32
High	49	54	53	58	56	68
Number of cases	(47)	(115)	(47)	(73)	(98)	(53)
	$X^2=.34, df=2,$ $p>.05, C=.03$			$X^2=2.14, df=2,$ $p>.05, C=.07$		

Further examination of the same table shows that the level of normlessness of all siblings is consistent across the different educational groups. Some differences begin to appear in the case of occupation, where first and last born children of a high white-collar background become more normless than their counterparts in the low white-collar group. Intermediate children approximately maintain the same level of normlessness in the two occupational strata. These results suggest that occupation is a more important variable than education in terms of its effect on the normlessness of different orders of birth.

Perhaps it should be noted that the high white-collar class in the social structure studied includes a large proportion of business managers and government officials. Moreover, in a largely agricultural society like the Middle East, achieved status, success, progress, etc. are not viewed as crucial for this socio-economic group as the case in an industrial society. Yet there seems to be some need on the part of first and last born children of this occupational group for manipulative attitudes even when this stratum represents government and business. However, it must be stressed that, in a comparative sense, this particular social class as a whole adheres to moral standards more than its counterpart in the American society (Tomeh, 1974).

Meaninglessness:

Unlike the other two dimensions of alienation, meaninglessness, in the context of college unsatisfaction, does not differentiate the population by birth order.   All siblings seem to report the same level of understanding of the educational system.   When college status is controlled (Table 5), the same findings are repeated except for sophomores where last born children appear to be slightly more satisfied with their college than first borns.   What is important, however, is that the degree of perceived meaninglessness for all sibling ranks decreases with an advance in college status.   College experience, therefore, has a positive effect on students in terms of their understanding of the college institution.

Further observation of the data in the same table shows that when the effect of religion is considered, no major differences appear for the Christian group, while for the Moslem group the expected birth order differential is reversed.   It is further noticed that all siblings of the former group perceive more meaning in what they are doing in college than Moslems.   Possibly the minority status of the Christians in the Middle Eastern society has compelled Christian parents to stress the internalization of standards of higher education in their children as contrasted to Moslem parents who, as a result of their majority status, may not necessarily conceive of their role as primarily eliciting specific attitudinal conformities from their children relative to their work in college.   This explanation based on differential socialization thought to be related to the transmission of values, may in part explain the above observed findings.

TABLE 5   BIRTH ORDER AND MEANINGLESSNESS BY DEMOGRAPHIC
                                                        CHARACTERISTICS

| | College Status (percent) | | | | | | | | |
| | Freshmen | | | Sophomore | | | Upperclasswomen | | |
Meaninglessness	First	In-between	Last	First	In-between	Last	First	In-between	Last
Low	41	36	39	42	47	50	54	54	51
High	59	64	61	58	53	50	46	46	49
Number of cases	(51)	(72)	(31)	(31)	(49)	(30)	(37)	(89)	(35)
	$X^2=.33, df=2,$ $p>.25, C=.03$			$X^2=.41, df=2,$ $p>.05, C=.07$			$X^2=.07, df=2,$ $p>.05, C=.02$		

(Contd)

Table 5 (Contd.)

	Religious Affiliation (percent)					
	Christian			Moslem		
Meaninglessness	First	In-between	Last	First	In-between	Last
Low	54	50	53	33	44	41
High	46	50	47	67	56	59
Number of cases	(67)	(88)	(66)	(51)	(124)	(34)
	$X^2=.25, df=2,$ $p>.05, C=.01$			$X^2=1.57, df=2,$ $p>.05, C=.06$		

	Size of Hometown (percent)								
	15,000 or less			15,000 to 99,000			100,000 or more		
Meaninglessness	First	In-between	Last	First	In-between	Last	First	In-between	Last
Low	58	49	48	33	48	59	43	44	44
High	42	51	52	67	52	41	57	56	56
Number of cases	(31)	(49)	(21)	(24)	(56)	(27)	(65)	(108)	(52)
	$X^2=.79, df=2,$ $p>.05, C=.09$			$X^2=3.44, df=2,$ $p>.05, C=.19$			$X^2=.02, df=2,$ $p>.05, C=.01$		

	Nationality of Father (percent)								
	Lebanese			Jordanian			Other Middle Eastern		
Meaninglessness	First	In-between	Last	First	In-between	Last	First	In-between	Last
Low	44	52	47	44	40	50	25	37	42
High	56	48	53	56	60	50	75	63	58
Number of cases	(48)	(96)	(53)	(27)	(50)	(18)	(24)	(51)	(19)
	$X^2=.96, df=2,$ $p>.05, C=.02$			$X^2=.57, df=2,$ $p>.05, C=.03$			$X^2=1.60, df=2,$ $p>.05, C=.13$		

	Size of Nuclear Family (percent)					
	Small: Five or Less Children			Large: Six or More Children		
Meaninglessness	First	In-between	Last	First	In-between	Last
Low	57	46	65	35	46	29
High	43	54	35	65	54	71
Number of cases	(37)	(48)	(49)	(40)	(110)	(24)
	$X^2=3.74, df=2,$ $p>.05, C=.09$			$X^2=3.27, df=2,$ $p>.05, C=.001$		

The results on size of hometown show that the birth order differential is as expected in the small city. A reversal takes place in the medium sized city, and no differences appear in the large city. The complexity of the large city seems to affect all orders of birth similarly in that even their college institution is perceived as an intricate and complex phenomenon. This argument is further supported by the fact that for each order of birth, meaninglessness increases with an increase in size of city except for last born children where a curvilinear relationship is noticed.

When nationality of father is controlled, the most noticeable effect is among the other Middle Eastern group where a reversal of the birth order differential occurs. Of course, the same was true for the other two dimensions of alienation. While the reversed differential by birth order cannot be explained in terms of other demographic characteristics or socialization patterns, because both of these sets of factors favor the low alienation of the first born, one can only conclude that the high club membership and mass media exposure of last born Middle Easterners (Tomeh, 1976) have a positive effect on their social psychological attitudes. Nonetheless, for each order of birth in the other Middle Eastern group, the level of meaninglessness is higher than those whose fathers are Jordanian or Lebanese.

When size of family is analyzed, results resemble those on powerlessness and normlessness in that the expected birth order differential holds only in the case of the large family, while in the small family, youngest children are more likely than their older siblings to find meaning in their college work. It seems that the role the first child plays in the large family is of tremendous importance to parents and other siblings. The significance of this particular role appears to have a positive effect on one's attitudinal outlook in terms of alienation.

It is further observed that in the small family, first and last born children perceive more meaning and clarity in the college system than their counterparts in the large family. For intermediate children, however, no differences are observed by size of family.

Unlike large families, small families are said to be particularly oriented towards status striving and upward mobility. Bearing in mind, of course, that these values are not of a very high priority in the Middle Eastern society. Nonetheless, families approximating this type of orientation would probably provide their children with a sense of clarity and coherence in society which, in turn, may be reflected in their view of the college institution. Furthermore, the relative stress on competition and achievement in the small family probably heightens the sense of rivalry which frequently exists between siblings, making parental attention an even more attractive object for the child. It is usually the last born who is the competitor and target for parental attention. These patterns of interaction between child and parent in the small family may explain in part the lower level of meaninglessness on the part of the last born as compared to older siblings as well as the lower level of meaninglessness of first and last born children as compared to the large family.

When socioeconomic status is controlled (Table 6), results are somewhat inconsistent. For example, it is observed that among those whose fathers have elementary school, first borns have a slightly greater tendency to perceive meaning in their educational system than youngest children. At the high school and low white-collar levels, a reversal of the expected birth order differential holds and as socioeconomic status increases beyond that stage, siblings of different orders of birth report almost the same rate of meaninglessness. In other words, when socioeconomic status is high, the effect of birth order is greatly reduced. It is also noticed that with an increase in education, older siblings maintain the same meaninglessness level, whereas last born children perceive the lowest level of meaninglessness at the high school level, after which there is a slight increase. Similarly, as occupational level increases, meaninglessness also increases for inbetween and last born children.

TABLE 6   BIRTH ORDER AND MEANINGLESSNESS BY SOCIO-ECONOMIC STATUS

	Education of Father (percent)								
	Elementary			High School			College		
Meaninglessness	First	In-between	Last	First	In-between	Last	First	In-between	Last
Low	45	45	37	42	46	59	46	46	50
High	55	55	63	58	54	41	54	54	50
Number of cases	(20)	(51)	(27)	(24)	(67)	(32)	(76)	(92)	(38)
	$X^2 = .52, df = 2,$ $p > .05, C = .06$			$X^2 = 2.09, df = 2,$ $p > .05, C = .13$			$X^2 = .22, df = 2,$ $p > .05, C = .02$		

	Occupation of Father (percent)					
	Low White-Collar			High White-Collar		
Meaninglessness	First	In-between	Last	First	In-between	Last
Low	43	49	55	47	43	43
High	57	51	45	53	57	57
Number of cases	(47)	(115)	(47)	(73)	(98)	(53)
	$X^2 = 1.53, df = 2,$ $p > .05, C = .09$			$X^2 = .25, df = 2,$ $p > .05, C = .03$		

Thus, for certain orders of birth and certain levels of socioeconomic status, comprehending the educational institution, remains to be intricate and unclear. The same is true of the other two dimensions of alienation.

Conclusion

The primary concern of this study is to analyze the relationship between birth order and alienation. Evidence shows that when first borns are compared to last born children, no significant differences in alienation are found. None-theless, the trend favors the low alienation of the oldest child in the family in terms of powerlessness and normlessness.

More specifically, on the dimension of powerlessness, first born children reveal slightly higher expectations for control of events regardless of demo-graphic variables except among sophomores, other Middle Easterners, and those whose fathers are of a middle socioeconomic level. In these specific instances, a reversal of the above described pattern is true. On the dimension of normless-ness, most first born children of different population groups are less normless than last borns except among other Middle Easterners and in the small family where a reversal also occurs. In some population groups the rates are rather similar.

The reversals in the relationship between birth order and forms of alienation in some population groups as compared to others, suggest the importance of maintaining the multivariate character of the alienation concept for specific orders of birth while seeking to determine the additive effects of social psychological variables in others. The control variables of population characteristics provide a background against which the operative effect of birth order on alienation may be determined. However, the dynamics of parent-child interaction as inter-vening variables between birth order and forms of alienation await further research.

On the dimension of meaninglessness, results on birth order do not follow a very consistent pattern; overall, however, there seems to be some similarity among the different orders of birth in the extent to which siblings perceive their college institution to be meaningful. Again, there are some exceptions to this pattern. Perhaps limiting the perception of meaninglessness to college work instead of viewing the broader social events as chaotic and without purpose may have reduced the effect of birth order and in some instances highlighted the low level of meaninglessness among last born children. One may raise the question as to whether alienation is a generic "trait" or whether it must be considered as a situationally related variable. It might be profitable to develop instead of a societal alienation component scale—scales to be specifically applied to various areas of social life. The first born might have a "low alienation" score, for example, in the familial aspect but a high one in regard to organizational or leisure life. In any event, our results perhaps raise some question as to the utility of the concept of alienation as it has been used.

It is important to point out, however, that on the various dimensions of alienation, the attitudinal pattern of intermediate children is not consistent. Possibly the lack of a fixed position in the birth order hierarchy and the avail-ability of multiple identification models may account in part for their unidentfiable social psychological inclination. It may be important in future research to make a distinction in the ranks and age spacing of inbetween children to be able to discern a typical attitudinal orientation.

Implicit in the findings, as well as in the larger theoretical framework based on differential socialization from which the hypotheses for this study have been extracted is the notion that birth order as a structural variable in the family affects one's social psychological outlook. This relationship is sometimes accentuated when combined with such factors as college status, religious perference, size of hometown, size of family, etc. the major premise being that children of a different ordinal position and sociocultural background are exposed to different interaction and social learning experiences which result in their attitudinal disposition. Despite the oversimplification of this statement, it is a firm basis for beginning a systematic analysis of the features and characteristics of interaction within the family which have bearing on the social psychological attitudes of children of different orders of birth. The unique features of the development process need to be identified empirically rather than speculatively.

When a comparison is made between the effect of birth order and that of the control variables, one is inclined to conclude that both sets of factors are important considerations in the study of alienation. Although the relationships are not significant, there is some evidence to suggest a birth order trend in the majority of cases. The fact does not conceal the intervening effect of demographic aspects of family structure as they also influence aspects of the socialization process, especially in instances where the birth order differential is reduced or reversed. The observed variability in some populatian groups implies that there is nothing fixed about birth order but that attitude and behavior are the same for children born into certain family places, because parents and other family and non-family members tend to maintain certain patterns of expectations. In any event, although birth order does not produce great alienative effects, it cannot be ignored in the study of the family. The small differences by birth order also suggest that the conditions in society described earlier pervade all orders of birth, and no one can greatly escape the impact of a changing society. At the same time, the traditional orientation of the first born and the peer orientation of the last born reported in previous studies are supportive elements that tend to reduce feelings of alienation among siblings. However, neither type of orientation always results in instant low alienation.

Important as this study is, it leaves some tasks undone. *First*, a sample composed of male and female Middle Eastern subjects may indicate that the effects of the ordinal position of siblings are probably subordinate to their sex with direct effects on the level of alienation. This is particularly applicable to the Middle Eastern culture where it still makes quite a difference whether the first born is a son or a daughter. The first son, though he may be born after his sister, is accorded the same position of importance as the first born child. He is expected to be the role model for younger siblings and act as a protector of an older sister (if any). He also receives priority in educational, occupational, and social opportunities (Tomeh. 1975:95-104, on family structure and sex roles). Hence, the extent to which sex as an intervening variable affects the relationship between birth order and alienation requires further study. The present study composed totally of a female sample may, in part, account for the low statistical support of the basic hypothesis of this analysis.

Second, we need to know about variations in the relationship between birth order and alienaton in the general population and in other societies and cultures taking into account structural and dynamic variables. For example, other factors besides those considered here may also be important—such as the number and ordinal position of male and female siblings, as well as the number of years separating each child. Furthermore, other adults besides parents, both in and out of the family, may play significant roles in the social psychological outlook of each child. Thus, more work remains to be done before the process through which values, attitudes, and behaviors are learned by each order of birth is adequately understood.

Third, and most important, is that future research must be directed toward the study of the interplay among family interaction, socialization, and order of birth. The effect of such factors are by no means simple or readily predictable. One reason for this is the substantial interactian between these variables particularly with some sociocultural and demographic aspects of the family. The complexity of this approach no doubt reflects the fact that many factors impinge upon the learning process. Such an attempt, however, will provide a theoretical and systematic analysis of the effect of birth order—a need which is pressing birth order research.

REFERENCES

Almond, Gabriel A. and Sidney Verba
  1963   The Civic Culture: Political Attitudes and Democracy in the Five Nations. Princeton: Princeton University Press.

Altus, William
  1966   "Birth order and its sequelae," Science 151 (January): 44-49.

Ansbacher, Hientz L. and Rowena R. Ansbacher
  1956   The Individual Psychology of Alfred Adler. New York: Basic Books:376-383.

Armstrong, Lincoln and Gordon Hirabayashi
  1956   "Social differentiation in selected Lebanese villages," American Sociological Review 21 (August): 425-434.

Bossard, James and Eleanor Boll
  1956   The Large Family System. Philadelphia, University of Pennsylvania Press.

Bradley, R.W.
  1968   "Birth order and school-related behavior," Psychological Bulletin 70 (July): 45-51.

Bragg, B.W. and V.L. Allen
  1970   "Ordinal position and conformity," Sociometry 33 (December): 371-381.

Brim, Orville A.
  1958   "Family structure and sex role learning by children: a future analysis of Helen Koch's data," Sociometry 21 (March) : 1-15.

Bronfenbrenner, Y.
  1958   "Socialization and social class through time and space." Pp. 400-425 in Eleanor E. Maccoby, T.M. Newcomb, and E.L. Hartley (eds.), Readings in Social Psychology. New York: Holt, Rinehart and Winston.

Camilleri, C.
  1967   "Modernity and the family in Tunisia," Journal of Marriage and the Family 29
          (August: 590-595.

Clausen, J.A. and J. Williams
  1968   "Sociological correlates of child behavior." pp. 62-107 in H.W. Stevenson, J. Kayan,
          and C. Spiker (eds.), Child Psychology, Yearbook National Society for the Study of
          Education, 62.

Connors, Keith
  1963   "Birth order and need for affiliation," Journal of Personality 31 (September):
          408-416.

Dean, Dwight
  1961   "Alienation: its meaning and measurement," American Sociological Review 26
          (October): 753-758.

Elder, Glen, Jr. and Charles Bowerman
  1963   "Family structure and child rearing patterns: the effect of family size and sex com-
          position," American Sociological Review 28 (December): 891-905.

Gerard, Harold
  1961   "Fear and social comparison," Journal of Abnormal and Social Psychology 62 (May):
          586-592.

Germani, Gino
  1966   "Soical and political consequences of mobility." pp. 364-394 in Neil Smelser and
          Seymour Lipset (eds.), Social Structure and Mobility in Economic Development.
          Chicago: Aldine.

Gillespie, James and Gordon Allport
  1955   Youth's Outlooks on the Future. New York: Doubleday. Papers in Psychology
          No. 15. Doubleday.

Groat, Theodore and Arthur Neal
  1967   "Social Psychological correlates or urban fertility," American Sociological Review 32
          (December) : 945-959.
  1973   "Social class and alienation correlates of Protestant fertility," Journal of Marriage
          and the Family 35 (February) :83-88.

Hall, Everette and Ben Barger
  1964   "Attitudinal structures of older and younger siblings," Journal of Individual Psycho-
          logy 20 (1) : 59-68.

Harris, Irving and Kenneth I. Howard
  1968   "Birth order and responsibility," Journal of Marriage and the Family 30 (August)
          427-432.

Hielbrun, Alfred, Jr. and Donald Fromme
  1965   "Parental identification of late adolescents and level of adjustment: the importance
          of parent-model attributes, ordinal position, and sex of child," Journal of Genetic
          Psychology 107 (September): 49-59.

Hirabayashi, Gordon and Fathalla El Khatib
  1958   "Communication and political awareness in the villages of Egypt," Public Opinion
          Quarterly 22 (Fall): 357-363.

Hirabayashi, Gordon and May Ishaq
  1958   "Social change in Jordan," American Journal of Sociology 64 (July): 36-40.

Kammeyer, Kenneth
  1966   "Birth order and the feminine sex role among college women," American Sociologi-
          cal Review 31 (August) : 508-515.

1967a   "Sibling position and the feminine role," Journal of Marriage and the Family 29 (August) : 494-499.

1967b   "Birth order as a research variable," Social Forces 46 (September): 71-80.

Kohn, M.L.
1959   "Social class and the exercise of parental authority," American Sociological Review 24 (June): 352-366.

Kornhauser, W.
1959   The Politics of Mass Society. Glencoe, Illinois: The Free Press.

Lasko, Joan K.
1954   "Parent behavior toward first and second children," Genetic Psychology Monographs 49 (February) 97-137.

Lerner, Daniel
1958   The Passing of the Traditional Society. New York: The Free Press.

MacArthur, Charles
1956   "Personalities of first and second children," Psychiatry 19 (February): 47-54.

Menzel, Herbert
1953   "A new coefficient for scalogram analysis," Public Opinion Quarterly 17 (Summer): 268-280.

Meier, Dorothy and Wendell Bell
1959   "Anomie and differential access to the achievement of life goals," American Sociological Review 24 (April): 189-207.

Merton, Robert
1957   Social Theory and Social Structure. Glencoe, Illinois: The Free Press.

Milikian, Levon and Jerry Prothro
1957   "Goals chosen by Arab students in response to hypothetical situations," Journal of Social Psychology 46 (August): 3-9.

Neal, Arthur and Theodore Groat
1970   "Alienation correlates of Catholic fertility," American Journal of Sociology 76 (November): 460-473.

Neal, Arthur and Salomon Retting
1963   "Dimensions of alienation among manual and non-manual workers," American Sociological Review 28 (August): 599-608.

Newcomb, Theodore
1950   Social Psychology. New York: Holt, Rinehart and Winston, pp. 205-207.

Palmer, R.D.
1966   "Birth order and identification," Journal of Consulting Psychology 30 (April): 129-135.

Radloff, Ronald
1961   "Opinion evaluation and affiliation." Journal of Abnormal and Social Psychology 62 (May): 578-585.

Rainwater, Lee
1965   Family Design. Chicago: Aldine Publishing Company, Chapter 6.

Roe, Ann
1953   "A psychological study of eminent psychologists and anthropologists, and a comparison with biological and physcial scientists," Psychological Monographs 62 (2): 47.

Rosen, Bernard C.
1956   "The achievement syndrome: a psychocultural dimension of social stratification," American Sociological Review 21 (April): 203-211.

1961   "Family structure and achievement motivation," American Sociological Review 26 (August): 574-585.

1964   "Family structure and value transmission," Merrill Palmer Quarterly 10 (January): 59-76.

Rotter, Julian
  1954   Social Learning and Clinical Psychology. Englewood Cliffs, New Jersey: Prentice-
            Hall.

Rossi, Alice
  1965   "Naming children in middle-class families," American Sociological Review 30
            (August) : 499-513.

Sampson, Edward
  1962   "Birth order, need achievement and conformity," Journal of Abnormal and Social
            Psychology 64 (February) 155-159.

Schachter, Stanley
  1959   The Psychology of Affiliation. Stanford: Stanford University Press.

Sears, Robert
  1950   "Ordinal position in the family as a psychological variable." American Sociological
            Review 15 (June) : 397-401.

Sears, R.R., E. Maccoby, and H. Levin
  1957   Patterns of Child Rearing. Evanston, Illinois: Ron Peterson.

Seeman, Melvin
  1959   "On the Meaning of alienation," American Sociological Review 24 (December):
            783-791.
  1966   "Alienation, membership, and political knowledge: a comparative study," Public
            Opinion Quarterly 30 (Fall): 353-367.

Singer, E.
  1971   "Adult orientation of first and later children," Sociometry 34 (September): 3,
            328-345.

Smelser, Neil
  1964   "Toward a theory of modernization." pp. 258-274 in Etzioni,, Amitari and Etzioni,
            Eva (eds.), Social Change: Source, Patterns, and Consequences. N.J.: Basic
            Books.

Stroup, Atlee and Katherine J. Hunter
  1965   "Sibling position in the family and personality of offspring," Journal of Marriage
            and the Family 27 (February): 65-68.

Sutton-Smith, *et al.*
  1964   "Sibling associations and role involvement," Merrill Palmer Quarterly 10 (January):
            25-38.

Tomeh, Aida K.
  1969   "Birth order and kinship affiliation," Journal of Marriage and the Family 31
            (February): 19-26.
  1970   "Birth order and friendship associations," Journal of Marriage and the Family 32
            (February): 360-369.
  1971   "Birth order and familial influences in the Middle East," Journal of Comparative
            Family Studies 11 (Spring) : 87-106.
  1972   "Birth order and dependence patterns of college students in Lebanon," Journal of
            Marriage and the Family 34 (May): 361-374.
  1974   "Alienation: a cross-cultural analysis," Journal of Social Psychology 94: 187-200.
  1975   The Family and Sex Roles. Toronto, Canada: Holt, Rinehart, and Winston.
  1976   "Birth order, club membership and mass media exposure," Journal of Marriage and
            the Family 38 (February): 151-164.

Warren, Johnathan
  1966   "Birth order and social behavior," Psychological Bulletin 65 (January): 38-49.

Wilensky, Harold
  1966   "Effects of mobility." pp. 48-140 in Neil Smelser and Seymour Lipset (eds.), Social
            Structure and Mobility in Economic Development. Chicago: Aldine.

7

Education of Muslim Women: Tradition Versus Modernity

M. INDU MENON*

A critical factor in the improvement of the status of women is education which is indispensable for many of the modern roles. Education not only equips women with the knowledge and expertise necessary for playing many modern roles and thereby enables them to rise in status; it also widens their cognitive map and enables them to compare their position in society vis-a-vis men. Accordingly, education has formed a key element in the Government of India's programmes for the improvement of status of women. The Government have also realised that education is basic to availing of many of their social welfare programmes and the enjoyment of many of the measures of social legislation passed since Independence. Government have initiated large scale educational programmes in the country, with special focus on the weaker section of the people. In spite of these, Muslim women continue to be one of the most backward sections of the people in India as far as education is concerned. This seems to be largely due to the presence of certain social structural and institutional factors in Islam which contribute to depress women's education and keep them in an inferior position.

This paper attempts to identify some factors which are responsible for hindering educational progress of Muslim women. We started with the assumption that the traditional attitude of the Muslim community is the most important reason for the low level of education among Muslim women. Here it is intended to find out the role of four major factors which hinder the educational progress of Muslim women viz. (1) insistence on religious education, (2) early marriage, (3) seclusion and (4) absence of socially defined occupational role for women in Muslim community.

Universe and Sample

The study was made on the Muslim women of Kerala. Though the Muslims are spread over the entire length and breadth of Kerala State, there are certain districts which have larger concentration of Muslims than others. Thus the districts of Malappuram, Calicut, Palghat and Cannanore account for 66 per cent of the total Muslim population of Kerala. These four districts were chosen for drawing up the sample. The population was stratified into rural and urban based on 1971 census data and representative panchayats (rural) and towns (urban) were

---

*Loyola College of Social Sciences, University of Kerala, Trivandrum, India.

selected from each of the four districts. From these panchayats and towns, wards were identified for selection of sample subjects. Since education is the critical variable in the study, the selection of panchayats and town wards was done on the basis of their comparatively higher literacy rate. From the voters list/register of households were identified (by the name of the head of the household). By using random sampling method, 450 women were chosen for interview.

Islam and Women's Education

Islam attaches great value to education and prescribes it as the duty of a woman as well as that of a man to acquire knowledge. According to Lichtenstadter (n.d.141) fundamentally it (Islam) has always considered learning at least a useful accessory to being a good Muslim...Islam thinks that education is a necessary condition which helps women to develop their faculties. In the words of Mohammed Qutb (1964:188) "acquisition of knowledge was as great a duty of women as of man, for, Islam wanted womenfolk to develop their rational faculties along with physical ones and thus ascend to higher planes of spiritual existence..." Mohammed preached to his followers: knowledge enables its possessor to distinguish what is forbidden from what is not, it lights the way to heaven; it is our friend in the desert, our society in solitude, our companion with benefits of friends; it guides us to happiness' (Gore, Desai and Chitnis, 1967:89). The four things which the Prophet commands the followers to do for their children are: (1) to circumcise them (2) to inform them of the principles of religion, (3) to educate them properly and (4) to marry them off when they reach the proper age. Thus we see that in Islam education is given an important position in the life of the people. Though Mohammed favoured women's education, in actual practice the injunctions of the Quran in this respect were completely ignored. The Muslim community, as it had misinterpreted many other principles of Islam, also considered the education of girls as an unnecessary step. As a result, 'a situation developed where Muslim societies are educationally perhaps the most backward in the contemporary world' (Kabir, 1969:8). In the absence of education, women in the Arab countries were considered inferior to men and consequently their status became accordingly low. Their status began to improve as a result of the spread of education. Berger (1962:152) points out that "emancipation of women in the Arab world has proceeded indirectly largely as a consequence of their greater education and freedom to work outside home, rather than as a result of direct legislation aimed at revolutionising their status."

In spite of the fact that the Government of India have provided girls with equal opportunity for education with boys and have given special considerations for the backward classes in the form of fee concessions, scholarships, seat reservations etc., the number of educated Muslim women is still less when compared with women belonging to other communities. One sample of 450 Muslim women contained only 66 persons (14.67%) who were educated high school and above. 35 per cent were illiterate. 27.55 per cent had primary school education and 22.67 per cent had middle school education. The conservatism of parents towards the education of girls, together with the practice of purdah or seclusion, early marriage, lack of socially defined occupational roles are the main factors which hinder the educational progress of Muslim women.

Place of Religious Education in Islam

One of the main things Islam commands a Muslim to do is to teach children the principles of their religion. So religious education is an imperative for a Muslim, man or woman. "These religious precepts have never been overruled by custom and are strictly observed by all classes of Mohammadans in India. It is this religious command that compels Mohammadans to instruct their children in Koran and other religious books" (Government of India, 1952, 311). Religious education is an essential part of the education to a Muslim and in many cases his education was limited to religious instruction only. It was one of the standing orders of the institution (Madrasai Azam) that Mussalman students should be first instructed on religious subjects in order that they might become acquainted with the laws of Islamism before they are instructed in those languages which would give them the means of livelihood (Government of Madras, 1894:4). As far as Muslim girls are concerned the main and sometimes the only education they were getting till recently was religious instruction. In the present study, it was found that out of 450 women 158 (35%) had only religious education and no formal school education what so ever. Without exception, all the respondents had religious education. About 35 per cent of the respondents said they studied religion for 1 to 3 years, 60 per cent said they had religious education for 4 to 6 years and 5 per cent had it for 7 to 9 years. The mean number of years spent on religious education by the respondents was 4.12.

Educational level of the respondents and the duration of their religious education are related to each other significantly. This is clear from the following table.

EDUCATION AND DURATION OF RELIGIOUS EDUCATION

General Education	Religious Education			Total
	1-3 years	4-6 years	7-9 years	
Illiterate	52 (33.33%)	94 (34.81%)	12 (50.00%)	158
Primary	20 (12.82%)	97 (35.93%)	7 (29.16%)	124
Middle	48 (30.77%)	50 (18.52%)	4 (16.67%)	102
High School and College	36 (23.08%)	29 (10.74%)	1 (4.17%)	66
Total	156 (34.67%)	270 (60.00%)	24 (5.33%)	450

Chi-square=80.639   Df=6
Table value at .01 =16.812

It is clear from the table that 23 per cent of the respondents who had religious education for only 1 to 3 years were high school and above educated. Only 4 per cent who had religious instruction for 7 to 9 years had high school and above education. So it is seen that as the duration of the religious education increases the educational level of the respondent decreases.

One of the after effects of this long duration of religious education is the late entry to school. It is a noteworthy fact that the age at which the Muslim girls first enter the school is 2 to 3 years older than the minimum age prescribed by Government for admission to school. The minimum age prescribed for admission to school when the oldest of our respondents were in school was 5. But in the case of our respondents, it was found that only 14.38 per cent of them entered the school at the age of 5 to 6, 31 per cent of the Muslim girls joined the school at the age of 6 to 7, 38.36 per cent at the age of 7 to 8 and 16.16 per cent at the age of 8 or above. So we see that a larger portion of the respondents first joined the school at the age of 7 to 8.

Thus we find that the average age at which the respondent entered school was 7 whereas the age prescribed by the state was 5. Our respondents had to undergo compulsory religious education for periods ranging from 3 to 5 years (in exceptional cases 9 years). Hence if the Madrasas and the State schools had concurrent working hours, children will have to postpone their school education until after the completion of the religious instruction. In that case after late entry they had to leave the school in 3 or 4 years as after maturity no Muslim girl was expected to be in school. If on the other hand the Madrasas are working outside the State school hours, a girl attending both of them will have to strain hard and this would result in poor performance at school. Consequently she will either fail in classes or will drop out from school, as education in these schools is considered less important than education in the Madrasas.

At present religious education is competing with the State educational system in so far as heavy demand is placed on the young child by both the Madrasas and the public school system simultaneously. Since priority has been given by the community to the first, this results in neglect of secular education. Actually there is no need for conflict between the two. Currently Arabic teachers are appointed in all schools where there is a sizeable number of Muslim students. Arabic instruction in the school could be expanded by provision of an extra hour or so per week to accomodate the curriculum followed in the Madrasas. This would avoid the need for a parallel system of religious schools along with the public schools and expenditure thereof and also the need to spend the first three or four years of a girls' school going life to be spend in religious schools to the neglect or subordination of secular education.

Early Marriage

In Islam no age limit is fixed for marriage. It was often seen that quite young girls may be legally married but a girl is handed over to the husband only after the attained puberty. According to Bevan Jones (1941:91) it is usual for orthodox muslims to claim that child marriage, though not enjoined in the Quran or the Traditions, is part of the very fabric of Islam and they contend that the custom is sanctioned by the practice of Mohammed who himself married a child wife... According to Muhammedan low majority is attained on puberty and even though a girl is under 15 years of age, she is free to marry after attaining puberty. But in India, after the passing of child Marriage Restraint Act of 1929, it is punishable offence to promote or permit the solemnisation of a marriage of a bridegroom under 18 years of age and a bride under 15 years. In spite of this, early marriage has continued to be widespread among the Muslim Community.

In the present study of 450 Muslim women, 36.22 per cent were married below 15 years, 58.22 per cent were married between 15 to 19 years and 5.56 per cent between 20 to 24 years and none above 24. When analysed on the basis of educational level of the respondents, it was found that age at marriage and the educational level of the respondents were significantly related. This is shown in the following table.

EDUCATION AND AGE AT FIRST MARRIAGE

Education	Age at Marriage			Total
	10 to 14	15 to 19	20 to 24	
Illiterate	73 (46.20%)	81 (51.27%)	4 (2.53%)	158
Primary	44 (35.48%)	77 (62.11%)	3 (2.41%)	124
Middle	37 (36.27%)	58 (56.86%)	7 (6.87%)	102
High School and College	9 (13.64%)	46 (69.70%)	11 (16.67%)	66
Total	163 (36.22%)	262 (58.22%)	25 (5.56%)	450

Chi–square=36.589   Df=6
Table value at 0.01 level=16.812

The table shows that out of 158 women who are illiterate 46 per cent were married below 15 years, 51 per cent between 15 and 19 years and only about 3 per cent were married between the age of 20 to 24. Out of 66 high school and above educated women only 14 per cent were married below 15 years, about 70 per cent between 15 and 19 and 17 per cent were married between 20 and 24. Thus it is clear that as the age at marriage decreases education also decreases.

So we find that early marriage continues to be a major hindrance to education of women. A good number (30%) of our respondents still believe early marriage is desirable for girls. Further, there were several cases where the daughters of our respondents who were married below 15. As Muslim women after marriage are not permitted to go out without escort, it is very difficult for them to continue their education after marriage—specially when educational institutions are located away from the place of residence. Most of the higher educational institutions fall in this category. As Muslim girls start their school education later on their life (due to the priority given for religious education) the combined effect of early marriage and late entry into schools is to leave the girls with very little education. Our respondents themselves felt that early marriage prevents girls from continuing their education. And our data have proved beyond doubt that early marriage has been a major deterrant in the education of Muslim women. This practice of early marriage could be easily checked at the time of registration of marriage, provided the state enforces this provision more strictly.

Seclusion

The Muslim community is one where the seclusion of women including purdah system was once strictly observed. They considered it as a sin to show themselves off to strangers. Freedom of movement is indispensable to attend the schools. In the present study it was found that when asked our respondents how much freedom of movement enjoyed in going out, 31.33 per cent of them had the freedom to go out with female friends only. None had the freedom to go out alone for any purpose (except for employment in the case of those who are employed). This seclusion including lack of freedom of movement discouraged Muslim girls from attending schools. The wealthy families arranged private tuitions in their own homes for teaching their women Quran and other religious books. But with the disappearance of purdah system this condition gradually changed. Now the number of Muslim girls going to schools and even attending mixed schools is on the increase. But the traditional attitude still remains.

Our respondents in general showed a positive preference for separate girls' schools for their daughters' education. This is clear from their answer to the question "to what type of institution would you like to send your daughters"? As religious instruction is being given in mixed classes, the respondents did not mind boys and girls studying together at the primary level. At the upper primary level 23 per cent of the respondents said they prefer girls' schools for their daughters, 38 per cent said they had no preference and 39 per cent said they prefer mixed schools. At the high school level, 81 per cent said they prefer girls' schools. In the case of college education, 95 per cent of the mothers preferred women's college. It is clear that as girls grow up, the mothers want them to be segregated from boys and this is most clearly pronounced at the college level. The preference of the large majority of respondents for girls' schools and colleges at the high school and college level makes it clear that they even now like to maintain seclusion of girls if possible.

Since very strong preference has been expressed by the majority of Muslim women for separate schools for girls it is desirable that separate educational institutions for girls be established in the Malabar area where the Muslims have the strongest concentration in the state. As girls' schools exist in large numbers in the state, the setting up of additional girls schools in the area will not violate any canon of state policy. As a matter of expediency, new schools to be opened may be earmarked as girls schools. This will certainly draw larger number of girls to schools than at present, without any compulsion.

The Muslim community protects the seclusion of women not only by insisting that women go out of home only with proper male escort and that even when they go out like this they should veil themselves. The majority of our respondents were found to scrupulously obey these two prescriptions. The result is that they are isolated from the society outside of their homes about which they have very little knowledge this state of affairs is perpetuated by the denial of education to them. Actually there is a vicious circle here. Seclusion compels them from going outside home except when absolutely necessary and then with escort. This deprives them of education which requires breaking of the seclusion rule and coming out of home to attend educational institutions. Lack of education deprives them of the capacity to engage in modern roles outside home and this contributes to their being confined at home. They (seclusion and lack of education) thus reinforce each other. This, in turn, dissuades them from having higher aspirations in life as a result of which they remain content with their low status.

Absence of Socially Defined Occupational Roles

When asked about the objectives of education of Muslim women, it was seen that the modern objectives have only a low order of priority for them. Out of 158 women who had education above the primary level (only those who were beyond the primary were asked about the aim of education because at the primary level no individual would have any specific aim in educating themselves), 8.86 per cent said they did not have any definite aim, 13.29 per cent stated that they aimed at getting a job, 21.52 per cent wanted to improve their status and 56.33 per cent said their aim was to acquire knowledge. Educational level of the respondents and their objective of education is found to be related to each other. It is clear from the following table.

LEVEL OF EDUCATION AND OBJECTIVE OF EDUCATION

Education	No aim	To get a job	To acquire knowledge	To improve status	Total
Middle school	12 (85.71%)	4 (19.05%)	58 (65.17%)	18 (52.94%)	92
High School and college	2 (14.29%)	17 (80.95%)	31 (34.83%)	16 (47.06%)	65
Total	14 (8.80%)	21 (13.29%)	89 (56.34%)	34 (21.57%)	158

The table shows that for the majority of the respondents (56%) education had only one purpose viz. to acquire knowledge. The second major aim was to improve status (22%). Only a very small number (13%) considered education as a means of securing a job. It is interesting to note that 17 out of 21 respondents (81%) who expressed this view belonged to the high school and above educated group. Probably they were deviating from contemporary social norms when they wanted to use education for getting a job. For the vast majority education was not intended as qualification for an occupational career.

When the data was analysed to find out what gain the Muslim women made from their education, it was found that 53 per cent of them said that their education had been of no definite use to them, while about 3 per cent said it helped them in acquiring knowledge, 7 per cent in getting a job and 34 per cent said it helped them in improving their position. It was also found that education has greatly contributed to the achievement of the goal, i.e. the higher the education the higher the percentage of respondents who achieved their goal. Nearly one half of those who aimed at a job through education were disillusioned with their hope, for education was helpful in securing a job only to 11 persons. All these makes it clear that socially defined occupational role is absent in Muslim Community. Education is a must for taking up an occupation and since occupational role is absent in traditional Muslim society education which is necessary for that is devalued.

Conclusion

Conclusions of this paper can be summarised as follows: There are some social structural and institutional factors in Muslim community which hinder the educational progress of their women. Insistence on religious education is one among them. Religious education which is indispensable for a Muslim lead to late entry to school after completion of a course of religious instruction. After entering the school at a comparatively later age she will be forced to discontinue her studies when she attains puberty as she is not allowed to go out freely after that. This will make her remain in school only for a short term by which time she will reach only 3rd or 4th standard.

Practice of early marriage which is widely prevalent among the Muslim Community is found to be another major factor preventing the women from continuing her education after marriage. A majority of the respondents and even their daughters were married below 15 years. As a Muslim woman is not permitted to go out without escort it will be very difficult for them to continue their education, so she will have to terminate her studies after marriage.

Seclusion of woman which is still observed by the Muslim Community prevents freedom of movement outside home and hinders her educational progress as she is not allowed to attend schools after attaining maturity.

Muslim community is one in which women are not expected to go out to work and earn but to remain at home looking after husband and children. Being born and brought up in such a society she does not consider the occupational role for a woman much important. Education is indispensible for taking up modern occupational roles and since occupational role is not considered important education is devalued. Thus lack of socially defined occupational role detracts from the importance of education as a tool for achieving occupational skills.

REFERENCES

Berger, Morroe
   1962   *The Arab World Today,* Weidenfeld and Nicolson, London.

Bevan, Jones, V. R. & L.
   1941   *Women in Islam. A manual with special reference to conditions in India.* The Lucknow Publishing House, Lucknow.

Chitnis, Suma and Gore, M.S., Desai, I.P.
   1967   *Papers in the Sociology of Education in India.* National Council of Educational Research and Training, New Delhi.

Government of India
   1952   *Muslims in India.* Ministry of Information and Broadcasting, Delhi.

Government of Madras
   1894   *Muhammadan Education.* Educational Department, G.O. No. 860, November, 12th.

Kabir, Humayun
   1969   *Education for Tomorrow.* Fiima, Mukbopadbyay, Calcutta.

Lichtenstadter, Ilse
           Islam and the Modern Age—An Analysis and an Appraisal. Vision Press Ltd., London.

Qutb Muhammed
   1964   *Islam. The Misunderstood Religion.* The Board of Islamic Publications, Jamamasjid, Delhi.

8

The Effect of Religious Affiliation on Woman's Role in Middle Eastern Arab Society*

PETER C. DODD**

I. *Introduction*

In 1963, William Goode reviewed the state of sociological knowledge about family structure in Arab Muslim society. He commented that:

"Anthropologists and sociologists have given little attention to the Arab family over the past half-century. There has been far more *systematic* field research among the Bantoid peoples of Africa. . . . It seems likely that a flood of sociological studies will appear in the next decade . . . " (pp. 87, emphasis author's)

Although the flood of sociological studies has yet to appear, a number of ethnographies and specialized papers have advanced our knowledge of Arab family structure in the years since Goode wrote. Among the various aspects of family structure, the status and role of women in society has received a modest amount of attention. Comparisons of Arab countries with countries at similar stages of development suggest that the participation of women in gainful employment is unusually low (Youssef, 1971). Other studies have begun to outline an "honor-modesty" code that tends to restrict women to their traditional roles as housekeepers and child-rearers (Antoun, 1968; Dodd, 1973). While wide-spread change is taking place, and women are in fact engaging in role-behaviors other than the traditional ones, the pace of change is slow. It appears that change has to take place in the face of strong resistance. The sources of this resistance are not fully known, but among them the role of religion is of special interest.

Islam is the dominant religion in nearly every Arab country. It is not uncommon for writers on Arab family structure to speak of Arab *Muslim* family structure, as did Goode. A further logical step, often made by students of Islam, is to see religion as the *major* determinant of family structure (Levy, 1957).

The question then arises of the role of religion in affecting change in the status and role of women in contemporary Arab society. This is part of a larger debate on Islam and social change, but the interest here is specifically on the structure of sex-roles and accompanying change.

The traditional society has imposed severe limitations on the public participation of women in society (Berger, 1962: 98 ff.; Berque, 1964: 155-

*A paper prepared for presentation at the Eighth World Congress of Sociology, Session on Sex-Roles and Society, Toronto, Ontario, August 1974.

The author wishes to acknowledge his deep debt to Ashod Amassian, for providing the basic data for this paper and for his knowledge of the topic.

**Department of Sociology and Anthropology, American University of Beirut, Beirut, Lebanon., United Nations Economic Commission for Western Asia, Beirut, Lebanon.

172, Goode, 1963). A number of scholars have linked these restrictions with the teachings of the Qur'an and the legal system based on the Qur'an, the Shari'a. However, the teachings of the Qur'an are general in nature and capable of varying interpretations with regard to the rights and responsibilities of men and women. The Qur'an enjoins modesty upon women, but it does not forbid them to engage in gainful employment nor does it forbid them to hold positions of authority. Some scholars maintain that Islam gives wide scope to women's activities in society and that there are few religious obstacles to change in the status of women in Muslim countries. Saleh says: ". . . a study of the Qur'an, the Hadiths, and the Shari'a laws . . . reveals that Islam idealizes the woman's status as one of equality and complementarity with males" (1972a:35; see also 1972b). Saleh maintains that the low status of women in traditional Muslim society represents a decline from the true ideals of Islam and attributes this decline to factors other than religion.

An unvoided assumption in this debate is that Muslim family and sex-role structure differs radically from Christian family and sex-role structure. Discussions of Muslim society frequently focus on points of difference, such as polygyny, which in fact are statistically rare, occurring in perhaps one per cent of the households. In other aspects of sex-role structure, such as the opportunity for married women to engage in gainful employment, few comparisons have been made between Christian and Muslim behavior. It is usually assumed that these are quite different, but careful comparisons are seldom undertaken. Often a comparison is latent in the mind of the observer, between the sex-role structure in Muslim Arab countries and the Sex-role structure in Christian Western countries. Such a comparison involves one level of development, that in Arab society, with a totally different level of development, that in Western society. Differences in sex-role structure, therefore, are more likely to be attributable to level of development than to religious teaching and doctrine.

A comparison of Muslim and non-Muslim societies at the *same* levels of development has been undertaken by Youssef (1971), comparing Egypt, Pakistan and Morocco with Mexico and Chile. After showing that these countries have reached equal developmental levels and structural similarities in the organization of their economies, Youssef compares them with respect to the participation of women in the non-agricultural work force. The three Muslim countries have a much lower level of woman's participation, at most 10% of the non-agricultural work force, whereas women in the two non-Muslim countries comprise about one-third of the work force. Youssef attributes the difference to "institutional arrangements", of which one is the influence of religion. She also sees religious affiliation as having a distinct influence on the position of women in traditional Middle Eastern society: "Until recently . . . women belonging to the religious minorities in the Middle East enjoyed a freer social life and higher educational standards than their Muslim counterparts." (1971: 437)

There appear to be two different methods of testing the difference due to religion. One, used by Youssef, involves the comparison between Muslim and non-Muslim societies at the same level of economic development. Another, suggested by this last quotation, is to compare Muslim and non-Muslim sex-role structure within a *single* society.

In this paper, the second approach is taken, the comparison of Christian and Muslim sex-role expectations within the same society, Lebanon. The Lebanese population is divided almost equally between Christians and Muslims. Very few comparisons have been made between aspects of the family structure of these two groups, the main exception being a carefully designed study of fertility (Yaukey, 1961). Yaukey's study shows that there is no significant difference in the fertility of Muslim women and Christian women in villages, but that in cities the Christian women have a slightly lower fertility rate. There is the suggestion, therefore, that in the traditional society sex-role structure may not differ radically between the two groups, if one is prepared to make the inference from fertility rates to sex-role structure.

In the present paper, the emphasis is on sex-role expectations, on the norms that people hold for the behavior of women. Most studies of these norms have been limited to the traditional sector of the society (Antoun, 1968, and references cited therein; 1972; Williams, 1968). The interest in this paper is on the modern sector of the society, on the norms held by educated youth.

One further question must be noted: the uniformity with which the norms are held. Many ethnographies give the impression that norms are supported equally by all members of the community and overlook the systematic sources of variation in agreement with the norms. In the case of sex-role expectations, a major source of variation is the sex of the respondent. For instance, Prothro and Diab (1972) surveyed Muslim women in four Arab cities: Beirut, Tripoli (Lebanon), Damascus, and 'Amman. Their respondents, some of whom had held jobs themselves, approved of women working both before and after marriage. They described their husbands, however, as being opposed to the employment of married women. This finding suggests the importance of the sex variable: women support liberal norms, men support traditional ones.

This paper focuses on the sex-role expectations held by individuals, both male and female, of differing religious affiliation. Since level of education may well affect the sex-role expectations held by an individual, this factor is controlled, by surveying a restricted population, all of whom have the same level of education.

II. *The Study*

An opportunity for inquiring into these norms and at the same time systematically comparing persons of different religious affiliation is to be found in the study of the attitudes and values of students. As students, these youth are elite, both actual and potential. They have a common educational experience, coming through the selective processes of the lower schools. Their future is such as to make it probable that they will enter middle- and upper-level occupations in the society and eventually assume positions of control. The opinions that they express are not only a function of their

education and exposure to society and the mass media; these opinions, especially at the secondary school level, often reflect the opinions of parents.
It is also likely that these opinions are more liberal than those of their
parents, especially when one notes that most secondary school students
have already attained a higher level of education than their parents.

It is important to note the role of religious affiliation in Lebanese social
structure. Lebanon's population is divided into Christian and Muslim, with
each religious group further subdivided by sect, or "confession". The con-
fessional system is essential to the Lebanese political system, and it also
has important social-structural features. Each sect, for instance, has its own
system of welfare and educational institutions. Family law is administered
through a system of religious courts. Civil marriage does not exist, religious sanction being essential to the legal validity of a marriage. (Hudson,
1968; cAbou, 1961).

In addition to these institutional features, religious affiliation is important to Lebanese as individuals. Residential patterns, friendships, and
marriage choices tend to follow lines of religion affiliation. In social interaction with strangers, an implicit question is the religious affiliation of the
other person. Once this is known, the lines of social interaction can be established. Religious affilation places the individual in a social milieu.

In this paper, data are presented from a survey of students in fifteen Lebanese secondary schools. The students were all in the baccalaureate class
(seventh secondary) of government secondary schools. The schools were
selected so as to include two or three from each of the five governorate (provinces) of Lebanon, and to include schools in communities of different
size, ranging from the metropolis of Beirut to the small towns in the mountains and in the plain of the Bequ'a. Given the conditions of the survey, a
representative probability sample of the government secondary schools of
Lebanon could not be obtained. Instead, the study included schools in a
wide variety of communities, especially those outside the metropolitan
area of Beirut. Since many schools are segregated by sex, it was possible
to select male and female students in the same proportion that they are
found in the secondary school population as a whole. It would appear that
this sample of youth is not very different from the population from which it
was drawn, the students in the Baccalaureate class in Lebanese government secondary schools.

Students in this class have passed the first part of the baccalaureate
examination and are preparing for the second part. Success on these two
examinations is required for most professional and administrative careers;
the first part is the more rigorous of the two. The students' ages range from
17 to 23, with the medians at 18 and 19. Students in this class were selected
because they are sufficiently mature to be aware of the system of sex-role
expectations, rewards and sanctions. Many of them, especially the girls,
have already begun to face conflicts involving the norms that are of interest
in this study, especially the norms about early marriage and child-bearing
and about work for women.

Government schools were deliberately chosen so as to include students from lower-class and lower-middle class families. In Lebanon, government schools enroll about one-third of all secondary school students. The other two-thirds are enrolled in private schools, where the fees restrict enrollment to students from the upper ranges of the income distribution. Students in government schools, by and large, are experiencing upward social mobility. Although their family backgrounds place them in the middle of the status range, their status as secondary school students place them in an elite category. Most of the children in the lower- and lower-middle classes, perhaps 90 per cent, fail to reach the final years of secondary school. Those who do succeed have a very good chance of moving into middle-class careers.

An indication of the social-class background of the students' families is shown in Table 1. This table compares the education of their parents with

Table 1.   Social Class Origin of the Students: Parents' Education.

1.	Father's Education	Students' parents (N=651)	Representative Sample Survey of Lebanese males aged 25 or more*
	Less than primary or primary only	76	82
	Secondary or university	24	18
2.	Mother's Education		
	Less than primary or primary only	86	88.5
	Secondary or university	14	11.5

*Source: *Population Active Au Liban.* Beirut: Direction Generale de la Statistique, 1972.
        Table 48, page 101.

the educational level attained by Lebanese adults. Since a population census is not available for Lebanon, the data on adults are drawn from a recent sample survey of 30,000 Lebanese   households. The education categories have been combined so as to make them comparable to the categories used in the present study.

A comparison of the students' fathers with the data for Lebanese men shows that the fathers have slightly higher educational attainments. The percentage of fathers who have attended secondary school is 24; for Lebanese men it is 18. If secondary school is seen as an aspect of middle-class status, a quarter of the students' fathers have this status. The remaining three-quarters come from families where the parents have at best a primary school education. This may be seen by a further examination of Table 1, where the education of the students' mothers is compared with that of all Lebanese women aged 25 or more. Of the mothers, 86% have not gone beyond primary school. The percentage is very close to that for all Lebanese women, 88.5.

The data on parental education indicate that this sample of students comes from families of about average status. This fact is important, especially when joined to the fact that most of the students (and their families) reside outside the metropolitan area of Beirut. The students — and the sex-role expectations that they hold — are likely to be representative of the society. The norms that they hold are likely to be more liberal versions of the norms held in the society, whereas the norms held by a private-school sample would be more likely to reflect elite norms. Students in the government schools may not be "common men", but they come from families of commoners.

The data on parental education permit a comparison of the social background of the Christian and Muslim students. Of the fathers of Christian students, 22% have had secondary education or more. Of the fathers of Muslim students, 21% have this level of education. Using this information as an indicator of social status, it appears that the Christian students and the Muslim students in this sample come from families of approximately equal social status. This fact is important for the comparison by religious affiliation: the students of the different religious groups come from families of the same social strata. In a sense, control is provided for possible differences due to social status of the student's family.

3. The Findings: Differences by Sex

Nine items in sex-role expectation were presented to the students, in the context of a longer questionnaire on career aspirations and family relationships. The response choices follow a simple agree/disagree format, except for two items where pre-testing and prior use indicated a wider range of choice. The language of the questionnaire was Arabic.

No study of the data can be undertaken without first taking into account the sex of the respondent. As Table 2 shows, the pattern of responses obtained from boys differs markedly and systematically from that obtained from girls. On every item, the girls are more likely to favor a "liberal" response than are the boys. Boys and girls differ most on working outside the home after marriage (item 2, a "general" statement, and item 8, which refers to one's own personal intentions). Forty-nine percent of the boys agree with item 2, and 79% of the girls. Fifty-nine percent of the boys approve of their own wives working outside the house, while 89% of the girls state their intention to do so. The girls not only favor work for married women, but they themselves want to work and plan to do so. The boys, in contrast; are almost evenly divided on the question of women working after marriage, both in general and for their own future wives.

It is thus clear that the norms held by boys differ from those held by girls. While this should come as no great surprise to anyone familiar with the literature on sex-roles, it is an important caution to those who speak freely of norms in a society and consensus on norms. The sexes do not agree on appropriate roles for men and women in Lebanon, any more than they do in other societies.

A second point that emerges from these responses, boys and girls, is that most of them are in favor of norms that imply *change* in behavior. Every

Table 2.   Attitudes on Woman's Role, By Sex.

	Item		Boys (N=425) %	Girls (N=226) %
1.	A woman should be able to work outside her home before marriage.	Agree	81	100
		"It depends"	2	0
		Disagree	17	0
2.	A woman should be able to work outside her home after marriage.	Agree	49	79
		"It depends"	3	1
		Disagree	48	20
3.	A woman should be able to work outside her home, even if she has children.	Agree	27	55
		"It depends"	2	1
		Disagree	70	43
4.	Women, like men, should be able to occupy high administrative posts in industry and finance.	Agree	70	79
		"It depends"	2	0
		Disagree	28	21
5.	Men should never be under women's supervision.	Agree	39	30
		"It depends"	1	0
		Disagree	59	61
6.	A woman should be less educated and less cultivated than her husband.	Agree	16	9
		"It depends"	2	0
		Disagree	82	91
7.	A woman's duty is to raise children and take care of the household work.	Agree	73	46
		"It depends"	2	1
		Disagree	25	52
8.	a) (Boys only) When you marry, will you approve of your wife, working outside the home?	Yes, full-time	7	17
		Yes, part-time	52	72
		No	41	11
	b) (Girls only) Do you intend to work after marriage?			
9.	Suppose that men and women are working in a factory and all of them are doing the same work, What pay do you think that each group should receive?	Equal pay	65	88
		Women-more	3	2
		Men a little more	27	9
		Men much more	4	0

one of the items, was deliberately designed to permit a response that would indicate change in the society as it presently exists. In nearly every case, the majority favored the response indicating change; change that would permit women to work, to have high positions, to have authority over men, to have equal pay. By and large, in the society with which these youth are familiar, women do not work outside the household for pay. They do not have high positions in "industry and finance". They seldom have authority over men and they infrequently receive equal pay for the same work. To favor these developments for women is to take a position in favor of change.

4. The Effect of Religious Affiliation: Boys' Responses

Since boys and girls differ so markedly in their expectations for sex-role, it is essential to separate them before attempting the analysis of the effect of religious affiliation. This has the further advantage of giving two independent tests of the effect of religious affiliation, since the two samples, boys and girls, are essentially independent.

In Table 3, the responses for boys are presented, divided by religious affiliation. The Muslim category combines Shi'a and Sunni Muslim and Druze. The Christian category combines the many Christian sects in Lebanon: Maronite, Greek Orthodox, and Greek Catholic predominate. It happened that the sample contains almost equal numbers of Muslims and Christians: 312 and 339. Among the Muslims, Sunni Muslims predominate, among the Christians, Maronites are most numerous.

Table 3.   Boys' Attitudes on Women's Role, By Religion (Percent Agreeing with the Item).

		Muslim (N=226)	Christian (N=199)	Percent Difference	X^2	Group giving more "liberal" responses
1.	A woman should be able to work outside her home before marriage.	82	80	2	0.4,2 df	Muslim
2.	A woman should be able to work outside her home after marriage.	52	46	6	2.07,2 df	Muslim
3.	A woman should be able to work outside her home even if she has children.	32	21	11	6.00,2 df*	Muslim
4.	Occupy high administrative posts	70	70	—	—	—
5.	Men should never be under women's supervision.	35	44	9	3.78,2 df	Muslim
6.	A woman should be less educated and less cultivated than her husband.	17	16	1	2.2,2 df	Christian
7.	A woman should raise children and take care of the house work.	66	80	14	9.3,2 df*	Muslim
8.	Approve of wife working (% "full" or "part" time)	63	55	8	3.81,2 df	Muslim
9.	What pay for same work in factory? (% "equal" or "women more")	66	74	8	6.59,4 df*	Christian

* = Chi Square significant at .05 level.

The data in Table 3 show no consistent pattern of differences by religious affiliation. In six items, the Muslim boys give more "liberal" responses, in two the Christian boys, and in one they are equal. The differences are modest in size, ranging from 0 to 14 per cent. Three of the nine com-

parisons show differences that, tested by Chi-square, are statistically significant. Of these three, two are items where the Muslims are more liberal
and one where the Christians are more liberal. (Given the sampling procedure, the chi-square statistic can only be taken as an indication of the magnitude of the difference.)

The item that provokes the greatest difference is "A woman should raise
children and take care of the house work". This is a "traditional" item,
where agreement indicates support for the traditional role definition, based
on sharp division of labor by sex. On this item, most boys agree; most of
them support the traditional role-definition. The Muslim boys, however, are
less likely to agree than are the Christian boys: 66% versus 80%.

A second item that provokes difference in response is item 3, permitting
a woman to work even if she has children. In general, the boys do not favor
work for a mother with children. This appears to reflect the norms in the
society, where the mother's role in child-rearing is very heavily emphasized.
Although no statistical data are available, deviation from these norms appears to take place only at the two extremes of the income scale. It takes
place among very emancipated women, who are educated enough to risk   cen-
sure while they work (and whose husbands, equally well educated, will support them in their deviation). It also takes place among the poor, where the
small children are turned over to an elder daughter or other relative while
the mother works to add to the family's income. This situation is a distinct
offense against the modesty code (Antoun, 1968; Dodd, 1973) and reflects
adversely on the husband.

On this item, the Muslim boys are somewhat more likely to favor work
for the married women than are the Christian boys, 32% versus 21%.

In summary, then, the boys' responses to the items on sex-role expectation do not seem to show any consistent effect that could be attributed to
religious affiliation. Of the nine items, only three showed "significant" differences. Of these three, the Muslims were more in favor of women with
children holding jobs and they were more opposed to the traditional "home-
and-children" role-definition for women. The Christian boys were more
likely to favor equal pay for equal work. None of the differences were large,
most of them were under 10%.

5. *The Effect of Religious Affiliation: Girls' Responses*

In the search for the effect of religious affiliation on sex-role expectation,
no clear pattern is found for the boys. A second test for the effect of religious affiliation is provided in the responses of the girl students in this study.
Of the 230 girls answering the questionnaire, information in religious affiliation was given by 226 girls. Grouped by religion, there are 140 Christians and 86 Muslims. Their responses are shown in Table 4.

A study of the data in Table 4 shows that the differences between Muslim and Christian girls are slight. For only one item, item 3, is there a difference that produces a chi-square of statistical significance. On the other
eight items, four of them show 1% differences, approaching zero. The other
four are all less than ten per cent.

Table 4.   Girls' Attitudes on Women's Role, by Religion (Percent who Agree with the item)

		Muslim (N=86)	Christian (N=140)	Percent Difference	X^2	Group giving more "liberal" responses
1.	Work before marriage	99	100	1	1.6,2 df	Christian
2.	Work after marriage	84	77	7	2.47,2 df	Muslim
3.	Work, even if she has children.	65	49	16	5.94,2 df*	Muslim
4.	Occupy high administrative posts.	74	63	9	2.46,2 df	Christian
5.	Men should never be under women's supervision.	35	41	6	.73,1 df	Muslim
6.	A woman should be less educated and less cultivated than her husband.	10	9	1	.02,1 df	Christian
7.	A woman should raise children and take care of the household work.	46	47	1	.06,2 df	Christian
8.	Do you intend to work after marriage (% "full" or "part" time).	91	88	3	2.06,2 df	Christian
9.	What pay for same work in factory? (% "equal" or "women more")	90	91	1	3.32,2 df	Christian

The direction of the differences also fails to show any consistent effect of religious affiliation. On the nine items, the Christian girls show the more "liberal" response pattern on six. Muslims are more "liberal" on three, including the one item that shows the largest difference, item 3.

Item 3 has to do with the propriety of a married woman with children holding a job. It is striking that this item alone shows consistent differences in response between Christian and Muslim students, both boys and girls. The Muslim students, both boys and girls, are more likely to agree with this item than are the Christian students. It is not clear whether this difference has any basis in religious teaching and doctrine. Both religious groups emphasize motherhood and the importance of childrearing, neither forbids or discourages work for women, both enjoin modesty upon women. It is worth noting this difference in attitudes towards working mothers, in the event that a similar difference should appear in further studies. Except for this difference, the responses of Muslim and Christian girls show similarity, perhaps even more so than that of the boys.

Conclusion:

The major question raised in this paper is whether youth of two very different religious groups also hold different patterns of role-expectations for women. The finding is that they do not, that the Christian students and the Muslim students hold *similar* patterns of role-expectations. Religious affiliation does not appear to have an effect on these attitudes regarding appropriate behavior for women.

On the other hand, sex does make a difference, and an important one. Girls are more liberal, boys more conservative. While this finding is not unexpected, it does indicate that opposition to women's emancipation is likely to be stronger among the men of the society than it is among the women.

Although the boys and girls hold different patterns of role-expectations, the finding on the effect of religious affiliation is true for both groups. The role-expectations held by Muslim boys do not differ substantially from those held by Christian boys. Similarly, the role-expectations held by Muslim girls do not differ substantially from those held by Christian girls.

These findings come as a surprise, in a society where religion and religious affiliation are important. While it must be stressed that they are not definitive, they also may indicate the effect of education, mass media and general social change in a hitherto conservative and traditional society. The youth in this study are not elite youth. They come from the "middle masses" of the society. On the other hand, they are "potential elites". The fact of receiving a secondary education places them in the top quarter of their age-group. Their attitudes, then, may be taken as a portent of change in the society, changes that may become extensive in coming years.

Three major reservations must be noted. One is that this study inquires into the effect of religious affiliation, but does not assess the effect of religiosity, the strength of the individual's belief in religion. The link between religiosity and sex-role expectations is important, for it may well be that persons with devout religious beliefs are more likely to have conservative role-expectations for women. While this is a common place assumption, it is essential to test it empirically.

A second is whether these role-expectations held by youth remain stable over time, or whether they change with age. As the students move into their twenties, they begin to form their own families of procreation. Will their sex-role expectations change? Only longitudinal studies can answer this question adequately. The ideas of youth, which appear in the relatively liberal patterns of role-expectations expressed by these students, must give way to the realities of adulthood. But it may be premature to assume that the effect of adulthood will be toward more conservative role-expectations and behavior.

Finally, there is the question as to the relationship between sex-role expectations and behavior. This is never a perfect relationship: there is always some slippage between what persons say they approve and what they will in fact do, whether it is permitting one's wife to work or accepting the authority of women in positions of responsibility. Studies of expectations must be complemented by studies of behavior, in the area of sex-role structure. The data presented in this paper can only serve as one indication of the relationship between religious affiliation and sex-role structure.

It is important, however, to note the trend of these data, in that they indicate the lack of major difference between persons of differing religious affiliations. If this trend is supported by further research, much of sociological thinking about the differences between Christian and Muslim family structure will have to be revised. The area of differences may be decreasing, as social change brings to the forefront common emphases on sex-role equality and participation in the larger society.

REFERENCES

Abou, Selim
    1961   *Le Bilinguisme Arabe-Francais au Liban*. Paris: Librarie Plon.

Antoun, Richard
    1968   "On the Modesty of Women in Arab Muslim Villages", *American Anthropologist, 70:671-697.*

    1972   *Arab Village*. Bloomington, Indiana: Indiana University Press.

Berger, Morroe
    1962   *The Arab World Today*. New York: Doubleday and Company, Anchor Edition.

Berque, Jacques
    1964   *The Arabs: their History and Future*. London: Faber and Faber.

Dodd, Peter C.
    1973   "Family Honor and the Forces of Change in Arab Society", *International Journal of Middle East Studies,* 4, 1: 40-54.

Goode, William J.
    1963   *World Revolution and Family Patterns*. New York: MacMillan, Free Press.

Hudson, Michael
    1968   *The Precarious Republic*. New York: Random House.

Levy, Reuben
    1957   *The Social Structure of Islam*. Cambridge, England: Cambridge University Press.

Prothro, E. Terry & L. Diab
    1972   *Changing Patterns of Family Life in the Arab Levant*. Mimeographed, American University of Beirut.

Saleh, Saniya
    1972   "Women in Islam: their Status in Religious and Traditional Culture" *International Journal of the Sociology of the Family,* 2, 1 (March 35-42.)

Snack, David R. and Audrey R. Smack
    1973   Political Fragmentation and National Accomodation: A Comparative Study of Lebanon and Ghana. (Mimeographed) 530 pages.

Williams, Judith
1968   *The Youth of Haouch al-Harimi, a Lebanese Village.* Cambridge, Massachusets: Harvard University Press.

Yaukey, David
1961   *Fertility Differences in a Modernizing Country: A Survey of Lebanese Couples.* Princeton, New Jersey: Princeton University Press.

Youssef, Nadia
1971   "Social Structure and the Female Labor Force: The Case of Women Workers in Muslim Middle Eastern Countries", *Demography,* 8, 4 (November): 427-439.

9   Attitudes of Women Towards Certain
            Selected Cultural Practices in
                      Kerala State, India

                GEORGE KURIAN AND MARIAM JOHN

INTRODUCTION

Study about women in India is getting more and more attention at present. The introduction of modern education in urban as well as rural areas
has changed authority patterns with less rigid socialization patterns.
Increasingly, women are working outside the home. While most of them
are still in lower paid and less prestigious occupations, there are quite
a few who are occupying prominent positions in all social, economic and
political spheres.

Some of the more recent studies where reference to the changes in the
role of women in India are found are Gore (1968), Kapadia (1966), Kapur
(1974), Rao (1975) and Ross (1961). There are also Masters and PhD.
dissertations and articles; a partial list of them is found in Kapur (1976).
These studies refer to social structure, marriage and family aspects, occupational mobility, etc. "Education and employment are beginning to be
viewed as tools which will lead to greater independence and more equality
for women. At the same time, the new freedom and opportunities are still
combined with old restrictions and traditional notions about women's
dependence on male protection" (Kapur, 1976:91).

This study is an attempt to assess the attitudes of rural women in a
Kerala village towards four selected areas of cultural practices: (1) rituals
during marriage ceremony, (2) dowry system, (3) aspiration towards
children's education and profession and (4) children's decision-making.
The attitudes have been studied in relation to *a priori* independent
variables, the educational and the occupational level to which the
respondents belong.

An attitude scale was constructed to elicit the responses of women on
these cultural practices. A stratified sample of 60 Christians, 60 Hindus and
30 Muslims was selected. Each community had an equal number from the
older and younger generations. The majority of the respondents were
educated at least up to primary school in all communities. They were
mostly from nuclear families. About one-third of them came from agricultural households, approximately one-third from households whose

head had teaching jobs or clerical jobs and about one-third from the
occupational class of semi-skilled labourers.

Community Influences

The religious community of the respondent was not found to be an
influencing factor, except in one area, namely, "Rituals during marriage
ceremony". Thus it may be said that the three communities show more or
less similar attitudes towards the cultural practices, although they belong
to three different religious faiths. It is generally believed that religion
regulates human conduct and behavior and sets "a limit which has
implications for the learning capacity of the society in which it is institutionalized" (Bellah, 1965:117). The finding of this study is not strictly in
conformity with the stated belief.

The similarity in attitude observed in the three communities may be
attributed to the mode of living which is typical in the state of Kerala.
Historically, these religious groups have been living together for generations. Christianity was introduced into Kerala as early as 52 A.D. when the
apostle Thomas went to India, preached the gospel and converted the local
inhabitants (Kurian, 1961:34-46).

The dominant socio-religious culture in India is that borne of Hinduism.
Thus, it may be surmised that through the generations of cultural linkage, the essential features of the dominant values and styles of living
came to be culturally assimilated into the minority groups who settled in
that area, in the process of seeking a harmonious identity with the
dominant pattern.

The three communities of Hindus, Christians and Muslims living
together use the same language (Malayalam) and are therefore exposed
to similar literature, which culturally binds the communities together.

In India, "these linguistic regions have considerable homogeneity of
culture and of family organization as language makes communication
possible and sets limits of marital connection, local folklore and literature" (Baig, 1969).

Furthermore, it can be seen from supportive information collected,
that these three communities have similar marriage customs. Most
respondents had their marriage arranged in the same form by the elders of
the family—for example—and the choice of marriage pattern was decided by the parents with the consent of the respondent. There is little
dissimilarity in the form of dowry payment among these communities.
Except in the case of Hindus whose dowry was paid in land, dowries were
paid in the form of money and gold. The exception in the Hindu community may be explained as a part of the matrilineal traditions which have
influenced a number of Hindu caste groups in Kerala.

Table 1

The Form of Dowry as Expressed by 120 Respondents

Community

S. No.	FREQUENCY Interval	HINDU Old	Young	MUSLIM Old	Young	CHRISTIAN Old	Young	Total
1.	Money alone	2 6.7%	8 47%	3 20%	1 10%	19 63.3%	14 77.8%	47 39.1%
2.	Money and land					3 10%	2 11.1%	5 4.1%
3.	Money, land and gold			3 30%	1 10%			4 3.3%
4.	Land and gold			1 6.6%	1 10%			2 1.7%
5.	Money and gold		2 11.5%	6 40%	4 40%	4 13.3%		16 13.3%
6.	Land alone	27 90%	6 35.8%	1 6.7%	2 20%	1 3.4%	2 11.1%	39 34.5%
7.	Gold alone							
8.	No Dowry	1 3.3%	1 5.7%	1 6.7%	1 10%	3 10%		7 5.8%
	Total	30 100%	17 100%	15 100%	10 100%	30 100%	18 100%	120 100%

From Table 1 it is evident that there seems to be a difference in the forms of dowry payment made in each community. The majority of the older Hindu's dowry was in the form of land, while a majority of the younger Hindu's dowry was in the form of money. Among the Muslims, the majority of both young and old paid money and gold; among Christians the majority of both generations paid the dowry in money.

Hence, socially, the Muslims and the Christians have retained some of the Hindu cultural customs such as dowry payments and marriage rituals. One of the most important Hindu customs among the Syrian Christians[1] is the marriage badge (thali) and among the "Mapillas"[2] of North Malabar, their matrilineal family organization (Rao, 1957:22). It has been observed by A.C. Mayer that "the Muslims have retained the

1. Syrian Christians - Christians of Kerala.   2. Mapillas - Muslims of North Malabar.

Hindu custom of inheritance" (Mayer, 1952:29). Perhaps because of their voluntary adjustments, the Muslims and Christians in the state have learned to live with their differences in religious faith.

The survival of the Church in Kerala is very much due to the fact that it developed an indigenous character and adapted itself to local conditions. Though the Christians in Kerala had Syriac liturgy and had much in common with the orthodox churches in the middle east, the Christians as such tried to fit into Indian or otherwise the Hindu social strata. In fact they show features of syncretism (Kurian, 1961:35).

The attitude towards "rituals during marriage ceremony" indicated that the Hindus were significantly more conservative than the Muslims and that the Christians were still less conservative. The Hindu community's conservative attitude may exist because the Hindus were the originators of these rituals and because rituals, which form a dominant part of the Hindu's way of living, were a means by which they maintained their cultural identity. The least conservative or progressive attitude on the part of the Christians may be related to a degree of Westernization as observed in Christians as a total group in India. The degree of progressivism could be compared very favourably with that most progressive Indian group, the Parsis (Kurian, 1961:103). The findings in the similarity of attitudes of the three communities in all cultural practices, except the marriage rituals, need further examination, particularly with respect to the impact of religious faith and close cultural proximity of living.

Generational Influences

Results of the findings regarding the generational differences in attitudes in the study confirm that there are differences between the two generations, the younger generation being far more progressive.

The results are in accord with an accepted social science theory as stated by Spicer (1952) that each generation behaves differently than the previous generation. Kapadia (1966) has attributed a capacity for changed outlook to the young people, especially in family relationships and family traditions and in that way shows a difference between the older and the younger generations.

In the state of Kerala, however, the educational level, particularly of the young, is high because of the increased number of incentives offered by the government and by private institutions. Therefore, the younger generation is better educated than the old, creating another difference.

Barnabas (1969) and Mahadeva (1969) claim that there are no major differences between the opinions of parents and their children. The discrepancy between their views and ours in this study may be due to the fact that the various samples were chosen from widely different areas, or that the two studies explored different dimensions of these attitudes with different types of questions.

Differences between generations in all four areas showed the highest mean difference in the area of "rituals during marriage ceremony". This was followed by "children's decision making", and "dowry system" and "aspiration towards children's education and profession". This finding indicates a general shift in the attitudes of the young away from "rituals during marriage ceremony" and the "dowry system". The young group seems inclined to give a great deal more freedom to the children.

What do these differences indicate since they exist consistently in four areas of cultural practices? Not only is there a difference in attitudes of the younger generation but their rate of change is much faster and hence may be one cause which may widen the gap between them with time. It is, therefore, not improbable that this difference in attitudes in such an important "core" value might lead to conflict between the young and the old. Technological change may be an important and additional catalyst.

Interaction of Community and Generation

In the investigation into the interaction between the communities and generations in regard to all four cultural practices taken together, it was found there was no significant difference between the communities. Further, in relation to each area of the dependent variable, namely, "rituals during marriage ceremony", "dowry system", "aspiration towards children's education and profession" and "children's decision making," it was also found that there was no significant differences.

These findings may be due to the fact that the amount of homogeneity in communities may have been modifying factors in the differences between generations when the two variables, community and generation, were taken together.

The Influences of Education

The *post facto* variable, education, appeared to have strongly influenced the attitudes of the respondents. The analysis clearly showed that the more highly educated the respondent, the more progressive the attitude. The university graduates and vocationally trained respondents were the most progressive, then came the matriculates, the primary school attenders and then the non-educated. The same pattern was found in all except the response to "children's decision making". There the matriculates had a higher score than the graduates indicating that in this area they were more permissive with children than the graduates.

In Mehta's (1969) study on need achievement in boys, the variables, low occupation and low education of the family, were related to high need achievement. The less educated in this study who had the highest mean score for progressivism in "children's decision making" were also from families of low occupational levels, i.e. low socio-economic status. One might question what the relationship (in this lower socio-economic group) might be between permissiveness towards children on the part of the parents and the need achievement as shown by their children.

A further probe into the influence of education shows that the higher the education of the respondent, the greater the progressivism expressed in "rituals during marriage ceremony". However, in the areas concerning the dowry system and the respondents' aspiration towards their children's education and profession, the differences were not so marked. Perhaps the deep rooted values about the dowry system are due to the long duration of the custom. Possibly the difference in ideas about women's aspiration towards their children's education and profession may be a manifestation of a high value attached to education in planning for children's future welfare at all levels of education.

Occupational Influences

The *post facto* variable, occupations, includes farming, teaching, clerical jobs, shop keeping and unskilled labor. The variance of attitude scores in relation to these occupations has shown no significant differences in total progressivism.

Even though the influence of occupation in all areas of progressivism was not found to be significant, a scrutiny of the mean shows that all occupational levels indicate a high aspiration for children's education and concern for their future profession.

Influence of the Generations Within Communities

When all respondents were grouped together, the interaction of community and generation showed no significant differences. However, differences between the two generations within each community did exist. The "T" test demonstrated that the mean differences in the total attitudes of the two generations in the Christian community and the Hindu community were found to be significant. Table 2 gives the "T" ratio for progressivism in each area.

Table 2

Tests of Significance for Attitude Scores on "Total Progressivism"
in Regard to the Four Cultural Factors

Community	PROGRESSIVISM				
	Dowry system	Ritual during marriage ceremony	Aspirations on children's education and profession	Children's decision making	Total attitudes
Hindu	2.08	2.53	1.55	2.27	3.41
Muslim	2.07	1.22	0.01	1.29	1.91
Christian	1.84	3.05	3.17	2.80	3.74

The mean score on total progressivism in both communities show
that the Christian young have a score higher than the Hindu young.
Perhaps this is due to the educational differences between the two communities, Christians and Hindus. When a "T" test was computed between
the two generations in all communities for all four areas of progressivism, only the Christian community showed significant differences.
These differences appeared in three areas but not in the area of the
"dowry system". This may be owing to concurrence in attitudes towards
dowry despite other factors such as strong differences between generations in the Christian community, where dowry is an almost compulsory
practice. People look down on a bride who does not bring a respectable sum as dowry. This is evident even among educated groups. However, modern education and accompanying liberal views are influencing
people, even some Syrian Christians, to question and often show dislike
for this system.

In all areas without exception, the Muslim community showed no significant differences between generations. Though the older generations
of Muslims have shown progressive attitudes, there seems to be a
tendency on the part of the older generation to keep the youth from
moving away from their own set of attitudes. This may be because
Muslims, in the locality where the study was conducted, were the
minority and may have wanted to maintain their identity.

Intercorrelation Between the Areas of the Dependent Variable for Community Generation

As an index of reliability, an intercorrelation between areas was
calculated for each sub-group (see Table 3).

Table 3

Summarizations of Correlations Coefficients (rs) Between Two
Generations in Each Community for the Areas of Progressivism

Community	Areas of progressivism	Rituals during marriage ceremony	Children's education and profession	Children's decision making
Old n = 30	Dowry system	.26	.02	.22
	Rituals during marriage ceremony		.27	−.18
	Children's education and profession			.15
Young n = 30	Dowry system	.27	.42	.05
	Rituals during marriage ceremony		.22	.07
	Children's education and profession			.12
Old n = 15	Dowry system	.42	.34	.56
	Rituals during marriage ceremony		.24	.07
	Children's education and profession			.68
Young n = 15	Dowry system	.45	.06	.60
	Rituals during marriage ceremony		−.31	.33
	Children's education and profession			.37

Old n = 30	Dowry system	.23	.14	.05
	Rituals during marriage ceremony		.09	.13
	Children's education and profession			.37
Young n = 30	Dowry system	.44	.19	.29
	Rituals during marriage ceremony		.38	.25
	Children's education and profession			.20

Only two patterns were found. One was differences between the old generation of the Muslims (significant at 1 percent level) and the old generation of Christians (approaching tendency towards significance in the areas "aspiration towards children's education and profession" and "children's decision making". This may be explained on the basis of (1) parents raised in a traditional society aspire for "better prospects" for their children in relation to their own socialization experiences and (2) a heightened awareness of the need for a change in their attitude in relation to the need for a change in their attitude due to the accelerated social changes in the world in which their children live.

Conclusions and Implications

From the above discussion, it is apparent that of the two *a priori* independent variables, (1) community and (2) generation, it is only the generation variable which significantly affects the progressive attitude of the respondents in all areas. The variable "community" was found to influence only one area significantly, i.e. "rituals during marriage ceremony". This indicates a variation in an area which seems to be deep-rooted in socio-religious norms. The Christians, being most progressive in this area and being somewhat Westernized, have perhaps adapted themselves more quickly to social change.

The younger generation is comparatively better educated than the older and is therefore more exposed to modernizing stimuli. Hence is is possible that education is a very significant influencing factor. This is bourne out by the fact that in all areas the *post facto* variable "education" was found to be a significant factor. The higher the education, the more progressive the attitude, except in the area of "children's decision making", where the matriculates were found to be most progressive. This implies a need for further investigation in other areas of aspiration for children in relation to education of the parents.

The second *post facto* variable "occupational level" did not significantly influence attitudes. In the discussion, an indication was given that this may have arisen due to two possibilities. The categorization was a compound of two criteria, (1) the skilled/unskilled dimension and (2) occupational classification. If instead, the index had been income, perhaps a more reliable result would have been obtained. Further, a compositive index of socioeconomic status including education, occupation, income and residential area might have been a more effective independent variable that the occupation.

The attitudes between generations in the communities indicate further areas of investigation. In the Christian community the two generations, old and young, were different in all areas except the "dowry system" owing to the earlier availability of modern education.

There was no significant difference in the Muslim community. The young educated Christian seems to be in the forefront of adaptability to social change in relation to the parent generation. One might hypothesize that there might be more conflicts in values and attitudes in this community than in others. The Muslim community showed the most similar responses. Perhaps the protected familial environment and strict socio-religious practices in this community create a common identification in attitudes.

There was no systematic pattern of intercorrelation within the community age-group sub-samples in the four areas, except in the older Muslim generation between areas "aspiration towards children's education and profession" and "children's decision making".

It should be stressed that, according to the cultural lag theory (Ogburn, 1954), all parts of culture do not show similar pace and speed of change. A group may be progressive in some areas and traditional in others.

In the case of Kerala the Christians have the advantage that they have been exposed to modern education. Unlike other communities such as the Muslims and the Hindus, Christians have been moving away from traditions. This was clearly shown in a study made by the senior author in Kerala in 1968 and 1972 (Kurian, 1975). However, with regard to dowry payments, Christians show little change in attitudes. From the woman's point of view, dowry is received in lieu of land, which sons inherit. Some of the recent changes in society tend toward giving equal rights to women with regard to inheritance. However, the emphasis on dowry is still dominant. This is a good case where cultural lag seems to apply.

REFERENCES

Baig, Tara Ali
  1969   Assignment Children. Reprint No. 10, UNICEF.

Barnabas, A.
  1969   Social Change in a North Indian Village. New Delhi: The Indian Institute
         of Public Administration.

Bellah, R.
  1965   Religion and Progress in Modern Asia. New York: The Free Press.

Cormack, Margaret
  1961   She Who Rides a Peacock. Bombay: Asia Publishing House.

Desai, I. P.
  1953   High School Students in Poona. Poona: Deccon College.

Gore, M. S.
  1968   Urbanization and Family Change. Bombay: Popular Prakashan.

Kapadia, K. M.
  1966   Marriage and Family in India. Bombay: Oxford University Press.

Kapur, Promilla
  1974   The Changing Status of the Working Women in India. New Delhi: Vikas
         Publishing House.
  1976   Studies of Urban Women in India, "Family and Change—Social Change
         in Modern India", ed. Giri Raj Gupta. New Delhi: Vikas Publishing House.

Kurian, George
  1961   Indian Family in Transition. The Hague: Mouton Publishers.
  1975   Structural Changes in the Family in Kerala, India, "Socialization and Com-
         munication in Primary Groups", ed. T. R. Williams, World Anthropology
         Series. The Hague: Mouton Publishers.

Mahadeva, B.
  1969   Achievements and Aspirations: People in Indian Universities. Jamshedpur:
         Xavier Labour Relations Institute.

Mayer, A. C.
  1952   Land and Society in Malabar. Bombay: Asia Publishing House.

Mehta, P.
  1969   The Achievement Motive in High School Boys. New Delhi: National
         Council of Educational Research and Training.

Natraj, P.
  1965 "Mental Pictures of College Girls of Hindus, Muslims and Christians."
        The Indian Journal of Social Work, Bombay, Vol. 26, No. 3, October,
        p. 287+.

Ogburn, W. F. and M. F. Nimkoff
  1954 Handbook of Sociology. Boston: Houghton Mifflin.

Rao, M. S. A.
  1957 Social Change in Malabar. Bombay: Popular Book Depot.

Rao, Prakash V. V. and Nandine V. Rao
  1975 "Differential Styles of the Employed and the Non-Employed Mothers in
        India." Journal of Comparative Family Studies, Vol. VI, No. 2.

Ross, Aileen D.
  1961 The Hindu Family in Its Urban Setting. Toronto: University of Toronto Press.

Singh, M.
  1968 "A Study of Attitudes of Rural Women Towards Selected Social Problems."
        M.A. thesis, Dept. of Rural Community Extension, Lady Irwin College,
        Delhi.

Spicer, E. H.
  1952 Human Problems in Technological Change. New York: Russell Sage Foun-
        dation.

10 Attitudes and Ideology: Correlates of Liberal Attitudes Towards the Role of Women*

ROGER GIBBINS**
J. RICK PONTING***
GLADYS L. SYMONS****

Introduction

The Canadian society is symbolically and ideologically structured by those people, generally men, who "govern, administer, and manage the community" (Smith, 1975). Because social structures emerge from the personal experiences of their creators, women have been largely denied ideological and symbolic ways of perceiving the world that reflect their own experiences. Instead, they have been relegated to being consumers of attitudes regarding women and women's roles that have been articulated by the male managers of the Canadian society. With the second wave of the feminist movement, however, some women, and some men, have begun to rethink prevailing ideological structures and to redefine the concept of "woman's role". Feminists have supplied us with a major critique of dominant ideological forms, and admonish us to re-examine societal beliefs, values and attitudes towards women.

In short, some of the natives are restless. But how restless, and who, are they? To what extent have new feminist perspectives penetrated the Canadian consciousness? To what particular groups may we look for the emergence and advocacy of new outlooks towards women and women's issues? Where within the social structure might we find sources of support for, or opposition to, feminist perspectives?

To a limited degree, these questions have been addressed previously. Using data collected by the Canadian Institute of Public Opinion between 1953 and 1973, Boyd (1974) examined the socio-demographic underpinnings of Canadian attitudes towards female professionals, gender of boss, equality of opportunity for men and women (including the equal opportunity of men and married women for jobs), working mothers, and the women's liberation movement in general.

*This Research was supported by grants from the Donner Canadian Foundation and The University of Calgary.
**Department of Political Science. ⌉
***Department of Sociology.   ⎬ The University of Calgary, Calgary, Alberta, Canada.
****Department of Sociology.   ⌋
Revision of a paper presented at the Annual Meetings of the Canadian Sociology and Anthropology Association, Fredericton, June, 1977.

The C.I.P.O. data also allowed Boyd to assess changes over time in some of these attitudes—changes that were by and large in the direction of greater egalitarianism between the sexes. In a second look at the 1964 to 1973 C.I.P.O. data, Boyd (1975) examined essentially the same set of dependent variables, although this time with the imposition of extensive language and gender controls. For the 1965 to 1972 period Schreiber (1975) also used C.I.P.O. data, along with American Gallup data, to examine the social bases of public opinion towards women and their roles.

These three studies broke important ground in the area of Canadian attitudes towards the condition of women, and we will return to their work for comparative perspectives on our own analysis. Both authors, however, faced serious analytical limitations inherent in the secondary analysis of C.I.P.O. data sets. For example, interrelationships among women's issues could not be explored, as the various dependent variables were spread over a large number of disjoint data sets. Furthermore, the range of independent variables that could be brought to bear on attitudes towards women's issues was restricted by the C.I.P.O. formating. In addition, the relatively small C.I.P.O. samples imposed other constraints on statistical controls that were not encountered here (Schreiber, 1975:64). As well, the quota sampling design employed by the C.I.P.O. raises considerable doubt about the representativeness of their data sets (Boyd, 1975:156), whereas we have a representative probability sample. Finally, Boyd and Schreiber were unable to assess attitudinal correlations between women's issues and other aspects of public opinion, whereas we shall focus on this in some detail. It is our intention therefore, both to submit the Boyd and Schreiber findings to a systematic re-examination in the light of more recent data, and to extend this analysis in new directions.

The data presented here are from a national public opinion survey conducted in early 1976. At that time personal in-home interviews of approximately forty-five minutes duration were conducted with 1832 randomly selected respondents aged 18 and over living south of the sixtieth parallel.[1] The interview focused primarily upon public opinion towards the native peoples of Canada. However, before this issue area was broached, respondents were asked a number of questions on other matters of contemporary concern. Among these were six questions relating to women's issues in Canada, and it is upon these six that the present analysis is based. Five of the six fit into three issue areas of central

---

[1]Sampling was disproportionate by province and proportionate by the rural-urban distribution of the population within provinces. Respondents were selected by the following procedures. First, census blocs were randomly selected within the provincial and urban-rural strata. Secondly, a walking path, starting point, and skip interval were determined for each selected bloc. Thirdly, the interviewer was instructed to select households according to the walking path, starting point and skip interval provided to her. Within the selected households, the interviewer used a selection grid to determine which specific individual to interview. If the individual refused to be interviewed, or if he/she could not be located after three more calls back, a replacement household was selected by the same path and skip procedures. A total of five interviews was collected from each census bloc. The randomness of this design is protected by denying the interviewer any latitude in the selection of respondents.

concern to the feminist movement, and we should thus like to begin by relating these five to those concerns.

Equality of Opportunity

In 1948, by adopting the United Nations' Universal Declaration of Human Rights, Canada publicly endorsed an ideology of equality which, theoretically, applies to women. It is against this backdrop of formal acceptance of the principles of equality and freedom that the inequities experienced by women are placed in bold relief. Since the disparity is most glaring, and perhaps most readily documented, in the public sphere of activity, a good deal of attention has been given to the position of women in the paid labour force.

In Canadian society, a sexual division of labour is very much in evidence. The sphere of economic and political activity is dominated by men, and women have been relegated, by and large, to the work in the home. Although more and more women are entering the paid labour force,[2] occupations continue to be sex-typed, and many are extensions of the gender role. Hence women pre-dominate in occupations such as nursing, teaching and secretarial work—all tasks requiring nurturing and helping relationships. Men, on the other hand, are over-represented in positions of power and dominance. A division of labour based on sex need not necessarily be inequitable, but when we notice that women tend to cluster in low-paying, low status jobs, inequality is in fact in practice. The Royal Commission on the Status of Women in Canada (1972) has clearly documented gender inequities in salaries, benefits and opportunities for advance-ment, to name only a few.

We might now ask how Canadians at large see these issues. Does the existing situation, despite its inequities, meet with public acquiescence, if not support, or has the feminist challenge to such inequities won the public's support? To shed some light on this question, we asked respondents to state the degree to which they agreed or disagreed with two statements, one descriptive and one prescriptive, relating to gender equality in the work place. The two statements, the replies to which will be taken up shortly, read as follows:

Canadian women, for the most part, enjoy equal economic opportunity with men, and
In the business world, more women should be promoted into senior management positions.

Traditional Gender Roles

Traditionally, men have been the primary wage earners and are charged by law with the support of their wives and children. The task of the woman becomes that of helping her husband advance in the public realm wherein any improvement in his status will theoretically improve hers as a dependent. In order to examine the extent to which Canadians espouse male dominance, we asked our respondents

---

[2]In 1974, 34.4% of the Canadian labour force was comprised of women, as compared to 28.4% in 1964 (Information Canada, 1975:7).

to state their degree of agreement or disagreement with the following prescriptive statement:

Although a wife's career may be important, she should give priority to helping her husband advance in his career.

Related to the issue of male dominance is the child-care role of women in Canadian society. Despite efforts and suggestions to the contrary,[3] women still take the major responsibility for child care. Although both the number and proportion of married women with children in the labour force have been increasing,[4] it remains to be seen whether Canadians have accommodated themselves attitudinally to this behavioural change. In order to tap attitudes in this area, we included the following agree-disagree statement:

When children are young, a mother's place is in the home.

Rights of Women

The abortion issue, while centred upon a woman's right to control her own body, is entangled in a wide array of medical, legal, religious and moral concerns, the intensity and scope of which have thrust abortion near the forefront of women's issues in Canada. We tapped public opinion in this area with the following agree-disagree statement:

A woman should have the sole right to decide whether or not to have an abortion.

The above statement completes the five questions that constitute the dependent variables for this study. With only five such questions, we cannot claim to offer a comprehensive examination of Canadian public opinion towards women's issues. We can, however, provide a useful porthole on the subject. To do so, we will begin by presenting the responses to the five questions, followed by an examination of gender and language correlates. The analysis will then be expanded, first to incorporate a broader range of socio-demographic variables and secondly to explore the attitudinal linkage between women's issues and orientations towards minority groups.

Findings

Table 1 presents the reactions of our respondents to the five statements discussed above. Close to a public consensus exists for three of the five statements.[5]

---

[3]One of the guiding principles of the Royal Commission on the Status of Women (1972:xii) states that "the care of children is a responsibility to be shared by the mother, the father and society. Unless this shared responsibility is acknowledged and assumed, women cannot be accorded true equality".

[4]In 1973, the proportion of working mothers as a percentage of all mothers (14 years of age and over) was 35.1% (Information Canada, 1975:269). By comparison, the proportion was only 20% in 1967 (Royal Commission on The Status of Women, 1972:263).

[5]This statement, and all other references to either the total sample or the gender subsamples are based upon data which are weighted to make the size of the sample from each province proportional to each province's contribution to the size of the total Canadian 1971 population. However, references and data pertaining to the gender-language subsamples (e.g., francophone females) are not based upon the results of any such weighting operation. We shall follow these conventions in both the tables and the text. See also the notes to Table 1.

Table 1   CANADIAN ATTITUDES TOWARDS THE CONDITION OF WOMEN

STATEMENT	SAMPLE	Agree Strongly %	Agree Moderately %	Neutral; Undecided %	Disagree Moderately %	Disagree Strongly %	Don't Know; No Opinion %	Total** %
1. In the business world more women should be promoted into senior management positions.	TOTAL*	37.7	34.5	13.2	8.1	5.7	0.9	100
	Male*	30.7	36.7	16.9	9.3	5.8	0.8	100
	Female*	42.7	32.9	10.5	7.3	5.6	1.0	100
	Anglo	28.8	40.5	16.6	8.2	5.1	0.8	100
	Franco	58.0	18.2	9.2	7.6	7.0	0.0	100
2. Although a wife's career may be important, she should give priority to helping her husband advance in his career.	TOTAL*	40.6	27.9	12.1	11.3	7.7	0.5	100
	Male*	36.2	28.6	13.9	13.2	7.5	0.7	100
	Female*	43.8	27.4	10.7	10.0	7.8	0.3	1C0
	Anglo	36.3	31.6	13.8	11.4	6.5	0.4	100
	Franco	52.1	22.1	5.9	9.0	10.9	0.0	100
3. Canadian women, for the most part, enjoy equal economic opportunity with men.	TOTAL*	19.2	25.2	8.6	25.7	19.3	1.4	100
	Male*	17.0	27.8	8.4	28.5	17.2	1.3	100
	Female*	22.0	23.3	8.7	23.8	20.8	1.5	100
	Anglo	16.5	28.6	8.5	27.6	17.9	0.8	100
	France	24.6	17.9	10.1	23.0	21.6	2.8	100
4. A woman should have the sole right to decide whether or not to have an abortion.	TOTAL*	43.4	12.8	8.8	11.6	22.2	1.4	100
	Male*	41.0	14.8	8.1	10.9	23.6	1.7	100
	Female*	45.1	11.3	9.2	12.1	21.2	1.2	100
	Anglo	39.2	15.7	10.6	13.0	20.2	1.3	100
	Franco	47.3	7.0	6.7	10.4	26.9	1.7	100
5. When children are young a mother's place is in the home.	TOTAL*	65.9	15.3	8.5	5.9	4.2	0.3	100
	Male*	66.0	16.6	8.1	5.6	3.6	0.2	100
	Female*	65.8	14.5	8.8	6.0	4.6	0.3	100
	Anglo	63.8	18.7	9.0	5.4	2.9	0.4	100
	Franco	73.4	7.3	6.4	7.8	5.0	0.0	100

*   Data from the total sample and from the male and female subsamples are weighted to make the size of the sample from each province proportional to each province's contribution to the size of the total Canadian population. In order to simplify the analysis, data from the Anglophone and Francophone subsamples are *not* weighted, since to do so would necessitate introducing a second and third weight factor and the advantages in precision gained are minute.

** The unweighted subsample totals are as follows: Males=775; Females=1052; Anglophones= 1413; Francophones=357. The total sample size was 1832. The sex of 7 respondents was not identified and 62 respondents were neither Anglophones nor Francophones.

That is, by large majorities respondents agree that more women should be promoted into positions of senior management, that a wife should give first priority to her husband's career, and that a mother's place is in the home when children are young. With respect to this last finding, Boyd (1974:17) had earlier concluded that "...negative attitudes towards married women who have young children and who work are still very strong throughout the 1960's and 1970's". Certainly our findings reinforce this conclusion, as almost two-thirds of our respondents *strongly* agreed that, when children are young, a mother's place is in the home.

Consensus breaks down for the statements on equal economic opportunity and abortion. On the existence of equal economic opportunity, public perceptions are far from being unitary. This is reflected in the balance between respondents who agreed and disagreed with the statement. This and the relatively moderate strength of opinion suggest that the public is ambivalent as to whether or not women do in fact enjoy equal economic opportunity with men. Public reaction to the abortion statement, on the other hand, was sharply polarized, with the majority favouring freedom of choice for women.

Clearly, the direction of Canadian public opinion towards the condition of women is mixed. On the one hand, Table 1 has shown that Canadians support a feminist position on both abortion and the promotion of women in the business world. Yet at the same time strong public support exists for the priority of the husband's career and for the desirability of women with young children staying home. Finally, perceptions of equal economic opportunity are balanced. It thus appears that any characterization of the public mood as opposed to, or supportive of, the feminist cause can only be made with reference to specific issues. Both traditional and feminist positions seem well-rooted in the public consciousness.

Gender and Language

Given the ambivalence present in public opinion at large, the question arises as to whether support for and opposition to the feminist cause are concentrated within specific segments of the social structure. In particular, the question arises as to whether the gender of respondents has any substantial impact upon opinion towards women's issues in Canada. This question is important to address since it so readily lends itself to contradictory hypotheses.

On the one hand, earlier studies such as those by Boyd (1974, 1975), Erskine (1971), Marx-Ferree (1974), and Schreiber (1975) have found a limited and contradictory impact of gender on opinion towards women's issues. Other studies (Chandler, 1972: 41-46) have offered substantial evidence that males display more liberal attitudes than do females. In addition, gender differences in other areas of public opinion have rarely been found. For instance, in the larger data set from which the present data derive, only negligible gender differences are to be found on questions relating to the protection of the natural environment, English-French relations, and sympathy towards native Indians. In the United States, Monroe (1975) and Erikson and Luttbeg (1973) conducted a comprehensive review of American public opinion studies spanning five decades and a wide variety of issue areas. They concluded that there are only slight and insignificant differences in the social and political attitudes of men and women.[6]

Nevertheless, there have been studies which have found marked gender differences. For instance, in his study of attitudes towards marital roles and female employment, Hobart (1973) found such differences, especially among French Canadians. In addition, differences in self-interest between men and women would suggest that the respondent's gender should be related to his or her opinions on women's issues. The fact that the most active and sympathetic supporters of the feminist movement have been predominantly women would also lead us to predict that women would espouse more egalitarian attitudes than men.

In the present study the impact of gender on opinion towards women's issues was rather slight. Significant male-female differences were present for only the first two of the five statements in Table 1. Even there, the character of the relationship was inconsistent. While female respondents were more likely to agree that more women should be promoted to positions of senior management, they were also more likely to agree that the husband's career should take priority over that of the wife.

In attempting to explain these findings it should be noted that our study, like those of Boyd (1974, 1975) and Schreiber (1975), did not tap attitudes towards male gender roles. It is possible, in this respect, that men and women may support relatively liberal positions on some women's issues while at the same time maintaining incompatible images of the male role. Another possible explanation (Monroe, 1975:76) comes from the fact that the distribution of most social variables (power being a notable exception) is virtually the same for men and women. It may be that this commonality of social characteristics over-rides class-type interests based upon gender alone. This, of course, raises the Marxian notion of "false consciousness" among women, but our data do not permit us to address it further.

Another respondent characteristic that is potentially related to most social outlooks in Canada, including outlooks on women, is language. Since French-English differences pervade Canadian political, social and cultural beliefs, there is little reason to anticipate that opinion on women's issues will be exempt. Previous studies, moreover, have revealed substantial linguistic effects in public opinion towards women's issues (Boyd, 1975; Hobart, 1972, 1973; Schreiber, 1975). Schreiber (1975:72), in fact, concluded that language was the single most important variable for explaining opinion in this area.

Language is defined here as the language spoken most often at home in conversation with one's family. In the sample there were 1413 Anglophone and 357 Francophone respondents; 86% of the Francophones resided in Quebec. The impact of language is demonstrated in Table 1 where some rather striking dif-

---

[6]Some evidence to the contrary, particularly with respect to the war in Vietnam, is provided in Harris (1973:90-98).

ferences are found. For example, only 29% of the Anglophone respondents strongly agreed that more women should be promoted into positions of senior management, compared to 58% of the Francophone respondents.

Table 1 shows that on all five variables Francophones are more likely than Anglophones to *both* strongly agree and strongly disagree. However, except on item one, the Francophones are no more liberal nor more conservative in outlook than are the Anglophones. Rather, the Francophones are simply more *polarized* than the Anglophones. It should also be noted that this polarization of the Francophones *within* any given item is accompanied by inconsistencies *across* items. For instance, while Francophones are adamant that more women should be promoted into senior management positions, they are also very inclined to strongly agree that a wife should give first priority to her husband's career over her own.[7] We shall briefly take up this point again below, when we simultaneously break down responses to these questions by gender and linguistic group.

We turn our attention now to an effort to locate particular perspectives on women within the Canadian social structure. In addition to differentiating our sample into four gender and linguistic subsamples, we shall examine a broad range of socio-demographic and attitudinal variables. In so doing, we shall streamline our anaysis in several ways. First we shall only report on differences between the gender-linguistic subsamples when those differences are statistically significant. Secondly, correlates with the statement on abortion will not be presented as a thorough analysis revealed a complete absence of socio-demographic correlates.[8] Thirdly, the statement dealing with equal economic opportunity for males and females will also be dropped from further analysis as it taps only descriptive perceptions about an existing situation rather than prescriptive opinion about the desirability or nondesirability of that situation. Finally, a feminist scale (described below) is constructed using the three remaining statements. Accordingly, these statements will not be subjected to independent analysis.

Feminist Scale

The three statements shown below have been collapsed into a Guttman scale measuring respondent outlook towards women's issues in Canada. The employment of any scaling procedure requires at the outset some agreement on the polarity of the scale to be constructed. In this respect Boyd (1974:5) notes

---

[7]Boyd (1975:159) has noted that French Canadians are relatively supportive of traditional male-female roles, particularly with respect to working wives and the dominance of the husband.

[8]Unfortunately, we did not determine our respondents' religious affiliations. However, in a study conducted by Ponting, in March 1977, of 203 randomly selected residents of Calgary Alberta, the abortion question was inserted in a battery of five Likert-type questions. Surprisingly, it was found that fewer Roman Catholics (29%) than Protestants (41%) or persons with no religious affiliation (58%) fell in the traditional range. Perhaps symptomatic of the turmoil currently occurring in the Roman Catholic Church is the fact that the modal response for Catholics was "Neutral, Undecided" (54%), while only 28% of the Protestants and 28% of those with no religious affiliation fell in this category. Only 14% of those with no religious affiliation fell in the liberal response range, compared to 17% of the Catholics and 31% of the Protestants.

that "discussions of equality between the sexes and attitudes towards women are all part of the concern with sex-role ideology". Following Lipman-Bluman (1972), she dichotomizes this sex-role ideology as "traditional" and "contemporary-egalitarian". Although we agree that the dichotomy is a useful one, we have opted for the more simplified terms of "traditional" and "liberal" to describe the two poles of our scale.

A traditional outlook towards women's issues in Canada is thus operationalized as disagreement with statement "A" below, and agreement with statements "B" and "C":

A —"In the business world more women should be promoted into senior management positions"

B —"Although a wife's career may be important, she should give priority to helping her husband advance in his career"

C —"When children are young a mother's place is in the home"

A liberal outlook would be operationalized as agreement with the first statement and disagreement with the latter two.

In constructing the Guttnam scale we were faced with the necessity of dichotomizing our original five-point Likert-type items. Thus, we collapsed the two agree and disagree categories, respectively. To minimize the loss of cases, the choice of the "neutral" response option was collapsed into the non-liberal response category. That is, a simple and necessarily arbitrary distinction was made between those who accept a liberal statement (or reject a non-liberal statement), and those who do not. The one percent of the sample with no opinion (as distinct from those with neutral opinion) on one or more of the three items was excluded from the scale and from the analysis. The resultant Feminist Scale met acceptable standards of unidimensionality, cumulativeness,[9] and reproducibility.[10] On the four point scale, 22% of the sample occupied the traditional pole with a scale score of zero. Fifty-eight percent had a score of one, 16% a score of two, and 4% fell at the liberal pole with a score of three.

Table 2 shows the mean scores of each of our subsamples on the Feminist Scale. Generally speaking, strong liberalism (as measured by this scale) does not

---

[9]For the sample as a whole, Pearsonian correlation coefficients between the three scale items, prior to dichotomization, were as follows: $r_{AB} = -.11$; $r_{AC} = -.16$; and $r_{BC} = .31$. These items were more strongly correlated among the most highly educated (i.e. university graduates). Nie et al. (1975:535) maintain that a scalability coefficient (CS) greater than .60 is indicative of an acceptable level of unidimensionality (and cumulativeness) for a Guttman scale. In our sample as a whole this criterion was met (CS=.66). It was also met in all of the language-gender subsamples except the francophone females. These subsample scalability coefficients were .67 for Anglophone males; .71 for Anglophone females; .67 for Francophone males; and .50 for Francophone females.

[10]The conventional indicator of the existence of a Guttman-type relationship among the scale items is the presence of a Coefficient of Reproducibility (CR) whose magnitude is .90 or greater. In our sample as a whole the CR was .94. In each of the four language-gender subsamples it also exceeded .90.

Table 2   MEAN SCORES ON FEMINIST SCALE FOR LINGUISTIC AND
                                                                   GENDER SUBSAMPLES

Subsample	Mean Score	Standard Deviation	N
Females	1.05	.733	1049
Males	0.98	.749	759
Anglophones	0.96	.726	1402
Francophones	1.09	.740	357
Anglophone Females	0.98	.718	783
Anglophone Males	0.94	.737	619
Francophone Females	1.11	.708	233
Francophone Males	1.06	·799	124
Total Sample	1.02	.740	1808

Notes : 1. Persons excluded from the subsample analysis included: (1) those who replied "Don't
            Know" or "No Opinion" to one or more of the constituent items of the Feminist
            Scale; (2) those for whom the main language spoken in the home is neither French
            nor English; and (3) persons whose sex was not identified.
        2. The scores of the subsamples are based upon unweighted data, while those of the
            total sample are weighted.
        3. The higher the mean score, the more liberal the response on the Feminist Scale.

emerge from the sample as a whole nor from the subsamples. In all cases the
mean score falls below the mid-point (1.5) of the scale. While women demonstrate slightly greater liberalism than do men, the difference is not statistically
significant at the .001 level of confidence. Francophones do demonstrate greater
liberalism than Anglophones ($\overline{X} = 1.09$ and 0.96 respectively; p = .003), while
Francophone females are the most liberal of all groups. One possible explanation
for this greater liberalism among Francophone females is that they have been
profoundly influenced by the radical changes that have taken place in Quebec
during the past two decades, particularly those changes associated with the
Quiet Revolution and the increased secularization of the Quebec society. The
reform lay feminism of the 1960's and the radical and socialist feminism of the
1970's (Jean, 1974:12-13) have transformed the attitudes and ideologies of the
Quebecoises, resulting in the greater liberalism of this group.

Socio Demographic Correlates

Although in one sense the feminist movement in Canada dates from the
suffragettes and Women's Christian Temperance Union, many aspects of the
movement, such as equality within both marriage and the business world, are
more contemporary in emphasis if not in origin.[11] There is thus good reason to
expect that young Canadians, who have come to maturity in a different social

---

[11]The discontinuity between the earlier suffragette movement and the contemporary feminist movement is noted in Samuel Clark et al., (1975:373).

climate than did their elders, should have relatively more liberal views towards women's issues. In the adoption of more egalitarian attitudes towards women's issues, young Canadians should be less constrained by more traditional patterns of socialization and experience. However, earlier work by Schreiber has revealed only weak and inconsistent relationships with age (1975:70). While Boyd (1974) also found generally negative relationships between age and liberal outlooks, these relationships were again neither powerful nor totally consistent.

In our data, age was moderately and negatively related to scores on the Feminist Scale ($r = -.22$). The younger respondents were, the more liberal their outlooks tended to be towards women's issues.[12] Interestingly, the relationship was somewhat stronger among Francophone respondents ($r = -.26$) than it was among Anglophones, ($r = -.19$), which supports the view that generational cleavages on women's issues are more pronounced within the Francophone culture. This finding serves to remind us of the existence within French Canadian society of rapid social change which is bound to leave generational cleavages in its wake.

A characteristic closely associated with age is the degree of formal education attained by respondents.[13] The generational change that has occurred in the Canadian educational system has meant that younger respondents tend to have more extensive formal education than their parents or grandparents. With respect to women's issues, furthermore, there are reasons, quite apart from multicollinearity with age, to expect some relationship between the respondent's formal education and his or her scores on the Feminist Scale. In the first place, exposure to advanced formal education, particularly at the university level, is thought to induce, by design or accident, more liberal outlooks towards social issues and concerns. Secondly, and related to the above point, advanced education enhances exposure to current ideologies of social change, among which falls the feminist movement. Finally, in the work by Schreiber (1975:70) and to a lesser extent in the work by Boyd (1974), generally moderate and positive relationships were established between formal education and attachment to non-traditional outlooks on the concerns of women.

Here, too, a moderate linear relationship exists between levels of formal education and scores on the Feminist Scale ($r = .18$, P $< .001$). The more formal education received by respondents, the more likely they are to express non-traditional outlooks. As we found with the age relationship, controlling for gender had little impact. However, and also similar to the finding with age, the education relationship was stronger among Francophones ($r = .32$) than among Anglophones ($r = .15$).[14] This undoubtedly reflects the central role played by

---

[12]For similar American findings, see Chandler (1972:45).
[13]The correlation between age and formal education was $r = -.30$. (In this sample, both age and education were unrelated to the sex of respondents).
[14]The Pearson correlations between the Feminist Scale and formal education were as follows for the four subsamples: anglophone males (.12), anglophone females (.18), francophone males (.32), and francophone females (.34).

educational change in the aforementioned rapid social change that has transformed the French Canadian society.

Given the relationship between education and the Feminist Scale, we might
well expect a parallel relationship to exist with levels of family income.[15] Theoretical support for such an expectation, however, is more difficult to muster, for
although relatively wealthy individuals may at times actively support civil rights
and social reform, wealth may also induce greater personal attachment to, and
identification with, the established social order that the feminist movement
confronts. It is interesting to note in this respect that Schreiber (1975:70) found
only weak and inconsistent relationships between income and outlooks towards
women's issues. Using American data, Chandler (1972:44) found consistent
negative relationships between respondent wealth and support for the feminist
movement.

One advantage of our data set over Boyd's and Schreiber's is that it enabled
us to approach the measurement of income and financial standing in a variety of
ways. However, in no instance did regular or powerful relationships emerge.
The relationship between the Feminist Scale and family income (adjusted for
family size and excluding students and retirees) was weak ($r = .12$) and irregular
across the six income categories.[16] Only among the Francophones did the relationship attain even moderate strength.[17]

Apart from family income, we collected a number of more subjective assessments of financial and social standing, such as self-assessed social class (both
at the time of questioning and when growing up), the respondent's view of
Canada's economic prospects over the next five years, and the respondent's own
financial prospects over the next five years. The comparison between the respondent's perceived present social class position and his/her perceived social class
when growing up provides us with a subjective measure of social class mobility.
Comparing the respondent's assessment of his/her own personal financial prospects to his/her assessment of the economic prospects of Canada as a whole
provides a subjective measure of the respondent's anticipated relative deprivation
or relative advantage vis-a-vis other Canadians.

---

[15]The Pearson correlation between formal education and the family income of respondents was
$r = .29$, $p < .001$.

[16]Due to our large sample size, weak relationships are frequently statistically significant. In this
instance, the correlation of $r = .12$ is significant at the .001 level. For this reason, significance
levels are of limited utility in assessing the data. However, to circumvent this problem, we use
different significance levels with different subsamples, depending upon the size of the subsample in
question. For instance, where the subsample N is 500 or greater (as in the total sample, the
Anglophone male subsample, and the Anglophone female subsample) a significance level of .001
is used. Where the subsample size is less than 100 (as the Francophone male subsample is on
one question) the .05 level is used, while for subsamples intermediate in size ($N = 101$-499),
which is to say the Francophone males and Francophone females, the .01 level is employed.
This method takes into account the fact that the level of statistical significance is influenced
by the subsample size, and permits meaningful comparisons across subsamples of quite different
sizes.

[17]The Pearson correlation for Francophone females was .22, compared to .22 for Francophone
males, .09 for Anglophone females, and .03 for Anglophone males.

Across this range of variables it was our expectation that financial security would make respondents more amenable to feminist demands for social change than would economic uncertainty and pessimism. Hence, we predicted that respondents who were optimistic about their own and/or Canada's economic prospects, who perceived themselves as upwardly mobile, and who saw their own financial prospects as being good relative to those of the economy as a whole, would be relatively liberal in their outlooks on women's issues. At best, however, our findings marginally confirmed such expectations. Although the relationships were generally in the predicted direction, they were feeble and frequently lacked statistical significance. Among male respondents, in fact, only the palest shadow of the predicted relationship existed. Overall, then, subjective assessments of financial prospects and social class contributed little of substance to scores on the Feminist Scale.

More consistent and powerful relationships were found between views on women's issues and the marital status of respondents. Single ($\bar{X} = 1.24$) and divorced or separated ($\bar{X} = 1.26$) respondents had significantly more liberal scores on the Feminist Scale than did those respondents who were married ($\bar{X} = .98$). Widowed respondents, in part because of their relatively advanced age, were the most traditional in their views ($\bar{X} = .90$).[18]

The final socio-demographic variable examined here is the employment status of female respondents. As paid employment represents a transgression of traditional roles, we should expect employed women to have more liberal attitudes on women's issues than would women who do not work outside the home. As noted earlier, it is in the public sphere that inequalities based on sex are the most glaring, and have been the most subject to feminist attack. Hence working women should be both more aware of the condition of women within the Canadian economic order and, from self-interest alone, should be more sympathetic to emerging feminist definitions of the role of women in Canada.[19]

These expectations were confirmed; employed women had more liberal scores on the Feminist Scale than did non-employed women ($\bar{X} = 1.21$ and 0.95, respectively, t-test $p < .001$). The failure of an even more striking relationship to emerge may perhaps be traced to the transient position of many women both within and outside the paid labour force. Undoubtedly many of the non-employed women in the sample had at one time been members of the paid labour force, and many will return to it. Similarly, many of the respondents within the labour force may be contemplating leaving paid employment, or may have only recently rejoined the labour force after a more or less prolonged absence. Thus, to a large extent, whether or not women are employed may reflect their position within life and family cycles (and their socio-economic status) more

---

[18]For supporting American evidence, see Chandler (1972:45).
[19]With reference to American data, Chandler (1972:44) notes that "of all the characteristics analyzed, the fact that a woman is not employed and does not want to be employed is the clearest indicator of resistance to Women's Liberation".

than any radical difference in work experience or in attitude towards paid employment.

Women's Issues and Indian Issues

The feminist movement in Canada co-exists with a multitude of other more or less organized movements for social change. As Canadians grapple with the issues raised by the feminist movement, they also confront minority group demands upon the social order and the perennial problems of inflation, American influence and national unity. Given this broader set of social concerns within which the feminist movement exists, it is interesting to explore the attitudinal linkages, if any, between women's issues and other social issues confronting the Canadian public. Thus we might ask whether women's issues stand apart, or whether there are broad ideological perspectives within the Canadian public that interweave opinion on women's issues with that on other matters of social concern.

In addressing this question we are limited by the content of the questionnaire within which the questions on women's issues were imbedded. As that questionnaire dealt primarily with public perceptions of Canada's native peoples, we shall now explore the association between that aspect of public opinion and women's issues.

One body of literature has emerged which approaches the condition of women from a minority group perspective (e.g., Hacker, 1951). The model has been borrowed and adapted from the minority group literature on race and ethnic relations. Its basic thesis is that women may be considered as a minority group, that is

a group of people who because of their physical or cultural characteristics, are singled out from the others in the society in which they live for differential and unequal treatment and who therefore regard themselves as objects of collective discrimination (Wirth, 1945:347).

Although this thesis is not without its shortcomings, it nevertheless suggests the interesting hypothesis that, to the extent that women are perceived as a minority group, opinion towards women and women's issues may be positively correlated with opinions towards other minority groups. More specifically, we might hypothesize that a relatively liberal outlook towards the concerns of women would reflect a broader sense of minority group liberalism that would also encompass sympathetic dispositions towards another more clearly delineated minority, the native Indians of Canada. In part this prediction is complicated by the rather bitter disputes that have broken out within the Indian community over the rights of Indian women. Indeed, for some members of the public, the recently established supremacy of the Indian Act over the rights of women as advanced in the Canadian Bill of Rights may well have blunted perceptions of a common minority group interest spanning Indians and women. Nevertheless, it is the minority group hypothesis of a positive relationship between feminism and sympathy towards Canadian Indians that we put to the test.

Although the survey collected voluminous data on public perceptions of Indians and Indian issues in Canada,[20] our analysis here is restricted to only two points of possible linkage with opinion towards women's issues. The first comes from an index of generalized sympathy toward Indian issues and Indian concerns in Canada. The Indian Sympathy Index, which has been described elsewhere (Gibbins and Ponting, 1977), incorporated ten agree-disagree statements such as "Indians, as the first Canadians, should have special cultural protection that other groups don't have". Scores on the ten statements were added together to form an index with values ranging from ten (very unsympathetic) to fifty (very sympathetic). The sample distribution closely approximated a normal curve with a mean score of thirty-two.

Table 3 presents the sample and subsample correlations between the Indian Sympathy Index and the Feminist Scale. Although the relationships are not strong, they are uniformly positive, as predicted by our minority group hypothesis, and the zero order relationships are statistically significant ($p < .001$) for all cases except Francophone males. The strength and statistical significance of the zero order relationships remain essentially intact when we simultaneously partial out the effects of age and education. Thus, a noticeable strand of minority group liberalism does interlace the two issue areas, albeit rather loosely.

Table 3   ATTITUDINAL LINKAGES BETWEEN FEMINISM AND SYMPATHY
                                           TOWARDS CANADIAN INDIANS

Subsample	Pearsonian Correlation Between Feminist Scale and Indian Sympathy Index	
	Zero Order	Second Order**
Total Sample	.17*	.16*
Males Only	.17*	.15*
Females Only	·16*	.14*
Anglophones Only	.16*	.14*
Francophones Only	.18*	.17*
Anglophone Males	.19*	.18*
Anglophone Females	.13*	.11
Francophone Males	.06	.00
Francophone Females	.26*	.27*

**Partialling out the effects of age and education.
*Statistically significant at the .001 level.

The second point of linkage relates to a battery of questions on the tactical options open to Indians in the pursuit of their objectives. Respondents were

[20]For an overview of this aspect of the study, see Gibbins and Ponting (1978).

presented a list of seven possible tactical options and were asked to state their degree of approval or disapproval of Indians actually using each tactic on the list.[21] Our concern here rests with only three of these tactics—holding protect marches, boycotting private businesses, and occupying government offices. These tactics were selected because they met two criteria. First, they are open to use by women in promoting their goals. Secondly, they fall at neither the extremely radical nor extremely conservative end of the protest continuum. These questions thus allow us to determine if approval of Indian assertiveness is linked to a relatively liberal stance on women's issues, or otherwise stated, whether approval of minority group assertiveness constitutes another thread tying together opinions towards Indians and the concerns of women.

Table 4   ATTITUDINAL LINKAGES BETWEEN SUPPORT FOR FEMINISM AND SUPPORT FOR INDIAN TACTICAL ASSERTIVENESS

| | Pearsonian Correlation Between the Feminist Scale and Approval of: | | | | | |
| | Protest Marches | | Boycotting Private Business | | Occupying Government offices | |
Subsample	Zero Order	Second Order	Zero Order	Second Order	Zero Order	Second Order
Total Sample	.21*	.17*	.17*	.12*	.09*	.06
Males Only	.21*	.16*	.19*	.13*	.11*	.07
Females Only	.22*	.18*	.17*	.11*	.07**	.04
Anglophones Only	.18*	.14*	.18*	.13*	.04	.00
Francophones Only	.29*	.23*	.26*	.14*	.26*	.24*
Anglophone Males	.19*	.16*	.19*	.14*	.05	.01
Anglophone Females	.18*	.13*	.17*	.13*	.03	—.01
Francophone Males	.22**	.08	.29*	.12	.32*	.25**
Francophone Females	.33*	.33*	.25*	.16	.22*	.23*

Note : The second order correlation coefficients indicate the magnitude of the association after partialling out the effects of age and education.
**Statistically significant at the .01 level.
*Statistically significant at the .001 level.

Table 4 presents the correlations between degree of approval of each of the three tactical options and scores on the Feminist Scale. Overall, these two phenomena are related in a positive direction. Although partialling out the effects of age and education reduces the magnitude of the associations in virtually all cases, they usually retain statistical significance. The table reveals negligible gender differences across the three items, but marked Anglophone-Francophone

[21]The seven tactical options are listed below with the percentage of the sample approving of each: requesting that a Royal Commission be formed to study Indian problems (83.5%), launching lawsuits in the courts (63.9%), holding protest marches (55.4%), occupation of government offices (34.8%), barricading railways or roads crossing Indian reserves (16.1%), boycotting private businesses (13.7%), and threatening violence (2.5%).

differences, especially for the tactic of occupying government offices. There the second order relationship with the Feminist Scale disappears altogether for the Anglophones, while remaining moderately strong among the Francophones.

The case of the Francophone women in Table 3 and Table 4 is rather interesting. The data support the interpretation that *as a "minority group" themselves*, Francophone women hold an empathetic understanding for women and Indians *as minority groups*.[22]   As Moreux (1973:179) reminds us, the French Canadian woman has historically faced a multi-faceted subordination involving subservience to her God, her priest, her parents, and her spouse (and, we might add, to Anglophones). Given that subordination, we might well expect a sharply developed minority-group consciousness on her part, with a corresponding integration of Indian and feminist concerns and means of bringing about change. This association is found in Table 3, and across all three tactics in Table 4. The data also suggest that this minority-group consciousness is more highly developed among Francophone women than among either the Anglophone women or the Francophone men.

To summarize Table 4, then, we find that approval of Indian tactical assertiveness is more pronounced among those respondents falling towards the liberal pole of the Feminist Scale, and we once again have evidence of a generalized, if not robust, liberalism in the attitudinal linkages spanning the two issue areas.

The Relative Importance of Feminist Concerns

There is a danger that an analysis focusing exclusively on public opinion towards women's issues may, by default alone, over-emphasize the importance of such issues within the public consciousness. Thus, in concluding our data analysis we should like to turn to the opening question of the interview, one that asked respondents to rank the priority of "several problems facing Canada today." Imbedded among the five problems posed to respondents was "the rights of women in Canada." The other four problems were "greater independence of Canada from the United States." "The social and economic problems of Canada's Indians and Eskimos," "conservation of energy," and "inflation." The priority assigned to "the rights of women in Canada" is examined in Table 5.

Within such a competitive context, concern for the rights of women in Canada fared poorly. The sample as a whole placed first priority on inflation, second priority on the conservation of energy, third on the economic and social problems of native peoples, fourth on greater independence from the United States, and fifth and last priority on the rights of women. As on the Feminist Scale, Francophone women once more stood out as being the most favourable to

[22]Earlier we hypothesized that to the extent women are perceived as a subordinated group, opinion towards women's issues will be positively correlated with opinions towards other subordinated groups. Here we are suggesting that Francophone women not only perceive other women and native Indians as being subordinated, but also perceive themselves as being particularly subordinated.

Table 5   PRIORITY ASSIGNED TO "THE RIGHTS OF WOMEN IN CANADA"

Priority	Total Sample	Anglophone Males	Anglophone Females	Francophone Males	Francophone Females
	SUBSAMPLE				
	%	%	%	%	%
First	4.4	2.4	4.8	4.0	10.3
Second	9.0	5.9	7.4	4.0	19.7
Third	18.8	14.1	16.8	21.0	25.8
Fourth	30.2	34.5	28.4	34.7	24.5
Fifth	37.5	43.1	42.6	36.3	19.7
	100%	100%	100%	100%	100%

women's issues. Also, while liberal respondents on the Feminist Scale tended to place a higher priority on the rights of women, the relationship was weak ($r = .14$; $p < .001$).

Discussion and Conclusions

It is useful to step back from the data and view it from a more general perspective on public opinion and public opinion research, research that has been justifiably criticized on a number of grounds. Critics point out that most forms of public opinion rest on a foundation of low awareness, little interest, and often even less information. Questions are frequently asked about issues that are peripheral to the concerns or life experiences of respondents; the opinion that is generated thus lacks any experiential base. Moreover, opinions are collected on issues about which the respondent, per se, is powerless to act; thus not only are the behavioral consequences of opinion seldom investigated, but in many cases there is simply no behavioral component to investigate. As Leo Bogart (1972:198) has stated in a powerful critique of the research field :

> When an interviewer confronts me with questions about my brand choice in beer or automobiles, he is dealing with preferences that relate to past and possible future actions over which I exercise the primary control regardless of influences that may be brought to bear upon me. When the same interviewer asks my opinions about China, Rhodesia, or the European Common Market, he is asking about matters on which my opinions can be translated into action only through the appropriate institutions of society or through expressive behavior that by-passes the institutions.

On one level, the type of public opinion under analysis here is less subject to these criticisms. That is, there is no reason to expect that interest, awareness and information should be low, as opinion is not being collected on a subject matter remote to the life experience of respondents. There is also the possibility of individual action to effect change in the realm of the woman's role in the family. The perceptions we hold, the roles we occupy, and the roles that we attempt to impose upon others are amenable in part to personal intervention and change. As a consequence, opinion here seems unlikely to be dichotomized into that held by an apathetic, indifferent and uniformed mass public, and that held by a relatively attentive opinion elite (Devine, 1970).

However, initiating change in social structures is not a simple task that can be accomplished by individual action alone. We are dealing here not only with "personal troubles of milieu," but also with "public issues of social structure" (Mills, 1967:8). Thus, at one level change can be affected by individuals, while on another plane structural modifications require organized intervention in the institutional sphere.

More empirically, we have found that the socio-demographic underpinnings of public opinion towards the role of women are not robust. (The multiple correlation between the Feminist Scale and age, income, education, gender, and language was ($R = .21$, $R^2 = .045$).[23] This finding is similar to that of Schreiber (1975)[24] in Canada, and of Marx-Feree (1974:394) in the United States. The potential significance of this lack of social structuring of opinion is that it may limit the impact of public opinion in the political process.[25]

We are still left, however, with the question: "If social roles, positions, and cleavages fail to organize opinion on women's issues, what *does*?" This question, unfortunately, is easier to pose than it is to answer. Part of the answer may lie in explanatory variables, such as religious affiliation, psychological traits, and organizational memberships, that were not incorporated into the survey. Part may lie in the relatively low priority assigned to the rights of women by the Canadian public; if the priority is low, the emergence of well defined social cleavages becomes less likely. It may also be the case that the absence of more visibly assertive feminist leadership has stiffled a more clearly articulated, and social defined, public mood.[26]

However, a more important key to the explanation may be found in the very scope and complexity of women's issues and concerns. The issue area is vast, encompassing a broad set of loosely entwined components that impinge upon virtually every aspect of the Canadian society. Yet at the same time, the issues are intensely personal, reaching into the most intimate corners of an individual's life. They have implications not only for interaction with the broader social order, but also for interaction with friends, lovers and relations. Perhaps few public issues

---

[23]For the statement of abortion, $R^2 = .003$; for the statement of perceived equal economic opportunity, $R^2 = .046$.

[24]Schreiber (1975:70), using similar socio-demographic variables reports multiple correlations ranging from .14 to .36 across six dependent variables. Across these six, the average $R^2 = .047$.

[25]This was Monroe's (1975:206) interpretation with regard to American public opinion towards the issue of the Vietnam war.

[26]This eschewal of a centralized "star" or charismatic leadership pattern in favour of a decentralized leadership pattern is determined in large part by the anti-hierarchical anti-elitist values of the movement's ideology.

encroach upon the individual to this extent. Thus when we consider the characteristics of both scope and intimacy it becomes less surprising that socio-demographic characteristics fail to provide useful route maps for the individual.   The issues are so complex, so vast, and so personal that one's age, education, social standing, or even one's gender, fail to provide guidelines that can be easily utilized.

One final point brings us full circle to our opening concern with ideological management in the Canadian society. Public opinion is frequently organized around a social actor or agent who is seen as having responsibility for, or control over, some state of affairs.[27] In the case of women's issues, however, traditional Canadian scapegoats are of little utility; one cannot blame the Americans, Eastern Canada, English Canadians, or French Canadians. Rather, the locus of responsibility is ill-defined and diffused. Is it the social order, the economic order, the political order, or aspects of them all? Ultimately, it seems that, whether we like it or not, we are all enmeshed in cultural and economic patterns that are so broad they make it impossible to lay the ·responsibility at the feet of a single target, against which opinion could consequently be mobilized, and about which that opinion could be organized.

In concluding, we harken back to Walt Kelley's comic strip philosopher of the swamp, Pogo, who once stated "we have met the enemy, and he is us". The point here is not simply that women themselves may frequently be adamant opponents of their own liberation.[28] More importantly, the responsibility for the condition of women lies deep within us all; within beliefs, values and expectations that have been well entrenched through multitudinous forms of socialization, and through cultural patterns that we often unquestionably accept as our own values, norms and ideals. The enemy, then, is not simply external, and because of this, external social characteristics appear to have a limited impact upon the way in which we order our beliefs and orientations. We react in the light of our own individual experiences and circumstances, and our more general social attributes impinge little upon our internal confrontation. The very nature of the issues forces a more personal, and hence more idiosyncratic form of resolution, a form that is unlikely to generate clearly discernible patterns of relationship in national surveys of disjointed individuals.

BIBLIOGRAPHY

Bogart, Leo
    1972   *Silent Politics: Polls and the Awareness of Public Opinion.* New York: John Wiley and Sons.
Boyd, Monica
    1974   "Equality between the sexes : the results of Canadian gallup polls, 1953-1973". Paper presented at the Annual Meeting of the Canadian Sociology and Anthropology Association, August 24.

[27]For an elaboration of this point see Butcher (1957). Bucher's findings appear to have generalizability far beyond the disaster context of her study.
[28]For example, Chandler (1972:46) notes that "in a number of respects, it appears that while Women's Liberation is a movement among women, it is viewed by many women as a movement against women".

7

1975 "English-Canadian and French-Canadian attitudes toward women: results of the Canadian gallup polls". *Journal of Comparative Family Studies.* 6, 2: 153-169.

Bucher, Rue
1957 "Blame and hostility in disaster," *American Journal of Sociology.* 62: 467-475.

Chandler, Robert
1972 *Public Opinion: Changing Attitudes on Contemporary Political and Social Issues.* New York: R.R. Bowker Company.

Clark, Samuel D., J. Paul Grayson, and Linda M. Grayson
1975 Prophecy and Protest : Social Movements in Twentieth Century Canada. Toronto: Gage.

Devine, Donald J.
1970 *The Attentive Public: Polyarchical Democracy.* Chicago: Rand McNally and Company.

Erikson, Robert S. and Norman R. Luttbeg
1973 *American Public Opinion: Its Origins, Content, and Impact.* New York: John Wiley and Sons.

Erskine, Hazel
1971 "The polls: women's role." *Public Opinion Quarterly,* 35, 2 (Summer) : 275-290.

Gibbins, Roger and J. Rick Ponting
1977 "Contemporary Prairie Perceptions of Canada's Native Peoples." *Prairie Forum: Journal of The Canadian Plains Research Centre.* 2, 1: 57-81.
1978 "Canadians' Opinions and Attitudes Towards Indians and Indian Issues: Findings of a National Study". Summary report prepared for and available from The Department of Indian and Northern Affairs, Ottawa, Canada.

Hacker, Helen Mayer
1951 "Women as a minority group". *Social Forces.* 30 (October): 60-69.

Harris, Louis
1973 *The Anguish of Change.* New York: Norton.

Hobart, Charles W.
1972 "Orientations to marriage among young Canadians". *Journal of Comparative Family Studies.* 3 (Autumn): 171-193.
1973 "Egalitarianism after marriage: an attitude study of French and English Canadians," pp. 138-156 in Marylee Stephenson (ed.) *Women in Canada.* Toronto: New Press.

Information Canada
1975 *Facts and Figures: Women in The Labour Force.* Ottawa.

Jean, Michele
1974 "Les Quebecoises, ont-elles une histoire?" *Forces* 27, Deuxieme Trimestre: 5-14.

Lipman-Blumen, J.
1972 "How ideology shapes women's lives". *Scientific America,* 226 (January): 34-42.

Marx-Ferree, Myra
1974 "A woman for president? changing responses: 1958-1972". *Public Opinion Quarterly.* 38, 3 (Fall): 390-399.

Mills, C.W.
1967 *The Sociological Imagination.* London: Oxford University Press.

Monroe, Alan D.
   1975   *Public Opinion in America.* New York: Dodd, Mead and Company.

Moreux, Colette
   1973   "The French Canadian family," pp. 157-182 in Marylee Stephenson (ed.) *Women in Canada.* Toronto: New Prers.

Nie, Norman H. et al.
   1975   *Statistical Package for the Social Sciences,* Second Edition. New York: McGraw-Hill.

Report of the Royal Commission on the Status of Women in Canada
   1972   Ottawa: Information Canada

Schreiber, E.M.
   1975   "The social bases of opinion on woman's role in Canada". *Canadian Journal of Sociology.* 1, 1: 61-74.

Smith, D.E.
   1975   "An analysis of ideological structures and how women are excluded: considerations for academic women." *Canadian Review of Sociology and Anthropology,* 12, 4 (November): 353-369.

Wirth, Louis
   1945   "The problems of minority groups." In Ralph Linton, (ed.) *The Science of Man and the World Crisis.* New York: Columbia University Press.

11 Feminist Egalitarianism, Social Action Orientation and Occupational Roles A Cross National Study*

LUDWIG L. GEISMAR, BENEDICTE CAUPIN and NEIL DeHAAN**

The set of ideas and social policies known as women's liberation has left visible marks on countless aspects of the social and economic life in the United States: Affirmative action in employment, equal rights legislation, women's study programs in colleges and universities, abortion reform, alternate marriage life styles, and the day care center movement are examples of phenomena that owe their existence at least in part to the movement. Some of them represent real gains such as the freedom of choice to have an abortion; others like the new egalitarianism in marriage are mostly symbolic, except for the few ideologically committed, and they will continue to be so until legislation and economic change make social reform possible.

While it would be difficult to assess the exact contribution of ideology versus such other factors as technology and economic need to social change, few would gainsay the proposition that in a free society personal beliefs of those affected by a given social situation will over time tend to affect that situation. Barring major upheavals such as wars, natural disasters or socio-economic revolutions, the beliefs of women in the desirability of change in their role in society will very likely make a contribution to the nature and degree of role change.

This paper concerns itself with two issues related to women's adherence to the idea of women's liberation: (1) the social context which generates egalitarian beliefs — particularly the role of culture and status in shaping women's ideology; (2) the relations between belief in the desirability of change versus maintaining the status quo and orientation which favors or opposes action to effect change. Beliefs in women's position in society revolve mainly around what Harriet Holter has termed sex norms (Holter 1970 p. 54). The concept connotes the application of evaluative standards to characteristics as well as activities of women in domestic, social, educational, occupational, political, and economic roles. These norms can be seen to arrange themselves on a continuum from the traditional to the egalitarian. The former emphasize such differences as have long been maintained in most of western society. The latter tend to ignore distinctions in the allocation of roles and responsibilities.

*We gratefully acknowledge the contributions of Barbara Berry, Diane Garcia, Martha Harris, Phyllis Salvato and Wilma Selenfried in all stages of the research, and we are greatly indebted to Harriet Fink for the computer analysis and to Harriette Johnson for aiding in the library research.
**Rutgers University,U.S.A.

Variations in Sex Role Norms

This study concerns itself with women as the group with the greater stake in a change of the status quo and, therefore, probably with a more favorable attitude toward change. Indeed, there is research evidence that women are more supportive of egalitarian norms than men (Payne 1956, Chombart de Lauwe 1962, Spence and Helmreich 1973, Holter 1970, p. 70-71). Our choice of women as research subjects does not imply that their views are more decisive than those of men in the change process. Instead, it could be argued that women's commitment to modifying traditional roles is a necessary condition for change.

In addition to sex as a factor influencing sex role norms, there is also some empirical evidence (Gavron 1966, Thompson and Finlayson 1963, Holter 1970 pp. 66-70, Komarovsky 1966) that egalitarianism is associated with a higher level of education. This is not an unexpected finding in view of the fact that advanced education entails the asssimilation of democratic and humanist values and a critical examination of traditional beliefs (Holter 1970, p. 65). The generally close association between educational and occupational status leads to the supposition that occupation likewise bears a direct relationship to attitudes favoring the equality of the sexes. This is borne out in a Norwegian study in which the occupational difference, however, was found to be largely a function of the variation due to formal education (Holter 1970, p.77). The present research will seek further proof of the influence of both education and occupation on sex role norms.

Sex Role Norms and Action Orientation

Since the present inquiry seeks to throw light on the possible relationship between women's beliefs and social reform, the question that must be posed first pertains to the relationship between sex role norms and ideological support of social action. Underlying this investigation is the assumption, not entirely without empirical foundation, (de Friese and Ford 1969, Fendrich 1967, Tittle and Hill, 1967, Linn 1965, De Fleur and Westie 1958) that an orientation favoring a cause is correlated with taking part in working for it.[1] This study, however, addresses itself to the attitudes toward, not participation in such action.

A postulated link between feminism and an action orientation can be explained readily by observing that low feminism implies an acceptance of those roles that have been traditionally allocated to women and, Women's Liberation not withstanding, continue as the dominant culture patterns in most of western society. A modification of women's role in society, by contrast, requires a variety of actions to reform or eliminate old norms and behaviors and institute new ones (Fowler et al. 1973).

Data analysis and findings are presented below in relation to three research hypotheses dealing with (1) the relationship of social conditions to feminist

---

[1]The literature on the relationship between attitudes and action is quite extensive and we have cited only some of the most relevant studies. By and large there is evidence that overt behavior is directly correlated with attitudes (Tittle and Hill 1967, Albrecht and Carpenter 1976), although the relationship is often mediated by such factors as reference group (DeFriese and Ford 1969), level of social involvement with the attitude object, amount of prior experience with it (Linn 1965), presence of social constraints (De Fleur and Westie 1958), and others.

beliefs, (2) the influence of occupational roles on egalitarianism, and (3) the nexus between feminist attitudes and action orientation.

Research Design

The study elicited the views — by means of a self-administered questionnaire — of sample of 230 American and 213 French women on three aspects of feminism: Attitudes toward egalitarianism, advocacy of action when experiencing discrimination personally, and advocacy of action vis-a-vis societal discrimination in general.

Attitudes toward egalitarianism were collected with the aid of a 24 item Likert Scale. The items were designed to assess respondents' views regarding a variety of domestic and career roles of women. Factor analysis (varimax rotated factor matrix — orthogonal rotation) did not bear out the intended clustering and yielded instead — after dropping out variables with loadings below ± .40 — three factors or sub-scales which were labeled role specialization (5 items), male superiority (6 items), and women's domestic role (4 items).[2]

The French version of the questionnaire paralleled the American one in every way. Both forms were given pre-tests before the start of the data collection. The American data were collected in the summer and early fall of 1973 while the French data collection took place in August and September of that year.

The respondents in both countries were selected from three occupational strata: Blue collar factory workers, white collar clerical workers, and students. This choice was aimed at creating status comparability across national boundaries. The ideal goal of representative sampling from the respective strata was beyond the capacity of this project. Instead, industrial plants and businesses were selected in northern France and northern and central New Jersey which were willing to cooperate in the project and allowed their workers to be interviewed in the plant during work hours or a luncheon break. Student respondents were selected randomly from the female student body of schools of social work in the region.

The 230 American respondents were sub-divided into 80 electrical products assembly plant workers, all members of a trade union; 71 clerical workers employed in a large library and a travel agency; and 79 graduate students in social work. The 213 French respondents were composed of 61 workers of a mail order house engaged in assembling, packing, and shipping orders; 73 clerical workers employed in this mail order house and in the office of the school of social work; and 79 students of the French School of Social Work. This school, in contrast to its American counterpart, was not university based, but merely maintained ties with a local university and its student body was considerably younger (mean ages differed by about 6 years).

---

[2]The scales are available on request from the senior author.

Feminism and Society

A comparison of French and American responses on feminist attitudes must take account of the cultural context within which beliefs have been generated in the recent past. Although France, often thought as the cradle of the western movement for the emancipation of women — during the revolution of 1789 the women of France demonstrated and rioted in the cause of equality — the country is best characterized by an abstract commitment to the quality of women. Catherine Bodard Silver, viewing developments in France in a historical perspective concludes that "French women are very far from that 'equality' proclaimed in the Republic's motto. . ." (Silver 1973, p.74). She observes that the egalitarian ideal coexists with a strong familistic tradition that stresses women's subordinate and domestic role (Silver 1973, p. 74). In summarizing developments, she writes that "despite the holding of an 'Estates-General'· of Women in Versailles in the fall of 1970 — an event which surprised many by the vigor and clarity of the complaints and demands that the delegates and leaders manifested — there is little sign of the emergence of a modern women's movement in search of expanded opportunities."[3] (Silver 1973 p. 88).

In the United States, feminist egalitarianism as a socially significant movement is of recent vintage. Although this country had a number of suffragette movements in the 19th century, they had either ceased to exist or were a pale shadow of their former selves by the middle of the 20th century (Freeman 1973). The 1960's and early 1970's saw the growth of an extensive popular literature, beginning with Betty Friedan's *The Feminine Mystique* (1963), the development of several feminist movements, and more significantly the passing of legislation ("sex" was added to Title VII of the 1964 Civil Rights Act, the Equal Rights Amendment passed by Congress) to protect the rights of women. By the late 1960's, the media had come to give prominent billing to the women's liberation movement and to issues involving the status and rights of America's female population.

While most objective indices of women's participation in economic life do not reveal sharp contrasts between France and the United Stated (Kievit p. 4, Sullerot 1973, p. 95, 115, for some seeming differences, see conclusions below), the rates of change since the beginning of the century vary considerably (the

---

[3]The appointment by French President Giscard d'Estaing of a Secretary of State for Women's Affairs has been viewed in the press as a symbolic rather than substantive move toward the emancipation of women.

---

[4]No claim is made that change in labor force participation fully reflects women's influence in economic life. Of equal or greater importance would be data on the socio-economic status of the jobs occupied by women. Our efforts to make longitudinal comparisons based on U.S. and French census data ran afoul of (1) differences between the two countries in the occupational categories used by the censuses; (2) different over time in the classification systems used in both countries. Shifts in categorization were particularly pronounced between 1900 and 1931. The best generalization that can be made from available census data is that both in France and the United States there has been a dramatic increase during this century in the proportion of women in white collar jobs. However, their share in the professional, managerial, and technical occupations has remained relatively constant between 1950 and 1970.

percent of women in labor force between the start of the century and the mid sixties ranged from 37% to 35% in France[4] and from 23% to 34% in the United States; (Goode 1963, p. 60; Sullerot 1973, p. 115).

In the United States public opinion poll data covering attitudes toward women's equality over a forty year period reveal a dramatic increase in the percentage favoring women working (20% to 64%) and willing to vote for a woman to be U.S. President (from 27% of men and 40% of women to 70% of both sexes; *Society* March/April 1974, 6-12). Two of the authors who have recently spent time in both France and the United States agree on their assessment of the greater strength and influence of the women's movement in America, and they see modern French egalitarianism sparked by developments in the United States.

Against this background of observations it is reasonable to hypothesize that Americans are more egalitarian than the French in their attitudes of feminism. This hypothesis receives considerable but not uniform support when the two national groups are compared on the three attitudinal dimensions (factors) and the two advocacy of action scales. This is shown in Table 1 which presents the significance of difference between total as well as occupational group means.

Gross comparisons between the national groups reveal that American respondents are significantly more likely than the French to reject attitudes marking males as superior and assigning women to domestic tasks. Differences are in the same direction but not significant on the issue of role specialization which addresses itself to the question of whether a division of labor among men and women would be a desirable arrangement. On the subject of advocating action to attain equal rights for women in society, French respondents show a significantly lesser inclination for such advocacy. On the other hand, French women were slightly but not significantly more ready to favor action to correct personal discrimination or injustice encountered at work.

Although the question of occupational differences will be addressed below a cross-national comparison with occupation controlled appears appropriate at this point because of the known association between education and sex role norms (see under "Variations in Sex Role Norms" above) and the close association in the study population between occupational level and education (American sample Gamma = + .96; French sample Gamma = + .94). Therefore, controlling in this study for occupation is tantamount to holding education constant.

Table 1 reveals a sub-group pattern of cross-national differences that is more or less in line with the total group differences. The male superiority and domestic role scales evoke significantly more liberal reactions from American than French respondents. On the question of role specialization, the two nationalities are not very far apart, and only the two student groups are differentiated at a level outside the realm of chance. The students, Table 1 shows furthermore, are the only group in which American egalitarianism is significantly more pronounced on every attitudinal dimension than its French counterpart. This is not surprising because American female students have been in the forefront of the national consciousness raising movement. Furthermore, to the

TABLE 1

SCORE DIFFERENCES BETWEEN AMERICAN AND FRENCH WOMEN

ON FIVE SEX ROLE ATTITUDE SCALES

Groups Compared	(N's in Brackets)	Significance of Difference T Scores for Each Scale *				
		Role Speciali- zation	Male Superiority	Woman's Domestic Role	Advocacy of Action- Personal	Advocacy of Action- General
Total American (230) Total French (213)		- 1.01	- 4.64 (3)	- 6.90 (3)	0.85	- 3.09 (3)
American (80) and French (61) Factory Workers		- 0.32	- 2.89 (2)	- 3.23 (3)	1.24	2.32 (2)
American (71) and French (73) Clerical		- 1.43	- 2.21 (2)	- 3.97 (3)	4.10 (3)	- 0.65
American (79) and French (79) Students		- 1.70 (1)	- 5.83 (3)	- 7.30 (3)	- 4.75 (3)	- 10.22 (3)

* Minus scores denote French more conservative than Americans

(1) Significant at 5% level

(2) Significant at 1% level

(3) Significant at 1% level

extent that years of formal education is a contributing factor to liberalism (see below), the American women students who in contrast to the French are engaged in graduate studies and have completed three more years of schooling on the average, might be expected to manifest a greater measure of female egalitarianism.

Advocacy of action to correct an injustice done to a person emerges as the dimension without a salient national characteristic. American students are significantly more action oriented than their French counterpart but the opposite holds true for clerical workers. This orientation, unrelated to attitudinal egaliltarianism may reflect the beliefs of the French employees that corrective action can yield results. Advocacy of action to effect changes in society in general receives significantly stronger endorsement from the French than the

American factory workers. We are left to conjecture that the French orientation is part of a wider ideology favoring social and political change. But American women students, as stated earlier, are consistently more vigorous advocates of social and political action than their French sisters.

A substantial mean age difference between American and French respondents of close to ten years, only partially accounted for by the younger age of the French students, posed the question whether national differences might not be understated because of the older age of the American sample. Such reasoning would be based on a not uncommon finding linking youth with liberalism on social, political, religious and moral issues. Test for the effect of age by comparing national differences shown in Table 1 with differences found when age of respondent is held constant yields the following results: With age not controlled 12/20 of the tests of differences were statistically significant in the hypothesized direction, while with age controlled (table not shown) 20/45 of the tests revealed such significant differences. With age not controlled, two significant differences are found in the reverse direction whereas four such differences are encountered when age is held constant. Shifts from the first to the second analysis reveal no systematic pattern, and there is every indication that age has no appreciable effect on the differences in feminist egalitarianism between French and American women.

Occupational Roles and Egalitarianism

A second research hypothesis postulates a direct relationship between occupational status and liberalism with regard to sex roles. The longer period of advanced formal education, usually associated with the higher status occupations, involved, as was stated above, the internalization of values favoring social change and acceptance of non-traditional forms of behavior. If this is true, we should expect to find a similar relationship between occupational status and sex role norms in the United States and France.

Table 2 furnishes substantial though not unqualified support for this thesis. Students in both societies are more egalitarian than either clerical or factory workers, and among the last two the former reveal more liberal leanings than the latter, although the white collar — blue collar worker contrast is less marked than the ideological gap between students and the two other groups. Differences in beliefs parallel differences in formal education, which show in both countries an ordinal progression from factory worker to office worker to student with the interval between the two groups of workers being smaller than between clerical workers and students. In both countries academic life and/or the sub-culture associated with the academic pursuit appear to produce a much more egalitarian set of sex role attitudes than life in the plant or clerical office.

French blue and white collar workers differed little — and their American counterparts differed least significantly — on the women's domestic role scale. Both leaned in the conservative direction and tended to agree with such statements as "a woman should not go on vacation without her husband and children" and "unless a family badly needed income, a woman with young children should not work." This is not strange if one considers that to a factory

TABLE 2

SCORE DIFFERENCES AMONG THREE OCCUPATIONAL STATUSES

ON FIVE SEX ROLE ATTITUDE SCALES

Occupational Groups Compared (N's in Brackets)		Significance of Difference T Scores for Each Scale *				
		Role Specialization	Male Superiority	Woman's Domestic Role	Advocacy of Action-Personal	Advocacy of Action-General
U.S. Students and Clerical Workers	(79) (71)	- 6.72 [3]	- 6.38 [3]	- 7.81 [3]	- 8.94 [3]	- 6.73 [3]
U.S. Students and Factory Workers	(79) (80)	- 10.06 [3]	- 9.88 [3]	- 10.95 [3]	- 7.41 [3]	- 8.26 [3]
U.S. Clerical and Factory Workers	(71) (80)	- 3.40 [3]	- 3.32 [3]	- 1.81 [1]	2.26 [2]	- 1.35
French Students and Clerical Workers	(79) (73)	- 7.95 [3]	- 3.32 [3]	- 4.80 [3]	- 1.64 [1]	0.30
French Students and Factory Workers	(79) (61)	- 12.24 [3]	- 8.78 [3]	- 5.96 [3]	- 1.77 [1]	2.19 [2]
French Clerical and Factory Workers	(73) (61)	- 3.17 [3]	- 4.67 [3]	0.30	- 0.40	1.62 [1]

* Minus scores indicate that the second group is more conservative than the first.

(1) Significant at 5% level

(2) Significant at 1% level

(3) Significant at .1% level

or clerical woman employee working in the home may not be nearly as unattractive as to a female professional or executive. The findings of a 1970 U.S. poll of a cross-section of American women supports this contention. Sixty eight percent of the respondents endorsed the statement that "taking care of a home and raising a family is more interesting than having a job."

On advocacy of social action likewise differences between the two working groups were neither sharp nor consistent. Being rather ambivalent on the question of favoring action to correct injustices or discrimination against women, factory and office workers in France as well as the United States seemed to formulate their attitudes on the basis of local work situations which defy generalizations concerning the beliefs of the two status groups.

Comparing occupational group differences in the United States with those in France, we observe that with few exceptions American women in the higher status jobs, when compared with those in the lower status positions, were relatively more liberal than their French counterparts. The reasons for this are a matter of conjecture, but the relative differences do not reflect greater discrepancies in American formal education. A likely explanation can be found in the relative exposure of the status groups to attitudes conveyed in the printed media. In America more than in France, the subject of women's liberation has been featured prominently in the journals and magazines appealing to the better educated. The above findings may simply mirror the differential effect of exposure to this material by the American occupational groups.

The third study hypothesis postulated a significant association between egalitarianism and advocacy of action. Inherent in this argument is the notion that beliefs supporting action furnish guidelines to action. Among the literature on this subject cited above, most relevant is the study by Fendrich (1967) who sought to compare the relative significance of attitudes and commitment as they are related to social action, and found commitment to be the better predictor. He contends that "unlike attitude measures, commitment incorporates in the measurement situation the fundamental aspect of overt behavior . . ." (Fendrich 1967, p. 355). At the same time, his own experimental research showed that attitudes and commitment to action are significantly associated, but the strength of this association varies with the conditions under which attitudes and commitment are juxtaposed.

Table 3 shows the correlations between egalitarian attitudes and two forms of advocacy of social action. It will be recalled that the first represents a nine item scale dealing wth action alternatives when a person has encountered discrimination. The second scale, composed of seven items, encompasses general strategies for attaining equal rights for women in society.

For American respondents as a whole there is a significant relationship between feminist liberalism and advocacy of both types of action. For the French, by contrast, the relationship is practically at a zero level. When occupational status is held constant additional differences emerge. American students' attitudes reveal a significant link with advocacy of personal but not general action. American women, except for students, show only a slightly greater tendency than French women to relate their action advocacy to feminist orientation. For both groups, sub-group correlations were in the main non-significantly positive or near zero negative (with a smattering of higher non-significant negative correlations).

Thus, the third hypothesis receives only stinting support. Despite an overall significant association for the U.S. sample between orientation and advocacy of action, the data in Table 3 show that this association holds true mainly for social work students, particularly in regard to action to correct injustice experienced

TABLE 3

RELATIONSHIP BETWEEN EGALITARIAN ATTITUDES AND ADVOCACY OF

SOCIAL ACTION +

National and Occupational Groups	Correlation (Gamma) Between Advocacy of Action-Personal and			Correlation (Gamma) Between Advocacy of Action-General and		
	Role specialization	Male Superiority	Woman's Domestic Role	Role Specialization	Male Superiority	Woman's Domestic Role
Total U. S. Group	0.37 (3)	0.48 (3)	0.50 (3)	0.52 (3)	0.59 (3)	0.62 (3)
Total French Group	0.06	0.20	0.00	- 0.17	- 0.05	- 0.08
U. S. Factory Workers	0.01	0.20	- 0.05	0.20	0.49 (2)	0.30
U. S. Students	0.48 (2)	0.57 (1)	0.67 (3)	0.06	0.36	0.61 (2)
U. S. Clerical Workers	0.08	0.14	0.15	0.36	0.24	0.32
French Factory Workers	- 0.31	0.00	- 0.07	0.43	0.46	0.15
French Students	0.26	0.49 (2)	0.24	0.10	0.04	- 0.03
French Clerical Workers	- 0.28	- 0.03	- 0.36	- 0.31	0.03	- 0.09

+
A positive correlation denotes that liberalism is associated with a commitment to social action.

(1) Significant at 5% level

(2) Significant at 1% level

(3) Significant at .1% level

by a person directly. It should be noted at the same time that advocacy of such action is further removed from the reality of student life than from the life of the office or factory worker. Hence, it might be argued that egalitarianism, not subject to the constraints of an employment framework (as in the case of American students), is more likely to generate advocacy for action focus than egalitarianism circumscribed by conditions of work.

If the foregoing rationale is a valid explanation for sub-group differences in the American sample, why does it not apply equally to the French study population? The difference may be partly a statistical artifact of the substantially weaker liberalism of French students (see Table 1 and 2) relative to the other French occupations, resulting in smaller correlation coefficients. Another possible explanation lies in the realm of French social work education which gives relatively more weight than does American social work training to agency-placed field instruction and less emphasis to theoretical learning and critical analysis of welfare systems. Furthermore, French in contrast to the U.S. social work education prepares students for work in industry (about 15% of French social workers are employed in industry) which is not noted for its liberal ideology. It is not far-fetched to assume that the reality of a more practice-centered training in France leaves its mark upon the students action orientation.

Conclusions

The data for this study were gathered from 443 women respondents in three comparable but not necessarily representative settings in the United States and France. The study population was composed of roughly equal numbers of factory workers, clerical workers, and students. They answered questions on three dimensions of feminist egalitarianism and two dimensions of action orientation.

The greater feminist egalitarianism of the American women in the study was seen to correspond to the relatively greater emphasis in the United States than France in recent years upon the theme of women's liberation. That theme has received backing from the media and support from new legislation, and it is kept alive by a number of women's organizations.

A substantial parallelism between the two societies marked the orientations of respondents from three occupational classes. Underlying the cross-national similarities are corresponding levels of education and socio-economic situations which give rise to similar belief systems. Egalitarian attitudes and action orientation, contrary to expectations, were not found to be strongly interrelated. Data from this study showed that in spite of the greater feminist liberalism of the American study population their action orientation (except for the students) did not differ consistently from that of the French. The explanation was seen to rest in the basic similarity or work situation confronting the workers, but not the students, in both countries. The research furnished indications that the culture in general and the work situation in particular mediate between attitudes and advocacy of social action.

Vis-a-vis our attempt to explain the differences in sex role norms between the two societies in terms of the vitality of the egalitarian ideology at the time this research was done, the question arises as to what structural factors might help explain the divergencies in the prevalent beliefs in the two countries.

If French women are more conservative than their American counterparts and yet, except for students, approximately equal believers in the efficacy of action to correct sex discrimination, does this not suggest that the former feel less deprived and handicapped than the latter. It is not irrelevant to note that during the past decade women constituted a larger percentage of professional technical and related workers in France (45.0% in 1968) than in the United States (40.7% in 1972; source *1973 Yearbook of Labor Statistics*). Moreover, more French than American women have held managerial positions in industry and commerce in recent years. The French 1962 census lists 36% of managers as being women. The corresponding figure for the U.S. 1960 census is 14.4% and the 1970 census is 16.5%.[5] It may be that the greater prevalence of women in superordinate positions influences the way in which blue and white collar employees assess their chances of receiving equal treatment. However, this relatively favorable position of French women is not equalled in other areas such as their share of higher paid jobs, professional higher status positions, and university faculties (Silver 1973, pp. 74-81). One anomaly similar to that found in the United States is their ready access, dating back to World War II, to higher education (with about 43% of French university students being women in 1968 as against 40% in the United States). The French women's educational opportunity stands in striking contrast to their career opportunities as measured by professional achievement. This discrepancy which has led to overt discontent and organized protest in the United States has failed to produce mass reaction in France.

An examination of other structural factors underlying American-French attitudinal differences such as salary differentials, fringe benefits, unionization, legislative protection, etc. is likely to lead one far afield without yielding conclusive results because of the lack of comparability of economic and labor data and the absence of theoretical guidelines on their relationship to women's belief systems.

The full significance of structural data could, in any case, be evaluated fully only against the background of such cultural factors as national tradition and social institutions, particularly the family.

The aforementioned lack of close association between sex role norms and advocacy of action, our analysis suggests, may be interpreted to mean that favoring change is not an inevitable concomitant of a critical evaluation of an existing situation. The link between the variables, as inferred from the sub-group analysis, can take such forms as confidence in the feasibility of change and the absence of risk in advocating a change in the status quo.

---

[5]For source see listings of U.S. and French censuses in the bibliography. These figures, nonetheless, need to be treated cautiously. In spite of our efforts to match specific occupational categories in the two countries, divergencies in the patterns of census taking such as the practice in France, but not the United States, of counting husbands and wives as managers in small family businesses and the relative frequency of such businesses may account in part for the large percentage dissimilarity.

The present research may be seen as relevant for the assessment of attitudes as a guide to action. If goal attainment in the cause of feminism calls for active involvement of women in social and political action, liberal attitudes alone do not serve as a good predictor of commitment to future involvement. The planners and organizers of this and other causes, who wish to project the extent of support from the rank and file, will do well to link their assessment of attitudes to a careful analysis of the incentives and impediments to action within the social structure.

BIBLIOGRAPHY

Albrecht, Stan L. and Kerry E. Carpenter
    1976   "Attitudes as Predictors of Behavior Versus Behavior Intentions: A Convergence of Research Tractions," Sociometry, 39 (March) 1-10.

De Fleur, Melvin L. and Frank R. Westie
    1958   "Verbal Attitudes and Overt Acts," American Sociological Review, 23 (December) 667-673.

de Friese, G. H. and W. S. Ford
    1969   "Verbal Attitudes, Overt Acts and the Influence of Social Constraints in Interracial Behavior," Social Problems, 16 (4) 494-505.

de Lauwe, M. J. Chombart
    1969   "The Status of Women in French Urban Society," Internatioinal Social Science Journal, 14 (1) 26-25.

Fendrich, James M.
    1967   "A Study of Association Among Verbal Attitudes, Commitment, and Overt Behavior in Different Experimental Situations," Social Forces, 45 (March) 347-355.

Fowler, Marguerite Gilbert; Robert L. Fowler and Hani Van De Riet
    1973   "Feminism and Political Radicalism," Journal of Psychology, 83 (March) 237-242.

Freeman, Jo
    1973   "The Origins of the Women's Liberation Movement," in Huber pp. 30-49.

Gavron, Hannah
    1966   The Captive Wife: Conflicts of Household Mothers, London: Routledge & Kegan Paul.

Goode, William J.
    1963   World Revolution and Family Patterns, Glencoe, Illinois, The Free Press.

Holter, Harriet
    1967   "Scandanavia" in Patai, pp. 437-462.

Holter, Harriet
    1970   Sex Roles and Social Structure, Oslo: Universitetsforlaget.

Huber, Joan (ed.)
    1973   Changing Women in a Changing Society, Chicago, Univ. of Chicago Press.

Institut National de la Statistique et des Etudes Economique
    1973   Annuaire Statistique de la France, Resultats de 1971, Paris.

International Labour Office
    1973   Yearbook of Labour Statistics, Geneva, 1973.

Jesser, Clinton J.
    1972   "Women in Society: Some Academic Perspectives and the Issues Therein," International Journal of Sociology of the Family, 2 (September) 246-259.

Kievit, Mary B.
    1972   Women in the World of Work, Review and Synthesis of Research, Columbus, Ohio: ERIC Clearinghouse on Vocational and Technical Education (March).

Komarovsky, Mirra
    1966   "Women's Roles" in Seymore Farber (ed.) The Challenge to Woman, New York: Basic Books, pp. 20-33.

Lehman, Andre
    1967   "France" R. Patai 229-246.

Linn, Lawrence S.
    1965   "Verbal Attitudes and Overt Behavior: A Study of Racial Discrimination," Social Forces, 43 (March) 353-369.

Oakley, Ann
    1972   Sex, Gender and Society, New York: Harper & Row, Publishers.
Patai, Raphael
    1967   Women in the Modern World, New York: The Free Press.
Payne, Raymond
    1956   "Adolescent Attiltudes Toward the Working Wife," Marriage and Family Living, 18
              (November) 345-348.
Seward, Georgene H. and Robert C. Williamson (ed.)
    1970   Sex Roles in Changing Society, New York: Random House.
Silver, Catherine Bodard
    1973   "Salon, Foyer, Bureau: Women and the Professions in France" in Joan Huber, 74-89.
Society
    1974   "Roundup of Current Research," March/April, 6-12.
Sullerot, Evelyn
    1973   Women, Society and Change, New York: World University Library.
Spence, Janet T. and Robert Helmreich
    1973   The Attitude Toward Women Scale: Washington, D.C. American Psychological
              Association (Journal Supplement Abstract Service).
Thompson, Barbara and Angela A. Finlayson
    1963   "Married Women Who Work in Early Motherhood," British Journal of Sociology, 4
              (June) 150-167.
Tittle, Charles R. and Richard J. Hill
    1967   "Attitude Measurement and Prediction of Behavior: An Evaluation of Conditions and
              Measurement Techniques," Sociometry, 30 (June) 199-213.
United States Department of Commerce
    1973   Statistical Abstract of the United States, 1973, 94th Annual Edition, Washington, D.C.:
              U.S. Government Printing Office.

12

English-Canadian and French-Canadian Attitudes Toward Women: Results of the Canadian Gallup Polls*

MONICA BOYD**

I. Introduction

Recent sociological research into the structure of the French-Canadian family tends to emphasize the increasing modernization and democratization of marital and parent-child relations. Elkin (1964), Tremblay (1966) and others suggest that conjugal role relations have become more modern with the husband now more involved in family life. These characterizations contrast with past depictions of the French-Canadian family. Compared to other types[1], the historical French-Canadian family, especially in rural areas, was said to be child-centred and to emphasize unity and solidarity. Authority was invested in the husband and father while the maternal role was the woman's vocation and the home was her domain (Garigue, 1962).

These current and past depictions of the French-Canadian family are important not only as insights into the diversity of Canadian family life, but also because of their implications for the status of women in French Canada. Emancipation within the household is often considered as a correlate of legal, political and economic changes in the status of women.

However, emancipation within the household need not be necessary for an egalitarian ideology concerning the participation of women in economic and political sectors of society. In French Canada, at least, the historical literature suggests the existence of two separate functions for women: 1) as wives, mothers, and maintainers of the family; and 2) as participants in the rural religious, and educational sectors of society. The literature suggests that women who participated in the economy or in the educational systems were perceived as equal to their male counterparts (D. Johnson, 1971; Labarge, 1971). Thus, on the assumption that current ideologies are in part products of past ones, it is possible that current French-Canadian attitudes still emphasize the family, and the wife and mother image while also supporting the idea of female economic participation.

*Polls analyzed in this paper were obtained from the Carleton University Social Science Data Archives, which is part of its data collection service acquired card data from the Canadian Institute of Public Opinion. The analysis was partially funded by the Department of Sociology and Anthropology, Carleton University. The author thanks Charles Hobart and Danielle Lee for their insightful comments on an earlier draft.
**Assistant Professor, Department of Sociology, Carleton University, Ottawa, Canada
[1]As Ishwaran (1971) observes, there are many types of families in Canada. However, most studies of the French-Canadian family are compared, often implicitly, either to the residual (the non-French-Canadian family), or to the Anglo family.

Varying support for this contention is offered by several recent studies. The persistence of the strong French-Canadian imagery of the mother who stays at home is documented by Moreux (1973) with respect to a working class community and in a marketing survey by Vickers and Benson Ltd. (1972). Carrisse and Dumazedier (1970) also show that despite the preference of innovative women for more egalitarian husband-wife relationships, considerable support is given to the family as a procreative and socializing unit of society. However, in comparing responses of French and English speaking students (college or technical) on marital role relations, Hobart (1972) found that the French students were more egalitarian than the English in areas concerned with the wife's authority, housework and gainful employment.

As indicated by Hobart (1972), French-English differences exist with respect to marital role relations. The above discussion also suggests that attitudes toward women differ between the two linguistic or ethnic groups. Specifically, the hypothesized emphasis in French Canada on both the wife-mother role and the economic participation of females contrasts with the assumed relocation of English-Canadian women from the home to the economic sector.

Differences in attitudes by language or ethnicity may also vary by gender. In his study of marital relations, Hobart observes that compared to English respondents, French-speaking females were more egalitarian and French-speaking males were less. This polarity of results among French-Canadians by sex is interpreted as reflecting a feminist influence which is egalitarian in orientation and a Church influence which is traditional in orientation (Hobart, 1972:189). While Hobart's results may be due to the subject (marital relations) or to the sample design (students), they may also reflect a general disparity in attitudes between French-Canadian men and women.

To date there has been no comprehensive examination of differences in Canadian attitudes toward women by language/ethnicity and gender; nor has there been an investigation of the proposition that French and English Canadians differ in their emphasis on the mother role and the participation of women in the public sector. However such studies are possible with data collected by the Canadian Institute of Public Opinion in the Gallup Polls. Between 1953 and 1973, a number of questions were asked : 1) on the acceptability of female physicians, lawyers, politicians; 2) on the acceptability of married women working, with and without young children; and 3) on equality of opportunity between men and women in general and in the labour force (see Boyd, 1974). Background characteristics of respondents were collected, including province of residence, and after 1960, mother tongue of respondents. Examination of these Gallup Poll questions on women should reveal both French-Canadian attitudes toward women and the similarities or differences in attitudes between French-Canada and Anglo-Canada.

II. The Gallup Polls

Much of the discussion on the Gallup Polls and their interpretations are found in an earlier inquiry into Canadian attitudes toward women (Boyd, 1974).

The Canadian Gallup Poll is conducted approximately every two months by the Canadian Institute of Public Opinion. Each poll is based on a random probability cluster sample using quotas (Canadian Institute of Public Opinion, no date; McIver, 1973). The use of quotas in the sample design prevents the use of statistical tests of significance, but generally differences of 5 per cent or greater may be considered larger than expected by chance.

Questions on women may be examined with respect to the province of residence or mother tongue of the respondents. Because Quebec includes English and other mother tongue residents, mother tongue rather than province of residence is selected as the measure of the cultural background of respondents. Mother tongue is determined by asking the respondents "What was the language you first spoke in childhood and can still understand?" It is coded in the Gallup Polls as English, French, and other. The results of the "other" category should be reviewed with some caution as the number of respondents often are small and the category includes a mixture of languages (such as Ukrainian, Dutch, German, Italian, or Chinese). For this reason, the attitudes of the other mother tongue respondents are not discussed in this paper although the answers are presented for the interested reader.

The choice of mother tongue as the indicator of respondents' cultural background reduces the number of Gallup Polls which serve as the data base for this study. Most of the polls discussed in the paper were conducted in the 1970's. As a result, the attitudes to be discussed in this paper are indicative of current attitudes toward women.

As discussed in an earlier study (Boyd, 1974), the examination of attitudes toward women is related to discussions of sex-role ideology. Attitudes may range along a continuum from traditional to egalitarian. The traditional view generally sees women as belonging in the home and as responsible for childbearing. The egalitarian view maintains women and men should participate equally in the home and in economic sectors. In this study, attitudes will be discussed as traditional or egalitarian depending on the majority response to each poll question. Because of the variety of poll questions, the operationalization of traditionalism or egalitarianism is specific to each poll.

In order to test for the sex-language interactions observed by Hobart (1972), responses to poll questions are presented by sex. It should be noted that responses to Gallup Poll questions by sex and language may not be representative of the larger Canadian population. The Gallup Poll samples are designed to obtain a cross-section of the Canadian population with respect to age, sex, occupation, province and similar background characteristics. Any tabulation of results by these characteristics alone may be considered representative of the Canadian population. But description of Gallup Poll sampling procedures suggest that detailed cross-classifications of the sample are not representative of the larger sub-populations. Accordingly, the tabulation of responses by mother tongue and sex is presented with considerable cautioning, for it suffers from the non-representative problem which exists in the Hobart (1972) study. It is also for this reason that additional detailed cross-classification (such as mother tongue by education and age) are not given in the tables. Even if non-representativeness was not an issue, responses are subject to sampling fluctuation in many cross-classified tables because of sample attention. Crude tabulations for the total Canadian population by sex, or age or education appear in Boyd (1974).

III. *English-Canadian and French-Canadian Response to the Gallup Polls*

The Canadian Gallup Polls analysed in this paper ask a number of different questions on women. Despite the diversity of questions, however, there appears to be three types of questions on women asked in the Gallup Polls. Family life is the theme for one group of questions. The second group of questions probes attitudes toward women as incumbents of male sex-typed roles. The third type of question focuses upon the equality of opportunity, in general and in the labour force, for men and women. A final poll, which does not fit into any of the areas, is one which asks respondents their perception of attitudinal change due to the impact of the Women's Liberation Movement.

A. *Women and the Family*

Table 1 and 2 present the results of three recent polls on the roles of men and women in the home. Two of these polls examine the attitudes toward the mother role, and another assesses the attitudes toward male dominance in the home. The 1970 poll asks respondents to distinguish between a woman with young children and a woman without young children. A comparison of French and English mother tongue responses to the question on married women without young children taking a job (Table 1) shows that when no young children are present, both groups have an identical percent (77%) believing that women should take a job.

However, there are differences in responses by sex with a higher proportion of women compared to men believing that women with no young children should take a job. Comparing responses by sex and mother tongue reveals the patterning of responses observed by Hobart (1972) in his study on English and French attitudes toward marital relations. In his study French-Canadian males were the least egalitarian and French-Canadian females were the most. Table 1 similarly shows that French-Canadian females (87%) are most likely to agree that married women with no young children should take a job outside the home, and French mother tongue males (68%) are the least likely to agree that married women should take a job outside the home. But in spite of these differences by mother tongue and sex, there is considerable support for the idea that work by married women is permissible if they have no young children.

However, the favourable attitudes of Canadians toward the labour force participation of married women changes considerably when young children are present. Four-fifths of the Canadian respondents to the 1970 poll stated that women shoul not take a job outside the home if they have young children, in contrast to the nearly four-fifths (77%) of Canadians who earlier agreed that women with no young children should be permitted to take jobs. The differences in responses by mother tongue are striking. The greater insistence of the French-Canadians that women with young children not take jobs may be interpreted as

TABLE 1   CANADIAN ATTITUDES TOWARD WOMEN WITH FAMILIES WORKING
             BY SEX AND MOTHER TONGUE. CIPO : GALLUP POLLS 1970-1973.

340 March 1970.   Do you think married women should take a job outside the home.
  (b) if they have no young children ?

	N(a)	Yes	No	Can't Say
Total	670	77	15	8
English	397	77	12	10
French	181	77	16	7
Other	92	75	21	4
Male	338	72	17	11
English	199	73	13	14
French	92	68	22	10
Other	47	75	23	2
Female	332	82	12	6
English	198	81	12	7
French	89	87	10	3
Other	45	76	18	7

(a) if they have young children

	N(a)	Yes	No	Can't Say
Total	670	13	80	7
English	397	16	75	9
French	181	7	88	4
Other	92	12	86	2
Male	338	12	81	7
English	199	15	75	10
French	92	8	89	3
Other	47	11	87	2
Female	332	14	79	7
English	198	17	74	9
French	89	7	88	6
Other	45	13	84	2

357, January 1973   There are more married women—with families—in the working world than
                    ever before. Do you think this has had a harmful effect on family life or
                    not ?

	N(a)	Yes Harmful	Not Harmful	Qualified	Undecided
Total	725	59	27	7	7
English	435	58	26	8	8
French	197	61	32	4	3
Other	91	62	20	8	11
Male	374	62	25	6	7
English	228	61	25	7	7
French	99	61	30	4	5
Other	46	65	17	4	13
Female	351	57	28	8	7
English	207	55	28	8	9
French	98	61	34	4	1
Other	45	58	22	11	9

(a) The sub-sample sizes for language and sex groups may not equal the total population because
of non-response to the question on respondent's characteristics.

revealing the continued importance of the mother in the home for French Canadians. It also suggests the persistence of the traditional female role in French Canada.

A more recent poll conducted in January 1973 does not mention the age of children nor their explicit presence. Instead, respondents were asked whether or not they felt labour force participation of married women had a harmful effect on family life. Over half (59%) of the Canadian sample agreed that it did have a harmful effect. As indicated in an earlier study (Boyd, 1974), these results should not be directly compared to the 1970 Gallup Poll. The inclusion of 18 and 19 year olds in the 1973 poll and the different wording in the questions may be partly responsible for the different results.

For the total population there is little difference in the proportion of English and French respondents who believe that labour force participation of married women is harmful to family life. Overall, the prevalent opinion, held by both French and English mother tongue respondents, is one which stresses the detrimental aspects of married women working. As Table 1 shows, the seemingly contradictory finding that French-Canadians are more likely to argue that the labour force participation of married women has a both harmful and non-harmful effect on families is due to the tendency of French-Canadian respondents not to give qualified or undecided responses compared to the English mother tongue respondents. This tendency is also evident in the earlier polls on working women with and without young children.

The January 1973 Gallup Poll also asked respondents to indicate whether they believed that the dominant role of the husband in the Canadian family is or is not declining in importance. Respondents were also asked to indicate if a decline was good or bad. Table 2 shows that while two-fifths of the Canadians polled believed no decline in husband dominance was occurring, nearly half (49%) believed a decline was occurring. Compared to women, men were slightly more likely to agree that the dominance of the husband had declined.

There were marked differences by mother tongue in opinions on the declining dominance of the husband. Even when sex was held constant. French mother tongue respondents were more likely than English mother tongue respondents to state that the dominant role of the husband in the family had not declined in importance. These differences in responses by mother tongue may reflect the French-Canadian emphasis on the authority of the husband-father which has been commented upon by sociologists (Garigue, 1962; Moreux, 1973). This interpretation suggests the continuation, at least normatively, of the traditional role of the husband-father in the French-Canadian family.

The continued importance of the dominant husband-father figure in the French-Canadian family is further suggested by answers to the question "Would you consider a decline in the husband's importance to be good or bad?" Although the majority (63%) responded that a decline would be bad, this belief is held by 72 per cent of the French mother tongue respondents compared to 59 per cent of the English mother tongue respondents. These differences persist when sex is held constant.

TABLE 2   CANADIAN ATTITUDES TOWARDS DECLINING DOMINANCE OF THE
HUSBAND, BY SEX AND MOTHER TONGUE, CIPO GALLUP POLL, 1973

357, January 1973   Do you think the dominant role of the husband in the Canadian family is, or is not, declining in importance ?

	N(a)	Declined	Not Declined	Undecided
Total	724	49	39	12
English	435	55	33	12
French	197	41	52	7
Other	90	42	39	19
Male	373	52	37	12
English	228	58	30	12
French	99	41	51	8
Other	45	40	44	16
Female	315	47	41	12
English	207	51	36	13
French	98	40	54	6
Other	45	41	33	22

357, January 1973   Would you consider a decline in the husband's importance to be good or bad ?

	N(a)	Good	Bad	Undecided
Total	722	20	63	17
English	433	23	59	18
French	196	14	72	14
Other	91	20	65	15
Male	371	23	58	19
English	226	27	53	20
French	98	12	70	17
Other	46	22	56	22
Female	351	17	68	5
English	207	18	65	17
French	98	15	74	11
Other	45	17	73	9

(a) See note for Table 1

Overall, responses by mother tongue to the Gallup Poll questions on married women working and on the declining dominance of the husband reveal the continued importance of traditional male-female roles in French-Canadian culture. Compared to English mother tongue respondents, French-Canadians are more likely to believe that the dominant role of the husband has not declined and that such a decline would be bad. French mother tongue respondents are also more likely to agree that married women with young children should not take a job, and to state that the labour force participation of married women has a detrimental effect on family life. Both French-Canadian males and females hold these views. With the exception of the responses for the question on whether or not married women with no young children should be permitted to take a job, there was no confirmation of the more egalitarian stance of French-Canadian women compared to English speaking respondents and male French speaking respondents, which Hobart (1972) observed.

B. *Attitudes Toward Women as Role Incumbents*

The results of the Gallup Polls on working women and husband dominance suggest that during the early 1970's, French-Canadians were more traditional in their attitudes toward women than were English respondents. However, the validity of this conclusion is questioned by the results of additional polls on confidence in women in medicine, law, politics and business.

Table 3 presents the results of these additional Gallup Polls on the acceptability of women in male sex-typed roles. As revealed in an August 1964 poll, most

TABLE 3   CANADIAN ATTITUDES TOWARD WOMEN AS ROLE INCUMBENTS, BY
SEX AND MOTHER TONGUE, CIPO GALLUP POLLS, 1964-1971

308, August 1964 If, in an emergency you had to call in an unknown doctor and it turned out to be a woman, would you have more or less confidence in her ability than in a male doctor ?

	N(a)	More Confidence	Less Confidence	Same	No Opinion
Total	724	5	13	81	1
English	414	4	14	82	1
French	197	8	11	80	2
Other	111	3	16	81	—
Male	364	2	15	82	1
English	205	2	15	81	2
French	97	3	12	84	1
Other	61	2	16	82	—
Female	360	7	12	81	1
English	209	5	12	83	—
French	100	12	9	76	3
Other	50	4	16	80	—

308, August 1964 What about a lawyer ? Generally speaking, would you have more or less confidence in a woman lawyer than a male ?

	N(a)	More Confidence	Less Confidence	Same	No Opinion
Total	724	8	25	65	3
English	414	8	30	59	4
French	197	9	17	72	2
Other	111	4	18	76	3
Male	364	7	27	62	4
English	205	7	33	55	5
French	97	9	20	69	2
Other	61	7	18	72	3
Female	360	8	23	68	2
English	209	9	27	62	2
French	100	9	15	74	2
Other	50	—	18	80	2

(Contd.)

Table 3 *(contd.)*

307, April 1964   If your party chose a woman as Federal leader and if she was qualified for the job of Prime Minister, would you vote for her ?

	N[a]	Yes	No	Can't Say
Total	715	71	25	4
English	428	71	26	3
French	200	72	24	5
Other	87	69	28	3
Male	363	70	26	4
English	214	70	26	4
French	101	67	27	6
Other	48	71	27	2
Female	352	72	24	3
English	214	72	26	2
French	99	76	20	4
Other	39	67	28	5

333, January 1969   Do you think Canada would be ruled better or worse if women had more say in politics ?

	N[a]	Better	Worse	No Difference	No Opinion
Total	711	32	24	37	8
English	401	37	22	32	9
French	197	24	24	44	8
Other	113	27	31	34	9
Male	352	29	26	36	9
English	197	33	24	32	11
French	90	23	27	46	4
Other	65	26	28	37	9
Female	359	34	23	35	8
English	204	41	21	32	7
French	107	25	22	43	10
Other	48	27	35	29	8

346, March 1971   Do you think women can run most businesses as well as men or not ?

	N[a]	Yes	No	Undecided
Total	720	58	36	6
English	419	55	37	8
French	191	68	29	3
Other	110	53	40	7
Male	358	53	40	7
English	209	51	42	8
French	93	57	37	6
Other	56	52	41	7
Female	362	63	31	6
English	210	59	33	8
French	98	79	21	—
Other	54	54	39	7

(a) See note to Table 1

Canadians appear to have equal confidence in a male or female physician or lawyer. The slightly higher proportion of French mother tongue women who state that they have more confidence in a female physician at first suggests they are more egalitarian than the remaining mother tongue sex groups, but when their replies are combined with the proportion indicating same confidence regardless of sex, the differences by gender and mother tongue respondents are not great.

Although there are no significant differences by mother tongue in confidence in a female physician, responses to the second question on the confidence in female lawyers (Table 3) suggests that regardless of sex, French mother tongue respondents hold more egalitarian attitudes toward female lawyers than do English mother tongue respondents. French-Canadian women display the most confidence in female lawyers.

Overall, the responses to the August 1964 poll support an egalitarian interpretation of Canadian attitudes toward women as role incumbents. Certainly, the majority of Canadians indicated equal confidence in a female or male physician or lawyer. Similar responses are obtained in an April 1964 poll on the acceptability of a female candidate for the job of Prime Minister. Table 3 shows that over two-thirds of the Canadian population indicated that they would vote for a woman if their party chose her as a federal leader, and if she was qualified for the job of Prime Minister. There are no real differences in responses by mother tongue and by sex for the English and French mother tongue respondents. If responses of "no difference" or "ruled better" are considered egalitarian, similar results are found in the January 1969 poll which queried: Do you think Canada would be ruled better or worse if women had more say in politics ? The rather small differences by mother tonque and sex of the respondents are not in the direction suggested by Hobart.

In addition to questions on female physicians, lawyers and politicians, Table 3 also includes responses to a poll which asked if women could run business as well as men. As with the other polls probing the acceptability of women in certain occupations, the majority response to this question could be considered egalitarian. A higher proportion of French mother tongue respondents, particularly women, gave egalitarian (yes) answers compared to the English mother tongue respondents.

In addition to questions on female physicians, lawyers and politicians, Table 3 also includes responses to a poll which asked if women could run business as well as men. As with the other polls probing the acceptability of women in certain occupations, the majority response to this question could be considered egalitarian. A higher proportion of French mother tongue respondents, particularly women, gave egalitarian (yes) answers compared to the English mother tongue respondents.

Overall, the data presented in Table 1, 2, and 3 confirm the earlier discussed expectation that French-Canadian attitudes toward women might be inconsistent with respect to the mother role and participation in the public sector. Compared

to the attitudes of English respondents, French Canadians are more likely to stress
the traditional home-oriented role of women when young children are present.
Yet, in terms of accepting women physicians, lawyers, politicians and business
women, French mother tongue respondents are slightly more egalitarian than
English speaking respondents.

C.   Attitudes Toward Females in the Labour Force

It should be noted that the egalitarian responses recorded in Table 3 for the
general Canadian population and by sex and mother tongue may be inflated by
the general and hypothetical nature of the question (Boyd, 1974).   Respondents
are asked to respond to a situation in which a female is already the role incum-
bent.   Furthermore, in the question on the acceptability of the female Prime
Minister, the situation is so unlikely that persons could answer in terms of a
general norm rather than their own situation-specific attitudes.   However, two
Canadian Gallup Poll questions probe situation-specific attitudes. The results from
these polls (Table 4) confirm the suspicion that egalitarian responses in Table 3
are inflated but re-affirm the greater tendency of French-Canadians compared to
English-Canadians to hold egalitarian attitudes toward the women in the public
sector.

As discussed in an earlier study (Boyd, 1974), the majority of Canadians (64%)
in the mid-1960's indicated that if they were taking a new job and had a choice
of a boss, they would prefer to work for a man (Table 4).   However, noticeable
differences exist by mother tongue.   Regardless of sex, English mother tongue
respondents are more likely to give traditional responses (preference for a male
boss) than are the French mother tongue respondents.   Other than a differing
cultural acceptability of women in work-authority roles, there is no readily available explanation for this finding.

The second question asked if married women should be given equal opportunity to compete for jobs with men. Responses to this 1965 poll also show that the
majority of Canadians believed that men should receive the first chance. However,
French mother tongue respondents agreed slightly more with the suggestion that
women should be given an equal chance with men than did English mother tongue
respondents.   This difference by mother tongue is caused by the fact that
proportionately fewer English mother tongue female respondents agreed with the
statement.

D.   Attitudes Toward Equal Opportunity of Women and Men

The above polls were conducted during the 1960's prior to the heated discussions on the status of women which occurred during the late 1960's and early
1970's.   Concomitant with this debate, the focus of the Gallup Poll questions on
women shifted from assessing attitudes toward female roles to assessing attitudes
toward equal opportunity of women with men.   As a consequence, the questions
asked became less situation-specific and more general.   Nonetheless, the responses
to these questions continue to differ by mother tongue.

The most specific of the questions on equal opportunity raised the issue of
whether or not a woman had as good a chance as a man to become an executive

TABLE 4   CANADIAN ATTITUDES TOWARD FEMALE LABOUR FORCE
                           PARTICIPANTS, BY SEX AND MOTHER TONGUE, CIPO
                                      GALLUP POLLS, 1964-1970

307, April 1964 If you were taking a new job and had your choice of a boss, would you prefer
                 to work for a man or a woman?

	N(a)	Prefer Male Boss	Prefer Female Boss	No Difference	No Opinion
Total	715	64	7	25	4
English	428	70	4	22	4
French	200	56	13	28	3
Other	87	54	7	34	5
Male	363	65	5	26	4
English	214	70	2	24	4
French	101	61	10	26	3
Other	48	48	10	33	8
Female	352	64	8	24	3
English	214	71	6	20	5
French	99	52	16	29	3
Other	39	62	3	36	—

315, November 1965 Do you think married women should be given equal opportunity to com-
                    pete for jobs or do you think employees should give men first chance?

	N(a)	Equal Chance with Men	Give Men First Chance	Qualified	Undecided
Total	1,928	40	53	4	4
English	1,129	39	52	6	3
French	540	44	51	1	5
Other	259	31	61	2	6
Male	952	41	51	4	7
English	561	42	49	6	2
French	252	43	51	1	5
Other	150	32	60	1	7
Female	976	38	54	4	5
English	568	36	54	6	4
French	288	44	51	—	5
Other	120	30	62	3	6

(a) See note to Table 1

of a company. As indicated in Table 5, slightly over one-half (52%) of the total
sample replied no. However, in contrast to the English speaking respondents, the
French mother tongue respondents hold more favourable views on the opportunity
of women to become executives.

Two additional questions asked during the 1970's probed the equality of
opportunity between the sexes (Table 5). One question which received nearly
universal approval asked if women who work should receive equal pay with men
for the same kind of work. Not surprisingly, women were slightly more likely to
agree with this statement than were men (89% versus 84%). In keeping with the
responses to previous questions, one would expect that French mother tongue res-

TABLE 5 CANADIAN ATTITUDES TOWARD EQUAL OPPORTUNITY OF MEN AND WOMEN, BY SEX AND MOTHER TONGUE, CIPO GALLUP POLL, 1971

346, March 1971   If a woman has the same ability as a man, does she have as good a chance to become the executive of a company or not?

	N(a)	Yes	No	Undecided
Total	720	41	52	7
English	419	29	63	8
French	191	63	31	6
Other	110	51	42	7
Male	358	42	50	8
English	209	30	62	9
French	93	60	32	8
Other	56	57	38	5
Female	362	41	53	7
English	210	28	64	8
French	98	65	31	4
Other	54	44	46	9

341, January 1971   Will you tell me if you approve or disapprove of these suggestions: a) that women who work should receive equal pay with men for the same kind of work

	N(a)	Approve	Disapprove	Undecided
Total	708	86	11	2
English	413	89	9	2
French	189	83	15	2
Other	106	81	14	5
Male	353	84	14	2
English	200	89	10	2
French	94	80	12	1
Other	59	76	17	7
Female	355	89	9	2
English	213	90	8	2
French	95	86	12	2
Other	47	87	11	2

346, March 1971   In your opinion do women in Canada get as good a break as men?

	N(a)	Yes	No
Total	720	64	36
English	419	59	41
French	191	78	22
Other	110	57	43
Male	358	71	29
English	209	65	35
French	93	88	12
Other	56	64	36
Female	362	57	43
English	210	53	47
French	98	69	31
Other	54	50	50

(a)   See note to Table 1

pondents would be somewhat more in favour of the principle of equal pay for equal work than would be the English mother tongue respondents. However, a smaller proportion of French mother tongue respondents approved and a large proportion disapproved compared to the English mother tongue category. This difference cannot be explained by education differences between respondents. The French-Canadian attitudes may be the response of a group which perceives itself as marginal to the dominant culture and to the economy. In a study of attitudes toward working wives in the United States, Axelson (1970) has observed that black males are less inclined than white males to pay women wages equal to theirs.

Although French mother tongue respondents are slightly more likely to disapprove of equal pay for men and women, they are more likely than English mother tongue respondents to assert that women have equal opportunities compared to men. The poll which questioned the chances of women to become an executive showed that nearly two-thirds (63%) of the French mother tongue respondents believe that a women had an equal chance compared to 29% of the English mother tongue respondents. Another question also asked in the same March 1971 poll also reveals that a higher proportion of French mother tongue respondents compared to English mother tongue respondents agree that women in Canada get as good a break as men. This difference in response by mother tongue exists regardless of sex of respondents.

E. *Women's Liberation*

The response of French-Canadian males to the polls on equal opportunity (Table 5) indicate that they are more likely than the English-Canadian males to approve of equal opportunity, but less likely to approve of equal rewards for labour force participation. This apparent contradiction may simply be due to the general nature of the questions and to their specific wording. However, it also may reflect the belief that men and women should have equal opportunities, but that males as head of the household should receive higher renumeration. This belief would be in keeping with the traditional French-Canadian importance of the family.

In actuality the traditional conjugal role relationships of French-Canadian families appear to be changing (Moreux, 1973). However, behavioural changes do not necessarily imply concomitant attitudinal changes, particularly when the attitudes are part of a normative ideology operating to maintain an institution such as the family. Further, attitudes may not change if the behaviour modification is caused by the behaviour of one group (women) rather than by the behaviour of both (men and women). In this case, males who are forced to undergo an alteration in conjugal role behaviour because of the altered behaviour of spouses may seek to deny such a change. Such denial may underlie the slightly greater tendency of French-Canadian males to disapprove of equal pay for men and women (Table 5). It also may underlie the discrepancy in male and female perception of changes in attitudes which is shown in the most recent poll on attitudes toward women (Table 6).

In this January, 1973 poll, women were asked if they found that the average man's attitude toward women had changed because of Women's Liberation. However, men were asked if their own attitude had changed. As shown in Table 6, over one-third (37%) of the women agreed that the average male's attitude had changed while less than one-sixth (13%) of the men indicated their own attitude toward women had changed. The differences in sex perception of attitude change by mother tongue are striking with the gap being greatest for French mother tongue respondents. Over half of the female French mother tongue respondents perceive a change in male attitudes toward women compared to less than 10 per cent of the male French-Canadian respondents. This discrepancy between perceived change by gender suggests the existence of a feminist influence which is not overtly acknowledged by men in general, and by French-Canadian men in particular.

TABLE 6   CANADIAN PERCEPTION OF CHANGES IN ATTITUDES TOWARD
                 WOMEN, BY SEX AND MOTHER TONGUE, CIPO
                 GALLUP POLL, 1973

357, January 1973   (Asked of women only). There has been a great deal of discussion in the past two or three years about Women's Liberation. Have you found the average man's attitude toward women has changed because of this?

	N(a)	Yes	No	Can't Say
Total	351	37	63	(b)
English	197	30	70	(b)
French	96	52	48	(b)
Other	42	31	69	(b)

357, January 1973   (Asked of men only) There has been a great deal of discussion in the past two or three years about Women's Liberation. Have you found that your attitude toward women has changed because of this?

	N(a)	Yes	No	Can't Say
Total	374	13	82	5
English	228	15	80	4
French	99	8	89	3
Other	46	11	80	9

(a) See note to Table 1
(b) Not a response category for women

IV. *Conclusion*

In conclusion, the results of the Gallup Polls, which probed attitudes toward women during 1964-1973, reveal differences between French and English Canadians. Compared to English mother tongue respondents, a higher proportion of French-Canadians express confidence in a female lawyer and say there is no difference in the ability of men and women to run businesses and politics. Furthermore, French mother tongue respondents are more likely to show no gender preference for bosses, and to view women as having equal chances to become executives, compete with men for jobs, and to obtain equal breaks. However, in certain areas, French-Canadians hold more traditional attitudes than do English Canadians. Both groups hold egalitarian attitudes toward women without young children working. But once the mother and husband roles are invoked, a larger proportion of French-Canadians concur with the traditional stance that women should remain at home and husbands should be dominant. Compared to English mother tongue respondents, French mother tongue respondents have a slightly higher proportion disapproving of equal pay for equal work although the majority of both mother tongue groups do approve of this principle.

For both the English and French mother tongue groups differences in responses by sex exist with women generally being slightly more egalitarian in their attitudes than males. However, the interaction between sex and language which was noted by Hobart (1972) in his study of marital relations is virtually absent. The lack of this interaction in the Gallup Poll data, in which female French-Canadians are the most egalitarian and French-Canadian males the least, could reflect the differing samples. The Gallup Polls generally include individuals aged 20 years and older while Hobart's sample consisted of students who were no older than 27 years of age. Thus, an investigation of attitudes by mother tongue and sex for the youngest age group in the Gallup Polls (age 20-29) might show a pattern more similar to Hobart's findings. Such an analysis, however, is prevented by the small size of the resultant age sex-language groups which render answers subject to fluctuation. The lack of interaction also could reflect the more general nature of the Gallup Poll questions which were spread over 9 years. Hobart's study was focused upon one topic, marital relations, and his scaling procedures permitted combinations of various questions, which were asked at one point in time.

Hobart's findings of a polarity of attitudes among French-Canadians is confirmed in a different way by this study. Rather than observing sex-ethnic differences, an examination of Gallup Poll data suggests the existence of two attitudinal complexes with respect to women. On the one hand, the idea of equality between the sexes is supported by French-Canadians, but only when the mother and husband images are not invoked. When these images are invoked, French-Canadians become more traditional in their attitudes toward the roles of women.

What are the implications of these findings for the status of French-Canadian women? Sociologists of the family will correctly observe that attitudes supporting the wife and mother role are not necessarily incompatible with attitudes favouring equality between the sexes. Such potential incompatibility is resolved by each sex performing tasks in equal but separate areas. However, attitudes which favour the location of women in the home and the dominance of the husband operate to keep married women out of the labour force. Data for 1972 show that Quebec was the only region in Canada in which married women were less than one-half of the female labour force. Furthermore, the labour force participation rate for single, widowed, divorced or separated women in Quebec was 1.5 times that observed for married women, compared to a comparable ratio of 1.3 for the Atlantic provinces and 1.1 for other regions in Canada (Labour Canada: Women's Bureau, 1974: Tables 18 and 19). Thus, the French-Canadian emphasis on the family and the mother role appears to reduce the labour force participation of married women. In this sense, the continuation of the French-

Canadian emphasis on married women in the home may be interpreted as being inconsistent with national and provincial attempts to advance social and economic equality between men and women.

BIBLIOGRAPHY

Axelson, L. J. 1970. The Working Wife : Differences in Perception Among Negroes and White Males. Journal of Marriage and the Family 32 (Aug) : 457-464.

Boyd, M. 1974. Equality Between the Sexes : The Results of the Canadian Gallup Polls 1953 1973. Presented at the 1974 meeting of the Canadian Sociology and Anthropology Association, Toronto.

Canadian Institute of Public Opinion. No Date. Canadian Cross Section. Toronto : CIPO.

Carrisse, C. and Dumazedier, J. 1970. Valeurs Familiales de Sujets Féminins Novateurs, Sociologie et Sociétés 2 (No. 2) : 265-281.

D-Johnson, M. 1971. History of the Status of Women in the Province of Quebec. In Studies of the Royal Commission on the Status of Women 8 : Cultural Tradition and Political History of Women in Canada. Ottawa : Information Canada.

Elkin, F. 1964. The Family in Canada. Ottawa : Vanier Institute of the Family.

Garigue, P. 1962. La Vie Familiale des Canadiens francais. Montreal : Presse de l'Université de Montreal. Excerpt appearing in B.R. Blishen et. al. (eds.). 1968. Canadian Society. Toronto: McMillan of Canada.

Hobart, Charles W. 1972. Orientations to Marriage Among Young Canadians. Journal of Comparative Family Studies. III (Autumn) : 171-193.

Ishwaran, K. (ed.), 1971. The Canadian Family. Toronto : Holt, Rinehart and Winston.

Labarge, M.W. 1971. The Cultural Tradition of Canadian Women : The Historical Background. In Studies of the Royal Commission on the Status of Women in Canada. 8 : Cultural Tradition and Political History of Women in Canada. Ottawa : Information Canada.

Labour Canada : Women's Bureau. 1974. Women in the Labour Force : Facts and Figures, 1973. Ottawa : Information Canada.

McIver, J. 1973. Would You Say the Gallup Poll is : Very Accurate; Sort of Accurate; Not So Accurate; Inaccurate. The Canadian Magazine edition of the Ottawa Citizen, July 21: 26.

Moreux, C. 1973. The French-Canadian Family in M. Stephenson (ed.) Women in Canada. Toronto: New Press : 154-182.

Tremblay, M.A. 1966. Modèles D'Autorité Dans la Famile Canadiénne—Francaise. Recherches Sociographiques 7 : 215-230.

Vickers and Benson Ltd. Marketing Department. 1973. The Lifestyles of English and French Canadian Women. (No place of publication given).

13

Comparative Attitudes About Marital Sex Among Negro Women in the United States, Great Britain and Trinidad

ROBERT R. BELL*

In recent years the writer has carried out studies among lower-class Negro families in Philadelphia (United States), Reading (England) and San Fernando (Trinidad).[1] In those studies the major interest was in the lower-class Negro woman and her various family roles. In previous papers the lower-class Negro families in each of the three societies have been examined as to subcultural variations with regard to their dominant societies as well as some aspects of the subcultures compared with respect to one another. The interest in this paper is to look at variations with regard to marital sexual values in the three societies. However, first a brief examination of the family setting in the three societies particularly with regard to their similarities, gives needed background material.

There is a strong body or research evidence to show that in the Negro lower-class in the United States there is limited value attached to marriage.[2] As a result it is very common for the family to be female headed. Even when there is a man present, he is often there for short periods of time and is functionally of limited importance. Furthermore, it is clear that these patterns have been maintained for many years. For example, the significance of the female head family among Negroes has its roots in the slavery system and was further developed and maintained by the caste system of the Negro in the South following the Civil War. As a result, the Negro male was often limited in family involvement because of low economic opportunity and because the climate of racial prejudice made his participation as the family head extremely difficult. An important characteristic of the family in the Negro lower-class continues to be the major role of importance being the mother. This implies that a variety of other role and behavior characteristics are greatly influenced by the importance of the mother in the Negro lower-class.

*Professor of Sociology, Temple University, Philadelphia, Penn., U.S.A.

[1]Robert R. Bell, "The One-Parent Mother In The Negro Lower Class," *Eastern Sociological Society,* New York, April 1965; "Lower Class Negro Mother's Aspirations For Their Children," *Social Forces,* May, 1965, pp. 493-500; "The Lower-Class Negro Family In The United States and Great Britain," *Race,* July, 1969, pp. 1173-181; and "Marriage and Family Differences Among Lower Class Negro and East Indian Women in Trinidad," *Race,* June, 1970, pp. 59-73.

[2]See: Bell, "The One-Parent Mother In The Negro Lower Class," *op. cit.,* and Lee Rainwater, *Family Design,* Chicago: Aldine Publishing Co., 1965, pp. 28-60.

The background of the American Negro as related to the plantation system is very familiar to the Negro family in the West Indies. In general, the similarities between the two groups are: both came from African origins into white dominated plantation systems as slaves, and for both groups slavery had the effect of destroying most of the traditional functions of the family.

There have been a number of studies made of the family in the West Indies, but few within the past ten years.[3] In general, the studies agree that the Negro lower-class family in the West Indies is commonly characterized by the female head with generally limited significance of the male in the family and little importance attached to birth legitimacy for either the mother or the child. These patterns are very similar to the ones found in the United States among lower-class Negro families.

However, for many West Indians who migrated to Great Britain there was the feeling and reality of having entered the middle class.[4] When the immigrant is contrasted with the lower-class Negro in the United States, he does not live an isolated life in ghettos. As a result, the West Indian generally feels himself to be a part of Great Britain. While he may feel somewhat different, he does not feel as isolated as does the American Negro. It was found that the West Indian immigrant could get jobs and live in areas in Great Britain that were about the same as was available to the white lower-middle class. As a result he saw himself as being more middle class in Great Britain than he had been in the West Indian country he had migrated from. It appears that for most of the migrants to England, their move represented upward mobility.

---

[3]Judith Blake, *Family Structure in Jamaica*, Glencoe, Illinois: The Free Press, 1961; Edith Clarke, *My Mother Who Fathered Me*, London; George Allen and Unwin, 1957; Yehudi A. Cohen, "Structure and Function: Family Organization and Socialization in a Jamaican Community", *American Anthropologist*, August, 1956; G. E. Cumper, "The Jamaican Family: Village and Estate", *Social and Economic Studies*, March, 1958, pp. 76-108; William Davenport, "The Family System of Jamaica", *Social and Economic Studies*, Jamaica, December, 1961, pp. 452-4; Sidney M. Greenfield, *English Rustics in Black Skin*, New Haven, Conn., College and University Press, 1966; F. M. Henriques, Family and Colour in Jamaica, London, Eyre and Spottiswoode, 1953; Dom Basil Matthews, *The Crisis in The West Indian Family*, University College of the West Indies, 1953; Keith F. Otterbein, "Caribbean Family Organization: A Comparative Analysis", *American Anthropologist*, February, 1965; Hyman Rodman, "Marital Relationships in a Trinidad Village," *Marriage and Family Living*, May, 1961, pp. 166-70; M. G. Smith, *Kinship and Community in Carriacou*, New Haven, Conn., Yale University Press, 1962; M. G. Smith, *West Indian Family Structure*, Seattle, Washington, University of Washington Press, 1962; Raymond Smith, "The Family in the Caribbean", in *Caribbean Studies: A Symposium*, Mona, Jamaica, Institute of Social and Economic Studies, 1957; N. Solien, "Household and Family in the Caribbean", Social and Economic Studies, Jamaica, March, 1960, pp. 101-6; and J. Mayone Stycos and Kurt W. Back, *The Control of Human Fertility* in Jamaica, Ithica, New York, Cornell University Press, 1964.

[4]See R. B. Davidson, *Black British: Immigrants to England*, London, Oxford University Press, for I.R.R., 1966; Mary Dines, "The West Indian Family," *Race*, Vol IX, No. 4, 1968, pp. 522-5; Katrin Fitzherbert, *West Indian Children in London*, Occasional Papers on Social Administration, No. 19, 1967; Ruth Glass, Newcomers: The West Indians in London, London, George Allen and Unwin, 1960; and Sheila Patterson, *Dark Strangers*, Harmondsworth, Penguin Books, 1965.

In general, the lower-class Negro family in Trinidad is similar to the family characteristics of the West Indies. The family tends to be female-centered, with late marriages (when marriages occur), low values placed in the interpersonal nature of marriage and with minimal concern about the legitimacy of offspring. In Trinidad there are no racial ghettos but homogeneous housing areas based on social class. Of the Island's population, 43 per cent are Negro and 37 per cent East Indian, and they frequently live intermingled with one another and share in common a similar social class level.

The people in the samples studied in the three different societies all have similar origins in that they come out of slave backgrounds and their development of adaptive family forms have been very similar. However, only two of the groups, the United States and Trinidad, continue to follow family patterns different from those ideally stated and/or followed by the dominant elements of their societies. In the United States this is due to a combination of racial discrimination and low social class status. In Trinidad it is primarily due to low social class factors. By contrast, the Negroes in Great Britain have reduced their differences from the broader society by being less racially discriminated against than their counterparts in the United States and less lower class restricted than their counterparts in Trinidad. Thus, the Negro in Great Britain is to a great extent a part of the middle class in that country. Given these differences it was therefore hypothesized that: the views about marital sex will be similar among Negro women in the United States and Trinidad and reflect their subcultural values while those of the women in Great Britain will be more conventional and middle class by British standards (as well as by United States and Trinidad standards).

SAMPLES

In the United States the sample was taken from parent lists in three elementary school districts in the city of Philadelphia in 1965. The districts were almost totally Negro, and on the basis of demographic data classified as lower class. There were interviews with 194 mothers who had at least one child in the four to seven year range. The interviewing was done by two Negro graduate students using a schedule consisting of 102 items. The two interviewers had grown up in the same general neighborhood and "could speak the language."

With a few minor changes the same interview schedule was used in the Reading, England study. In 1968 a sample was drawn of 200 West Indian women living in Reading, all of whom had one child under ten years of age. There were no residential records of where the West Indians live in Reading but in consultation with several people who knew the West Indian community, the population distribution in Reading was estimated and divided up by residential areas. The percentage of the total Reading West Indian population in each area was estimated and a proportionate number of interviews were assigned. For each area an interviewer went to a house where she knew the woman would meet the sample requirements.   When the interview was finished she would get the names of other eligible West Indian women in that area, add those to the list she already had, and randomly select the next interview.   All 200 of the interviews were done by West Indian women who were trained and supervised throughout the interviewing period.

The Trinidad study was carried out in 1969 in central Trinidad.   The sample studied was from an area not far from the second largest city on Trinidad, that of San Fernando with a population of about 40,000.   However, the area where the respondents lived was primarily rural.   To qualify for the sample a woman had to live within the defined area and have at least one child between one and ten years of age.   In the area chosen for study, streets were picked at random and the interviewers went to each house on the street and interviewed the woman if she met the requirement of having at least one child under ten years of age.   The interviews were done by two trained Negro female interviewers who lived in the area.   There were 200 interviews done using the same schedule as used in the United States and Great Britain samples.

BACKGROUND

The ages of the two samples of women in the United States and Great Britain were exactly the same, 30 years old.   However, the women in Trinidad were on the average seven years older.   About 90 per cent of the women in the United States and Great Britain were Protestants, but neither group showed any strong tendency for church attendance.   By contrast, two-thirds of the Trinidad women were Roman Catholics and they were characterized by a high level of church attendance.

TABLE 1

Marital Status (Number and Percent) of the Women in the Three Samples at the Time of the Interview

	United States		Great Britain		Trinidad	
	No.	%	No.	%	No.	%
Single (Never Married)	48	26	16	8	49	25
Married	72	40	177	90	120	60
Widowed, Divorced or Separated	62	34	4	2	31	15
Totals	182	100%	197	100%	200	100%

Table 1 shows the marital status of the women in the three samples.   It will be noted that the marriage rate in Great Britain is as high as for that population in general, while in the United States and Trinidad the marriage rate in the two samples is below that found in their overall respective societies.   There are also important differences between the three samples on the number of children they have.   The mean number of children in the United States was 5.8, in Great Britain 3.2 and in Trinidad 6.3.   So the Negro women in Great Britain have a much higher marriage rate and a much lower number of children than did their counterparts in the other countries.

A more positive definition and view of marriage was found among the Great Britain women than among those in the other two samples. For example, 60 per cent of the British sample rated their marriages as "very good" or "good", compared to 48 per cent of the United States women and only 28 per cent of the Trinidad women. For a large number of women in all three groups, there was little positive identification with marriage. To illustrate, over a third of the women in all three samples said they would never marry if they had it to do all over again. There was an even stronger rejection of their specific husbands by the American women (46 per cent) and the Trinidad women (50 per cent) as compared to the British women (35 per cent) who said that if they had it to do all over again they would never marry the same man.

One important consequence of sexual behavior in all societies is the legitimacy or illegitimacy of offspring. An important part of the middle class values common to all three societies is the assumption that legitimacy is very significant. But in the Negro sub-cultures that developed out of slavery this was often an area of irrelevancy. That is, one would ideally marry to make a child legitimate but in reality if one didn't it wasn't very important. Personal experience with illegitimacy was an experience common to many women in all three samples about two-thirds of all the women in each sample had at least one child before they were married. As indicated, this has been a pattern for many generations and as a result social stigma tends to be minimal. This is reflected in several findings. For example, 81 per cent of the women in the United States, 77 per cent in Great Britain and 78 per cent in Trinidad said that within their social setting there were no negative feelings directed at women who were not married and had a child. However, there were some sharp differences among the women to attach some stigma to the illegitimate child. This is reflected in the findings that 36 per cent of the American, 50 per cent of the British and 95 per cent of the Trinidad women felt that it was imp. · nt for a woman to marry for reasons of making her child legitimate. These findings indicate that for the woman the concern with legitimacy when it occurs is centered on the child rather than the mother. However, the evidence suggests that the Negro woman in Britain was becoming increasingly concerned with legitimizing the role of the mother. In this area at least the pressures of the dominant values of Great Britain appeared to exert a rapid and strong influence on the Negro migrants.

Before looking at some of the specific responses with regard to marital sexuality it is important to discuss some general values in this area. A basic part of marriage is that of the sexual rights and obligations the partners have to one another. In the middle-class in the three societies studied the ideal values restrict all sexual experience in marriage to the partners and any deviance from that is usually seen as extremely threatening to the overall marriage relationship. However, the low expectations associated with marriage role relationships in the Negro lower-class in the U.S. and Trinidad would not lead one to expect there to be very strong values associated with the exclusive nature of sexual expression in marriage. In general, the lower class places much less importance on sexual behavior than does the middle class. This is probably because sex is more open and does not usually take on the highly emotional and psychological dimensions that it does in the middle class. In the lower class, sex is usually engaged in for immediate gratification and not as an expression of a strong emotional commitment between the couple.

It is often assumed that because the lower class is permissive about some heterosexual relations that the subculture is characterized by a general sexual permissiveness. But such is not the case because many types of sexual intimacy common to the middle class are minimized or even rejected in the lower class. For example, extended sexual foreplay and petting are not common sexual patterns in the lower class of the Negro or the White in the U.S. The sexual act tends to be the entire focus, with little foreplay or variation in sexual techniques. In part these limitations are related to the fact that most individuals in the lower class have limited knowledge about sex.

With the greater importance and sense of satisfaction reached by the Reading women in their marriage roles and role relationships than was found for the Philadelphia and Trinidad respondents, it would also be expected that more positive notions about the sexual aspects of marriage would be found among those women than the ones in the other two samples.

TABLE 2

Number and Percent Responses in the Three Samples to the Question: "How Do You Feel About the Importance of Sex in Marriage for the Husband? (and the Wife?)"

For the Husband	United States		Great Britain		Trinidad	
	No.	%	No.	%	No.	%
Very important	99	54	83	41	147	76
Important	82	45	107	54	47	23
Not Important	2	1	10	5	1	1
Totals	183	100%	200	100%	195	100%
For the Wife						
Very Important	52	28	66	33	66	33
Important	119	65	101	51	90	45
Not Important	11	7	33	16	44	22
Totals	182	100%	200	100%	200	100%

The respondents were asked two questions about the relative importance of sex in marriage for the spouses. They were asked: "How do you feel about the importance of sex in marriage for the husband? and the wife?" Table 2 shows the significant differences given by the three populations for both questions. The Philadelphia women more often said sex was "very important" for the husband (54 per cent) than did the Reading women (41 per cent). However, of the Trinidad women 76 per cent said it was "very important" to the man. The Trinidad women were more apt to define sex as "not important" for the woman (22 per cent) than were the Reading women (16 per cent) or those in Philadelphia (7 pecent).

An examination of Table 2 indicates that the Reading women were more apt to suggest equal importance of sex in marriage for *both* the husband and the wife than were the other two groups of women. In the Philadelphia sample, the women said sex was "very important" for women in only 28 per cent of the cases. Among the Reading and Trinidad respondents it was 33 per cent. This difference is also seen in a related question asking about the relative importance of sex in marriage for the husband and wife. For example, among the Philadelphia sample 42 per cent of the women said sex in marriage was more important for the man as compared to 23 per cent of the Reading and 25 per cent of the Trinidad respondents. Very few in either group suggested sex was more important for the wife. Five per cent in Philadelphia, two per cent in Reading and one per cent in Trinidad. But there was a significantly greater number of women in Reading and Trinidad than in Philadelphia holding to an equalitarian point of view about sex. In the Reading and the Trinidad samples 75 per cent said they thought sex in marriage had about equal importance for both the husband and wife as contrasted to only 53 per cent in the Philadelphia sample.

Extra Marital Sexual Values

For many, if not most, middle class women in the three societies nothing would be more threatening to her marriage than to find that her husband was sexually involved with another woman. If a husband or wife shows a romantic or sexual interest in someone else, this is often viewed as catastrophic to the ego-relationship of marriage. However, in the middle class there are male and female differences. Many middle-class men feel that adultery on the part of the woman is an irreparable blow to their marriage. Women are less inclined to see adultery in the same extreme way. The middle-class husband who has what is seen by the wife as a single sexual encounter may be forgiven; however, if he has an affair of some length, the wife is much more threatened because, to her, a lengthy affair implies that her husband must care about the other woman — thus the "other" woman becomes an emotional threat. In the Negro lower class, marriage has not usually assumed these values and therefore the views about adultery have been quite different from those of the middle class.

A "folk" notion that probably has been common to most cultures of the world is the belief that men are incapable of being sexually monogamous.

This has long been a belief held by many women as well as men in the lower class. Liebow found among the men he studied, that not only was there the belief that men could not be sexually monogamous over time but that they were also incapable of it at any point in time. That is, that no man could be sexually satisfied with only one woman at a time.[5] This belief provides a rationalization for the man not restricting himself to one woman — a kind of folk biological determinism that makes him incapable of being monogamous because it goes contrary to his very biological nature.

The lower-class Negro man in the United States is more apt to also see the rights of sexual freedom for women than is the male in the middle class. Rainwater found that in the Negro lower class the men, when compared to lower-class whites, were more apt to think that a wife would seek sexual gratification elsewhere if relations did not go well.[6] However, there is no complete agreement among Negro men as to how much sexual freedom a woman should have. Liebow found that the men in his study felt that in marriage the man had the right to exclusive sexual access to his spouse. But there was no agreement between the lower-class men on other relationships. "Some streetcorner men feel that a partner in a consensual union has a right to demand exclusive sexual access; others deny this."[7]

Among lower-class Negro women in the United States a common belief is that they have the same sexual rights as the man. And whatever the husband or boy friend does with another woman they have the same right to do with another man. "If the husband indulges himself, they have the right to indulge themselves. If the husband steps out on his wife, she has the right to step out on him." Or as Lewis points out the lower status females show a great deal of sex initiative and independence and often say, "I don't have to worry about no man" or "Anything he can do, I can do."[8] These liberal views about sex in marriage are much less apt to be found in the West Indies, particularly in Trinidad. This is because the Trinidad woman places a high value on eventual marriage and therefore believes in strong monogamous restrictions as to sexual behavior. Also their views are a reflection of the strong conservative sexual values that many of them have as a result of being Catholics. The following discussion shows some of the differences between the three groups in their views about extramarital sexual behavior.

The three groups of women were compared in their responses to questions about restricting sexual expression to marriage. The respondents were asked: "Is there any time when you think a married man is justified

[5]Elliott Liebow, *Tally's Corner: A Study of Negro Streetcorner Men*, Boston: Little Brown and Co., 1969, p. 120.

[6]Rainwater, *op. cit.*, p. 116.

[7]Liebow, *op. cit.*, p. 104.

[8]Hylan Lewis, *Blackways of Kent*, Chapel Hill, N.C.: University of North Carolina Press, 1955, p. 83.

in 'running around' with another woman?" The same question was also asked about a married woman ever being justified in "running around."

TABLE 3

Number and Percent Responses in the Three Samples to the Question: "Is there any time when you think a Married Man, (Woman) is justified in 'running around'?"

Man "Running Around"	United States No.	%	Great Britain No.	%	Trinidad No.	%
Yes	108	59	22	11	62	32
No	75	41	178	89	130	68
Totals	183	100%	200	100%	192	100%
Woman "Running Around"						
Yes	77	41	11	6	45	22
No	109	59	189	94	155	78
Totals	186	100%	200	100%	200	100%

There were very sharp differences in the responses given by the three samples. Fifty-nine per cent of the women in Philadelphia and 32 per cent in Trinidad as compared to only 11 per cent of the Reading women felt men were ever justified in "running around". The same wide difference was also found with regard to married women ever justified in "running around", with 41 per cent of the Philadelphia respondents, 22 per cent in Trinidad and 6 per cent of those in Reading answering "yes". It is of interest that the three groups of women hold to essentially single standards although the standards were different. The Reading women believed that *neither* the married man or woman was justified in "running around", while the Philadelphia women very often believed that *both* the man and woman were often justifield in "running around". The Trinidad women fall in between in having a distinct minority saying *both,* but most of them saying *neither.*

The women were also asked: "Should a wife expect 'running around' at one time or another regardless of how good the husband has been?" And the same question was also asked about the wife. On these questions there were also wide differences in the responses of the women in three samples. As to expecting a husband to engage in "running around" the answer was "yes" by 56 per cent of the Philadelphia women but by only 6 per cent of the women in both the Reading and the Trinidad samples.. There were also significant differences in the responses for expecting "running around" by a wife. In Trinidad 33 per cent said "yes" as compared to 30 per cent in Philadelphia and 12 per cent in Reading. In England there is for most a single standard of not expecting "running around" for either the husband or the wife. However, in Philadelphia there is more a double standard with a greater expectation of "running

around" by the husband than by the wife, while in Trinidad just the opposite is true with greater expectation of the wife than the husband
running around.   The findings indicate that the Reading women have
more of a shared or equal view of the sexual aspects of marriage than do
the Philadelphia or Trinidad women.

SUMMARY

The overall findings in all three samples leads to the conclusion that
there is a higher positive view toward marriage among the Reading
women than among the women in the other two samples.   This is further
reflected in the evidence suggesting that the Reading women see a greater
equality in the rights and obligations of marriage than do the Negro
women in the other two samples.   So the views about sexual rights among
the women in Great Britain can be seen as a part of their changing view
as to the egalitarian nature of marriage.   That is, the egalitarian beliefs
that men and women have equal sexual needs and rights in marriage and
these needs are to be met within the exclusive setting of monogamy.

The findings of this study indicate that values about sexual behavior
in marriage are strongly influenced by social class position.   All of the
evidence suggests that the West Indians who migrated to Great Britain
shared values very similar to those of the Trinidad women when they
lived in the islands.   However, of the three groups of women studied they
were the one group subjected to significant social change.   That is, the
women in the the United States and Trinidad were living in a social setting
that for most of them had existed all of their lives and even for at least
several generations.   So the women in the United States and Trinidad
followed their life long socialization to sexual values where the women in
Britain were resocialized into the middle class values and as a result
strongly identified with and followed the new values.

TABLE 4

Number and Percent Responses in the Three Samples to the Question:
"Should a wife (husband) expect 'running around' at one time or another regardless of how good the husband (wife) has been?"

Expect of Husband	United States No.	%	Great Britain No.	%	Trinidad No.	%
Yes	102	56	13	6	6	3
No	81	44	187	94	193	97
Totals	183	100%	200	100%	199	100%
Expect of Wife						
Yes	54	30	23	12	66	33
No.	129	70	177	88	134	67
Totals	183	100%	200	100%	200	100%

What generalizations can be made about the three groups? Clearly the historical backgrounds are somewhat different but there is one important sociological difference between the sample in Great Britain and the other two. This is related to the subculture and ghetto-like life patterns found in the United States and Trinidad. In the United States, the women studied lived in the lower class and their ghettos were physical, social and psychological. These women lived in large areas that were almost completely Negro and lower class and were in almost complete isolation from the dominant white world. So the subcultural values were important in her dealing with life as she encountered it. Essentially the same social phenomena was found in Trinidad. However, the one important difference is that the ghetto-like way of life there is not due to racial discrimination, but rather to social class restrictions. By contrast, the Negro in Great Britain is much less isolated either for racial or social class reasons. As a result he feels himself to be a part of Great Britain. While he feels somewhat different, he does not feel as isolated as do the American or the Trinidad lower-class Negroes. Therefore, the acceptance of middle class values about sex in marriage is an indication of the degree of assimilation into society. It also indicates that significant changes may occur with reference to basic family values *if* individuals enter new social patterns that are important and valuable to them.

PART II
WOMEN IN THE ECONOMY

WOMEN IN THE ECONOMY
Introduction

RATNA GHOSH

Women have always had a relationship to the means of production but this relationship has generally been restricted to the domestic sphere. And being extra-economic, women's labor has always been underestimated. With industrialization and modernization women are increasingly making significant contributions in the economic sphere. Although both the rate of female labor force participation and women's employment opportunities vary strikingly in different countries of the world, the influx of women into the employment market in general is perhaps causing one of the most significant changes in contemporary thought.

The collection of articles in this section deal with women and employment. Several factors are evident universally with regard to women's gainful employment. Women's participation in the work force has led to the emergence of altered marital satisfaction, conjugal power, sex-role attitudes and fertility behavior. Yet there is a cultural lag in adjusting attitudes and behaviors to altered socio-economic circumstances. Women still face conflicts because they bear the greater responsibility of combining roles at home and at work. Even in countries which have official ideologies promoting sex equality women still face the pressures of work overload and are subjected to sex segregation in employment, which is a worldwide phenomenon.

While sex is a criterion, the economic factor is the other significant dimension in stratification and in achieving status and privilege. Economic independence, for example, distinguishes the status of the working from the non-working woman. But because the work experience is not limited to the economic aspect and involves a social experience, the attitudinal and behavioral implications are many.

The first eight articles in this section discuss how the employment status of the wife affects several aspects of her life. In terms of the power to control decisions the wife's labor force participation does much to alter her position. The comparitive study of changing female roles in the United States and Venezuela by Robert T. Green found that regardless of cultural differences, the employment of the wife has a pronounced impact on family roles, and leads to increased participation and power in family decision-making. Large differences were observed in the roles played by non-working wives in the two countries.

Bruce W. Brown studies the widely assumed causal relationship between employment of married women and the emergence of egalitarian marital role prescriptions. The marital advice articles studied, though far from advocating complete husband-wife equality, provided evidence that wife's employment influenced egalitarian marital role prescriptions in respect to decision-making in the United States.

Based on the argument that the greater the resources of the wife the more her power therefore the more egalitarian the marriage, D. Ian Pool examines whether there has been an evolution towards the egalitarian family structure in Canada. It was found that female labor force participation, taken here as the key dimension of conjugal bargaining, has not changed dramatically over the years and the author stresses the need for longitudinal and retrospective studies to validate the notion of evolution towards egalitarian family structures in North America.

The effects of wife's employment status and sex-role attitude on marital satisfaction is the theme of the article by Stephen J. Bahr and Randal D. Day. The employment status of the wife was found to have s small influence on marital satisfaction. Attitudes made the difference. If both the husband and the wife were against female employment and role reversal, marital satisfaction tended to be high when the wife was not employed. In the case of working wives, marital satisfaction was high when the husbands favored employment of mothers or when the wives favored role reversal.

Mothers' income and education have been related to mothers' aspirations for their children. Roberta H. Jackson found that in her sample of lower class black mothers three independent variables, namely, income, education and family size, had a significant influence on their attitudes towards the future success of their children. Refuting the common assumption that indigent black mothers have very few positive aspirations for their children, data indicated that increase in levels of mothers' income and education corresponded with increase in positive aspirations for their children.

The relationship between women's labor force participation and their fertility behavior has been of great interest to social planners. P. M. George, G. E. Ebanks and Charles Nobbe examine this relationship among a national sample of women in Barbados. Further, they seek to determine whether their labor force participation has an impact on their attitudes towards family planning. Women's labor force participation was associated with low expected and actual fertility, with more positive attitudes, knowledge and practices toward fertility control.

A factor influencing fertility is the economic structure which affects the economic value of children. In rural Iran, where the economic value of children is high, the decision about the number of children to have is an economic one. Akbar Aghajanian tests a set of propositions based on the relationship of fertility and the economy. He concludes that when the family is the unit of economic production, high fertility indicates the demand for the economic value of children. While differential fertility by education, occupation and size of landholding was apparent, in general, when the woman's economic activity is within the family, such activity does not affect her fertility.

How does women's employment outside the home affect fertility? Albert W. Niemi, Jr., examines the economic costs borne by females as a result of child bearing and rearing. While recognizing the non-economic factors associated with market employment this study focusses on the most rational procedures of maximizing female earnings. The results suggest that it is most economical for females with low educational attainment to stay at home until children reach school age, while women with high educational attainment should put children in day care centers and return to work.

The next few articles discuss the role conflicts and wide variety of problems faced by working women. Aileen D. Ross comments on the conflicts entailed in the spheres of authority, responsibility and personal relations when carrying on a career with the roles of wife, household manager and possibly mother. Examining the situation of businesswomen in India, Australia and Canada the author asks: What price is a woman willing to pay to have a career?

In an exploratory study of female professionals in the Soviet Union and East Germany, Marilyn Rueschemeyer discusses how conditions of work affect personal relations, especially in marriage. Despite the structural supports which encourage women's education, labor force participation and equality, the women in these two socialist countries are overloaded with work because they still have the ultimate responsibility for house and children while maintaining the same ambitions and work interests as their husbands.

Female academicians in Israel and their occupational role images are the subjects of the study by Rina Shapira, Evan Etzioni-Halevy and Shirra Chopp-Tibon. Despite Israel's egalitarian ideology the authors found that female academicians in Israel are subjected to cross-pressures of expectations in their professions and familial roles.

The impact of ideology on the status of women has been a matter of much discussion. Sex-segregation is evident universally. Women earn low levels of pay and occupy positions having lower prestige. How does ideology affect this phenomenon? Four articles in this section examine this issue. In the Israeli study the authors found that although the female academicians had been exposed to the ideology of equality between the sexes they were characterized by distinctively "feminine" patterns of occupational choice. A sizeable minority did not conform to these patterns but women were still inclined to emphasize the feminine role image. These images have been shaped by the constraints of social reality which operate in Israel as in other contemporary societies.

Three articles examine the position of women in socialist societies. Rueschemeyer concludes that despite the many supports working men and women are given in the Soviet Union and East Germany, the possibilities of incorporating the two important aspects—one's working life and personal relationships—are limited. William T. Liu and Elena S. H. Yu assess the impact of the official Chinese policy of sex equality on family life and fertility patterns. There exists great disparity between urban and rural lifestyles. Moreover, women are expected to successfully combine productive labor and political work with household chores. The authors note that policy-makers have established a complex set of institutional support for alternative careers for women and propose that fertility rates are likely to come down for a combination of factors. Yet homemaking and private production are the same today as they were three decades ago. In the rural areas women's work points are often half of men's. In urban areas women are concentrated in light industries where wage scales are lower and fewer fringe benefits are provided and where the retirement age for women is earlier than that for men. In addition, women who are prevented from working at the factory site (for lack of nurseries, etc.) get much less pay in neighborhood workshops for similar work. The authors conclude that (1) different wage systems are not due to difference in skills; (2) women-intensive industries have much lower wage scale than less women-intensive industries and (3) there are fewer facilities for women and especially for married women.

The consequence of what Benigno E. Aguirre calls the "political myth" that women's freedom has been achieved in Cuba is analyzed in a study of women in the Cuban bureaucracies. In Cuba a socialist revolutionary movement's ideological tenet has significantly increased female labor force participation. Data presented indicate that sex-segregation nevertheless exists in the occupational structure and that women are under-represented in administration and decision-making positions. Aguirre suggests that the cultural roots of women's oppression and low status have not been adequately dealt with in Cuba. Even the Family Code which redefines family tasks and obligations cannot be enforced without changing existing stereotypes and re-education about social attitudes and practices which have emphasized male supremacy.

The degree of change in status of women in a traditional Muslim society is examined by J. Henry Korson. Pakistan prepares women for careers by making higher education available to them but the constraints of *purdah* not only segregate females from males in the social and employment worlds; it also calls for minimum participation in community affairs. The author suggests that the greater degree of labor force participation leading to great degrees of economic and social independence which is evident now will undoubtedly affect traditional relationships in marriage.

Another potent force in determining female roles and family structure is ethnicity. In the last article in this section Ratna Ghosh analyzes the combination of difficulties faced at the occupational level by South Asian women in Canada. As a group of minority women they experience negative and sometimes positive effects of multiple repressions according to race, ethnicity, sex and social class. In addition to general barriers resulting from racism, sexism and their immigrant status, they are likely to encounter problems specific to them because of their cultural differences. All of these factors combine together to make their position in relation to the employment situation very complex.

This cross-cultural collection of articles indicates some general patterns and trends. While there is tremendous under-utilization of human resources represented by women in the economic sphere due to sex-segregation in the labor force and barriers to occupational achievement, employed women are overworked, overburdened and face complex role conflict situations. Women's work is of less value socially because the husband is thought of as playing the more instrumental role as provider—whereas the wife, in Parson's words, "is primarily the giver of love". The studies in this section demonstrate that in addition to her important function of providing love, the woman is making significant economic contributions. Although equality of opportunity and conditions is still far from being achieved, there is evidence of change towards greater egalitarianism both in the family and occupational structures in all countries. Indeed, structural supports and ideological commitments have helped considerably but they have not eliminated discrimination against women because the universal need is to strike at the roots by changing attitudes and behaviors of men and women.

14

Working Wives in the United States and Venezuela: A Cross-National Study of Decision Making*

ISABELLA C. M. CUNNINGHAM**
and
ROBERT T. GREEN**

The entry of the wife into the labor force does much to alter her position in the family (Blood and Wolfe, 1960; Heer, 1963; Hoffman, 1963; Kenkel, 1961). The economic contribution which the working wife makes to the family puts her in a decidedly different position vis-a-vis her husband compared with the nonworking wife. The working wife is in a better position to participate in decisions which concern how the money is spent. In addition, she often brings skills into the family which she has acquired through her work experiences that can contribute to family functioning. Further, the very fact that the wife is spending a large portion of her day away from the home will often force changes in husband/wife roles since the working wife physically does not have the time to perform all of the same traditional home tasks as the nonworking wife.

All of the preceding statements are subject to qualification. For instance, it has been found that husbands, regardless of their wives' work status, are the dominant decision makers in some areas, while wives are the decision makers in other areas (Green and Cunningham, 1976). It has also been found that working wives have to combine both work and home roles to a much greater extent than their husbands (Fogarty, et al., 1971; Meissner, et al., 1975). However, at a general level, the idea that some reorientation of family roles will accompany the employment of the wife is well established.

The study reported in this paper represents an investigation of the extent to which the phenomena discussed above are also manifested in working wife families in Venezuela. Most of the findings regarding the changes which occur in family roles when the wife is employed have emanated from either the United

*The study reports the results of research projects conducted in the United States in 1973 and in Venezuela in 1977. The authors gratefully acknowledge the assistance of the administration and students at the Universidad de Carabobo, Valencia, Venezuela throughout the study. The authors also thank the Institute of Latin American Studies and the University Research Institute of The University of Texas at Austin for providing funds which made the study possible.
**Isabella C.M. Cunningham is associate professor of Advertising, and Robert T. Green is associate professor of Marketing and International Business, both at The University of Texas at Austin, Texas, U.S.A.

States or Europe. Little is known about how the wife's employment affects family decision-making structures within a Latin American cultural context. The present paper reports a cross-national study of purchasing decisions, and compares husband and wife decision-making roles in families with employed and non-employed wives.

International Studies of Wive's Employment

Studies conducted in Europe indicate the same tendency found in the United States toward a restructuring of sex roles when the wife is employed. Michel (1976), in a study of Parisian working-wife families, found that a remolding of sex roles directly attributable to the employment of the wife seemed to occur among these families. Douglas (1976), in a cross-national study of U.S. and French working and nonworking wives, found that cross-national differences are more influential than wives' employment in explaining differences in decision-making patterns. Outside of Europe, Wadhera (1976) conducted a broad study of working wives in India. While his findings were not compared with work from other countries, Wadhera found that working women in India enjoyed considerably more freedom than their non-working counterparts.

Rodman (1972, 1975) reviewed the literature in the area of cross-national family decision making in which he attempted to explain the findings in terms of the theory of resources. This theory, in essence, depicts marital decision roles as a function of the resources which the marital partners bring into the marriage. The greater the resources of the husband relative to the wife, the greater his decision-making power, and vice versa. A working wife, therefore, would have more decision-making power than a nonworking wife, all else being equal, since she brings more resources into the marriage. Rodman also distinguishes between family decision-making roles in societies characterized by equalitarian family structures. Decision making in patriarchal societies tend to be husband dominated, although the amount of husband dominance may be negatively correlated with social class (Rodman, 1975). Decision roles of husbands and wives in equalitarian societies tend to be more flexible than in patriarchal societies, although here there may be a positive correlation between the husband's decision-making power and social class (Rodman, 1975).

Few studies have been conducted that pertain to decision making in Latin American families in which the wife is employed. However, considerable literature does exist which gives a general picture of family decision making in Latin America. Sex role structures in Latin America are portrayed as being well defined, with little overlap in male and female roles (Cardenas, 1974). In addition, these role structures are seen as being relatively stable (as compared with the United States), and many writers foresee little general change occurring in them. For instance, Chaney (1973) describes men and women of all classes as being in basic agreement about certain boundaries for 'women's proper activities. These boundaries give women control in the prescribed feminine fields, and therefore make them less likely to demand equality in other areas. Stevens (1973), after a brief analysis of social and economic conditions in Latin America, concludes that such women's liberation movements as have characterized the North Atlantic nations are not likely to be found in the near future in Latin America.

Women in Latin America have also been found to be less affected by the changes associated with industrialization than are their husbands. Gans, Pastore, and Wilkening (1970), in a study of the effects of modernization on women in the Brazilian family, found that modernism among men was significantly higher than among women. They attributed these findings to the rigidly defined role of women that limits them to the household.

With respect to working wives in Latin America, Nash and Safa (1976, p. 105) make the point that, " . . . women's entry into the labor market at every class level is conditioned by their primary identification as wives and mothers." Men are viewed as the primary providers, and work is seen by most women as being only a temporary necessity. Such feelings toward work by married women are reinforced by structural barriers that exist which limit women's entry into the job market for all but the most menial jobs (Chaney and Schmink, 1976).

One study which did explore decision-making differences between working and nonworking wives within a Latin American context was conducted by Saffioti (1976). This study compared decision making on a very general level between employed and unemployed wives in poor families in Ararguara, Brazil. This study found that among working wives:

1. 36.7 percent are completely subject to their husbands' decisions (compared to 51.9 percent among nonworking wives);

2. 25.1 percent can decide only minor items (compared with 21.5 percent of nonworking women); and,

3. 38.2 percent have the authority to make any decision (compared with 26.6 percent for women who do not work).

Therefore, it appears that the general trend of more equality associated with working wives may also be present in the Latin American context, although the sample case came from a highly restricted subsegment of the population.

Hypotheses

Based on the preceding findings, three hypotheses were developed to be tested in the present study. The first hypothesis states that:

H_1—Venezuelan working wives make more decisions in the family than Venezuelan nonworking wives.

This hypothesis is based on the theory of resources and is supported by the findings that working wives in the United States and Europe have been found to make more decisions than their nonworking counterparts.

The second and third hypotheses are concerned with a comparison of the decision-making roles that are played by working and nonworking wives in the United States and Venezuela:

H_2—Working wives in the United States make more family decisions than working wives in Venezuela.

H_3—Nonworking wives in the United States make more family decisions than nonworking wives in Venezuela.

These two hypotheses emanate from the description of sex roles in Latin American cultures being more patriarchal and more rigidly prescribed than those in the United States. It should be expected that women in Venezuela, regardless of their employment status, will participate less in family decision making than is the case in the United States.

Method

The samples employed in the study were drawn from Houston, Texas and Valencia, Venezuela, both large industrial cities, although Houston has a greater population (2,000,000 inhabitants versus 700,000). Both samples were comprised of married women ranging in age from 18 to over 70; 255 were included in the U.S. sample, and 170 were in the Venezuelan sample. The U.S. data were gathered in the Fall of 1973 through the use of a self-administered mail question-naire. The Venezuelan data were collected during the Winter and Spring of 1977.

Collection of the Venezuelan data presented the special types of problems long associated with cross-national research. First, in order to make comparisons with the U.S. sample, the Venezuelan sample had to be as closely matched as possible in terms of the more important demographic characteristics. This is a difficult task, particularly in the case where the two countries do not have directly equivalent educational systems or living standards. It was decided that since the U.S. sample came primarily from middle and upper-middle income groups, it would be best to draw the Venezuelan sample from the middle and upper-middle residential sections of Valencia. Thus, these areas were identified, and an area sample was selected by numbering the individual blocks and randomly selecting the blocks to be surveyed.

The second problem encountered in the collection of the Venezuelan data concerned the selection of a data gathering technique. The use of market surveys of any type is not common in Venezuela, which can lead to cooperation problems. Such problems are enhanced by the apparent distrust of strangers—it is common to believe that an interviewer may actually be a disguised felon or a salesman. Furthermore, structural problems exist which effect the data-gathering options: mail service is unreliable as is the telephone system. Within these constraints, the data-gathering technique selected consisted of having students hand deliver questionnaires to the selected households and retrieving them at a time conveni-ent to the respondents. This method was the most feasible under the environ-mental conditions, and it came the closest to approximating the procedure used in the United States, especially in maintaining the self-administered aspect of the questionnaire.

Research Instrument

The questionnaire employed in the study was developed in the United States for use in the original study. It contains questions pertaining to decisions associated with the purchase of nine products and services (see Table 1). The respondents were instructed to identify whether the individual decisions were normally made by the husband, the wife, or by both the husband and wife in their families.

Table 1   PRODUCTS AND PRODUCT-RELATED DECISIONS
                                            EMPLOYED IN THE STUDY

GROCERIES
   When to shop
   How much to spend
   Which store
   Which grocery products to buy

FURNITURE
   When to buy
   How much to spend
   Where to buy
   Which piece of furniture to buy
   Which style
   What color and fabric

MAJOR APPLIANCES
   When to buy
   How much to spend
   Where to buy
   Which brand
   Which model

LIFE INSURANCE
   When to buy
   Amount to buy
   From whom to buy
   Type of policy

AUTOMOBILE
   Which make
   Which model
   What color
   When to buy
   Where to buy
   How much to spend

VACATION
   When to go
   How much to spend
   Where to go
   How long to take
   Form of transportation

FAMILY SAVINGS
   When to save
   How much to save
   How to invest savings

HOUSE OR APARTMENT
   Size
   Price
   Location

WHO SELECTS THE FAMILY DOCTOR?

Back translation was used when translating the questionnaire into Spanish. In this method, one bilingual Venezuelan was employed to translate the English questionnaire into Spanish, and a second bilingual Venezuelan translated it back into English. The discrepancies in the original questionnaire and the retranslated version were then resolved. This method helps ensure comparability of the research instruments in both countries.

Data Analysis

To test the first hypothesis the number of husband, wife and joint decisions were summed for each product and service and across all products and services. These values then served as the dependent variables (or cell values) in a one way analysis of variance, with employment serving as the independent variable (or treatment). The hypothesis anticipates significant differences to exist between the employed and nonemployed Venezuelan respondents. The employed Venezuelans are expected to make more decisions than the nonemployed.

Also involved in testing the first hypothesis is a comparison between the employed and nonemployed Venezuelan subjects on their responses to some of the more important decisions associated with the specific products and services. Within the present study, the decisions which are clearly among the most important with regard to purchasing are those pertaining to "how much to spend" for a particular item. Such decisions are associated with eight of the products and services. Chi square analysis was used to determine if differences in response patterns exist on these items between the employed and nonemployed Venezuelans. Support for the hypothesis would be gained if the employed wives tend to participate in these decisions to a greater extent than the nonemployed wives.

The second and third hypotheses are tested in the same general manner as the first. For the second hypothesis, the mean number of decisions made by the husband, the wife, and jointly are compared between employed U.S. and Venezuelan wives using one-way analysis of variance. In addition, these two groups were tested for differences in responses to the "how much to spend" decisions. The hypothesis is supported if the U.S. sample indicates greater wife participation in decision making than the Venezuelan sample. The third hypothesis was tested in the same manner as the second using the nonemployed members of the U.S. and Venezuelan samples as the test groups. In this hypothesis it is also anticipated that the U.S. sample will indicate greater decision making participation than the Venezuelan sample.

Findings

The analysis of variance associated with the three hypotheses are presented in Table 2. The Table shows the decision-making means for each of the groups being analyzed and the F-ratios which correspond to the differences that exist between the means for each set of groups. The results are presented below with reference to the individual hypotheses.

Hypothesis 1

Table 2 indicates several significant differences between employed and nonemployed Venezuelans in terms of who makes decisions on the various items used in the study. The general pattern of the results is for fewer decisions by the husband and/or more joint decisions in families where the wife is employed. This pattern exists for six of the nine products and services and for the total number of decision category. For one of the decision areas, groceries, the results show a tendency

Table 2 ANALYSIS OF VARIANCE RESULTS FOR EMPLOYED AND NON-EMPLOYED
VENEZUELAN SAMPLES, EMPLOYED VENEZUELAN AND U.S. SAMPLES,
AND NON-EMPLOYED VENEZUELAN AND U.S. SAMPLES

	Venezuelan Employed vs. Non-Employed			Venezuelan Employed vs. United States Employed			Venezuelan Non-Employed vs. United States Non-Employed		
	Employed (n=43)	Non-Employed (n=125)	F	United States (n=117)	Venezuela (n=43)	F	United States (n=137)	Venezuela (n=125)	F
Groceries									
Husband	0.07	0.27	3.72a	0.22	0.07	1.75	0.24	0.27	0.11
Joint	0.53	0.74	1.10	0.84	0.53	2.27	0.38	0.74	7.09b
Wife	3.37	2.95	3.78a	2.93	3.37	3.58	3.38	2.95	7.22b
Furniture									
Husband	0.65	1.33	6.22a	0.29	0.65	6.06a	0.51	1.33	23.70b
Joint	3.16	2.52	2.68	3.21	3.16	0.00	3.54	2.52	14.42b
Wife	2.16	2.13	0.02	2.50	2.16	0.71	1.95	2.13	0.71
Major Appliance									
Husband	1.34	2.15	5.87a	0.78	1.34	5.41a	1.14	2.15	23.54b
Joint	2.86	1.79	8.93b	3.30	2.86	2.30	3.07	1.79	30.59b
Wife	0.77	0.98	0.63	0.91	0.77	0.25	0.78	0.98	1.47
Life Insurance									
Husband	3.12	3.47	2.46	2.34	3.12	6.36a	2.87	3.47	11.22b
Joint	0.88	0.44	4.32a	1.47	0.88	3.88a	1.01	0.44	11.43b
Wife	0.00	0.07	1.19	0.19	0.00	2.32	0.12	0.07	0.49
Auto									
Husband	3.14	4.43	15.24b	2.28	3.14	5.87a	2.80	4.43	48.88b
Joint	2.35	1.09	14.78b	3.16	2.35	5.39a	2.91	1.09	60.21b
Wife	0.49	0.37	0.98	0.56	0.49	0.08	0.28	0.37	2.20
Vacation									
Husband	1.05	1.63	2.72	0.78	1.05	1.26	1.05	1.63	4.50a
Joint	3.65	2.90	3.92b	3.74	3.65	0.19	3.53	2.90	6.56a
Wife	0.30	0.44	0.47	0.47	0.30	0.52	0.32	0.44	0.90
Savings									
Husband	0.50	1.26	11.82b	0 79	0.50	2.38	1.15	1.26	0.31
Joint	2.10	1.40	8.92b	1.70	2.10	2.96	1.48	1.40	0.13
Wife	0.40	0.32	0.66	0.50	0.40	0.26	0.36	0.32	0.61
Housing									
Husband	0 65	0.91	1.42	0.27	0.65	8.32b	0.38	0.91	17.69b
Joint	2.02	1.67	2.05	2.41	2.02	4.59a	2.25	1.67	15.88b
Wife	0.33	0.40	0.33	0.31	0.33	0.03	0.36	0.40	0.54
Family Doctor									
Husband	0.12	0.09	0.28	0.03	0.12	9.99b	0.04	0.09	4.06a
Joint	0.37	0.44	0.52	0.40	0.37	0.19	0.31	0.44	4.47a
Wife	0.51	0.48	0.16	0.57	0.51	0.67	0.66	0.48	9.37a
Total Decisions									
Husband	10.56	15.48	18.50b	7.80	10.56	7.81	10.17	15.48	39.96b
Joint	17.88	12.91	13.03b	19.95	17.88	2.86	18.28	12.91	28.89b
Wife	8.33	8.06	0.06	9.09	8.33	0.88	8.36	8.06	0.15

$a_p \leqslant .05$
$b_p \leqslant .01$

for the husband to make fewer decisions and the wife to make more decisions in families where the wife is employed. Thus, the overall pattern of the analysis of variance results provides support for the hypothesis of greater wife participation in family decision making when she is employed. The qualification which must accompany this conclusion is that the wife's increased participation is manifested in conjunction with her husband rather than autonomously; only in the case of groceries is a significant difference found in the number of wife-only decisions between the employed and nonemployed groups.

Further support for Hypothesis 1 is found in Table 3, which presents the findings of the chi square tests run between the employed and nonemployed Venezuelan wives on the "how much to spend" decisions. Of the eight product and

Table 3   CHI-SQUARE RESULTS ON "HOW MUCH TO SPEND" DECISIONS FOR EMPLOYED AND NON-EMPLOYED VENEZUELAN SAMPLES
(Stated in percentages)

	Husband	Joint	Wife
1. How much to spend on groceries:			
Employed	7.0	25.6	67.4
Non-Employed	18.3	19.8	61.9
$x^2=3.30$, d.f.$=2$, p$=$n.s.			
2. How much to spend on furniture:			
Employed	32.6	60.5	7.0
Non-Employed	52.4	32.5	15.1
$x^2=10.58$, d.f.$=2$, p $\leq$ .01			
3. How much to spend on appliances:			
Employed	32.6	58.1	9.3
Non-Employed	63.2	30.4	6.4
$x^2=12.37$, d.f.$=2$, p $\leq$ 0.1			
4. How much to spend on insurance:			
Employed	81.0	19.0	—
Non-Employed	90.4	8.0	1.6
$x^2=4.55$, d.f.$=2$, p$=$n.s.			
5. How much to spend on the car:			
Employed	60.5	37.2	2.3
Non-Employed	92.7	7.3	—
$x^2=25.96$, d.f.$=2$, p $\leq$ .01			
6. How much to spend on vacation:			
Employed	27.9	69.8	2.3
Non-Employed	45.2	47.6	7.3
$x^2=6.58$, d.f.$=2$, p $\leq$ .05			
7. How much to save:			
Employed	19.0	64.3	16.7
Non-Employed	44.3	45.9	9.8
$x^2=8.60$, d.f.$=2$, p $\leq$ .05			
8. How much to spend on housing:			
Employed	32.6	65.1	2.3
Non-Employed	50.4	43.1	6.5
$x^2=6.41$, d.f.$=2$, p $\leq$ .05			

service areas for which these decisions are included, six show significant differences including the "how much to spend" decisions for one of the areas, housing, in which no differences were found by the analysis of variance. The differences are all in the predicted direction of more participation by employed wives, although once again it seems that this participation is in conjunction with the husband and not autonomously. In sum, the analysis of variance and chi square findings provide strong support for the hypothesis of more decision making by working wives than nonworking wives in Venezuela.

Hypothesis 2

The second set of columns in Table 2 present the findings associated with the second hypothesis concerning employed U.S. and Venezuelan wives. The findings indicate significantly more joint and/or less husband decision making among the U.S. sample for six of the nine products and services. These findings provide some support for the hypothesis, although it is not as strong for the previous hypothesis. While the husband was reported by the Venezuelan sample to make more decisions than his U.S. counterpart, in only two cases were significant differences found on the number of joint decisions between the two samples, thus suggesting substantial wife input in most instances.

The results of the chi square analyses run on the "how much to spend" decisions provides further evidence which is contrary to the hypothesis. Table 4 shows significant differences between the samples on only two of the eight "how much to spend" decisions. While the two significant differences run in the hypothesized direction, the total findings do not provide strong support for the hypothesis. Therefore, it has to be concluded that the findings provide, at best, weak support for the hypothesis that U.S. working wives have greater participation in purchasing decisions than Venezuelan working wives.

Hypothesis 3

The third set of columns in Table 2 present the findings associated with the third hypothesis which predicts more participation in decision making among U.S. nonworking wives than Venezuelan nonworking wives. In this case, the findings run strongly in the predicted direction. Differences between the two groups are found for eight of the nine products and services. In most of these cases the findings reflect the pattern of less husband and more joint decisions among the U.S. sample exhibited in the tests of the other hypotheses. However, in this case, this pattern appears considerably strong both in terms of the number of significant differences that exist between the groups and in the magnitude of the mean differences.

The chi square analyses on the "how much to spend" decisions also reflect the considerable difference that exists in decision-making patterns between the U.S. and Venezuelan nonworking wives. Table 5 shows that significant differences exist between the two groups on seven of the eight "how much to spend" decisions. All of these findings run in the predicted direction, with more wife

Table 4   CHI-SQUARE RESULTS ON "HOW MUCH TO SPEND" DECISIONS FOR
                 EMPLOYED VENEZUELAN AND U.S. SAMPLES
                 (Stated in percentages)

	Husband	Joint	Wife
1. How much to spend on groceries:			
United States	7.7	25.6	66.7
Venezuela	7.0	25.6	67.4
$x^2=.02$, d.f.$=2$, p$=$n.s.			
2. How much to spend on furniture:			
United States	12.8	67.5	19.7
Venezuela	32.6	60.5	7.0
$x^2=10.11$, d.f.$=2$, p $\leq$ .01			
3. How much to spend on appliances:			
United States	20.5	67.5	12.0
Venezuela	32.6	58.1	9.3
$x^2=2.54$, d.f.$=2$, p$=$n.s.			
4. How much to spend on insurance:			
United States	61 5	33.3	5.1
Venezuela	81.0	19.0	—
$x^2=6.03$, d.f.$=2$, p $\leq$ .05			
5. How much to spend on the car:			
United States	44.4	50.4	5.1
Venezuela	60.5	37.2	2.3
$x^2=3.39$, d.f.$=2$, p$=$n.s.			
6. How much to spend on vacation:			
United States	22.4	68.1	9.5
Venezuela	27.9	69.8	2.3
$x^2=2.54$, d.f.$=2$, p$=$n.s.			
7. How much to save:			
United States	20.9	60.9	18.3
Venezuela	19.0	64.3	16.7
$x^2=0.15$, d.f.$=2$, p$=$n.s.			
8. How much to spend on housing:			
United States	18.3	75.7	6.1
Venezuela	32.6	65.1	2.3
$x^2=4.24$, d.f.$=2$, p$=$n.s.			

Table 5   CHI-SQUARE RESULTS ON "HOW MUCH TO SPEND" DECISIONS FOR
NON–EMPLOYED VENEZUELAN AND U.S. SAMPLES
(Stated in percentages)

	Husband	Joint	Wife
1. How much to spend on groceries:			
United States	12.3	9.4	78.3
Venezuela	18.3	19.8	61.9
$x^2=9.00$, d.f.$=2$, p $\le$ .05			
2. How much to spend on furniture:			
United States	18 1	71.0	10.9
Venezuela	52.4	32.5	15.1
$x^2=41.86$, d.f.$=2$, p $\le$ .01			
3. How much to spend on appliances:			
United States	32.6	60.9	6.5
Venezuela	63.2	30.4	6.4
$x^2=26.15$, d.f.$=2$, p $\le$ .01			
4. How much to spend on insurance:			
United States	70.1	27.0	2.9
Venezuela	90.4	8.0	1.6
$x^2=17.05$, d.f.$=2$, p $\le$ .01			
5. How much to spend on the car:			
United States	57.2	42.8	—
Venezuela	92.7	7.3	—
$x^2=40.99$, d.f.$=2$, p $\le$ .01			
6. How much to spend on vacation:			
United States	27.0	64.2	8.8
Venezuela	45.0	47.6	7.3
$x^2=9.41$, d.f.$=2$, p $\le$ .01			
7. How much to save:			
United States	34.8	50.0	15.2
Venezuela	44.3	45.9	9.8
$x^2=3.19$, d.f.$=2$, p=n.s.			
8. How much to spend on housing:			
United States	21.7	70.3	8.0
Venezuela	50.4	43.1	6.5
$x^2=23.73$, d.f.$=2$, p $\le$ .01			

participation among the U.S. sample. On the basis of these results, it appears that the third hypothesis can be accepted with a high level of confidence.

Discussion

Regardless of cultural heritage, the findings of the present study suggest that the employment of the wife has a pronounced impact on family roles. Such a restructuring of roles can be inferred through an integration of the three sets of analyses used to test the hypotheses in this study.

The interpretation of the findings, however, must also take into account the nature of the two samples used in the study. Both were primarily middle class samples, and Rodman (1975) had observed the possibility of a positive relationship between social class and wife decision-making power in partiarchal societies and a corresponding negative relationship in equalitarian societies. It is therefore uncertain whether the findings of the present study would apply to lower class families. The differences in decision making between lower class families in the United States and Venezuela may be considerably more extreme, even among families in which the wife is employed. The effect which social class has upon the relationship between the wife's working status and her role in family decisions could be the subject of future cross-national research.

The middle class nature of the samples may also be a factor in explaining the relative lack of differences that exist between U.S. and Venezuelan working and the large differences that exist between nonworking wives in the two countries. The expansion of the middle class is a comparatively recent phenomenon in Venezuela. Thus, many, of the families in this group are the product of upward mobility. Yet, the small size of this class in the past may imply that behavioral patterns and norms associated with the middle class are not well established; nor are they well understood by those who have recently attained middle class status. Under these conditions, Venezuelan families in which the wife performs her traditional home-oriented role should be expected to continue in the traditional decision-making format, while the roles of working wives would be less predictable.

If the traditional family in both the U.S. and Venezuela can be assumed to consist of a working husband and a nonworking wife, then the tests between nonworking wives probably reflect traditional role structures in the two countries. These tests indicated substantial differences in the structuring of roles in the two countries, with the U.S. wives showing more participation in purchasing decisions than the Venezuelan wives. When working Venezuelan wives are contrasted with Venezuelan nonworking wives, the results indicate significantly more participation in purchasing decisions among the former group. Finally, the comparisons of working wives in the United States and Venezuela yielded relatively few differences between these two groups.

The cultural differences inherent to the two countries are probably responsible for the large differences in the roles played by nonworking wives both in the United States and Venezuela. The Latin American wife's behavior appears to confirm the conclusions of Cardenas (1974) that sex role structures in Latin America are well defined and do not overlap.

The study shows, however, that employment appears to produce a significant change in the family structure in Venezuela. Consistent with the theory of resources, the employed wife gains participation and power in the family decision-making process. In fact, the decision role of the Venezuelan employed wife appears similar to its United States counterpart, as not many differences were found between the two samples. Thus, what political ideology may not bring about through a women's liberation movement (Stevens, 1973), could very well be implemented subtly by changing wives' employment status.

REFERENCES

Blood, R., and D. Wolfe
  1960   Husbands and Wives: The Dynamics of Married living. Glenco: Free Press.

Cardenas, Marta Cecilia Osorno
  1974   Mujer Colombiana y Latino Americana Pareja y Familia. Medellin, Colombia: Impresos Marin.

Chaney, Elas M.
  1973   "Old and new feminists in Latin America: the case of Peru and Chile." Journal of Marriage and the Family 35 (May): 331-343.

Douglas, Susan P.
  1976   "Cross-national comparisons and consumer stereotypes: A case study of working and nonworking wives in the U.S. and France." Journal of Consumer Research 3 (June): 12-30.

Fogarty, Michael, Rhona Rapoport, and Robert N. Rapoport
  1971   Sex, Career, and Family. Beverly Hills, California: Sage.

Gans, Marjorie, Jose Pastore, and Eugene A. Wilkening
  1970   "La mujer y la modernizacion de la familia Brasilena." Revista Latinoamericano de Sociologia 6 (December): 389-419.

Green, Robert T., and Isabella C.M. Cunningham
  1976   "Employment status, feminine role perception, and family purchasing decisions." Journal of Business Research (November).

Heer, D.M.
  1963   "Dominance and the working wife." In Nye, F.I. and L.W. Hoffman (eds.), The Employed Mother in America. Chicago: Rand McNally.

Hoffman, L.W.
  1963   "Parental power relations and the division of household tasks." Pp. 215-230 in Nye, F.I., and L.W. Hoffman (eds.), The Employed Mother in America. Chicago: Rand McNally.

Kenkel, William F.
  1961   "Family interaction in decision-making on spending." Pp. 140-164 in Nelson N. Foote (ed.), Household Decision Making. New York: University Press.

Meissner, Martin, Elizabeth W. Humphries, Scott M. Meis and William J. Scheu
  1975   "No Exit for Wives: Sexual Division of Labour and the Cumulation of Household Demands." Canadian Review of Sociology and Anthropology 12(4): 424-439.

Michel, Andree
1971   "Interaction and goal attainment in Parisian working wives' families." Pp. 43-65 in Andree Michel (ed.), Family Issues of Employed Women in Europe and America. Leiden: E.J. Brill.

Nash, June, and Helen Icken Safa
1976   Sex and class in Latin America. New York: Praeger.

Rodman, Hyman
1972   "Marital Power in France, Greece, Yugoslavia, and the United States: A Cross-National Discussion." Journal of Marriage and the Family 29 (May): 320-324.
1975   "Marital Power and the Theory of Resources in Cultural Context." Journal of Comparative Family Studies 3 (Autumn): 50-69.

Saffioti, Heleieth Iara Bongiovani
1976   "Relationships of sex and social class in Brazil." Pp. 147-159 in J. Nash and H.I. Safa (eds.), Sex and Social Class in Latin America. New York: Praeger.

Stevens, Evelyn P.
1973   "The prospects for a women's liberation movement in Latin America." Journal of Marriage and the Family 35 (May): 313-321.

Wadhera, Kiron
1976   The New Breadwinners. New Delhi: Kendra.

15   Wife-Employment and the Emergence of Egalitarian Marital Role Prescriptions: 1900-1974*

BRUCE W. BROWN**

Wife-employment in itself is not a new phenomenon. Wives have always worked alongside their husbands in supporting the family. However, it was not until the twentieth century that a substantial proportion of wives began working away from home and receiving monetary compensation for their labors. "The labor force participation rate of married women in the United States more than doubled from 1900 to 1940 and then doubled again from 1940 to 1960" (Cain, 1966:11), and since 1960 has risen from 30.1 percent to 43.9 percent in 1974.

The general public and most researchers have assumed that there is a causal connection between wife-employment and the emergence of egalitarian marital ideology. However, we know very little about this relationship or whether in fact one even exists. A number of authors have commented on the difficulty of establishing the causal direction between these variables (Hoffman, 1960:215; Goode, 1963:115; Heer, 1963:137; Scanzoni, 1970:161). As Scanzoni (1970:161) points out, it is difficult to know whether egalitarian values preceded or followed wife-employment.

The main purpose of this investigation is to determine whether or not wife-employment is correlated with the emergence of egalitarian marital role prescriptions, and if so, which variable causally influences the other, and what length of time is required for this variable to appreciably influence the other. This is not to suggest that wife-employment is the only cause of the emergence of egalitarian marital role prescriptions, or vice versa. Rather, it is a relationship which needs to be clarified because much recent research has assumed or implied a causal relationship.

Theoretical Framework

The causal significance of the increased resources of working wives on marital role prescriptions becomes clear in light of resource theory. Blood and Wolfe (1960:12) assert that the balance of power is based on the resources which marital

---

*Revision of a paper presented at the annual meeting of the National Council on Family Relations, New York, October 1976. The author is indebted to Arnold Linsky, Stephen Reyna, Howard Shapiro, and in particular Murray A. Straus, for their assistance in critiquing earlier drafts of the paper.

**Assistant Professor of Sociology, Wilkes College, Wilkes-Barre, Pennsylvania 18703, U.S.A.

partners contribute to the marriage.   Since money is a resource in marriage, it is assumed that as a greater proportion of wives contributed to the family income, the power of employed wives increased and they were in a better bargaining position to suggest or demand a more egalitarian marital role organization.   A number of studies have found that when the wife is employed her power and/or authority within the family is increased (Heer, 1958:347; Wolfe, 1959:109; Blood and Wolfe, 1960:40; Blood, 1963:294; McKinley, 1964:149; Blood, 1965:195; Scanzoni, 1970:160; Bahr, Bowerman, and Gecas, 1974:366).   The previously cited studies have all been investigations of American families.   However, similar results have been found in cross-cultural studies (Blood, 1967:159; Buric and Zecevic, 1967: 328; Safilios-Rothschild, 1967:346; Weller, 1968:439; Lupri, 1969:144; Michel, 1970:159; Oppong, 1970:678; Abbott, 1976:172; Richmond, 1976:262).   In contrast to the general trend of most findings. several studies have found no relationship between wife-employment and family power and/or authority (Blood and Hamblin, 1958:352; Hoffman, 1960:224; Centers, Raven, and Rodrigues, 1971:276; Kandel and Lesser, 1972:134).   One study actually found opposite results.   Middleton and Putney (1960:608) observed that working-wife families are more patriarchial in terms of decision-making than non-working-wife families.

Another possible consequence of wife-employment is a change in the division of labor in the home.   The results of most studies support the notion that wife-employment causes the husband to become more involved in household tasks and the wife less involved (Blood and Hamblin, 1958:351; Nolan, 1959:244; Hoffman, 1960:222; Blood and Wolfe, 1960:62; Axelson, 1963:191; Blood, 1963:289; Nye, 1976:94).   Cross-culturally, similar results have been found (Blood, 1967:162; Michel, 1970:160; Szalai, 1972:119; Richmond, 1976:263).   But, again, there are findings contrary to the general trend.   Powell (1963:233) found that in families with adolescents, husbands of working wives do less housework than husbands of non-working wives.

It is assumed that the egalitarian suggestions or demands of employee wives would eventuallyy be reflected in the marital role prescriptions of our culture. Nye and Hoffman (1963:5) concur when they suggest that:

> ...as the proportion of employed married women increased, the relative power of these women increased as well as adding further to the development of an egalitarian ideology.

Therefore, it is hypothesized that the proportion of employed wives has causal priority over the emergence of egalitarian marital role prescriptions.   Both the contradictions between some of the previous research and the weakness of their cross sectional designs for questions of causality, leave many questions unanswered.   The longitudinal design of the present investigation will hopefully provide some insight concerning the relationship between wife-employment and the emergence of egalitarian marital role prescriptions.

Proportion of Employed Wives

The information on the proportion of employed wives was obtained from the decennial United States Census Reports for the years 1900 to 1970. Because it was necessary to obtain an employment figure for every even-numbered year from 1900 to 1974, linear interpolation was used to estimate the proportion of employed wives for non-census years. Employed wives were classified into those employed in middle-class and working-class occupations in order to see if wife-employment increases in these separate occupation groups affected marital role prescriptions in significantly different ways.[1]

Marital Role Prescriptions

Marital role prescriptions are defined as normative rules concerning which spouse should be responsible for specific aspects of married life. As such, the prescriptions do *not* indicate how marital partners actually interacted, but rather, they provide an idea of what people thought was appropriate marital behavior.

Several studies have supported the idea that popular literature tends to reflect cultural norms (Inglis, 1938; Albrecht, 1956). Middleton (1960:142), in a content analysis of mass circulation magazine fiction, found that fertility values expressed in these stories paralleled the changes in actual fertility rates. Webb, et al. (1966:77), commenting on Middleton's research concluded:

> This research suggested that the media, if carefully selected, can serve as a mirror of the society's values—or at least of some selective elements within the society.

It would seem that if popular fiction is a good indication of cultural norms, then non-fictional literature, i.e., marriage advice in women's magazines would be as valid in terms of reflecting cultural norms.

Sample of Women's Magazines

The *Reader's Guide to Periodical Literature* was used as a primary source of marital advice article titles. All articles which appeared under the subject heading of "marriage" were considered for the final sample. Four articles from every even-numbered year from 1900 to 1974 were randomly selected, resulting in 152 individual marital advice articles. When the *Reader's Guide to Periodical Literature* failed to provide four appropriate articles for a given year, individual magazine issues were searched to make up the difference. In order to be included in the final sample an article had to meet the following criteria:

1. The article must have appeared in a women's magazine. "Women's

---

[1]One limitation in the comparability of the census data is that from 1900 to 1930 employed wives were classified as "gainfully occupied," while for the census tabulations for 1940 and after employed wives were classified as belonging to the "labor force." Gainfully occupied wives were those who worked with some regularity for money income. On the other hand, wives in the labor force were those "who worked for pay or profit for any length of time during the given week or who seek such work; and those who work for fifteen hours a week or more in a profit-making family enterprise, even if not paid" (Smuts, 1959:157). Edwards' (1943) work did much to increase the comparability of occupation statistics for employed women. However, at present, comparable statistics only exist for employed women and not for employed wives. Therefore, the original census tabulations were felt to be the best estimate.

magazine" is defined as a periodical whose content is designed to appeal primarily to females.[2]

2. The article must have been published during an even-numbered year from 1900 to 1974.[3]

3. The article must have been written as a guide to married life.

It is assumed that the marital advice analyzed reflects the dominant values of middle-class wives. This assumption is based on the work of Morgan and Leahy (1934) and Kass (1949) who analyzed nine of the ten women's magazines used in the present study in terms of what they referred to as the "cultural level" of the magazines.

Content Coding

Before the actual coding was undertaken, all indications of the publication dates were removed from the articles. Articles were then placed in random order. Each article was coded for each of the following marital roles:

1. Economic Provision—Which spouse should provide the monetary support for the family.

2. Decision-making—Which spouse should have the "final say" in major family decisions.

3. Household Task Performance—Which spouse should be responsible for the everyday household tasks such as cooking, cleaning, shopping, maintenance, etc.

4. Interpersonal Supportiveness—Which spouse should be expected to show understanding, respect for wishes, affection, companionship, etc. for the other.

5. Child Rearing—Which spouse should be responsible for discipline, teaching, physical care, entertainment, etc. of the children.

Each sentence, relevant to one of the preceding marital roles, was coded according to the following scale which is a modified version of that used by Blood and Wolfe (1960:21).

Marital Role Responsibility Scale

 2 Wife only
 1 Wife more than husband
 0 Husband and wife equally
−1 Husband more than wife
−2 Husband only

---

[2]The following women's magazines were the source of the marriage advice articles: Good Housekeeping, Ladies Home Journal, Harpers Bazar, Parent's Magazine, McCall's, Better Homes and Gardens, Redbook, House and Garden, Mademoiselle, ahd Woman's Home Companion.
[3]It was not possible to obtain four articles from the desired year in four cases. Therefore, articles from adjacent odd-numbered years were chosen to make up the difference. When this was the case, monthly issues closest to the desired year were searched first as a better approximation.

Since all of the coding was done by the author, a check of interrater reliability was made.[4]

Role responsibility score. This is essentially a measure of which marital partner should be responsible for a specific marital role. The sum of the scores divided by the total number of sentences coded for an individual marital role comprised this measure.

Role differentiation score. Role differentiation is defined as the style of sharing a marital role in which the husband is responsible for certain aspects of the role and the wife is responsible for others. A marital role characterized by a *lack* of role differentiation is synonymous with Blood and Wolfe's (1960:23) "syncratic" type of sharing, where the husband and wife share in the individual aspects of the role. This measure was computed by adding the absolute values, i.e., disregarding the sign, of the marital role responsibility scores and dividing the total by the number of ratings for individual roles.[5]

Trends in Marital Role Prescriptions: 1900-1974

Essentially, most authors, until the mid-thirties, agreed that responsibility for *economic provision* belonged solely to the husband. It was stressed that any self-respecting man ought to be able to provide adequately for his family. Around the mid-thirties, the idea of wife-employment had become more acceptable and yet, the husband was still primarily responsible for this marital role. The picture has changed little since the mid-thirties with wife-employment being acceptable only under certain conditions.

Women with skills they love to employ, with training they mourn not to use, have every right to exert them; so long, that is as the family is not essentially harmed. (McGinley, 1964:32).

Although the role responsibility scores for economic provision were strongly correlated (.66, $p < .00001$) with the passage of time, indicating increased support to share this responsibility, normatively an equal sharing of economic provision has not come about. Even during the "liberated" seventies, the number of authors suggesting that husband and wife share this responsibility equally was minimal (2 out of 12 authors).

Contrary to popular belief, as early as 1900, marital role prescriptions were suggesting the sharing of *decision-making* by husbands and wives. However, there have been two types of sharing advised. The first is where the husband

---

[4] Ten articles were coded by both the author and another trained coder. The overall agreement was 68%. This fairly low level of agreement resulted from some disagreement concerning whether or not certain sentences dealt with any of the marital roles under investigation. This is one place where the more subjective nature of content analysis emerges. Some sentences clearly dealt with one of the marital roles being investigated, while others did so in a less explicit manner. However, sentences coded by both coders had a high level (92%) of inter-rater reliability.

[5] Role differentiation scores were only computed for the following marital roles: decision-making, household task performance, and child-rearing. The other marital roles investigated, i.e. economic provision and interpersonal suppo лt.do not conceptually seem capable of a varying degree of role differentiations. These role are either shared or not shared.

is responsible for certain decision areas and the wife is responsible for others (autonomic). This viewpoint, although still popular today, was the type of sharing of decision-making which most authors advised during the early part of the century. This type of sharing stemmed from the notion that men were inherently more capable than women in certain decision areas, and vice versa.

> There are differences of point of view between men and women; their logic is different; women are most governed by their desires, and men by their laws. (George, 1923:90)

Even those authors who suspected that men were not necessarily any more capable than women in terms of certain decision areas, suggested that wives should know their place nonetheless. Around the mid-thirties authors began to advise a second type of decision-making, where the husband and wife jointly make family decisions (syncratic). Use of the *Role Responsibility* method of scoring does not differentiate between the two types of decision-making and therefore produced results which seem to show essentially no change in decision-making role prescriptions over the 74-year period studied ($r = .004$). This came about because the "autonomic" pattern, typical of the early period, was replaced by the current emphasis on a "syncratic" pattern of decision-making. The change which actually occurred is shown when the *Role Differentiation* method of scoring is used. These scores declined during the period under study ($r = -.39$, $p < .01$), indicating that a syncratic type of decision-making has been increasingly advocated since the turn of the century.[6]

Household task performance has been thought of as almost exclusively the wife's responsibility. At least part of the reason for this can be found in the fact that women were thought of as especially "designed" for this type of work.

> Woman's work is home work — not for "my" husband and "my" child because of "my" love for them; but for humanity, because Nature has destined woman for this service. (Editorial, Harpers Bazar, 1900:250).

There has been a sharp decrease in this pattern since 1900 as shown by the negative correlation ($-. 57$, $p < .00001$) between the household task performance role responsibility scores and the passage of time. Furthermore, the correlation of $-.56$ ($p < .0001$) between the role differentiation scores for household task performance and the passage of time indicates that authors have been advising an increasingly less differentiated pattern since 1900. Despite the changes shown by these correlations, a qualitative analysis of the marriage advice suggests that essentially, house-work has been and continues to be seen as primarily the wife's responsibility. For example:

> Husbands may be thoughtless, or even a little lazy, but a wife who finds herself struck shouldn't hesitate to yell for help. (Brothers, 1966:26)

---

[6]The *negative* correlations between the marital role scores and the passage of time are due to the fact that as the time variable increases most of the marital role scores (with the exception of economic provision) decreased towards zero, indicating advocacy of increased role sharing.

Even though both husbands and wives see *interpersonal supportiveness* as important to their relationship (Levinger, 1964:447), wives have been expected to be the more supportive marital partner. Again, the wife's predominance in this role has been based largely on the idea that women are inherently better suited:

> Women are more yielding ... Therefore they fall naturally into the role of the one who oils the machinery, so to speak. (Hohman, 1952:221).

By the mid-fifties, authors began to suggest that husbands and wives should assume responsibility more equally for interpersonal supportiveness. These changes are summarized by the correlation of —.48 ($p. < .001$) between the interpersonal supportiveness role responsibility scores and the passage of time.

Similar to other marital roles which wives have been primarily responsible for, *child-rearing* has been thought of as best handled by the wife because of woman's basic nature. This idea was not only popular during the early part of the century, but remained so well into the century.

> Nature has destined her to be emotionally responsive, yielding, warm, sympathetic, and sensitive. For these are the emotions that make for motherhood ... (Holmes, 1952:9).

Nevertheless, the correlations show that since the turn of the century child-rearing has progressively become recognized as more of a shared responsibility between the husband and wife (—.45, $p < .004$ for the role responsibility scores, and —.42, $p < .006$ for the role differentiation scores). However, the wife is still primarily responsible for child-rearing. The husband's responsibility in child-rearing has been to help with those aspects of child-rearing which a man was assumed to be better qualified to perform.

Wife-Employment and Marital Role Prescriptions

Having shown the extent of the changes in marital role prescriptions in this sample of women's magazines for the period 1900 to 1974, the question of the extent to which these changes are a result of increases in the employment of married women is at issue.

Lagged correlations (Fishman, 1969: Pelz and Andrews, 1964) were employed to test the hypothesis that the proportion of employed wives influences the emergence of egalitarian marital role prescriptions. A series of correlations were computed, starting with the usual time series correlation (lag of 0) in which scores for the marital roles were correlated with the percentage of wives employed during the same year. Then the lagged correlations were computed by relating the marital role scores to the wife-employment data two years previously (lag of 2), four years before (lag of 4), etc. up to a maximum lag of 18 years. The lag of two years tested the hypothesis that it takes two years for the effect of an increase in wife-employment to affect the marital roles advocated in women's magazines, and a lag of 18 tested the hypothesis that the effect of such changes in employment are not felt in this form of mass media until 18 years later. The lag at which the *highest* correlation occurs indicates the best estimate of the causal interval, i.e., the time which is required for one variable to appreciably affect the other.

The lagged correlation analysis can provide data on the issue of whether egalitarian values preceded or followed increases in the proportion of employed wives. This is done by first using the marital role prescriptions as the dependent variable and the proportion of employed wives at some previous year as the independent variable (i.e., lagging employment on marital role prescriptions). The resulting correlations can then be compared with the correlations based on using the proportion of employed wives as the dependent variable and the marital role prescriptions which occurred in some previous year as the independent variable (i.e., lagging marital role prescriptions on employment). The *highest* of the correlations indicates which variable has the causal priority. Of course, as Peltz and Andrews (1964:839) explain, this method does not establish one variable as the sole cause of the other, but rather, it indicates which hypothesis is more plausible.

The Causal Sequence

The data presented thus far show that over the 74-year period covered, marital role prescriptions became increasingly more egalitarian, even though they are still far from equal. During this same period, ever larger proportions of married women became employed ($r=.93$, $p<.00001$). But the question remains as to whether increased wife-employment produced a more egalitarian view of marriage (as reflected in the marital advice presented in the women's magazines studied), or the reverse; i.e., did the increasingly egalitarian view of marriage lead to greater employment of married women.

The strongest lagged correlations are underlined in Table 1.[7] The lagged correlation analysis provides evidence that wife-employment may have causal priority, but only in respect to the decision-making role. Furthermore, the results presented in Table 1 indicate that it takes approximately fourteen years after an increase occurs in the proportion of employed wives for the decision-making role prescriptions to advise that husbands and wives should share more decisions in a "syncratic" sense (i.e., joint decision). Although the causal direction just presented is supported by the strongest and only significant correlation (for decision-making), this very same significant correlation is not significantly different than some of those produced at other lag lengths or some of those produced in the opposite causal direction. Therefore, these results must be interpreted cautiously.

---

[7]The lagged correlation analysis, using the *Role Responsibility* method of scoring, produced evidence that wife-employment may have causal priority over the emergence of egalitarian decision-making role prescriptions. However, these lagged correlations were *not* significant. The other marital roles, as measured by the *Role Responsibility* method, were found to become more egalitarian at approximately the same time that the proportion of employed wives was increasing; results essentially the same as those produced using the *Role Differentiation* method of scoring. Therefore, only the lagged correlation analysis using the *Role Differentiation* method are reported in the text of this paper.

TABLE 1 LAGGED CORRELATIONS BETWEEN MARITAL ROLE DIFFERENTIATION SCORES AND THE PROPORTION OF EMPLOYED WIVES IN ALL OCCUPATIONS

Marital Role	Lag in Years									
	0	2	4	6	8	10	12	14	16	18
A. Wife-Employment as Independent Variable										
Decision-Making	—.31	—.22	—.14	—.11	—.21	—.34	—.27	—.43*	a	a
Household Task Performance	—.64**	—.54**	—.45**	—.49**	—.56**	—.43*	—.36*	—.27	—.24	—.15
Child-Rearing	—.34*	—.21	—.14	—.21	.28	—.30	—.25	—.29	—.30	a
B. Wife-Employment as Dependent Variable										
Decision-Making	—.31	—.28	—.23	—.17	—.06	.06	—.003	—.10	a	a
Household Task Performance	—.64**	—.61**	—.60**	—.58**	—.56**	—.52**	—.48**	—.43*	—.36*	—.31*
Child-Rearing	—.34*	—.33*	—.30	—.30	—.28	—.23	—.16	—.09	—.01	a

* significant at .05 level.

** significant at .01 level.

a insufficient data to lag at this length.

The other marital role prescriptions become more egalitarian at approximately the same time that the proportion of employed wives was increasing, indicating that neither variable was necessarily causally prior. This suggests that possibly some other factor or factors may have causal priority over the increasing proportion of employed wives as well as the emergence of egalitarian marital role prescriptions. This may also indicate that, in terms of these other marital roles, both wife-employment and role prescriptions may be causally affecting each other at a length of time too short for the present lagged correlation analysis to capture. No significant differences were found between the lagged correlations computed with the proportion of wives employed in middle-class occupations as opposed to those computed with the proportion of wives employed in working-class occupations, indicating that increases in both of these groups are related to the emergence of egalitarian marital role prescriptions in about the same fashion.

Summary and Conclusions

This study investigated changes in marital role prescriptions as expressed in marriage advice articles published in women's magazines for the period 1900 to 1974. Bearing in mind that marital role prescriptions set forth recommended rather than actual behavior, it was found that marital role prescriptions became more egalitarian. However, even at the end of the period studied, the role prescriptions were far from advocating complete husband-wife equality. A recurrent theme throughout much of the marriage advice was the notion that responsibility for marital roles should be allocated to husbands and wives in terms of the inherent natures of males and females. A main issue of the study was the question of whether the emergence of egalitarian marital role prescriptions was a result of the rise in the proportion of employed wives or the reverse, i.e., the proportion of employed wives increased as a result of the emergence of egalitarian marital role prescriptions.

Data on the question of causal priority was obtained by means of a series of lagged correlations. This provided evidence that the normative prescriptions for four of the five marital roles became more egalitarian at approximately the same time as the proportion of employed wives was increasing, indicating that neither variable was necessarily causally prior. However, the lagged correlations also show that wife-employment may have causal priority over the emergence of egalitarian marital role prescriptions in respect to decision-making.

In conclusion, these findings provide support for the resource theory of marital power, on a macrosociological level. They show that of the marital role prescriptions which were studied, those which were found to be influenced by wife-employment are precisely those concerning the aspect of marriage which resource theory argues should be most affected, i.e., sharing in power as indexed by normative prescriptions concerning joint decision-making.

REFERENCES

Abbott, Susan
  1976   "Full-time farmers and week-end wives: an analysis of altering conjugal roles."
          Journal of Marriage and the Family 38 (Feb.): 165-174.

Albrecht, Milton C.
  1956   "Does literature reflect common values ?"   American Sociological Review 21 (Dec.):
          722-729.

Aldous, Joan
  1974   "The making of family roles and family change."   The Family Coordinator 23
          (July): 231-235.

Axelson, Leland
  1963   "The marital adjustment and role definitions of husbands of working and nonwork-
          ing wives."   Marriage and Family Living 25 (2): 189-195.

Bahr, Stephen J., Charles E. Bowerman, and Viktor Gecas
  1974   "Adolescent perceptions of conjugal power."   Social Forces 52 (March): 357-367.

Blood, Robert O.
  1963   "The husband-wife relationship."   Pp. 282-308 in F. Ivan Nye and Lois W. Hoffman
          (eds.)   The Employed Mother America.   Chicago: Rand McNally.

Blood, Robert O.
  1965   "Long-range causes and consequences of the employment of married women."
          Journal of Marriage and the Family 27 (Feb): 43-47.

Blood, Robert O.
  1967   Love Match and Arranged Marriage.   New York: Free Press.

Blood, Robert O. and Robert L. Hamblin
  1958   "The effects of the wife's employment on the family power structure."   Social Forces
          36 (May): 347-352.

Blood, Robert O. and Donald M. Wolfe
  1960   Husbands and Wives: The Dynamics of Married Living.   Glencoe, Ill.: Free
          Press.

Brothers, Joyce
  1966   "Why shouldn't husbands dry the dishes!"   Good Housekeeping 162 (March): 26+.

Buric, Olivera and Andjelka Zecevic
  1967   "Family authority, marital satisfaction, and the social network in Yugoslavia."
          Journal of Marriage and the Family 29 (May): 325-336.

Cain, Glen G.
  1966   Married Women in the Labor Force.   Chicago: University of Chicago Press.
Centers, Richard, Bertram H. Raven, and Aroldo Rodrigues
  1971   "Conjugal power structore: a re-examination."   American Sociological Review 36
          (April): 263-278.

Editorial
  1900   "Women and their work: the truth."   Harper's Bazar 33 (March): 250.

Edwards, Alba M.
  1943   Comparative Occupation Statistics for the United States 1870-1940.   Washington,
          D.C. : U.S. Bureau of the Census.

Fishman, George S.
  1969   Spectral Methods in Econometrics.   Cambridge, Mass.: Harvard University Press.

George, W.L.
   1923   "No housewives, no homes."   Good Housekeeping 76 (May): 90+.

Goode, William J.
   1963   "World revolution and family patterns."   Pp. 111-122 in Arlene S. Skolnick and
             Jerome H. Skolnick (eds.) Family in Transaction. Boston: Little, Brown & Co.

Hedges, Janice N.
   1970   "Women at work."   Monthly Labor Review 93:19-29.

Heer, David M.
   1958   "Dominance and the working wife."   Social Forces 36 (May): 341-347.

Heer, David M.
   1963   "Measurement and bases of family power: an overview."   Marriage and the Family
             Living 25 (May): 133-139.

Hoffman, Lois W.
   1960   "Parental power relations and the division of household tasks." Pp. 215-230 in F.
             Ivan Nye and Lois W. Hoffman (eds.) The Employed Mother in America. Chicago:
             Rand McNally & Co.

Hohman, Leslie
   1952   "On getting along."   Ladies Home Journal 69 (April): 200+.

Holmes, Marjorie
   1952   "What became of the man I married ?"   Better Homes and Gardens 30 (May): 6+.

Inglis, Ruth A.
   1938   "An objective approach to the relationship between fiction and society."   American
             Sociological Review 3 (Aug.): 526-531.

Kandel, Denise B. and Gerald S. Lesser
   1972   "Marital decision-making in American and Danish urban families: a research note."
             Journal of Marriage and the Family 34 (Feb.): 134-138.

Kass, Babette
   1949   "Overlapping magazine reading: a new method of determining the cultural levels."
             Pp. 130-151 in Paul Lazersfeld and Frank N. Stanton (eds.) Communication Research
             1948-1949. New York: Harper and Brothers.

Levenger, George
   1964   "Task and social behavior in marriage."   Sociometry 27 (4): 433-448.

Lupri, Eugene
   1969   "Contemporary authority patterns in the West German family: a study in cross-natio-
             nal validation."   Journal of Marriage and the Family 31 (Feb.): 134-144.

McGinley, Phyllis
   1964   "Wives and the moonlight adventures."   Ladies Home Journal 81 (Aug.): 30+.

McKinley, Donald Gilbert
   1964   Social Class and Family Life.   London: Free Press.

Michel, Andree
   1970   "Working wives and family interaction in French and American families."   Inter-
             national Journal of Comparative Sociology 11 (June): 157-165.

Middleton, Russel
   1960   "Fertility values in American magazine fiction."   Public Opinion Quarterly 24
             (Spring): 139-143.

Middleton, Russel and S. W. Putney
  1960   "Dominance in decisions in the family: race and class differences." American Journal of Sociology 65 (May): 605-609.

Morgan, W. L. and A.M. Leahy
  1934   "The cultural content of general interest magazines." Journal of Educational Psychology 25 (Oct.): 530-536.

Nolan, Francena L.
  1959   "Rural employment and husbands and wives." Pp. 241-250 in F. Ivan Nye and Lois W. Hoffman (eds.) The Employed Mother in America. Chicago: Rand McNally & Co.

Nye, F. Ivan
  1976   Role Structure and Analysis of the Family. Beverly Hills: Sage.

Nye, F. Ivan and Lois W. Hoffman
  1963   The Employed Mother in America. Chicago: Rand McNally & Co.

Oppong, Christine
  1970   "Conjugal power and resources: an urban African example." Journal of Marriage and the Family 32 (Nov.): 676-680.

Pelz, Donald and Frank M. Andrews
  1964   "Detecting causal priorities in panel study data." American Sociological Review 29 (6): 836-847.

Powell, Kathryn S.
  1963   "Family variables." Pp. 231-240 in F. Ivan Nye and Lois W. Hoffman (eds.) The Employed Mother in America. Chicago: Rand McNally & Co.

Richmond, Marie L.
  1976   "Beyond resource theory: another look at factors enabling women to affect family interaction." Journal of Marriage and the Family 38 (May), 257-266.

Safilios-Rothschild, Constantina
  1967   "A camparison of power structure and marital satisfaction in urban Greek and French families." Journal of Marriage and the Family 29 (May): 345-352.

Safilios-Rothschild. Constatina (ed.)
  1972   Toward a Sociology of Women. Pp. 63-70, "Instead of a discussion: companionate marriages and sexual equality: are they compatible?" Lexington, Mass.: Xerox Corp.

Scanzoni, John
  1970   Opportunity and the Family. New York: Free Press.

Smuts. Robert W.
  1959   Women and Work in America. New York: Columbia University Press.

Szalai, Alexander
  1972   The Use of Time. Netherlands: Mouton and Co.

Webb, Eugene J., Donald T. Campbell, Richard D. Schwartz and Lee Sechrest
  1966   Unobtrusive Measures: Nonreactive Research in the Social Sciences. Chicago: Rand McNally & Co.

Weller, Robert H.
  1968   "The employment of wives, dominance, and fertility." Journal of Marriage and the Family 31 (Aug.): 437-442.

Wolfe, Donald M.
  1959   "Power and authority in the family." Pp. 99-117 in D. Cartwright (ed.) Studies in Social Power. Ann Arbor, Mich.: University of Michigan Institute for Social Research.

16 Changes in Canadian Female Labour Force Participation and Some Possible Implications for Conjugal Power*

D. IAN POOL**

Labour Force Participation and Conjugal Power

In analyses of conjugal relations, emphasis is often laid on the links between female labour force participation and the relative amount of leverage enjoyed by wives in situations where bargaining occurs. Stated briefly the argument runs: the greater the resources of a wife the more her power, and the more egalitarian the marriage. Labour force participation is seen to provide her with remuneration so that she can contribute to the family's income. Such a resource is considered a key element of conjugal power (e.g. the hypotheses of Blood and Hamblin, 1958: 348ff)†. Egalitarian marriages will be possible in Canada, so Eichler argues (1975), only when there is equality of access by men and women to the labour market. However, it has been further noted, both in the popular press and by researchers using public statistics, that there has recently been an increase in female labour force participation, at least in North America. Thus, by inference, there has been an increment in the resources wives have at their disposal, and, accordingly, a movement towards egalitarian marriages.

The primary aim of this paper is to evaluate whether or not, female labour force participation, this key dimension of conjugal bargaining, has increased in Canada. If not, this raises major questions about a theme commonly put forward in the literature, namely that marriages are everywhere becoming more egalitarian, as a result of the improved bargaining position of wives. There are, however, few data on this 'trend' as most studies of conjugal power are synchronic. If they purport to be diachronic, often changes over time will, in reality, be assumed rather than demonstrated empirically. The basis of this assumption is

*I wish to thank Linda Pettit who carried out the interviews on which this study is in part based (see Appendix). I was fortunate to have recourse to cross-comparative data on conjugal power in unpublished manuscripts by Janet Sceats Pool, to whom acknowledgement is made. The project was supported by a research grant from Carleton University, to which grateful acknowledgement is made. Finally, I am grateful for the constructive comments of the anonymous reviewers of the paper.

**Department of Sociology and Anthropology, Carleton University, Ottawa, Ontario—Canada, December 1977. (From July 1st, 1978, Dept. of Sociology, University of Waikato, Hamilton, New Zealand).

†Their paper is apparently a "major contribution" as it has been reprinted. Its rather strong conclusions do not support their hypotheses. Curiously, their conclusions also appear to contradict the weak but consistent results emanating from the data.

a rather pervasive notion of an evolution towards more egalitarian structures, usually resembling the North American type of family. Even in the clearest exposition on conjugal power, the key diagram lacks an empirical base (Scanzoni, 1972: Fig. 2-1).

Empirical Data on Changes Over Time

If we seek to employ empirical data on labour force participation we encounter yet another problem. Very often these must be drawn from official statistics, and may well be based on definitions which either (i) suit economic or administrative ends rather than sociological; or (ii) have been developed by one group in the community. This is composed of professional statisticians, often economists, usually middle-class males, who base their definitions on what they consider to be community or cultural norms. Most importantly their definitions are often formulated around salaries, wages or some other form of economic gain.

Recognising the fact that such definitions lead to an under-reporting of unpaid members of family economic units, and, in particular, of wives, Denton and Ostry (1967) attempted to provide estimates of historical Canadian labour force data. Their estimates were based on conversion ratios drawn from 1951, at which date it was possible to adjust the census "gainfully occupied" question with the labour force survey data for May-June 1951. These ratios were applied to the "gainfully occupied" in earlier years. A major problem is that they still had to rely on official definitions as a basis for their estimates and these definitions, while different, did reflect the bias noted above.

Unfortunately, because of a lack of age detail in survey data, it was decided to use the 1951 census unpaid family workers figure of 18,166 females in agriculture for women 20 and above, as against 80,000 in the labour force survey (presumably 14+ years of age) (Denton and Ostry, 1967, pp. 32-33). This decision had the effect of reducing their conversion ratio to roughly $\frac{1}{4}$, which is obviously critical in earlier years (e,g. Census of 1921). The effect of this bias can be gauged if one compares the Prairie Census of June 1946, which enumerated 8,000 women in agriculture, with the Labour Force Survey data for the same month which reported a figure of 103,000 (Denton and Ostry, 1967, fn, p.12). These Prairie data thus indicate, very forcefully, that we are not dealing with minor or merely semantic differences. Moreover, the fact that Canada was heavily rural in early decades of the 20th century by comparison with other industrialized countries (Stone, 1969, Table 2.3), must be taken into account in any interpretation of societal change. Therefore, although Denton and Ostry's estimates are a major contribution for many analytical purposes, it is doubtful whether they provide useful indexes for the case being made here; that is, one must question, at least for family economic units, their brief conclusion based on these re-estimates. They argue that the historical statistics demonstrate a "rise in labour force participation of women, especially middle aged and older married women" (Denton and Ostry, 1967, p. 14; see also Ostry, 1968, p. 47). They have been able to re-arrange the data, but not to confront the real issue of the conceptualisation of labour force participation.

The question then arises whether a definition, which more fully reflected the labour force contribution of rural Canadian women would show a substantially different trend. In this paper we do not intend to provide a definitive answer for it is essentially an exploratory study.

Alternative Definitions of Labour-Force Participation

It is possible to take an alternative approach to the collection of data which would permit one to investigate more adequately the proposition that in some sectors of the economy female labour force participation has always been high. For the present paper we can employ data derived from a small quota sample discussed in the appendix and undertaken in the Ottawa Valley in 1973. Three cohorts of English-speaking married women were interviewed: (i) those born from 1890-1900 and in the peak of their child raising in the 1920s and early 1930s; (ii) those born in the period 1920-1930 and representing early "baby boom" mothers (1940-1955); and (iii) those born in the early "baby-boom" and currently at the peak of their reproductive span. They correspond approximately to Campbell's "Three Generations of Parents" (Campbell, 1973). The quotas were further drawn so that for each cohort there were rural and urban respondents. Residence was assessed in terms of the *place of residence of the women when they were in their main period of childbearing and childraising (i.e. 20-35 years of age).* The data are thus retrospective cohort information on the two major sectors of the Canadian economy. The women were asked a labour force question (see appendix) which attempted to determine all types of participation including performance of dual role (e.g. home and farm). It must be stressed that this modest survey was not a probability sample; it merely attempted to determine if it were possible to overcome some of the problems inherent in the use of published data where one is so bound by official definitions.

Cohort Differentials in Labour Force Participation

If we use the data in Table 1 drawn from the Ottawa Valley study, we can infer several interesting phenomena which suggest thet we may need to re-assess our views of changes in family structure. Firstly, in all 3 rural cohorts labour force participation during the peak child-bearing period is very high; but for urban cohorts this increases monotonically towards the present. Working rural wives were normally part of the farm-family unit except in the case of the most recent cohort. This last factor may, however, be merely an artifact of the retrospective data collection process: earlier cohorts, rural residents at ages 20-35, were interviewed both in rural locations and in Ottawa urban area, and may have lived in any rural region when aged 20-35 years. By contrast, the young, by definition, had to be residents of rural locations (in this case farms) at the time of the interview, and by living near Ottawa urban area they have access to a non-farm job market. The 18% of the 1920-30 birth-cohort of rural women working in non-farm jobs had worked mainly part-time, but we do not

Table 1.A.   OTTAWA VALLEY FAMILY COHORT STUDY, LABOUR FORCE
                                                       PARTICIPATION OF WIVES

Cohort by residence	O/U	O/R	M/U	M/R	Y/U	Y/R
(N=)	(34)	(31)	(40)	(40)	(44)	(23)
% Working at peak of reproductive span	29	74	45	93	50	86
% Rural wives working on family farm at peak of reproductive span	N/A	74	N/A	75	N/A	55
% of wives earning "pin money" at peak of reproductive span*	32	29	20	20	16	26

Table 1.B.   NATIONAL LEVELS OF LABOUR FORCE PARTICIPATION

(a) National level based on official statistics, adjusted for definitional problems:			*Year*		
age group**	1921	1931	1941	1951	1961
20-24	39.8	47.4	46.9	48.4	50.7
25-34	19.5	24.4	27.9	25.4	29.4

(b) Expected national level at ages 25-34 if the Ottawa Valley definition had been employed***	1920's	1940's/50's	1960's/70's
	52	65(58)	59(50)

* "When you were 25-35 years of age did you earn your own "pin-money" by activities such as baby-sitting; dress-making; selling eggs, crafts and preserves; typing or the like".

** Adjusted by a ratio using 1951 labour force survey and census data (Denton & Ostry, 1967).

*** Weighting for rural-urban distribution of population. Figures in parentheses take account of part-time component of non-family farm workforce.

Samples: O=Oldest, born 1890-1900; M=Middle, born 1920-1930; Y=Youngest, born 1940-50;
           U=Urban residence at the peak of the reproductive span; R=Rural residence, peak of
           reproductive span.

know whether they were rural-farm or rural non-farm residents. Similarly, one-quarter of the young urban cohort were in part-time employment. It is also interesting that all cohorts earn(ed) "pin-money".

The survey data differ markedly from Denton and Ostry's adjusted and unadjusted data. A very general idea of this can be gauged by pro-rating the Ottawa Valley data by the percentage of the population rural or urban in the decade at which the particular cohort was at the peak of child-bearing. This gives the "expected" national figure were the Ottawa Valley data to have applied to Canada. Of course, the reader must be warned that is not an extrapolation based on statistical inference, but is merely an illustration of the reasoning which might be directed towards the development of propositions to be tested with a much better data base.

In thinking about this survey, and particularly with Campbell's recent perceptive paper (1973) in mind, a working hypothesis had been that the baby-boom mothers, a high fertility cohort, would have remained outside the labour force. Participation should have been highest in the 1920's and again in the 1960's/70's, but the results showed the middle cohort to have the highest rates. This holds true even when one takes account of the high levels of part-time employment (figures in parentheses adjust for this factor in the rural cohorts of the 1940's/50's and urban cohorts of the 1960's/70's). Perhaps, the problem is that our 1940's/50's data are affected by the fact that women often had to run family farms in the war period; a larger sample and more refined dating may have produced a different result supporting the hypothesis.

Implications for Conjugal Power

Above it was noted that labour force participation provides a resource for conjugal bargaining. In family economic units such as farms or small businesses, the resource will take the form of a share in the generation of the gross family income or subsistence; if the spouses are wage or salary earners it is their earnings which are critical. Therefore, if female labour force participation has not increased radically over recent years, is it reasonable to argue that power relations may also have remained relatively unchanged? Again we can only explore this subject and suggest some issues requiring further intensive research.

As every student of sociology of the family will immediately recognise, the study of conjugal power, the amount of leverage in a system of marital exchange and reciprocity, is beset by theoretical, conceptual and measurement problems, all of which have been widely debated recently (e.g. Bahr, 1972; Scanzoni, 1972; Safilios-Rothschild, 1970 and 1972; Sprey, 1972; Olson and Rabunsky, 1972; Turk and Bell, 1972). For my purposes, it is convenient to adopt Scanzoni's notion of conjugal power which, in turn, is derived directly from a general definition of power, framed by Blau: "A person on whom others is dependent for vital benefits has power to enforce his demands. He may make demands on them that they consider fair and just in relation to the benefits they receive for submitting to his power" (1972:67, citing Blau) Moreover, and still following Scanzoni, I deal here with "legitimate power" (or "authority") for "it is the provision of resources [rather than "punishments"] that is the key element in compliance and approval" (1972:80).

The present paper follows the orthodox strategy of attempting to index conjugal power by studying decisions facing families: (a) relatively minor decisions, such as in the area of recreation activities; the purchase of both luxury items and necessities; household expenses; the disciplining and naming of children; (b) two major decisions, a job change by the husband; and a decision for the family to move.

In measuring decision-making some acute problems arise. A number are relevant to the present study, but cannot be taken up in detail here. However, two should be noted for they are of direct import for the interpretation of the data presented below. Firstly, there is the problem that respondents are likely to be biased as they have been participants in this decision-making, a difficulty greatly compounded by selective recall in retrospective studies. There is no way we can control for this in the present study, but the reader should be aware that we are reporting the wife's view of their bargaining. Secondly, if decision-making is taken as the basis for an analysis of power, various types of decisions carry differential weights. For example, decisions made by the wife relating to the purchase of necessities are often used, yet these are of little importance if the husband as the sole income-earner, decides how much money to give her, can change jobs, and will even decide on a family move without consulting her. In fact, the Ottawa Valley data demonstrated no clear pattern for the minor decisions, such as purchases of household items, so they will not be analysed here. Instead data will be presented on two basic decisions which may well determine the fate of a family.

These are presented in Table 2(a) and are: (i) a job change by the husband, and (ii) a move by the family. The N's are very small, representing merely those ever-exposed to these situations. Nevertheless, they do suggest for all cohorts that the rural wife may have more input than the urban to both of these two areas of family decision-making. It is also important to note in this regardt hat three-quarters of working older rural women worked on their own family farm (Table 1). For the urban sample there is a monotonic increase in bi-lateral decision-making towards the present. One can point to the possible significance of the higher levels of labour participation among rural than among urban respondents at earlier dates, and to the fact that, across the sample, work status definitely affects the level of input to crucial aspects of decision making (Table 2(b)). These data imply, therefore, that labour-force participation in the past was a resource as it is today. More importantly they suggest that we may need to modify our notions of a monotonic evolution towards egalitarian unions.

Kin, Friends and Community Involvement

Of course, economic resources do not constitute a unique determinant of marital power. Perhaps the inter-cohort differences we have pointed to here are confounded by the availability of social-emotional resources, gained from kin,

Table 2   OTTAWA VALLEY FAMILY COHORT STUDY: WHEN AT THE PEAK OF CHILDBEARING. DID THE WIFE PARTICIPATE IN DECISIONS RELATING TO (i) THE HUSBAND CHANGING HIS JOB AND (ii) TO A SHIFT? (a) BY COHORT AND RESIDENCE (b) BY LABOUR FORCE PARTICIPATION
(Percentage of eligible respondents)

			Job Change		Shift	
			Yes	No	Yes	No
(a)	Cohort/Residence :	O/U	12	9	24	4
		O/R	6	0	10	1
		M/U	23	6	30	5
		M/R	15	1	17	0
		Y/U	32	4	31	6
		Y/R	11	0	14	0
(b)	Work Status:					
	Working		61	8	76	7
	Not Working		38	12	50	9

Table 3   WHEN AT PEAK OF CHILDBEARING (SAY 25-35 YEARS), CHOICE OF FRIENDS AND INVOLVEMENT IN THE COMMUNITY

	O/U	O/R	M/U	M/R	Y/U	Y/R
Choice of Friends:						
Wife's choice domianant	32	22	38	20	36	35
Husband's choice dominant	9	—	10	13	23	9
Joint choice	24	19	38	8	27	31
"Just people in the community"	35	55	15	55	14	17
Total (%)	100	96*	101	97*	100	100
Mean No. of Organisations belonged to be wives:	0.8	1.3	1.3	1.6	1.3	1.4
% of Women belonging to *no* organisations:	50	23	43	25	43	35

friends and the community.   The Ottawa Valley data provide some information
on this subject (Table 3)*.

The rural respondents generally had taken up patri-local residence.   For the
urban women there was no apparent residential pattern, but they clearly preferred
their own kin to their affines.   By contrast, the rural women showed no clear-cut
pattern of preferences for either kin or affines.

Choice of friends was the wife's or made jointly in the urban samples, except,
interestingly enough, in the better educated, better-off youngest cohort where the
husband's choice assumed a more important position than in any other sample.
Is this choice significant? It may merely be a function of factors such as duration
of marriage.   But if it were a real difference it might indicate a weakening of one
power base for wives.   In particular, wives outside the labour force are often
reduced to maintaining contact with the wider world vicariously through their
husbands.   Yet it is this very group which is frequently taken as the model for
egalitarian families.   By contrast, in the older rural samples the availability of
friends in the community was of major importance.

Two sets of data are given on membership in organisations.   The second is
probably the more telling, for the first is obviously affected by the "chronic
joiners".   In the second set, there is a rather clear rural-urban difference:
65% to 75% of rural women belonged to non-kin associations, as against only
50% to 57% of urban women.   In the rural sample there is a decrease in membership over time.

In brief, in the past, rural women more obviously had a community basis for
support if this were necessary, and the weakest position was that of the youngest
cohort.   If one can draw inferences from Margaret Laurence's novels on rural
Prairie Canada, of the 20's and 30's the community knew about its members
(1975, "The Nuisance Grounds"), while her character, Mrs. Cameron, took a
clear position about what was acceptable or unacceptable (1972).

Conclusion

The present results are tentative as the study is merely exploratory.   Nevertheless, one can suggest a series of propositions, which relate to sociological interpretations of social change and conjugal structures and power.   The ·first 2 relate
to macro-level socio-demographic change:

(1) That changes in labour force participation of women are less than is
     suggested by official empirical data.   This can be implied from Ottawa
     Valley data, as has been discussed already.

(2) That, at least in rural Canada, in which the majority of Canadians lived
     earlier this century, female labour force participation took the form of

---

*It should be noted that 93% of respondents used as a first language the language spoken in the
community they had lived in while at the peak of child-bearing.   All data refer, of course, to that
period in the respondent's life cycle.

involvement in family economic units.   Again Ottawa Valley data support this.

These two propositions in turn suggest one other which relates more to the micro-level and to interspouse relations.

(3) Let us accept, as our data on decision-sharing imply, that conjugal power is related to labour force participation. Our data also show that the levels of labour force participation may not have changed dramatically. Therefore, it can be postulated that the notion of an evolution towards egalitarian family structures, as propounded by some recent American writers, may not be entirely valid, at least for Canada.

Unfortunately, this evolutionary model is most persuasive, but one must recognise that it may be more a derivative of polemics than of empirical research. Goode, one of the leading practitioners in this field, links the conjugal family to industrialization, seeing this evolution not merely as inevitable, but as highly desirable. He appears not to question whether his model, the contemporary North American family, is in reality the most egalitarian, while he also confounds egalitarianism with libertarianism (Goode, 1963; 1967). Such a strongly ideological view, itself a subset of the "modernization" theme, has probably influenced both American and Canadian sociology, as well even as the development and implementation of social engineering, particularly family planning programmes in the Third World (See Raulet, 1970, esp. p. 213: Notestein, 1966.)

If the postulate of evolution towards egalitarian unions cannot be supported substantively we have a situation which is undesirable academically, and could have even more severe consequences in applied fields. Yet the problem remains that, to a large degree, such a major proposition and its underlying assumptions rest on few empirical bases.

Of course, it is also essential to investigate the availability of a wide range of resources. The present study has indicated one of further proposition relevant to this aspect of power.

(4) That, often non-economic factors, such as participation in the community and propinquity of kin, may have reinforced economic dimensions of conjugal power. Indeed, the effect of this factor may be assumed as a pre-condition for the enforcement of some norms relating to family life.

Finally, this study indicates a n overwhelming need for diachronic studies: longitudinal, if possible, or retrospective if not. As a basis for data collection and analysis the cohort is a useful tool and, one can compare between these. Of course, we must recognize that there are problems at the analytical stage with retrospective data, and particularly with the interplay between response effects (e.g. recall lapse), and the effects of social change *per se*, but these difficulties need not prove insurmountable, particularly with purely structural (as against attitudinal) variables.

APPENDIX I
The Ottawa Valley Family Cohort Study

The data used here were collected in Summer 1973 in rural and urban locations in the Ottawa Valley. The interviews were conducted by Linda Pettit, mainly to determine whether or not labour force participation rates as shown by official data sources were an artifact of the narrow definitions employed officially, rather than a result of substantive changes over time.

The aim was very modest, for the intention was exploratory, to see whether or not a researchable issue existed. For this purpose we employed quota sampling, selecting 3 birth cohorts of ever-married women (1890-1900; 1920-1930; 1940-1950), further divided by rural and urban residence *at the peak of their reproductive span.* The sample was small ($N = 212$), but, except for the young rural groups, the N for each sub-group was over 30. These are given in Table 1A.

Copies of the data-file and of coding and questionnaires have been lodged with the Social Science Data Archive at Carleton University.

Eighty-two per cent of the women were born in Canada, 8% in the U.K., 5% in N.W. Europe and the rest elsewhere. Only 11% had lived in Canada less than 20 years, 3% less than 10 years. When their children were young 92% had spoken English in the home, 4% French, 4% English and French. For 93% the language spoken in the home had been the language of the locality. Sixty-three percent were Protestant, 29% Catholic, the remainder other or no religions. For each cohort the urban sample was markedly less Protestant than the rural, while the youngest cohort was more strongly Catholic than the others. This may reflect the fact that the young cohort was interviewed where it had lived most of its life, (some sections of the rural Anglophone Ottawa Valley Community is strongly Catholic) whereas the older cohorts could well have lived in more Protestant regions of Canada prior to coming to Ottawa.

The wives in rural samples were better educated than their husbands, if exposure to post-secondary education is considered. The reverse is true in urban samples. In older samples the modal educational level was secondary; it is overwhelmingly post-secondary for husbands in the young urban sample.

For wives working the modal occupational group was the major category 4 on the Blishen Scale weighted downwards, but more evenly dispersed than for husbands. The distribution is weighted upwards for husbands except for category I, but is highly concentrated at category 4, which is hardly surprising as many of the husbands are/had been farmers. A major variation is that, paralleling education, the young urban husbands' cohort is concentrated at Blishen categories 2 and 3, a function perhaps more of a general shift to white collar industry than of sampling. Finally, few described their families or those of their husbands as "wealthy" when they had first married. When at the peak of their reproductive span most had enjoyed comfortable means, if urban, but rather more limited means if rural, particularly for the middle cohort. By contrast, and reflecting education and job, 21% of the young urban cohort described itself as "well off".

Most of the questions were of a standard format. However, given the importance of labour force participation this question is reproduced in full here. (Appendix II).

Finally, a number of the results discussed in the text could be supported by tests of statistical significance, but to reproduce these would be to impute confidence levels which cannot be borne by data collected purely for the purposes of an exploratory study. Thus, the data are used here to suggest propositions, but not to investigate hypotheses.

APPENDIX II

Section of the Questionnaire Relating to Labour Force Participation

The following questions relate to the period *when you were aged 25-35 years* (or to the present if you are less than 35 years of age)

*13. (Please read all the categories in this question before checking the correct response)

When you were 25 to 35 years old did you:

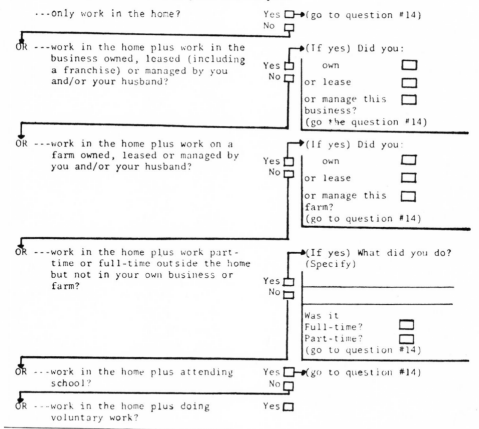

---

* This was intended as a drop-off and pick-up questionnaire. However, and particularly for older women, often it was completed as an interview. Many respondents, probably as a first reaction based on norms, automatically completed the first category, in spite of the directive, but then later erased it and checked one below.

REFERENCES

Bahr, Stephen J.
1972   "Comment on 'The Study of Family Power'", *Journal of Marriage and the Family* (J.M.F.), May. pp. 239-62.

Blood, Robert O, and Hamblin, Robert L.
1958   "The Effects of Wife's Employment on the Family Power Structure, *Social Forces*, Vol. 36, May. pp. 347-52.

Campbell, Arthur A.
1973   "Three Generations of Parents", *Family Planning Perspectives*, 5(2). pp. 106-12.

Denton, Frank T. & Sylvia Ostry
1967   *Historical Estimates of the Canadian Labour Force* (Ottawa: DBS),

Eichler, Margrit
1975   "The Egalitarian Family in Canada?" in Wakil, Parvez (ed) *Marriage, Family and Society: Canadian Perspectives* (Toronto: Butterworth & Co.). pp. 223-36.

Goode, William J.
1963   *World Revolution and Family Patterns* (Glencoe: Free Press).

Goode, William J.
1967   "The Family as an Element in the World Revolution" in Rose, Peter I (ed.), *The Study of Society*, (N.Y.: Random House). pp. 528-38.

Laurence, Margaret
1972   *A Jest of God* (Toronto: McClelland & Stewart).

Laurence, Margaret
1975   *The Diviners* (Toronto: Bantam).

Notestein, Frank W.
1966   "Closing Remark s" in Berelson, Bernard, *et al*, (eds.) *Family Planning & Population Programmes*, (Chicago: University of Chicago Press), pp. 827-30.

Olson, David H. and Rabunsky Carolyn
1972   "Validity of Four Measures of Family Power" *JMF.*, May. pp. 224-33.

Ostry, Sylvia
1968   *The Female Worker in Canada* (Ottawa: DBS).

Raulet, Harry M.
1970   "Family Planning and Population Control in Developing Countries", *Demography* 7(2), May. pp. 211-34.

Safilios-Rothschild, Constantina
1970   "The Study of Family.   Power Structure: A Review 1960-69". *JMF*, pp. 539-52.

Safilios-Rothschild, Constantina
1972   "Answer to Bahr's Comment...", *JMF*, pp. 245-46.

Scanzoni, John
1972   *Sexual Bargaining* (Englewood Cliffs, N.S.: Prentice Hall).

Sprey, Jesse
1972   "Family Power Structure: A Critical Comment", *JMF*, pp. 235-38.

Stone: Leroy O
1967   *Urban Development in Canada*, (Ottawa: D.B.S.).

Turk, James L. and Norman W. Bell
1972   "Measuring Power in Families", *J.M.F,*, May. pp. 215-3

17 Sex Role Attitudes, Female Employment, and Marital Satisfaction*

STEPHEN J. BAHR**
RANDAL D. DAY***

STEPHEN J. BAHR**
RANDAL D. DAY***

Substantial increases in the proportion of married females in the labor force have occurred during the past 25 years (Carter and Glick, 1976; U.S. Bureau of Census, 1975). This has prompted family scholars to ask whether or not the employment of the wife might affect marital satsifaction. Although this question has been examined by a number of scholars, research on this topic needs to be extended in at least two ways. First, sex role attitudes of husband and wife would appear to be important but have not been examined thoroughly. Second, other variables known to be associated with female employment have not been adequately controlled (Nye, 1974). The purpose of this paper is to examine with appropriate controls the effects of sex role attitudes and the wife's employment status on marital satisfaction.

Hypotheses

There are at least three alternative hypotheses relevant to the present problem. We have labelled these the role accumulation hypothesis, the role congruence hypothesis, and the neutralization hypothesis.

It is assumed in the role accumulation hypothesis that employment of the wife produces stress which decreases the level of marital satisfaction. Role conflict is viewed as more probably since the wife's occupational role is added to the other family roles. Rapaport and Rapaport (1969) and Bebbington (1973) observed that some stress is often encountered when couples attempt to integrate two occupational roles with the role of maintaining the household. Traditional norms may also be violated when both partners are employed and this may result in guilt feelings and/or informal pressures from significant others.

*This research was supported by the Family Research Institute and the College of Family Living, Brigham Young University, Provo, Utah and in part by Public Health Service grant number RO1 MH 27560 awarded by the Nationa. Institute of Mental Health. We are grateful to F. Ivan Nye for his suggestions during the development of the questionnaire and for permission to use selected items from his questionnaire on family roles. An earlier version of this paper was presented at the annual meeting of the National Council on Family Relations, New York City, October 1976.
**Department of Child Development and Family Relations, Brigham Ycung University, Provo, Utah 84602—U.S.A.
***Department of Child Development and Family Relations, South Dakota State University, Brookings, South Dakota 57006—U.S.A.

Existing data lend modest support to the role accumulation hypothesis. Most studies have found that satisfaction tends to be higher when the wife is not employed but the differences are small (Gianopulos and Mitchell, 1957; Feld, 1963; Axelson, 1963; Gover, 1963; Powell, 1963, Nye, 1963, 1974). This hypothesis appears more characteristic of the lower than middle class (Nye, 1974), perhaps because lower class families do not have the resources to take on an additional role. In recent research Burke and Weir (1 976) found that working wives were more satisfied than housewives, indicating that the expansion of roles had positive benefits for their middle class sample. However, the husband's satisfaction appeared to be less when the wife was employed.

The role congruence hypothesis assumes that the employment status of the wife is relatively unimportant by itself. The important factor is whether her behavior is congruent with the attitudes of the husband and wife. It is hypothesized that among employed wives, the more the attitudes of husband and wife favor employment of the wife, the greater their marital satisfaction. Among housewives it is hypothesized that, the more the attitudes of husband and wife favor employment of the wife, the less their marital satisfaction. This hypothesis is a special case of the more general hypothesis that role congruence has a positive relationship with marital satisfaction (Burr, 1973; Hawkins and Johnsen, 1969; Kotlar, 1965; Mangus, 1957; Sarbin and Allen, 1968).

Avaialable data appear generally consistent with the role congruence hypothesis. When the husband's or wife's attitude was consistent with behavior, whether or not the wife was employed, satisfaction was higher (Nye, 1963, 1974; Gianopulos and Mitchell, 1957). For example, Nye (1961) found that marital satisfaction tended to be less (1) if the wife was employed and the husband and/or wife wished she were not, or (2) if the wife was not employed and the husband and/or wife favored her employment. Nye (1961:118) also compared employed women whose husbands approved of their working with non-employed women whose husbands approved of their not working. He found that marital satisfaction was significantly higher among the non-employed wives. This suggests that there may be some validity to both the role accumulation and role congruence hypotheses.

The neutralization hypothesis states that marital satisfaction is independent of female employment status and attitudes toward female employment. Employed females who do not favor female employment are not necessarily expected to be less satisfied maritally than employed females who favor employment. It is assumed that the particular situation neutralizes the effect of any attitude-behavior discrepancy. For example, one may not favor female employment even though she considers it justifiable in her particular case. Her justification for employment could take many forms, including monetary need or type of child care available. The fact that substantial numbers of mothers of young children are employed when norms proscribe employment (Retert and Bumpass, 1974) indicates that this hypothesis might have some validity. A similar hypothesis has been used by Sykes and Matza (1957) to explain rule violation among juveniles. They maintained that individuals who have internalized a norm use neutralization techniques to rationalize norm violation. Although the neutralization hypothesis has not been discussed in the literature on employed females, it appears plausible and deserves examination.

In this paper we examine female employment status and the attitudes of both husband and wife as they relate to the marital satisfaction of both husband and wife. The data will be useful in assessing the validity of the above three hypotheses. This analysis appears particularly important since in existing data controls for relevant background variables have been inadequate, and differences between the satisfaction of employed and non-employed wives may have diminished in the middle class (Nye, 1974; Burke and Weir, 1976).

Definition and Measurement of Variables

Following Spanier (1976) and Burr (1973), marital satisfaction is viewed as one aspect of overall marital adjustment. It is separate from marital consensus, cohesion, or affection, although it may be influenced by these qualities. Marital satisfaction is a feeling about how one's marriage is doing and may be defined as "the subjectively experienced contentment or gratification with the marital situation as a whole (Burr, 1971:369)." Although there is a debate over the utility of the concept of marital satisfaction (Burr, 1973; Hicks and Platt, 1970; Lively, 1969), it appears to be one useful way to assess the subjective perception an individual has of the quality of his or her marriage. This subjectivity is also the concept's greatest weakness since highly satisfied marriages may vary greatly when assessed by some objective criterion.

Sex role attitudes were divided into two types: (1) Attitude toward a mother of young children being employed; (2) Attitude toward husband and wife role reversal. The first refers to the feelings concerning the acceptability of a mother of preschool children becoming employed if it is not really necessary. Role reversal is the acceptability of the wife becoming the provider while the husband stays home and cares for the children and house. Factor analysis was used as a guide in constructing scales of these dimensions.

Twelve items on various aspects of female employment and role reversal were factor analyzed separately for husbands and wives.[1] A summary of this factor analysis is presented in Table 1. In both analyses two factors emerged, attitude toward mother's employment and attitude toward role reversal.

In constructing scales three criteria were used. First, it was necessary that the items in each scale were consistent conceptually in that they all appeared to measure the intended dimension. Second, a varimax rotated factor loading of .60 was chosen as the minimum for including an item in the scale. Third, only those items that met these criteria for both husbands and wives were included.

Four items in factor one met these criteria and were combined to form an index of attitude toward women's employment. Factor two included two items on

---

[1]The type of factor analysis used was principal factoring without iteration (Nie, et al., 1975:469). Our aim was to determine if some number of items accounted for most of the variance in the data. The coefficients presented in Table 1 are the varimax rotated factor leadings, which in this case are the same as the correlation coefficients between questionnaire items and factors.

attitude toward role reversal which met the criteria for inclusion, and these were added together to form an index.[2]

TABLE 1   SUMMARY OF FACTOR ANALYSIS ON ATTITUDE TOWARD
                        EMPLOYMENT OF MOTHER AND ROLE REVERSAL

	Husbands		Wives	
	Factor 1*	Factor 2*	Factor 1*	Factor 2*
Attitude Toward Mother's Employment (Factor 1)				
1. How do you feel about a married woman with preschool children taking a full-time job outside the home—				
A. If she wants to work and her husband agrees even though they could get along without her income?	.80	.16	.80	.30
B. If she wants to work but her husband does not particularly like the idea and they don't need her income to make ends meet?	.72	.14	.65	.40
C. If the children can be cared for by a close relative or grandmother or aunt?	.84	.13	.71	.26
D. If there is very good care by a neighbor or center nearby?	.82	.25	.80	.31
Attitude Toward Role Reversal (Factor 2)				
2. If the wife is able to earn a better living for the family than the husband, should she go to work while the husband stays home and cares for the children and house?	−.09	−.83	−.20	−.63
3. How would you personally like the arrangement where the wife is mainly responsible for earning the living and the husband is mainly responsible for housekeeping and child care?	.07	.86	.06	.84

*Varimax rotated factor loadings.

To construct an index of marital satisfaction five items which appeared to measure this dimension were factor analyzed. Table 2 shows the results of this analysis.[3] All five items met our criteria of inclusion and were summed to form

[2]In constructing the scales, the items that met the criteria of inclusion were added together (items with negative coefficients were subtracted). This is a commonly used method of scale construction and justification for this type of procedure is given by Alwin (1973). Alwin noted that there was a very high correlation between factor score procedures and the method of equal weighting, which was the method used in the present paper.
[3]A factor analysis was also performed on the 10 items together (5 for husbands and 5 for wives). Two factors emerged with the 5 items of the husband forming one factor and the 5 items of the wife making up the second factor. All factor loadings were greater than .60. This indicated that the five items form a single dimension but that the satisfaction of the husband does not necessarily coincide with the satisfaction of the wife.

the scale of marital satisfaction. This scale is similar to the dimension "dyadic satisfaction" identified by Spanier (1976) in a recent factor analysis of another sample.

TABLE 2   FACTOR ANALYSIS OF FIVE MARITAL SATISFACTION ITEMS

	Husbands*	Wives*
1. Have you ever wished you had not married?	.79	.82
2. If you had your life to live over again would you marry the same person?	−.76	−.77
3. Do you and your mate generally talk things over?	.72	.76
4. Number of items that have caused serious difficulties in your marriage (16 items)	−.77	−.74
5. The degree of happiness of your marriage	.74	.71

*This is the unrotated factor matrix since only one factor emerged and rotation made no sense.

Sample

The sample consisted of 539 names randomly drawn from the telephone and Polk directories of metropolitan Salt Lake City. During the Fall of 1974, two questionnaires were mailed to each name with a letter requesting responses from both husband and wife. Usable questionnaires from both spouses were returned by 232 couples, a return rate of 42%.[4] A comparison of the sample with U.S. Census data on education and income is shown in Table 3. Although the sample had a number of similarities to the U.S. Census data, individuals with low incomes were underrepresented while those in the middle income category (10,000 to 14,999) were overrepresented. There was also an underrepresentation of the highly educated.

Analysis

Multiple regression analysis was used because it allowed us to estimate the effects of sex role attitudes while controlling for nine relevant background varia-

[4]Both types of directories were used in an attempt to compensate for the deficiencies of each. Actually 408 names were originally drawn from the telephone directory but 108 were eliminated because they were found to be single, widowed, deceased, divorced, unable to read, or not locatable and thus were not in the population under study. The Polk directory was used to draw 279 names of which 40 were eliminated for the same reasons. This left 300 and 239 names from the telephone and Polk directories respectively. Two questionnaires were mailed to each name with a letter requesting that both husband and wife fill them out independently and return them. The first questionnaire was followed by a reminder post card, a second questionnaire, and finally a third questionnaire sent by certified mail. There may have been some nonrespondents who were not married as only those who could positively be identified as not currently married were eliminated. Thus, 42% return rate is conservative and might have been higher if the married population could have been identified more precisely.

TABLE 3   FAMILY INCOME AND EDUCATION OF HEAD FOR SALT LAKE
                           SAMPLE, CENSUS DATA OF SALT LAKE CITY, AND CENSUS
                           DATA OF UNITED STATES (in percent)

		Sample: Salt Lake City	Census: Salt Lake City*	Census: United States**
Family	Less than $3.000	3.1%	4.8%	3.8%
Income	$3,000—4,999	1.3	6.7	6.5
	5,000—6,999	11.1	10.8	8.0
	7,000—9,999	13.7	24.6	12.7
	10,000—14,999	40.3	31.9	24.7
	15,000 and over	30.6	21.2	44.3
Education	Less than 8 years	2.2%	4.8%	10.1%
	8 years	8.7	6.0	10.4
	9-11 years	26.1	18.6	14.6
	12 years	30.0	33.0	34.2
	13-15 years	21.7	19.1	13.4
	16 or more years	11.3	18.4	17.3

*Source: U.S. Bureau of Census, *Census of Population: 1970, Vol. 1, Charcteristics of the Population, Part 46, Utah*, U.S Government Printing Office, Washington, D.C., 1973, Table 198, page 545 and Table 202, page 559.

**Source: U.S. Bureau of Census, *Statistical Abstract of the United States: 1975* (96th edition). Washington, D.C., 1975, Table 646, page 396.

bles including income and occupation of husband, age and education of wife, age at marriage of husband and wife, religious status, number of children, and stage of family life cycle. As mentioned earlier, these controls are critical because there are known differences between employed and non-employed females on these characteristics (Nye, 1974).

The location of the sample resulted in 75 percent of the respondents being members of the "Mormon" religion. Therefore, religion was dichotomized into Mormon and non-Mormon for this control. Age at marriage was dichotomized into teenage marriage and those who married at age 20 or above. Since previous research has shown that the presence of preschool children may be important, life cycle was dichotomized into those with and without preschoolers. The controls, age, education, occupation, and income were all entered as continuous variables.

Findings

Initially, we examined the relationship between female employment and marital satisfaction. The data indicate that both husbands and wives were slightly more satisfied when the wife was not employed (r=.01 for wives and .09 for husbands). The zero-order and partial correlations were almost identical, indicating that this relationship is not due to the nine control variables. It may be concluded that modest support for the role accumulation hypothesis exists.

The next step in the analysis was to estimate the effects of sex role attitudes on marital satisfaction within the housewife and employed-wife categories. This allowed us to determine whether the interaction between attitudes and employment status existed as expected by the role congruence hypothesis. The findings are presented in Table 4.

TABLE 4   SUMMARY OF REGRESSION OF MARITAL SATISFACTION ON ATTITUDE TOWARD EMPLOYMENT OF MOTHERS AND ROLE REVERSAL

Employment Status of Wife	Dependent Variable	Independent Variable	r	β**
Wife Not Employed (N=139)	Wife's Satisfaction	Wife's attitude toward employment of mother	—.10	.09
		Husband's attitude toward employment of mother	—.17*	—.13
		Wife's attitude toward role reversal	—.13	—.15*
		Husband's attitude toward role reversal	—.17*	—.08
	Husband's Satisfaction	Wife's attitude toward employment of mother	—.17*	—.02
		Husband's attitude toward employment of mother	—.26*	—.17*
		Wife's attitude toward role reversal	—.20*	—.18*
		Husband's attitude toward role reversal	—.23*	—.13
Wife Employed (N=86)	Wife's Satisfaction	Wife's attitude towards employment of mother	—.21	—.40*
		Husband's attitude toward employment of mother	.16	.34*
		Wife's attitude toward role reversal	.03	.15
		Husband's attitude toward role reversal	—.06	—.23*
	Husband's Satisfaction	Wife's attitude toward employment of mother	—.20	—.39*
		Husband's attitude toward employment of mother	.06	.22
		Wife's attitude toward role reversal	18	.33*
		Husband's attitude toward role reversal	—.08	—.22*

* Probability less than .05

** The control variables were income and occupation of husband, age and education of wife, age at marriage of husband and wife, religious affiliation of husband, number of children, and stage of family life cycle.

Among couples in which the wife was employed the data were only partially consistent with the role congruence hypothesis. As expected, the more the husband favored the employment of mothers, the greater the satisfaction of both husband and wife. However, contrary to the hypothesis, the more the wife's attitude favored female employment, the lower the satisfaction of both husband and wife.

When working wife favored role reversal both she and her husband tended to be more satisfied than if she was less inclined toward role reversal. This relationship was considerably stronger for the husband's than wife's satisfaction. Contrary to the role congruence hypothesis, satisfaction of both husband and wife tended to be less if the husband of an employed wife was inclined toward switching roles with his wife.

Among couples in which the wife was not employed the relationships were small but generally consistent with the role congruence hypothesis. Marital satisfaction tended to have a negative relationship with the attitudinal variables. However, the only independent variable that had a significant effect on the satisfaction of both husband and wife was the wife's attitude toward role reversal.

Discussion

Although marital satisfaction tended to be higher when the wife was not employed, the differences were small. Support for the role accumulation hypothesis is at best modest and it may be concluded that employment status of the wife has a small influence on marital satisfaction. Perhaps the role accumulation hypothesis could be characterized as incomplete, since it appears more realistic to assess attitudes in conjunction with employment status.

The lay observer might say that the role congruence hypothesis is an elaboration of the obvious, that of course satisfaction will be higher when attitudes and behavior are congruent. The fact that many previous studies did not take attitudes into account suggests that the hypothesis is less obvious than it appears on the surface. The present data suggest that the "obvious" should not necessarily be accepted at face value but should be subjected to empirical tests.

One might ask why satisfaction among employed wives would tend to be less when the wife favored female employment. The neutralization hypothesis provides a possible explanation. Retert and Bumpass (1974) found that a norm proscribing the employment of mothers of preschool children is strong and pervasive in America. A mother who works may use neutralization techniques to justify her violation of the norm. However, if her attitude is favorable to female employment the discrepancy might be magnified rather than neutralized. Her attitude might create and/or intensify conflicts between her and her husband or elicit subtle sanctions from significant others. In this way her attitude might adversely affect the marital satisfaction of both partners even though her attitude (favoring employment) and behavior (employment) are consistent.

The attitude of the husband may have different effects, however. If his attitude favors female employment it may be perceived as support in return for her willingness to share the provider role. This type of support may be helpful to the wife given the general norm against female employment. If the husband's attitude is against female employment this might be viewed as a lack of appreciation for her attempt to help the family economically, while the opposite may occur if he is more positive toward female employment.

If the above explanation is correct, one might ask why attitude toward role reversal does not operate in the same fashion. Recall that satisfaction decreased as the husband's attitude toward role reversal became more positive, while satisfaction tended to increase as the wife's attitude became more favorable toward role reversal. Given that a strong norm exists which prescribes the provider role to the male (Nye, 1976), his favoring role reversal might be perceived as an abdication of his primary responsibility. This may result in subtle sanctions from significant others and could increase conflict between husband and wife. Some wives might perceive it as an attempt to place too much of the provider role on them and a lack of appreciation for their monetary contribution. On the other hand, a wife whose attitude is favorable to role reversal might be perceived as supporting her husband. Her attitude may signify her willingness to help in the provider role while he helps in the housekeeper role.

In summary, we have explained the present findings by referring to norms which prescribe the provider role to the man and the child care role to the wife. It appears that employed females may adhere to the norms attitudinally by using neutralization techniques to justify their employment. However, a woman who attitudinally refutes this norm may meet with resistance while a similar attitude by the husband may be perceived as support for his wife. Circumstances may justify norm violation, but attempts by a female to discount the norm are another thing. Similarly, a husband who favors role reversal is probably seen in a different light than a wife who favors role reversal. She may be seen as a competent female who is able to contribute to the family income and expects household help from her husband. On the other hand, his attitude might be viewed as a serious violation of the norm and an attempt to relinquish a male responsibility.

We emphasize that these explanations are speculative and post hoc. They have been offered after-the-fact as plausible explanations of the data and need to be subjected to empirical tests. Hopefully, our discussion will stimulate an examination of these issues.

There are at least two other possible interpretations of the data. First, the results might be due to the nature of the sample since it had a middle class bias and 75 per cent of the respondents were members of the Mormon religion. Second, some might argue that the results are an artifact of an invalid measure of marital satisfaction.

To minimize the sample limitation, occupation and income of husband, education of wife, and religious status (Mormon, non-Mormon) were entered as control variables. Thus, the results do not appear to be explainable by the sampling limitations. There is also evidence available that Mormon couples do not differ from non-Mormon couples on marital satisfaction and other family variables (Bahr and Bahr, 1977; Rollins and Cannon, 1974). Furthermore, since it was within the middle class that the effects of female employment appear to have diminished (Nye, 1974), it appears justifiable to use a middle class sample.

The measure of marital satisfaction used in the present study is similar to those often used in the literature (Locke and Wallace, 1959; Spanier, 1976). The major limitation of these instruments is the tendency for individual to respond in a socially desirable manner (Laws, 1971; Edmonds, 1967; Edmonds, Withers, and Dibatista, 1972). Despite this limitation, there is evidence that social desirability accounts for a relatively small amount of the variance in marital satisfaction scales (Hawkins, 1966). In addition, Spanier (1976:22-23) recently provided evidence of content, criterion, and construct validity for his dyadic adjustment scale. Therefore, it appears unlikely that the present findings can be discounted because of social desirability.

A Replication

One of the ways to overcome sampling and measurement problems is to replicate a finding using a different sample and measurement technique. In the present paper we attempted to do this using data from the National Longitudinal Survey (NLS) of Labour Market Experience. The NLS data set contains a question on attitude toward the employment of mothers that is very similar to one used in the Salt Lake sample.

The NLS data were obtained from a national probability sample in which four different age-sex groups were sampled, males' age 45-59, males' age 14-24, females' age 30-44, and females' age 14-24. In each group approximately 5000 individuals were interviewed, 1500 blacks and 3500 whites. Only the two female cohorts contained data relevant to the present problem. Each of the younger females was interviewed annually for a period of five years beginning in 1968, while each of the older females was interviewed five times over a six year period beginning 1967.[5] Our analysis was restricted to individuals who were married at the time of the first interview, and this reduced the samples of the younger and older cohorts to about 1200 and 3300 respectively.

In their initial interview the NLS respondents were asked if a married woman with children under twelve should take a full-time job outside the home, if she wants to work and her husband agrees.[6] The comparable question in the Salt

---

[5]For a more complete description of the sample and data collection procedures see the "National Longitudinal Surveys Handbook" which is available from the NLS Users Center, Center for Human Resources Research, 1375 Perry Street, Suite 585, Ohio State University, Columbus, Ohio 43201.

[6]The question was phrased somewhat differently for the two cohorts. The younger females were asked how they felt about a woman with several children under school age taking a full-time job outside the home, if she prefers to work, her husband agrees, and a trusted relative who can care for the children lives nearby. The older females were asked how they felt about a woman with a child between 6 and 12 taking a full-time job outside the home, if she wants to work and her husband agrees.

Lake data had a factor loading of .80 in the factor analysis reported in Table 1.

The NLS survey did not include data on marital satisfaction but information regarding marital stability was collected. It is reasonable to assume that individuals who divorce or separate are dissatisfied with their marrige, and therefore, stability was used as an indicator of marital satisfaction. The limitation of using marital stability in this manner is that many individuals who are dissatisfied with their marriages may nevertheless remain in that marriage.

Those individuals who were married at the initial interview and remained married during all subsequent interviews were classified as stable. Those who were married at the initial interview and were separated or divorced at a subsequent interview were classified as unstable. The question on attitude toward female employment was obtained during the initial interview when all the respondents were married and living with their spouses. This allowed us to determine how their attitudes at the initial interview affected subsequent marital stability.

To replicate the findings of the Salt Lake sample tabular analysis was used. Multiple regression analysis was not used because the dependent variable, marital stability, was dichotomous and highly skewed (the rate of instability was 15% and 7% for the young and mature females respectively).

The females who were employed at the initial interview dissolved their marriages at a slightly higher rate than the non-employed females. Among the older cohort the rate of instability was 8% and 5% for the employed and non-employed females respectively. For the younger group the comparable percentages were 16% and 14% respectively.

The respondents were also asked how their husband felt about their working, or if they were not employed, how he would feel about their becoming employed. The data from both cohorts were consistent with the role congruence hypothesis. For example, the rate of instability for the older females was 7% among housewives whose husband would like it very much if she went to work, while it was only 3% if the husband would strongly dislike the employment of his wife. Among employed wives, the trend was reversed; if the husband was pleased that his wife was employed the instability rate was 8% while it was 13% if the husband had a strong dislike for the employment of his wife.

Perhaps the most important aspect of the NLS analysis is the data from the employed females. Recall the intriguing finding of the Salt Lake data that marital satisfaction tended to be *less* when *employed* wives favored female employment The NLS data relevant to this question are shown in Table 5. Marital dissolution tended to be less when the employed females felt it was not all right for mothers to be employed. The trend was not as strong among the older females, but those who felt employment was "definitely not all right" had a dissolution rate at least 3 percent less than the other categories.

TABLE 5 PERCENT OF EMPLOYED FEMALES WITH UNSTABLE MARRIAGES BY ATTITUDE TOWARD EMPLOYMENT OF MOTHERS: NLS DATA*

Cohort	Attitude Toward the Employment of Mothers**			
	Definitely All Right	Probably All Right	Probably Not All Right	Definitely Not All Right
Young	17%	17%	12%	11%
Females	(205)	(215)	(73)	(74)
Older	8%	10%	9%	5%
Females	(746)	(561)	(124)	(144)

* The question was phrased somewhat differently for the two cohorts. The younger females were asked how they felt about a woman with several children under school age taking a full-time job outside the home, if she prefers to work, her husband agrees, and a trusted relative who can care for the children lives nearby. The older females were asked how they felt about a woman with a child between 6 and 12 taking a full-time job outside the home, if she wants to work and her husband agrees.

** The numbers in parentheses are the base from which the percentages were computed. Thus, 17% of the 205 young females who responded "definitely all right" to the question became divorced or separated. Data from the neutral response category were omitted because the number of cases was extremely small.

Summary and Conclusion

In this paper we examined the effects of sex role attitudes and female employment status on the marital satisfaction of 232 Salt Lake City couples. The findings may be summarized as follows: (1) When the wife was not employed the marital satisfaction of both husband and wife tended to be slightly higher than when the wife was employed fulltime. (2) Among couples in which the wife was not employed marital satisfaction tended to be slightly higher if husband and wife were attitudinally against female employment and role reversal. (3) Among couples in which the wife was employed marital satisfaction tended to be higher if (a) the wife's attitude did not and the husband's attitude did favor female employment and (b) the wife's attitude did and the husband's attitude did not favor role reversal. Some speculative interpretations of the findings were given. As a check on the findings, particularly when the wife was employed, data from the National Longitudinal Survey of Labor Market Experience were analyzed and found to be consistent with the results from the Salt Lake sample. This lends credibility to the findings and suggests that they are not the result of sampling bias or invalid measurement of marital satisfaction.

In the present study only two types of sex role attitudes were examined. Future research needs to explore this problem using other attitudinal variables. For example, a more extensive study of attitudes toward role sharing would be valuable.

REFERENCES

Alwin, Duane F.
1973   "The use of factor analysis in the construction of linear composites in social research." Sociological Methods and Research 2 (November): 191-211.

Axelson, Leland J.
1963   "The marital adjustment and marital role definitions of working and non-working wives." Marriage and Family Living 25 (May): 189-195.

Bahr, Stephen J. and Howard M. Bahr
1977   "Religion and family roles: a comparison of Catholic, Mormon, and Protestant families." Pp. 45-61 in Phillip R. Kunz (ed.), The Mormon Family. Provo, Utah: Family Research Center, Brigham Young University.

Bebbington, A.C.
1973   "The functions of stress in the establishment of the dual-career family." Journal of Marriage and Family 35 (August): 530-537.

Burke, Ronald J. and Tamara Weir
1976   "Relationship of wives employment status to husband, wife and pair satisfaction and performance." Journal of Marriage and the Family 38 (May): 229-287.

Burr, Wesley R.
1971   "An expansion and test of a role theory of marital satisfaction." Journal of Marriage and the Family 33 (May): 368-372.
1973   Theory Construction and the Sociology of the Family. New York: John Wiley.

Carter, Hugh and Paul C. Click
1976   Marriage and Divorce: A Social and Economic Study (Revised Edition). Cambridge, Massachusetts: Harvard University Press.

Edmonds, Vernon H.
1967   "Marital conventionalization: definition and measurement." Journal of Marriage and the Family 29 (November): 681-688.

Edmonds, Vernon H., Glenne Withers, and Beverly Dibatista
1972   "Adjustment, conservatism, and marital conventionalization." Journal of Marriage and the Family 34 (February): 96-103.

Feld, Sheila
1963   "Feelings of adjustment: Pp. 331-352 in F. Ivan Nye and Lois W. Hoffman (eds.), The Employed Mother in America. Chicago: Rand McNally.

Gianopulos, Artie and Howard E. Mitchell
1957   "Marital disagreement in working wife marriages as a function of husband's attitude toward wife's employment." Marriage and Family Living 19 (November): 373-378.

Gover, David A.
1963   "Socio-economic differentials in the relationship between marital adjustment and wife's employment status." Marriage and Family Living 25 (November): 452-456.

Hawkins, James L.
1966   "The Locke marital adjustment test and social desirability." Journal of Marriage and the Family 28 (May): 193-195.

Hawkins, James L. and Kathryn Johnsen
1969   "Perception of behavioral conformity, imputation of consensus, and marital satisfaction." Journal of Marriage and the Family 31 (August): 507-511.

Hicks, Mary W. and Marilyn Platt
1970   "Marital happiness and stability: a review of the research in the sixties." Journal of
        Marriage and the Family, 32 (November): 553-574.

Kotlar, Sally L.
1965   "Middle-class marital role perceptions and marital adjustment." Sociology and
        Social Research, 49 (April): 283-293.

Laws, Judith Long
1971   "A feminist review of marital adjustment literature; the rape of the Locke." Journal
        of Marriage and the Family, 33 (August): 483-516.

Lively, Edwin L.
1969   "Toward concept clarification; the case of marital interaction." Journal of Marriage
        and the Family, 31 (February): 108-114.

Locke, Harvey J. and Karl M. Wallace
1959   "Short marital adjustment and prediction tests: their reliability and validity."
        Marriage and Family Living, 21 (August): 251-255.

Mangus, A.R.
1957   "Role theory and marriage counseling." Social Forces, 35 (March): 200-209.

Nie, Norman H., C. Hadlai Hull, Jean G. Jenkins, Karin Steinbrunner, and Dale Bent
1975   Statistical Package for the Social Sciences (Second Edition). New York: McGraw
        Hill.

Nye, F. Ivan
1961   "Maternal employment and marital interaction: some contingent conditions."
        Social Forces, 40 (December): 113-119.
1963   "Marital interaction." Pp. 263-281 in F. Ivan Nye and Lois W. Hoffman (eds.)
        The Employed Mother in America. Chicago: Rand McNally.
1974   "Husband-wife relationship." Pp. 186-206 in Lois W. Hoffman and F. Ivan Nye,
        Working Mothers. San Francisco: Jossey-Bass.
1976   "Role Structure and Analysis of the Family." Beverly Hills, California: Sage
        Publications.

Powell, Kathryn S.
1963   "Personalities of children and child-rearing attitudes of mothers." Pp. 125-132 in F.
        Ivan Nye and Lois W. Hoffman (eds.), The Employed Mother in America. Chicago:
        Rand McNally.

Rapaport, Rhona and Robert N. Rapaport
1969   "The dual career family: a variant pattern and social change." Human Relations
        22(1): 3-30.

Retert, Sandra L. and Larry L. Bumpass
1974   "Employment and approval of employment among mothers of young children."
        Madison, Wisconsin: Working paper 74-4, Center for Demography and Ecology,
        University of Wisconsin.

Rollins, Boyd C. and Kenneth L. Cannon
1974   "Marital satisfaction over the family life cycle: a reevaluation." Journal of Marriage
        and the Family 36 (May): 271-282.

Sarbin, Theodore R. and Vernon L. Allen
1968   "Role theory." Pp. 488-576 in G. Lindzey and E. Aaronson (eds.) The Handbook of
        Social Psychology (2nd ed.), Volume 1. Reading, Massachusetts: Addison-
        Wesley.

Spanier, Graham B.
  1976   "Measuring dyadic adjustment: new scales for assessing the quality of marriage and similar dyads." Journal of Marriage and the Famliy, 38 (February): 15-28.

Sykes, Gresham M. and David Matza
  1957   "Techniques of neutralization: a theory of delinquency." American Journal of Sociology, 22 (December): 664-670.

U.S. Bureau of Census
  1973   Census of Population; 1970, Volume 1, Characteristics of the Population, Part 46, Utah. U.S. Government Printing Office, Washington, D.C.
  1975   Statistical Abstract of the United States: 1975 (96th edition). Washington, D.C.

18

Some Aspirations of
Lower Class Black Mothers

ROBERTA H. JACKSON*

A common assumption in many quarters is that indigent black mothers produce offspring for whom they have few or no positive aspirations. The assertion that low aspirations develop during early socialization in the black family is not consistent with the fact that "three-fourths of the blacks enrolled in college during 1970 came from homes in which family heads had no college education," (Hill, 1971 : 40). The findings from the study of Williams and Stockton (1973:46) reveal that 90 per cent of the ghetto dwelling parents in 111 families hoped that their children would attain a college degree.

Rainwater and Yancey (1967) suggest that some of the current controversial issues covering life among black families, and especially those within the lower class, have been influenced by Moynihan's (1965) report. While contrasting old and new views about the black family, Lieberman (1973:10) states that in the past the research revealed an underlying strain of ethnocentrism. More specifically, he maintains that black families were seen as if they were all lower class.

Family size helps to perpetuate the allegation that indigent black mothers have very low aspirations for their children. On an average, ghetto dwelling black families are often headed by female parents who tend to have several children. According to the *U.S, Bureau of the Census* (1974:3), "In 1973, black female heads of families were more likely than their white counterparts to have children to support, and of those with children, a larger proportion of blacks than whites had 2 or more children...However, the total fertility rate in 1970 of 3.10 children per black woman was still substantially higher than that of 2.34 for white women." In speaking of the bases for the patterning of life among lower class black families Billingsley (1968:143) reports family size may serve as both an obstacle and a facilitator of achievement.

A myth in many quarters is that inadequate education causes many indigent black mothers to have no positive aspirations for their offspring. This is an unfair accusation, for research has shown that lower class mothers, both black and white, have expressed interest in the future of their children. Data from a study made by Bennett and Gist (1964) reveal that two-thirds of 114 lower class black mothers and a similar per cent of 90 indigent white mothers often discussed education with their offspring. The majority, or 88 per cent, of 77 poor white mothers and 63 per

* Associate Professor, School of Education, University of North Carolina at Chapel Hill, Chape Hill, North Carolina, 27514, U.S.A.

cent of 102 indigent black female parents were also directive in specifying the kind of school their children should attend. In reference to maternal intensity to attempt to influence occupational choice of their offspring, 90 per cent of 77 lower class white female parents and 70 per cent of 100 black mothers performed in the same manner.

Hyman (1953:432) discussed the findings of Roper's 1945 study which dealt with parental desire for children to attend college. The following question was asked : "After the war, if you had a son (daughter) graduating from high school would you prefer that he (she) go on to college, or would you rather have him (her) do something else, or wouldn't you care one way or another?" A majority, or 91 per cent, of the wealthy and 68 per cent of the poor parents desired a college education for their offspring. When Roper's respondents were grouped according to age, sex and social class, mothers appeared to be more conscious of their social class level than fathers when they expressed educational desires for their children. A comparison of Roper's finding in a national survey of high school youth (1942:9) with data from his study in 1945 suggests that regardless of social class and age, mothers tend to have more influence than fathers upon the educational aspirations for their offspring.

Data collected by the National Opinion Research Center (1947) in a nation-wide survey show that within a sample of approximately 2,500 adults and 500 youths, about one-half of the entire group indicated that they regarded "some college training" as their answer to the question : "About how much schooling do you think most young men need these days?" Only 39 per cent of the 856 lower class respondents felt that "some college training" was necessary, but 68 per cent of 512 upper class respondents felt the need for a college education. The differential emphasis between upper and lower classes upon college education as an essential to advancement reveals that the lower class emphasized college training much less.

In Bell's (1965:497) study of Negro mothers' aspirations for their children, lower class female parents were placed in two categories. Those assigned "low status" had 0-8 years of education and 7 or more children. Mothers who had 9 or more years of formal training and 6 or fewer children were given "high status." There was a significant difference between the female parents' educational aspirations for their daughters in that 61 per cent of the high status and only 39 per cent of the low status mothers desired a college education for their female offspring. Educational aspirations for sons revealed a statistically significant difference between the high and the low status mothers. A desire for sons to attend college was expressed by only 44 per cent of the low status mothers, but 65 per cent of the female parents with high status wanted their children to receive a college degree. By sex of the child, there were no differences in the educational aspirations for offspring among the two groups of mothers.

In Bell's study, regardless of status, the mothers showed no significant differences in their occupational preferences for sons. Forty seven percent of all the mothers wanted professional jobs for their male children. The low status mothers were more definitive in their occupational aspirations for daughters than for sons. Only 10 per cent of the mothers responded, "don't know" about job preferences for daughters, but 29 per cent gave similar responses for sons. However, there were no significant differences in the occupational aspirations for male and female offspring among the high status mothers.

In describing the relationship of the sexual roles adopted by boys and girls to the separate and curious effect that American attitudes have had on the past, Grier and Cobbs (1968:121) had this to say : "It has often been observed that black parents push girls in the family to remain in school and in many ways encourage them and make higher education more accessible to them. On the other hand, the family may discourage its sons, urge them to drop out of school, and make it difficult for them to obtain an education." The explanation of the significance of sex differentials in educational aspirations of low income black mothers, especially in the past, is simple. Often the sons worked in order to help their sisters to remain in school. The black mother was concerned about all of her children, but the daughters in the family had to be protected from those who would exploit them, which was common in the event that they had menial jobs.

Many black mothers have worried about the safety of their sons and have also felt that their male offspring without the benefits of eduction, stood little chance of becoming self sustaining citizens. The description given by Grier and Cobbs (1968:122-124) provides further explanation of sex differentials in education :

...For the boys, the world was quite a different place. It was exceedingly dangerous, and the first task was to develop a style of life which allowed one to survive...This played a part in the division of roles in girls who went to school and boys who dropped out. For in one sense school was seen by black families in a very special way. Beset on all sides by a cruel enemy, school was often primarily a refuge—a place of safety for those who were to be protected —and in a sense it was a case of women and children first...

Education serves as a force to gain both family stability and mobility. During the past 4 years some gains in education have been made by a small segment of the black population, but there is need for greater progress in this area. This necessity is revealed in a report of the U.S. *Bureau of the Census* (1974:3): "By 1973, about 8 per cent of black adults 25 to 34 years old had completed a college education. Despite these continuing gains, the proportion of black adults completing high school or college was still well below that of whites." With respect to the wishes of black parents Billingsley (1968:181-182) had this to say, "Ask almost any Negro family head what he (or she) wishes for his family, and the response will be 'a decent house in a decent neighborhood.' Ask that same perent what he wishes most for his children and the response will be 'a decent effective education'."

Some critics of lower class familles maintain that black mothers have children without any thought to their future success, because 'welfare is a way of life'. Many lower class black female parents with unemployed husbands, find jobs and refuse to subject their children to the stigma which is often associated with public welfare. In a number of states when the father loses his job, he must desert his family in order for it to qualify for public assistance. While discussing the importance of the instrumental functions of the family, Billingsley (1968:24) reminds us that the recently developed and expanded legal protections for low income blacks have revealed family break-up following the loss of the job of the husband and the father.

"In 1973 the median income of black families was $7,270, about 58 per cent of the $12,600 for white families...The proportion (16 per cent) of families with less than $3,000 was lower than the 1965 level...The proportion of black families at the lower end (under $3,000) of the income distribution had not changed over the last 4 years," (*U.S. Bureau of the Census*, 1974:15). Within black families, Billingsley (1968:143) suggests that, "A second basis for patterning is socio-economic. Even among the lower class, there are at least three major groupings, the working *nonpoor, the working poor* and the *nonworking poor*." Unfortunately in our economy, lower class blacks are the last to be hired and the first to be fired.

Limited information is available on the aspirations for offspring of lower class black mothers. This study was made in an effort to advance our knowledge in one segment of the many problems which have a tendency to plague lower class black families. This report is focused toward determining whether family size, education and income have any influence upon the aspirations for offspring of lower class black mothers.

SAMPLE AND PROCEDURES

The sample consisted of 441 subjects randomly selected from lower class black female parents who lived in low-income housing projects in a small southeastern city with a population of almost 100,000.

The instrument for data collection was a questionnaire administered by interview to each of the 441 mothers. Contained in the instrument were items which dealt with faimly size, education, and income. In addition, each mother was asked : "What kind of job would you like your child to have once he (or she) has become an adult?"

The aspirations which the mother expressed for a daughter and a son 18 years of age or younger were classified as positive, democratic, undecided or negative. A positive response included the preference for any job or profession. The decractic response involved the mother's desire for the child to chose a profession. An undecided response represented replies such as: "I'm not quite sure just now," "My child's future depends upon how long I have a job," or "If my health remains good, I will decide just what I want my child to do." A negative response had to do with complete indiference on the part of the mother, for example, some mothers said, "I don't care what he (or she) does."

Since family size, education and income constituted 3 independent variables, and the data in terms of frequencies were in discrete categories, the chi-square test of independence was used to determine any influence of the 3 independent variables upon the aspirations for offspring of the 441 lower class black mothers.

RESULTS

When the maternal aspirations were tabulated according to family size, education and income, the majority of the responses were positive. Each of the 3 independent variables were significantly related to the aspirations for offspring of the mothers (chi-squares significant beyond .01).

Family Size. Within the 441 families there were 2,362 individuals among whom were 168 fathers, 441 mothers, 1690 siblings (856 brothers and 834 sisters) along with 63 relatives of either the mothers or the fathers. Family size ranged from 3 to 11 members with the average household containing 5 persons. The mean number of siblings per family was 4. On an average, the total fertility rate of the 441 lower class black mothers was higher than the 1970 total fertility rate of 3.10 children per black woman.

Table 1 shows that 367, or 83 per cent, of the 441 mothers gave information about family size and aspirations for their daughters. Almost three-fourths, or 73 per cent, of the 367 responding female parents expressed positive aspirations for their female children. That is, these mothers wanted their daughters to have definite occupations and careers. Positive aspirations for daughters were almost equally divided between mothers in families with 7 or more members and those with 6 or fewer individuals. Among the 208 mothers who desired professional employment for their daughters 127, or 61 per cent, of them were in large families with 7 or more persons, and each mother was gainfully employed. This finding is

TABLE 1   FAMILY SIZE AND MATERNAL ASPIRATIONS FOR OFFSPRING

FAMILY SIZE	Maternal Aspirations for Daughters					Maternal Aspirations for Sons				
	P*	D**	U***	N****	Total	P*	D**	U***	N****	Total
11-12	7	0	0	0	7	5	1	0	1	7
9-10	36	0	0	0	36	20	9	0	4	33
7-8	92	5	0	4	101	113	10	0	30	153
5-6	61	20	17	18	116	55	14	5	15	89
3-4	73	18	12	4	107	22	9	4	13	48
Total	269	43	29	26	367	215	43	9	63	330

* Positive
** Democratic
*** Undecided
**** Negative

(Daughters) $X^2 = 67.46$

Significant beyond .01 at 12 d.f.

(Sons) $X^2 = 33.03$

Significant beyond .01 at 12 d.f.

comparable to that of Bell's "high status" mothers (1965). However, 118 or 53 per cent of the mothers in families with 6 or fewer members also expressed desires for their daughters to become professionals such as doctors, dentists, lawyers, teachers, nurses, and so on.

In comparison to Bell's (1965) report that 10 per cent of the mothers in large families responded "I don't know" when asked about occupational aspirations for their daughters, none of the 144 mothers in families of 7 or more individuals gave similar responses. Contrary to the findings of Bell, 13 per cent of the 223 mothers in families of 6 or fewer members said that they "did not know" or were "undecided". These findings tend to support the idea that lower class black mothers of large families are more definitive in their occupational aspirations for daughters than indigent black female parents in smaller families. A chi-square of .01 indicates that a definite relationship exists between family size and the occupational aspirations for daughters of lower class black mothers.

Table 1 also shows that 330 of the 441 female parents stated both family size and aspirations for their sons. Within this group 215, or 65 per cent, of the mothers were positive in their aspirations for male offspring. This group of female parents wanted their sons to have useful and respectable lives. These findings also suggest that family size has a definite influence upon the aspirations of lower class black mothers for their sons. The degree of this relationship is indicated by chi-square significant beyond the .01 level. Three-fifths, or 129, of the 215 mothers who expressed positive aspirations for sons hoped that their male offspring would obtain work of a professional nature. Within the group of 129 mothers, 116 of them lived in families of 7 or more members. These data imply that lower class black mothers with large families are becoming increasingly aware that daughters as well as sons should be urged to remain in school.

The near majority (60 per cent) of professional aspirations for sons among mothers in large families is higher than the 47 per cent of professional occupations desired for sons by mothers in large families as reported by Bell (1965 : 497). Of interest was the fact that among 137 mothers in families of 6 or fewer individuals, 44 per cent of them desired professional careers for their sons. A small group of 9, or 6 per cent, of the 137 mothers in small families were not definitive in their aspirations for male offspring in that they gave responses such as, "I don't know," or "undecided." On the other hand, 10 per cent of the mothers in families with 7 or more persons were not definitive in their job preferences for their sons. Again, the findings in this study appear to be more favorable than those of Bell's (1965) in reference to definitive aspirations of mothers for sons in large families, for 29 per cent of Bell's mothers in similar households were not definitive about aspirations for their male children.

An analysis of positive maternl aspirations for offspring, according to family size, reveals that lower class black mothers in both large and small families show no differences in their positive aspirations for daughters. Female parents in large families were more definitive in their job preferences for daughters than mothers in small families. The female parents showed no differences in their democratic responses for male and female offspring. More than 3 times as many of the mothers were lacking in decisions about aspirations for their daughters than for their sons. Less than 10 per cent of the female parents felt negatively about the future success of their daughters, while one-fifth of the mothers gave similar responses concerning their male children. Lower class black mothers are slightly more positive in their occupational aspirations for daughters than for sons. This finding is a corroborant for a statement made by Grier and Cobles (168 : 121), "It has often been observed that black parents push girls in the family to remain in school and in many ways encourage them and make higher education more accessible to them."

Education. On an average, the 441 mothers had obtained a mean grade level of 8.1 years. Educational attainment for these female parents ranged from 5-6 years of formal training (less than 10 per cent) to those who had attended institutions of higher learning for 1-2 years (3 per cent). A tabulation of maternal aspirations for daughters with educational attainment of the mothers revealed that 367 female parents responded. (See Table 2). Within this group, almost three-fourths, or 73 per cent of them expressed positive aspirations for their daughters.

The data in Table 2 also show that certain patterns are found in the relatoinship of aspirations for offspring to the educational attainment of indigent black female parents. Mothers who had completed 9 or more years or formal education were more positive in their aspirations for daughters than mothers in lower educational levels. On the other hand, all of the negative aspirations expressed for daughters came from mothers who had attended school for 7-8 years. The weight of available evidence indicates then, that the educational attainment of the

TABLE 2   EDUCATION AND MATERNAL ASPIRATIONS FOR OFFSPRING

GRADE LEVEL	Maternal Aspirations for Daughters					Maternal Aspirations for Sons				
	p*	D**	U***	N****	Total	p*	D**	U***	N****	Total
13-14	9	1	0	0	10	7	3	0	0	10
11-12	41	3	1	0	45	24	2	2	2	30
9-10	124	16	13	0	153	111	10	1	9	131
7-8	73	21	8	26	128	46	23	1	24	94
5-6	22	2	7	0	31	27	5	5	28	65
Total	269	43	29	26	367	215	43	9	63	330

* Positive   (Daughters) $X^2=35.9$ (Sons) $X^2=82.01$
** Democratic
*** Undecided   Significant beyond .01 at 8 d.f.   Significant beyond .01 at 12 d.f.
**** Negative

280 WOMEN IN THE ECONOMY

mothers correlates significantly with aspirations for female offspring of lower class black mothers (chi-square significant beyond .01).

A desire for professional occupations which required college training for daughters was expressed by a majority, or 78 per cent, of the mothers who had 9 or more years of formal training along with a near majority, or 63 per cent, of the female parents who had 8 or fewer years of education. The occupational aspirations for daughters among this group of mother were higher than those cited by Bell (1965 : 497). A small group, or 10 per cent, of the mothers with 9 or more years of formal training gave democratic responses, but a larger group (14 per cent) with less than 8 years of education felt that their female children should choose their own occupations. Very little difference was found between mothers with 9 or more years of education and those in the lower educational range in reference to undecided responses which dealt with occupational aspirations for female offspring.

Two-thirds, or 215, of 330 mothers who responded to education also expressed positive aspirations for sons. (See Table 2). A large group, or 83 per cent, of the mothers who had remained in school for 9 or more years expressed positive aspirations for their male children. Among this same group, 78 per cent hoped that their sons would eventually obtain professional employment. Unlike some lower class black mothers during past decades, these mothers showed no difference in their desires for professional occupations for their sons and their daughters. Perhaps this finding helps to explain why "three-fourths of the blacks enrolled in college during 1970 came from homes in which family heads had no college education" (Hill, 1971 : 40).

Among the 73 mothers who had remained in school between 5 and 8 years, only 46 per cent of them expressed positive aspirations for their male offspring. Within this same group of female parents only 41, or 56 per cent, of them hoped that their sons would secure professional employment. But even so, this particular group of mothers had higher occupational aspirations for their sons than the low status mothers in Bell's study (1965 : 497). Almost 5 times as many mothers with lower educational attainment (5-8 years) expressed negative aspirations for their sons than female parents who had remained in school for 9 or more years. Approximately twice as many of the mothers with 5-8 years of formal training were undecided on occupations for their sons than those mothers who had remained in school for 9 or more years. This same situation existed in the case of female parents who wanted their male offspring to choose their own professions.

An analysis of data indicates that the educational attainment of the mothers correlates significantly with aspirations for their male offspring (chi-square significant beyond .01).

Even though 97 per cent of the mothers had never attended college, the majority of them hoped that both their sons and their daughters would eventually have occupations or careers which required a college education or other professional training. Although mothers who had never attended high school were less definitive and more negative about occupational aspirations for their children than female parents who had attended high school or college, the majority of these responding mothers were definitely interested in the future success of their children.

Income. Only 331, or almost three-fourths, of the 441 mothers responded to the item on annual income. Approximately one-half, or 168, of the reported yearly earnings were in households which contained employed husbands and wives. However, in some cases, husbands and/or wives worked on a seasonal or part-time basis. The average annual income for the 331 families was $2,678.40, or three-fifths of the $4,540 poverty index which was adopted by the Federal Interagency Committee for a nonfarm family of four (*U.S. Bureau of the Census,* 1974 : 29). Yearly earnings for the reporting families ranged from below $800 for 3 families to above $9,000 for another 3 families. These data are shown in Table 3. The 331 families subsisted on an average monthly income of $233.20 or $51.50 per week.

A rough division of the responding mothers into 2 groups revealed that one-fourth of them lived in families which had annual earnings above $3,703. Unfortunately for approximately three-fourths of the remaining families, members in these households managed to exist on annual incomes below $3,700. A vast majority, or more than three-fourths, of the mothers in both the upper and lower income categories had positive aspirations for their children. It was of interest that none of the mothers reported negative aspirations for their female offspring, and only 3 per cent of the upper income mothers along with 10 per cent of the lower income female parents expressed negative aspirations for their sons. There was a tendency for mothers in the lower income category (13 per cent) to be more democratic in their aspirations for children than mothers in the upper income group. Regardless of income group, the mothers were less definitive in their aspirations for daughters than for sons; however, these differences were negligible. Family income level and the maternal aspirations for offspring were significantly related (chi-square significant beyond .01). These data are shown in Table 3.

The importance of income is highlighted further when one considers the following patterns which were found during an examination of occupational aspirations for children and income levels of the female parents. More than two-thirds (69 per cent) of the mothers in the upper brackets of income (above $3,700) and educational attainment (9 or more years) wanted their children to pursue professional careers. Among 226 mothers with less than 8 years of formal training and living in households with less than $3,700 annual income, almost two-thirds (63 per cent) of the group expressed a desire for their daughters to obtain professional work and more than three-fifths (61 per cent) of these mothers gave similar responses for their sons. These data indicate that as levels of income and education increase, there is also an appreciable increase in the positive aspirations for offspring among lower class black mothers.

CONCLUSIONS

Several conclusions may be derived from the analyses of data which dealt with the relationship of family size, education and income to the aspirations for offspring of lower class black mothers. First, contrary to some allegations, the

TABLE 3.   INCOME AND MATERNAL ASPIRATIONS FOR OFFSPRING

INCOME LEVEL	Maternal Aspirations for Daughters					Maternal Aspirations for Sons				
	P*	D**	U***	N****	Total	P*	D**	U***	N****	Total
$7401-9250	7	0	0	0	7	9	1	0	0	10
$5551-7400	24	0	6	0	30	23	2	0	0	25
$3701-5550	42	2	2	0	46	43	2	0	3	48
$1851-3700	134	30	10	0	174	138	20	6	4	168
$1850 Below $800-	48	1	3	0	52	37	5	3	17	62
Total	255	33	21	0	309	250	30	9	24	313

*Positive   (Daughters) $X^2=41.68$ (Sons) $X^2=49.65$
**Democratic
***Undecided   Significant beyond .01 at 6 d.f.   Significant beyond .01 at 6 d.f.
****Negative

majority of indigent black mothers have positive aspirations for their children. Second, contrary to common expectation, indigent black female parents in families of above average size tend to think more positively about the future success of their offspring than mothers in smaller families. Third, black mothers of low socioeconomic status who have attained an educational level of nine or more years of formal training appear to be more positive in their aspirations for children than mothers with less formal training. Fourth, the percentage of positive aspirations for offspring increases as levels of income and education become higher in the families of lower class black mothers. Fifth, female parents in low socioeconomic black families have become increasingly aware of the necessity of encouraging their children, regardless of sex, to obtain an education. Finally, the findings in this report should provide a more objective basis for future examination of the relationship of family size, education and income to some of the problems which confront low income black families.

REFERENCES

Bell, Robert R.
    1965   "Lower Class Negro Mothers' Aspirations for their Children." *Social Forces.* 43 (May): 497.

Bennett, Jr., Williams and Noel P. Gist
    1964   "Class and Family Influences on Student Aspirations." *Social Forces.* 43 (December): 169-173.

Billingsley, Andrew
  1968   *Black Families in White America.* Englewood Cliffs, New Jersey: Prentice Hall, Inc.
Hill, Robert
  1968   "The Strengths of Black Families." Research Department, National Urban League.
Grier, William H. and Price M. Cobbs
  1968   *Black Rage.* New York: Bantam Books
Hyman, Herbert H.
  1953   "The Values Systems of Different Classes: A Social Psychological Contribution to the
          Analyses of Stratification," in Reinhard Bendix and Seymour Martin Lipset, *Class,
          Status and Power.* Glencoe, Illinois: The Free Press.
Lieberman, Leonard
  1973   "The Emerging Model of the Black Family." *International Journal of Sociology of
          the Family.* 3 (March): 10.
Moynihan, Daniel
  1965   *The Negro Family: The Case for National Action.* Office of Policy Planning and
          Research. Washington, D.C.: U.S. Department of Labor.
National Opinion Research Center
  1947   "Opinion News." *National Opinion Research Center.* University of Chicago
          (September 1).
Rainwater, Lee and William Yancey
  1967   *"The Moynihan Report and the Politics of Controversy.* Cambridge, Massachusetts:
          MTI Press.
Roper, Elmo
  1942   "National Survey of High School Youth." Fortune. XXVI, No. 6.
U.S. Bureau of the Census
  1974   Current Population Reports, Special Studies, Series P-23, No. 48, *The Social and
          Economic Status of the Black Population in the United States, 1973.*
Williams, J. Allen Jr. and Robert Stockton
  1973   "Black Family Structures and Functions: An Empirical Examination of Some Sugges-
          tions Made by Billingsley." *Journal of Marriage and Family.* 35 (February): 39-49.

19

Labor Force Participation and Fertility, Contraceptive Knowledge, Attitude and Practice of the Women of Barbados

P. M. GEORGE*
G. E. EBANKS*
CHARLES NOBBE**

Introduction

It has been variously documented that the labor force participation of women is related to their fertility (Namboodiri, 1964:65-77; Zarate 1967:213-18; Miro and Rath, 1965:36-62; Miro and Mertens, 1968:89-117; Macisco, *et. al.*, 1970:51-70; and Cain and Weininger, 1973:205-23). The realization that female labor force participation might depress fertility became a matter of special interest for those interested and involved in social planning. Collver and Langlois (1962:367-85), maintained that if recruitment of women in the labor force will help to induce a decline in fertility by changing the character of the family and its reproductive behavior, it should be something of high priority in development strategies. However, Stycos (1965:42-45) found no basis for the statement that increased entry of females into the labor force would act as a solution to high fertility, from his analysis of data from Peru.

Though there is generally a well-established negative relationship between female employment and fertility in the industrialized countries, research focusing on less developed countries indicate no such uniform pattern, a contrast which is well-documented by several demographers (e.g. Goldstein, 1972:419-36; Weller, 1968:507-26). Of interest in this paper is the relationship between female labor participation and fertility in Barbados, an island nation which falls between the developed and the developing nations in its stage of development.

It has been argued (Goldstein, 1972:419-36) that labor force participation *per se* may not be acting as an agent to depress fertility but that a series of variables associated with labor force participation on the part of women, such as age at marriage, longer periods of schooling, etc., might be the ones which are affecting fertility. In fact, there have been several attempts to link labor force participation with intervening variables, which in turn are related to low fertility. For example, Speare *et. al.*, (1973:323-34) noted that work experience acts mainly

*Dept. of Sociology, University of Western Ontario, Canada.
**Canadian International Development Agency, Ottawa, Canada.

to delay marriage and childbearing. Stycos (1965: 42-45) in his study found that age at first sex union was somewhat higher for working women. Westoff *et. al* (1969: 11-37) noted more "liberal" views on abortion on the part of the working women. Work experience is something more than simply earning a living. It is a social experience with many behavioural implications.

This paper examines, in addition to the above relationship that between labor force participation and the role perception of women with respect to family planning. It attempts to answer the additional question as to whether women who work still consider it their duty to be responsible for family planning, compared to those women who do not work.

In summary we intend to see:

(i)   whether or not the traditional inverse relationship between the female labor force participation and their fertility exists in the case of Barbadian women;

(ii) whether or not a set of intervening variables could account for the relationship between labor force participation and low fertility; and

(iii) to what extent the role perception regarding family planning of the working women are different from the role reception of the non-working women.

Data

The data on which this paper is based came from a national sample of Barbadian women aged 16-50 excluding those under 20 who have never been pregnant and are still in an educational institution. A probability sample of enumeration districts was selected, and within each all women meeting the above criteria were eligible to be interviewed. The 54 sampled enumeration districts yielded 4199 interviews with women of what we classify as lower and lower middle socio-economic status women and an additional 200 women of the middle—middle and above socio-economic status women. The smaller sub-sample involving a mailed questionnaire is not used in this study. Comparisons made between the larger sample and the national population prove it to be representative on several socio-demographic variables.

Analysis of Data

That labor force participation is associated with low fertility in the case of lower and lower middle class women in Barbados can be seen in the Table 1. Also whether the woman works part-time or full-time makes a difference with respect to fertility. Women currently in the labor force have lower fertility than those who are not. Those who work part-time have higher fertility than those who work full-time. The work experience of the women tends to have a similar relationship with expected fertility (Table 2), but is not related to the number of children the respondents would like to have. The relationship between the number of children the respondents think others should have and the work experience is in the expected direction, though not as pronounced as above (Table 3). The above findings support previous ones which documented the inverse relationship between labor force participation and fertility.

TABLE 1 LABOR FORCE PARTICIPATION BY THE NUMBER OF LIVE-BIRTHS
CONTROLLING FOR THE AGE OF THE RESPONDENTS

| | Age of Respondents | | |
	29	30-39	40+
Presently Employed:			
Yes	1.06 (912)	3.84 (412)	4.81 (412)
No	1.64 (1340)	4.55 (512)	5.00 (510)
Nature of Work			
Full-time	1.41 (1362)	4.24 (584)	4.85 (561)
Part-time	2.03 (176)	4.47 (114)	5.04 (96)

TABLE 2 LABOR FORCE PARTICIPATION BY THE EXPECTED AND IDEAL
FERTILITY OF THE RESPONDENTS

Expected Fertility

Presently Employed:
Yes 3.17 (1317)
No 3.33 (1786)

3.27 (3103)

Nature of Work:
Full-time 3.23 (1912)
Part-time 3.56 (320)

3.31 (2232)

How Many Children Would You Like to Have or Would Like to Have Had

Presently Employed:
Yes 2.6 (1968)
No 2.6 (2265)

2.6 (3963)

Nature of Work:
Full-time 2.6 (2428)
Part-time 2.7 (371)

2.6 (2799)

TABLE 3   LABOR FORCE PARTICIPATION AND THE FERTILITY VIEWS
                                        OF THE RESPONDENTS

The No. of Children a Woman of Your Position Should Have

Presently Employed:
    Yes   2.62   (1727)
    No   2.65   (2301)

                                                                     2.64   (4028)

The Nature of Employment:
    Full-time   2.65   (2472)
    Part-time   2.75   (381)

                                                                     2.67   (2853)

The No. of Children a Bajan Woman Should Have

Presently Employed:
    Yes   3.33   (1684)
    No   3.47   (2264)

                                                                     3.41   (3948)

The Nature of Employment:
    Full-time   3.40   (2411)
    Part-time   3.50   (366)

                                                                     3.42   (2777)

Labor force participation in influencing fertility or vice versa must be operating through some intermediate variables. An examination of the differences between working and non-working women in such areas as attitudes, practices and values should give us some insights into what account for the differences in fertility between working and non-working women. We will look at contraceptive attitudes, values, practice and knowledge as intervening variables between labor force participation and fertility. As pointed out by Collver (1968: 55-60) and Sweet (1970: 195-209) it is possible that women with smaller families could be more attracted to work since they have more time to work and fewer constraints on work. Thus it is important to look into the "intervening" variables such as contraceptive attitudes, values, knowledge, and practices assuming that work experience introduces the woman to a new social world of expanding horizons, a world which in turn changes her values, attitudes, practices, and knowledge. In other words one would expect greater contraceptive knowledge and more favorable attitude toward contraception on the part of the working women compared to their non-working counterparts.

In Table 4, it can be seen that labor force participation is associated with greater contraceptive knowledge. For example, the women who are presently employed know on the average of 3.41 contraceptives while the average for their counterparts, those who are not presently employed is 3.05. Similarly those who usually work on a full-time basis have a slightly better cantraceptive knowledge compared to those who work usually on a part-time basis.

TABLE 4   CONTRACEPTIVE KNOWLEDGE BY THE LABOR FORCE PARTICIPATION OF THE RESPONDENTS

No. of Contraceptives Known

Presently Employed	
Yes	3.41 (1756)
No	3.05 (2371)
	3.20 (4127)
Nature of Employment	
Full-time	3.34 (2511)
Part-time	3.26 (388)
	3.32 (2399)

One of the major arguments for expecting that female labor force participation would tend to reduce fertility is based on the assumption that work experience would change the women's attitudes towards fertility. In fact there is some evidence to indicate that labor force participation of the women is associated with liberal attitude toward contraception. For example, Westoff *et. al.*, (1969: 11-37) noted more liberal views on abortion on the part of working women compared to non-working women. Data in Table 5 deal with some dimensions of the attitude

TABLE 5   LABOR FORCE PARTICIPATION AND ATTITUDE TOWARD CONTRACEPTIVE PRACTICE

	Would you Advise Anyone to Use Contraception?		
	Yes	No	Total
Employment Status			
Yes	1448 (84.2)	272 (15.8)	1720 (100.0)
No	1845 (80.2)	455 (19.8)	2300 (100.0)
	3293 (81.9)	727 (18.1)	4020 (100.0)
Nature of Employment			
Full-time	2052 (83.6)	404 (16.4)	2456 (100.0)
Part-time	304 (80.6)	73 (19.4)	377 (100.0)
	2356 ( )	477 ( )	2833 (100.0)

(Contd.)

TABLE 5 (Contd.)

| | The Government Should Approve Abortion | | | |
	Agree	Neutral	Disagree	Total
Presently Employed				
Yes	618 (35.3)	326 (18.6)	806 (46.1)	1750 (100.0)
No	827 (35.1)	356 (15.1)	1171 (49.7)	2354 (100.0)
	1445 (35.2)	682 (16.6)	1977 (48.1)	4104 (100.0)
Nature of Employment				
Full-time	907 (36.3)	409 (16.4)	1183 (47.3)	2499 (100.0)
Part-time	119 (30.8)	69 (17.9)	198 (51.3)	386 (100.0)
	1026 ( )	478 ( )	1381 ( )	2885 (100.0)

toward contraception.   Though the relationship noted between labor force participation and the attitude toward contraception is not very strong, it is still in the
expected direction.

There is evidence (Micro and Mertens, 1968: 89-117) to indicate that labor
force participation is associated with contraceptive practices.   Data on the
contraceptive practice of the respondents are noted in Table 6, and it can be seen
that labor force participation is related to contraceptive use.   For example, more
working women than non-working women are presently using contraceptives;
more full-time workers than part-time workers are using contraceptives.   Thus
the association between contraceptive practices and labor force participation is in
the expected direction.   Moreover, the nature of the contraceptive practices of
the respondents is even more revealing.   According to the data in Table 6, the
nature of the contraceptive use of the working women compared to their non-
working counterparts is more conducive to lowering fertility.   For example,
among those who work, only 30% take chances whereas 37% of those who do not
work take chances while using contraceptives.   Similarly among those who work
on a full-time basis only 32% of them take chances whereas the corresponding
figure for those who work part-time is 42%.   This finding is consistent with other
findings which indicate a more efficient use of contraceptives on the part of the
working women (Macisco et. al; 1970)

The association between labor force participation and the age at first use of
contraceptives is also in the expected direction.   Those who usually work on a
full-time basis have started to use contraceptives at an average age of 23.5 years
whereas the corresponding figure for their counterparts who work on a part-time
basis is 24.6 years — a finding which is consistent with the findings of Miro and
Mertens (1968).   However, there is no difference in age at the first use of contraceptive between those who presently work and those who do not.

TABLE 6   LABOR FORCE PARTICIPATION BY THE CONTRACEPTIVE PRACTICE
OF THE RESPONDENTS

	Presently Using Contraceptives		
	Yes	No	Total
Presently Employed			
Yes	574 (59.2)	396 (40.8)	970 (100.0)
No	623 (48.3)	668 (51.7)	1291 (100.0)
	1197 ( )	1064 ( )	2261 (100.0)
Nature of Employment			
Full-time	769 (53.8)	661 (46.2)	1430 (100.0)
Part-time	122 (51.5)	115 (48.5)	237 (100.0)
	891 ( )	776 ( )	1667 (100.0)

	Age at First Use of Contraceptives	
Presently Employed		
Yes	23.6 (939)	
No	23.6 (1239)	
Nature of Employment		
Full-time	23.5 (1380)	
Part-time	24.6 (231)	

	Take Chances While Using Contraceptives		
	Yes	No	Total
Presently Employed			
Yes	276 (30.1)	641 (69.9)	917 (100.0)
No	447 (37.4)	749 (58.4)	1196 (100.0)
	723 (34.2)	1309 (65.8)	2113 (100.0)
Nature of Employment			
Full-time	432 (32.1)	913 (67.9)	1345 (100.0)
Part-time	91 (41.6)	128 (58.4)	219 (100.0)
	523 ( )	1041 ( )	1564 (100.0)

There is ample evidence to substantiate the generalization that the working women tend to get married later than the non-working women (Miro and Mertens, 1968: 89-117; Goldstein, 1972: 419-36; Speare *et. al.*, 1973: 323-34; and Stycos, 1965: 42-45). The data in Table 7 support this. Though those who are presently employed began their first partnership later those who are not presently employed, those who work on a full-time basis had their first partnership a little earlier than those who work on a part-time basis. One should not over emphasize this small difference as contradictory evidence.

There is some evidence (Speare *et. al.*, 1973: 323-34) to indicate that the working women tend to get pregnant later than those who are not working. According to the data presented in Table 7, the relationship between labor force participation and the age at first pregnancy is as above. Those who are at present employed got pregnant at a much later age than those who are at present not working, but those who work on a full-time basis got pregnant a little earlier than those who work on a part-time basis. Again this latter difference is too small to draw any firm conclusion from it.

TABLE 7   LABOR FORCE PARTICIPATION BY THE AGE AT FIRST PARTNERSHIP AND AT FIRST PREGNANCY, AND THE NUMBER OF PARTNERSHIPS OF THE RESPONDENTS

Age At First Partnership	
Presently Employed	
Yes	17.32 (952)
No	16.79 (1255)
Total	17.01 (2207)
Nature of Employment	
Full-time	16.96 (1434)
Part-time	17.26 (246)
Total	17.00 (1670)
Age At First Pregnancy	
Presently Employed	
Yes	19.57 (1250)
No	18.96 (1893)
	19.20 (3143)
Nature of Employment	
Full-time	19.16 (1250)
Part-time	19.38 (342)
	19. (2283)

To summarize, those who are presently working not only entered their first partnership later, but also had their first pregnancy later than those who are not working at present. However, those who work full-time had their first pregnancy a little earlier than those who work part-time. However, on the average those who are working full-time have taken 2.20 years between their first partnership and first pregnancy whereas those who work part-time took slightly less time (i.e. 2.12 years) between the two above-noted events in their lives. So the earlier pregnancy on the part of those working full-time as opposed to those who work part-time is a function of the former's earlier partnership.

Data presented in Table 8 deal with the contraceptive views of the respondents regarding their sons and daughters. The right age respondents think for a

TABLE 8   LABOR FORCE PARTICIPATION BY THE VIEWS OF THE RESPONDENTS ABOUT THE RIGHT AGE AT MARRIAGE AND AGE AT FIRST PREGNANCY

The Right Age for a Girl to Get Married

Presently Employed

Yes	22.16	(1728)
No	21.66	(2323)
	21.87	(4051)

Nature of Employment

Full-time	21.89	(2475)
Part-time	21.87	(384)
	21.89	(2859)

The Right Age for a Boy to Get Married

Presently Employed

Yes	24.38	(1722)
No	23.75	(2318)
	24.01	(4040)

Nature of Employment

Full-time	24.00	(2464)
Part-time	23.93	(384)
	23.98	(2848)

The Right Age for a Girl to Get Pregnant

Presently Employed

Yes	21.00	(1694)
No	20.30	(2255)
	20.58	(3949)

Nature of Employment

Full-time	20.67	(2436)
Part-time	20.50	(372)
	20.63	(3046)

boy as well as for a girl to get married is related to the respondents' work experience as one would expect. The same thing is true with respect to the right age for a girl to get pregnant. In other words, according to those who are presently employed, the right age for a girl or a boy to get married and for a girl to get pregnant is later than the right age given for such events by those who are not working at present. Similarly, according to those who work full-time, the right age for the above-noted events is slightly later than the ages noted by those who work part-time. Though the difference between the two groups of women is not great, it remains that the difference is in the expected direction.

The role perception of the working women (Table 9) is consistent with what one would expect. Those who are presently employed, compared to those who are not, give a greater role for the joint responsibility of the husband and wife in contraceptive practice. A similar difference is noted, though a rather small one, between those who work full-time and those who work part-time. The significance of the greater role of joint responsibility in contraceptive matters becomes clear when we realize that those who believe in joint responsibility have fewer children than those who leave such responsibility in the hand of one partner (Kiser and Whelpton, 1953: 95-110).

TABLE 9   LABOR FORCE PARTICIPATION BY THE ROLE PERCEPTION OF
                                              THE RESPONDENTS

Who Should Decide on How Many Children a Family Should Have?

	Man	Woman	Both	God	Total
Presently Employed					
Yes	153 (8.7)	70 (4.0)	1357 (77.6)	169 (9.7)	1749 (100.0)
No	277 (11.7)	133 (5.6)	1695 (71.8)	256 (10.8)	2361 (100.0)
	430 (10.5)	203 (4.9)	3052 (74.2)	425 (10.4)	4110 (100.0)
Nature of Employment					
Full-time	264 (10.6)	103 (4.1)	1868 (74.7)	266 (10.6)	2501 (100.0)
Part-time	41 (10.6)	23 (5.9)	286 (73.9)	37 (9.6)	387 (100.0)
	305 ( )	126 ( )	2154 ( )	303 ( )	2888 ( )

Who Should be Responsible for Birth Control?

	Man	Woman	Both	Total
Presently Employed				
Yes	47 (2.7)	179 (10.3)	1520 (87.1)	1746 (100.0)
No	92 (3.9)	304 (13.0)	1942 (83.1)	2338 (100.0)
Nature of Employment				
Full-time	80 (3.2)	282 (11.3)	2128 (85.5)	2490 (100.0)
Part-time	10 (2.6)	50 (13.0)	325 (84.4)	385 (100.0)

It has been noted that the more educated women have a better representation in the labor force compared to that of the less educated women (Carleton, 65: 233-39; Miro and Mertens, 1968: 89-117). In the light of the above-noted findings it has been suggested (Goldstein, 1972: 419-36) that the working women's lower fertility may be partly due to their higher education, since education is negatively related to fertility. The higher educated women have a higher representation in the labor force compared to the representation of those who are less educated, as can be seen from Table 10. Thus it is quite likely that at least part of the influence of labor force participation is due to the higher education of the working women. A similar inference can be made about the repondents' social class position as indicated by their partners' monthly income (Table 10).

TABLE 10   LABOR FORCE PARTICIPATION BY THE EDUCATION OF THE RESPONDENTS AND THE SALARY OF THE PARTNERS

	*Education of the Respondents**		
	Primary	Secondary	Total
Presently Employed			
Yes	955 (55.7)	760 (44.3)	1715 (100.0)
No	1445 (62.1)	883 (37.9)	2328 (100.0)
Nature of Employment			
Full-time	1448 (58.9)	1010 (41.1)	2458 (100.0)
Part-time	250 (66.5)	126 (33.5)	376 (100.0)
	Partner's Monthly Salary		
	$0-200	$200+	Total
Presently Employed			
Yes	406 (46.1)	475 (53.9)	881 (100.0)
No	738 (57.2)	552 (42.8)	1390 (100.0)
Nature of Employment			
Full-time	693 (50.4)	683 (49.7)	1376 (100.0)
Part-time	131 (62.1)	80 (37.9)	211 (100.0)

*The numbers of those who have had no formal education and those who have had college education are less than 5; therefore they are not included in the table.

Summary and Conclusions

The data from a probability sample of 4199 lower and lower middle class women from Barbados were used to examine the relationship between female labor force participation and fertility. In general labor force participation is associated with low actual and expected fertility, as one would expect based on the literature in the area of fertility and female labor force participation. Similarly labor force participation is associated with better contraceptive knowledge, more positive attitude towards fertility control, and contraceptive practices. Though the magnitude of the relationship is not too strong, the fact remains that the relationship is in the expected direction.

No one would deny that involvement of women in the labor force is likely to depress their fertility, and we find the plan of action that emerged from the World Fertility Conference held in Bucharest in 1974 recognizing this by calling for an uplifting in the status of women. But countries that have high fertility tend to have high rates of female employment. Employing all women in order to depress fertility, is not feasible and perhaps is putting the emphasis in the wrong place.

REFERENCES

Cain, Glen G. and Adriana Weininger
    1973   "Economic Determinants of Fertility: Results from Cross-Sectional Aggregate Data" *Demography* Vol. 10 No. 2, pp. 205-223

Carleton, Robert O.
    1965   "Labor Force Participation: A stimulus to Fertility in Puerto Rico?" *Demography* Vol. 2, pp. 233-39

Collver, O. Andrew
    1968   "Women's Work Participation and Fertility in Metropolitan Areas" *Demography*, Vol. 5, No. 1, pp. 55-60.

Goldstein, Sidney
    1972   "The Influence of Labor Force Participation and Education on Fertility in Thailand" *Population Studies* Vol. 26, pp. 419-436.

Kiser, Clyde V. and P.K. Whelpton
    1953   Resume of the Indianapolis Study of Social and Psychological Factors Affecting Fertility *"Population Studies* Vol. 7 part 2, pp. 95-110.

Macisco, John J., Jr., Leon F. Bouvier, Robert H. Weller
    1970   "The Effect of Labor Force Participation on the Relation Between the Migrant Status and Fertility in San Juan Puerto Rico". The Milbank Memorial Fund Quarterly Vol. 48 part 1, 51-70.

Miro, Carmen, and Ferdinand Rath
    1968   "Preliminary Findings of Comparative Fertility Surveys in Three Latin American Cities" *The Milbank Memorial Fund Quarterly* Vol. 46 part 2 No. 3 pp. 89-117.

Nambroodiri, N. Krishnan
    1964   "The Wife's Work Experience and Child Spacing" The Milbank Memorial Fund Quarterly Vol. 42 No. 3, part 2, pp. 65-77.

Speare, Alden, Jr., Mary C. Speare and Hui-heng Lin
    1973   "Urbanization, Non-Familial Work, Education and Fertility in Taiwan" Population Studies Vol. 27, pp. 323-334.

Stycos, J. Mayone
    1965   "Female Employment and Fertility in Lima, "Peru" The Milbank Memorial Fund Quarterly Vol. 43 part 1, No. 1 pp. 42-54.

Sweet, James A.
    1970   "Family Composition and the Labor Force Activity of American Wives", *Demography* Vol. 7 No. 2, pp. 195-209.

Weller, Robert H.
    1969   "The Employment of Wives Role Incompatibility and Fertility: A study among Lower—and Middle-class Residents of San Juan, Puerto Rico" *The Milbank Memorial Fund Quarterly* Vol. 47 No. 1, part 1, pp. 11-37.

Zarate, Alvan O.
    1967   "Differential Fertility in Monterry, Mexico: Prelude to Transition" *The Milbank Memorial Fund Quarterly* Vol. 45 No. 2, part 1, pp. 213-28.

20

Fertility and Family Economy in the Iranian Rural Communities

AKBAR AGHAJANIAN*

Introduction

Children as a potential source of psychic satisfaction for parents, may be considered as consumption goods (Becker, 1960). They may also be economically valuable in two ways: as participants in the productive activities of the household and as the potential source of security to the parents. Leibenstein (1957) hypothesizes that with the rise of per capita income, the value of children as consumption goods remains more or less stable, but their value as productive participant and as a potential source of security declines. Thus, to causal observers and social scientists, the direct benefits of children loom much larger in the economically less developed countries and particularly in rural areas of such countries (Demeny, 1972; Nag, 1972).

Rural community, as an ideal type, has been characterized as having the following characteristics: relatively low population density, isolation, low degree or role differentiation and homogeneity of internal structure. However, rurality as described is a matter of degree. Recent studies on the social structure of villages and rural communities in developing countries, have revealed that homogeneity of internal structure is not an accurate description of these communities (Albert, 1963; English, 1966; Ajami, 1969, Brandes, 1973). In fact, with the widespread governmental effort toward the modernization of rural areas of developing countries, a relatively different occupational and economic structure appears in these areas. It is possible to assume that differentiation in the occupational and economic structure affect the economic value of children. Accordingly, it seems natural that economic differences be partly responsible for the fertility differences across families in rural communities. The present research provides an empirical examination of this line of reasoning, using data from a rural area in Iran.

Economic Aspect of Fertility in the Rural Community

One of the most potent structural factors affecting fertility is the type of economy within which the population function. If the economy is of the household unit type where the family itself is the exclusive unit of production, the compulsion to have a larger number of children is strong. Since the household

---
*The Department of Sociology, Duke University, Durham, NC, USA.
The author is supported financially by Pahlavi University (Iran) as a trainee at the Center for Demographic Studies, Duke University, Durham, NC.

unit's major source of labor power is the family members, its strength as a producing unit varies with its size (Hawley, 1950). A large number of children are
desired not only because they may satisfy some inherent psychological need of the
parents or the "normative pressures" of the society, but also because they are
economic necessities (Kasarda, 1971).

A main dimension of rural communities is agricultural production as the
dominant economic activity, with family as the unit of production. The major
imputs for this production are family land and members of family, children and
parents, as labor. Thus, the economic value of children is an important factor
affecting the family size of rural couples (Mamdani, 1972; Caldwell, 1976). The
more the family is involved in agricultural production and dependent on income
from such kind of activity, the more the economic necessity of children and hence
the higher the fertility of rural couple. In addition, the size of family landholding,
as a fixed factor of production, is directly related to the economic necessity of
children. Thus, a larger farm encourages a larger family size and those families
that have more landholding have a higher level of fertility.

An important economic aspect of fertility is the wife's labor force participation.
The question of the relationship between fertility and female employment has
been of considerable importance in the literature of differential fertility and
population policy (Collver and Langlois, 1962; Blake, 1965; U.N. 1973). However,
opinions vary concerning the "existence of the relationship between fertility and
employment, the direction of the relationship, and the explanation of the relationship." The family-activity-ratio hypothesis, assumes that as long as the wife's
labor force participation does not involve expenditure of time and energy away
from the family, it cannot affect fertility of employed women (Freedman, 1962).
It has been also stated that in the situations where the role of mother and employed women are compatible, a relationship between fertility and employment should
not be expected (Stycos and Weller, 1967). Since in most rural areas, the wife's
economic activity is within the family, as in cottage or family carpet industries,
such activity does not affect the fertility of the rural wife. In fact, there is not
conflict in the role of worker and mother for the rural woman.

Drawing from this theoretical background, the following set of propositions
will be tested in this study :

1. The more the family is involved in agricultural production and dependent
    on income from such kind of activity, the higher the fertility level of
    the couple. Thus, farmers should have a higher level of fertility in
    compare to the non-farmers in the villages.

2. The size of family landholding is directly related to the family size.

3. As long as a woman's economic activity is within the family, such
    activity does not affect the fertility of the rural wife.

4. The relationship between the dependent variable and the three inde-
    pendent variables stated in the above propositions, are influenced by
    other intervening factors such as education and the age of marriage.

Education, particularly husband's education, leads to changes in the life-style and the occupational structure of the rural family, which reduces the perceived economic utilities of children and hence fertility. Thus, education should be controlled for its indirect effect on fertility of rural couples. In addition, the exposure effect of age of marriage is obviously to be controlled for testing the above propositions.

Methodology

The data for this study are part of a larger data set collected during the summer of 1974. To establish a dual registration system in twenty-five villages of a rural area in Fars Ostan, a southern province of Iran, all households were surveyed and in each household, all husbands and wives were interviewed. For the purpose of the present study a 50% random sample of all once-married women, age 15-50, who were currently living with their husbands, were considered. This selection criteria produced a sample size of 505 rural couples.

The villages differed from each other in size of population ranging from 70 to 500. However, they did not differ with regard to access to city. The city of Noorabad, which is the headquarter for Mammassani district with a population of less than 10,000 in 1974, is the nearest city to the villages. None of the villages had regular transportation service to the city and their distance to the city ranged from 14 to 20 kilometers. As they were located in clusters of five to six, they shared such amenities as the health clinic, rural midwife, school and other public services. It should be noted that basic cultural differences did not exist for the couples in different villages because they were all originally from the same tribe (Mammassani) who settled in different villages in the area.

Information was gathered by means of personal interview. Separate questionnaires were used for collecting the information from each husband and wife. Questions about demographic characteristics, family income and size of land-holding appeared in the usband's questionnaire. For women, a pregnancy history was collected among other information. As all villagers were Moslem, the question on religion was ignored.

Measurement of Variables:

A. Fertility

In this study fertility behavior, is measured by the number of children ever-born, is considered the dependent variable. This is a continuous variable and is recorded as reported by wife.

B. Wife's Age and Age of Marriage

Age of wife at the time of interview and age of marriage, as reported by her, are two continuous variables which are controlled for exposure factor.

C. Level of Education

The educational level of the husband is one important explanatory variable. It is an ordinal variable with three levels—illiterate, primary education, and one year or more of high school.   The wife's education was excluded because of the very few cases of literate wives.

D.   Occupation of Husband

Another important independent variable is occupation of husband.   It is a categorical variable with two categories: farmers and non farmers.

E.   Wife's Economic Activity

This variable has two categories.   If the wife reported that she has some kind of economic activity in addition to her normal work of taking care of domestic animals and housework, she was considered to have economic activity.   An example of such kind of economic activity is rug weaving which is very common in rural areas of Iran.

F.   Size of Landholding

Size of landholding, as reported by husband, is the main explanatory variable with three catagories: no land, small landholders (less than five hectars), and large landholders (five hectares or more).   It should be noted that, while measurement of farmers' income is related to problems or reliability, data on size of the land-holding can be readily and reliably gathered.

Findings

1.   Fertility Behavior

Currently married rural women have had, on the average, 5.69 live births. Women in age group 40-44, have had 8.20 babies.   The same figures for all rural areas of Iran are 5.48 and 8.23. (Table 1)

TABLE 1   MEAN NUMBER OF LIVE BIRTH BY AGE GROUP OF WOMEN IN THE SAMPLE VILLAGES AND ALL RURAL AREAS OF IRAN

Age group	Mean number of live birth	
	Sample Villages	Rural areas*
15—19	1.60	1.78
20—24	2.56	3.52
25—29	4.73	5.15
30—34	6.34	6 56
35—39	7.60	7.72
40—44	8 20	8.23
All ages	5.69	5.48

*Figures are calculated by author from Nehapetail, W., Prelimiary Report of Fertility & Mortality Survey, Part I (Rural Areas), Iran, Tehran University, 1972.

Table 2 shows the age specific martial fertility rates for the women in the villages and all the rural areas of Iran.   The rate for the villages are adjusted by

Brass method (Brass, 1968). A total fertility rate from data can be calculated. This is 7.766 children per mother which is comparable to the 7.815 total fertility rate calculated for all the rural areas of the country.

TABLE 2   AGE-SPECIFIC FERTILITY RATES FOR MARRIED WOMEN IN THE SAMPLE VILLAGES AND IN ALL RURAL AREAS OF IRAN

Age of women	Age-Specific Fertility Rates	
	Sample Villages*	All rural areas**
16—19	.375	.290
20—24	.385	.349
25—29	.313	.326
30—34	.220	.276
35—39	.215	.211
40—44	.045	.122
Total fertility	7.766	7.815

*Estimated rates from Brass method.
**Figures are from Nehapetial, W., Preliminary Report of Fertility and Mortality Survey, Part I (Rural Areas), Iran, Tehran University: 1972.

2. The Effect of Economic Factors on Fertility

The basic statistical technique used here is multiple classification analysis (Andrews, et. al., 1967). This procedure provides a measure of association between each independent variable and the dependent variable after controlling for all other independent variables in the equation. Using additive multiple least-squares regressions, the procedure adjusts the mean of the dependent variables for each category of the independent variables by the amount of deviation from the total sample (grand) mean that is due to the interrcorrelation with other independent variables in the analysis.

Occupation

This section contrasts the fertility of farm rural couples, whose main source of income is agriculture, with non-farmers. It is expected that nonfarmers have lower fertility than farmers. The underlying hypothesis is that the economic necessity of children is more for those rural families who are involved in agriculture.

Table 3 shows the effect of occupation of husband on the fertility of rural couples. Considering the gross effect, the difference between farmers and non-farmers

is a little more than two children. When other variables are controlled, it shows
that farmers have a higher fertility level than non-farmers.

TABLE 3.   GROSS AND NET EFFECT OF OCCUPATION, EDUCATION AND
                            AGE OF MARRIAGE ON NUMBER OF LIVE
                            BIRTHS FOR ALL WOMEN

Categorical variables	N	Gross effect	Net of Age and all other variables
Occupation of husband			
Farmer	449	0.24	0.07
Non-farmers	56	−1.92	−0.57
Education of husband			
Illiterate	372	0.14	0.07
Primary school	77	0.24	0.01
More than primary school	56	−1.26	−0.31
Wife's age of marriage			
15 or less	300	0.18	0.22
16 or more	205	−0.26	−0.32
Total N	505		
Grand mean	5.69		

Size of Farm

Other things being equal, the larger size of the farm, the more labor is needed.
Accordingly, the economic value of children and hence fertility level should
increase as size of landholding increases. Past studies stressing the determining
effect of size of farm on fertility include Hawley (1955), Stys (1957), Drive (1963),
and Ajami (1976). The relationship between size of farm and fertility for the
present study can be seen in Table 4. From these findings it appears that large
landholders have the highest level of fertility among the farmers. When all
other factors were controlled, the original finding did not alter.

Wife's Economic Activity

A large number of women in Iranian villages have some kind of economic
activity, such as carpet weaving. It is expected that such kind of activity, which
is within household, does not affect fertility of rural women. Past studies by Jaffe
and Azumi (1960), and Stycos and Weller (1967) support this notion. Findings
from the present study show that the effect of wife's economic activity on fertility
of rural couples is negligible. Controlling for all the variables, the active women
have only 0.02 children below the grand mean (Table 4).

TABLE 4   GROSS AND NET EFFECT OF SIZE OF THE FARM, WIFE'S ECONOMIC ACTIVITY, EDUCATION, AND AGE OF MARRIAGE ON NUMBER OF LIVE BIRTHS FOR FARMERS

Categorical variables	N	Gross effect	Net of age and all other variables
Size of landholding			
Landless agr. worker	52	—2.59	—0.77
Less than 5 hectars	247	—0.09	—0.18
5 hectars or more	146	1.07	0.59
Wife's economic activity			
Active	48	—0 13	—0.02
Inactive	401	0.01	—0.00
Education of husband			
Illiterate	330	0.04	0.08
Less than primary school	71	0.30	—0.14
More than primary school	44	—0.75	—0.34
Wife's age of marriage			
15 or less	273	0.12	0.13
16 or more	176	—0.18	—0.22
Total N	449		
Grand mean	5.93		

3. The Effect of Education

Since few women were literate, wife's education was ignored in the present study. However, husband's education was considered to be an important variable to be controlled when analyzing the effect of economic variables on fertility of rural couples. Husband's education is mainly important for its indirect effect on fertility as it leads to a change in the occupation of the husband from farmer to non-farmer. Moreover, education reduces fertility of farmers through its impact on perceived economic utilities of children. It may also be effective in creating positive attitude toward effective use of modern birth control techniques, though it is not a necessary condition for birth control and family size limitation among the rural couples.

Summary and Discussion

These findings indicate the existence of high level of fertility as well as considerable variation among couples in the Iranian villages. While fertility is high, differential fertility by education, occupation, and size of the landholding is apparent. The evidence seems consistent with the following proposition: in the agrarian community, where family economy is the major type of economic unit, the positive relation between family size and size of farm may be interpreted as showing the demand for children for their productive services. It has been claimed that such relationship is partly attributable to the pressure of more children stimulating farmers to acquire more land for cultivation. However, the relative importance of the latter factor is not known. In fact, under the present condition of the agricultural sector in Iran, the former proposition is more likely to hold true. For many villagers, land purchases require capital which is not available to the peasants who have very recently gained the status of ownership of land. Children, on the other hand, require low "down payment" and their full cost to parents is automatically spread over a long period. More importantly, they will be a source of economic benefit from very young ages.

An alternative explanation of the positive relation between fertility and size of farm is that, this is the mechanism through which the same product per family is maintained as the rate of population growth increases (Davis, 1963). As reduction of mortality brings population pressure to the fixed land, the poor peasants limit their fertility to maintain the old balance between production of food and population.

Acknowledgements

The data collection for this study was financially supported by Pahlavi Population Center (Iran). I would like to acknowledge unlimited help of Professor George Myers and Charles Hirschman, Assistant Professor, Department of Sociology, Duke University. The helpful comments of two anonymous referees are gratefully acknowledged.

REFERENCES

Ajami, I.
    1969   "Social Class, Family Demographic Characteristics and Mobility in Three Iranian Villages." Sociologica Ruralis 9 (1)
    1976   "Fertility Differentials in Peasant Communities: A Study of Five Iranian Villages." Population Studies 30 (3)

Albert, R.C.
    1963   Social Structure and Cultural Changes in An Iranian Village. Ann Arbor: University Microfilm.

Andrews, Frank M., James M. Morgan, and John A. Soaquist
    1967   Multiple Classification Analysis : A Report on A Computer Program for Multiple Regression Using Categorical Predictors. Ann Arbor : Survey Research Center.

Becker, G.
    1960   "An Economic Analysis of Fertility." in Universities—National Bureau of Economic Research (ed), Demographic and Economic Change in Developed Countries. Princeton: Princeton University.

Blake, J.
    1965   "Demographic Science and The Redirection of Population Policy." Journal of Chronic Disease 19 (4).

Brandes, S. H.
    1975   Migration, Kinship, and Community: Tradition and Transition in a Spanish Village. New York: Academic Press.

Caldwell, J.C.
    1976   "Fertility and The Household Economy in Nigeria." Journal of Comparative Family Studies 5 (2).

Coller, A. and E. Langlois
 1962 "The Female Labor Force Participation in Metropolitan Areas." Economic Development And Cultural Change 10 (4).

Davis, K.
 1963 "The Theory of Change and Response in Modern Demographic History." Population Index 29 (3).

Demeny, P.
 1972 "Economic Approach to The Value of Children : an Overview." in James T. Fawcett (ed), The Satisfaction and Costs of Children: Theories, Concepts, Methods. Honolulu: East-West Center.

Driver, E.D.
 1963 Differential Fertility in Central India. Princeton: Princeton University.

English, P.W.
 1966 City and Village in Iran. Madison: The University of Wisconsin.

Freedamn, R.
 1962 "American Studies of Family Planning and Fertility: A Review of Major Trends and Issues." in C. V. Kiser (ed), Research in Family Planning. Princetion: Princeton University Press.

Hawley, A.H.
 1950 Human Ecology a Theory of Community Structure. New York: Ronald Press.
 1955 "Rural Fertility in Central Luzon." American Sociological Review 20 (1).

Jaffe, A.J. and K. Azumi
 1960 "The Birth Rate and Cottage Industries in Underdeveloped Countries." Economic Development And Cultural Change 9 (1).

Kasarda, J.D.
 1971 "Economic Structure And Fertility: A comparative Analysis." Demography 8 (3).

Leibenstein, H.
 1957 Economic Backwardness and Economic Growth. New York: John Wiley.

Mamdani, M.
 1972 The Myth of Population Control. New York: Monthly Review.

Nag, Moni
 1972 "Economic Value of Children in Agricultural Societies: Evaluation of Existing Knowledge and an Anthropological Approach." Honolulu: East-West Center.

Stycos, J. and Robert H. Weller
 1967 "Female Working Role and Fertility." Demography 4 (2).

Stys, W.
 1957 "The Influence of Economic Conditions on the Fertility of Peasant Women." Population Studies 11 (2).

United Nations
 1973 The Determinants and Consequences of Population. New York: United Nations.

21   The Impact of Children on Female Earnings

ALBERT W. NIEMI, Jr.*

Introduction

Recently, there have been several studies concerned with housewives' labor force participation and the value of housewives' time [3, 5, 6, 8, 10, 13, 14]. It is generally recognized that housewives' labor force participation decisions depend on their knowledge and evaluation of expected earnings and opportunities in the market sector. Housewives who choose against employment outside the home place a greater value on their nonmarket activities than is offered in the market; housewives who leave the home for market activity place a greater value on the market's reward than on their time in the home. Statistical evidence for 1970 shows that the majority of married women (52%) chose against employment outside the home, and only 21% of all married women worked in the market sector full time.[1] A much higher percentage of single females worked in the market sector, but only 50% of single females in the prime labor force ages of 25-44 worked full time.[2] Data show that female employment outside the home tends to increase with education, and, in 1970, the following labor force participation rates were reported: eight years or less, 30.7%; high school, 59.7%; and four or more years of college, 67.5%;[3]

Many explanations for the low labor force participation of females have been offered, and it is generally agreed that female participation habits reflect a combination of employer prejudices and employee attitudes [10]. In most families, married females place primary emphasis on their work inside the home and secondary emphasis on employment in the market sector. Married females generally bear primary responsibility for child rearing, and their life-style is moulded by family considerations, and their mobility and geographic location are determined by their husband's occupation. Family restrictions interfere with the normal decision-making regarding employment and result in part-time and irregular female labor force participation. It is difficult for employers to predict

---

*University of Georgia, U.S.A.

[1]Full time employees were defined to include those who worked 50-52 weeks. For married females, the figures showed the following increase in full time labor force participation with age: 25-34, years, 17.8%; 35-44 years, 24.0%; and 45-54 years, 28.0%. See U.S. Bureau of the Census [16], Table 19.

[2]For single females, the following participation rates (full or part-time) were shown: 25-34 years, 81.7%; 35-44 years, 76.7%; and 45-54 years, 75.4%. See U.S. Bureau of the Census [16], Table 19.

[3]See U.S. Bureau of the Census [16], Table 24.

the expected work-life of female employees, and this factor, in conjunction with employer prejudice, limits the job opportunities open to females.

Purpose and Methods

This paper presents estimates of the present value of lifetime female earnings in a variety of family and domestic situations. These estimates are used to gauge the approximate loss in market earnings that results from the presence of children. The calculations indicate that the economic costs of children are substantial. For females with low educational attainment, it appears that the costs associated with child bearing and rearing can be minimized by remaining at home until the children reach school age. For females with high educational attainment, it appears that the costs associated with child bearing and rearing can be minimized by putting the children in day care centers and returning to the labor force as soon as possible.

Estimates of lifetime female earnings have been calculated for the following five hypothetical situations involving females without children and females with two children:

Y_1 : a female bears two children after her education is completed, puts the children in a day care center, and enters the labor force immediately after the second child is born

Y_2 : a female bears two children after her education is completed and enters the labor force after both children are in school[4]

Y_3 : a female bears no children and enters the labor force after completing her education

Y_4 : a female enters the labor force for three years after completing her education, leaves the labor force to have two children, puts the children in day care, and returns to the labor force

Y_5 : a female enters the labor force for three years after completing her education, leaves to have two children, and returns to the labor force after both children are in school.

For each of the above cases, estimates of lifetime female earnings have been calculated for four levels of educational attainment: eight years, high school, four years of college, and five or more years of college.[5] The basic data on female income by age-education cell are available in the 1970 census.[6] As they are reported, the income figures show average earnings by age and education for all females who worked, both full and part time. In order to measure the approxi-

---

[4]School age is defined here as age 6.
[5]Hereafter, five or more years of college is designated as post-college.
[6]The following education levels were included: less than 5 years, 5-7 years, 8 years, 1-3 years of high school, 4 years of high school, 1-3 years of college, 4 years of college, and 5 or more years of college. For each level of educational attainment, the following age groupings were included: 18-24 years, 25-34 years, 35-44 years, 45-54 years, 55-64 years, and, 65 years and over. See U.S. Bureau of the Census [15], Table 249.

mate loss in female market earnings due to the presence of children, the income figures were adjusted to reflect potential earnings of full-time female workers.[7] For each age-education cell, it was assumed that male work habits were the full-time norm, and the ratio of male/female average participation was used as a coefficient to inflate the female income data into full time male equivalent units.[8]

Employment in the market sector involves certain direct expenditures for items such as additional clothing, dining, domestic service, and day care.[9] For each of the measures cited above, Y_1-Y_5, it was assumed that market employment would result in approximately $700 of additional expenditures per year on food and clothing.[10] The average cost of formal day care programs was estimated at approximately $30 per week.[11] The cost of domestic service was approximated on the basis of a recent study by Mattila [12]. Mattila estimated the average wage of domestics in 1967-68 at approximately $1.00 per hour, and he suggested that this figure could be extended into the present according to the consumer price index. The consumer price index for household services showed an increase of 26.8% between 1967 and 70, and, therefore, I used $1.30 as the average wage for domestics.[12]

The following six variants of the direct costs of market employment were estimated:

X_1 : $700 per year for food and clothing

X_2 : $700 per year for food and clothing
maid one day per week=$645 per year[13]

X_3 : $700 per year for food and clothing
maid three days per week=$1935 per year

---

[7]The calculations in this paper only include earnings associated with employment in the market sector; gains or losses in psychic income associated with market employment are not included.

[8]The adjustment was calculated from the U.S. Bureau of the Census [16], Table 24. A similar adjustment was used by Gwartney and Stroup [7, p. 579] to derive female earnings in full time equivalent units.

[9]The estimated costs of market employment only include those expenditures incurred as a result of employment in the market sector. No attempt was made to measure the costs of rearing children, and only those child related expenditures (day-care) that were required in order to work outside the home were included.

[10]It was assumed that market employment would lead to an increase in dining outside the home and that this would cost at least $10 per week. The cost of additional clothing required by market employment was assumed to be approximately $200 per year. A check on the direction of bias introduced by the food and clothing allotment showed that the size of the allotment was inversely related to the estimated loss in income due to children. However, it was also clear that a doubling of the estimated food and clothing expenditures would have no substantial effect on the results.

[11]See [14, 17, 19, and 28]. There are many informal day care arrangements, and the U.S. Department of Labor [19] suggests that the majority of day care is provided in a private household by a relative. In order to include upper and lower bound estimates of the costs of children, I have used the extreme situations of no day care and formal day care.

[12]For the consumer price index, see U.S. Department of Labor [20].

[13]For each day of employment, it was assumed that a maid worked eight hours ($1.30 per hour) and charged $2.00 for transportation.

X_4 : $700 per year for food and clothing
eleven child-years of day care=$1500 per year[14]

X_5 : $700 per year for food and clothing
maid one day per week=$645 per year
eleven child-years of day care=$1500 per year

X_6 : $700 per year for food and clothing
maid three days per week=$1935 per year
eleven child-years of day care=$1500 per year

Many other possible combinations of family situation and work-related expenditures could be specified. However, this paper only attempts to provide rough approximations of the loss in female market earnings that result from child bearing and child rearing, and the combinations of family status, work-life, and work related expenditures cover a broad spectrum and provide upper and lower bound estimates of the potential loss in female income due to the presence of children.

In calculating the present value of lifetime earnings, the future earnings stream was adjusted for mortality and taxes.[15] The mortality adjustment was necessary in order to take into the account the probability that an individual might not survive to age 65 and receive the full benefits accruing to a normal worklife.[16] The tax adjustment was necessary in order to reduce that portion of the expected future income stream that wonld go toward payment of increased taxes associated with higher income levels.[17] In addition to the tax and mortality adjustments, it was necessary to depreciate the earning power of females who defer entry into the labor force after their education is completed or who drop out of the labor force for a period and then reenter. A recent study by Mincer and Polachek [13] pointed to the depreciation of skill that results from non-participation in the market and provided some tentative estimates of the annual percentage rate of depreciation for various education levels. Based on Mincer and Polachek's findings, I used one per cent (eight years and high school) and three per cent (college and post-college) as annual rates of depreciation in female skill during periods of non-participation.[18]

---

[14]It was assumed that children were clustered and day care expenditures commenced shortly after the second child was born and continued until both children entered the first grade.

[15]See Wilkinson [24, pp. 561-62] and Becker [1, pp. 74-88]. Hines et al [9] adjusted future earnings streams to take into account secular productivity growth and native ability and found that the adjustments had no significant effect on the estimates.

[16]The mortality adjustment was made by multiplying the earnings for the various age-education groupings by a coefficient constructed as the ratio of the number of estimated survivors at those ages relative to the number of survivors at age 18 (eight years and high school) and at age 22 (college and post-college). The life tables are available from U.S. Department of Health, Education, and Welfare [18].

[17]Since all states do not tax income, the tax adjustment only takes into account federal taxes associated with income levels. Effective tax rates for adjusted gross income classes, calculated as the ratio of actual taxes paid to gross income, are available from the U.S. Department of the Treasury [23].

[18]The depreciation of female skills was calculated by reducing female earnings by one per cent (eight years and high school) and three percent (college and post-college) during each year of non-participation.

In order to preserve the upper and lower bound character of the estimates, three rates of discount (6%, 9%, and 12%) were used in the calculations of the present value of lifetime female earnings. The estimates were derived through use of the standard present value formula:

$$P = \sum_{j=0}^{n} \frac{Y_j}{(1+r)^{j+1}}$$

where Y equals the expected future earnings stream for females, r represents the rate of discount, and j represents the number of years of expected work-life.[19] In each instance, the present value of the earnings stream was calculated to age 65.

Results

The Y_3 estimates show the present value of life time earnings of females who enter the labor force upon completion of their education and have a continuous work life uninterrupted by children. The difference between the Y_3 estimates and the other combinations (Y_1, Y_2, Y_4, and Y_5) yields an approximation of the present value of the loss in earnings due to the presence of children.

The Y_1 combinations show the present value of earnings of females who have children right after their education is completed and immediately enter the labor force and incur expenditures for day care and domestic help. The figures in Table 1 reveal that day care is very costly at low education levels. For example, at a twelve percent discount rate, the present value of lifetime earnings with no domestic help and formal day care until school age ($Y_1 X_4$) is $697 for eight years of education and $2,436 for a high school education. At high education levels and high rates of discount, the costs of day care are greatly diminished. For example, the present value of lifetime earnings with post-college training and a twelve percent discount rate is $16,125 for combination ($Y_1X_4$) compared to $16,891 for combination ($Y_3X_1$).

The Y_2 combinations involve non-participation in the labor force from the time education is completed until children enter school. For low education levels, deferring entrance into the labor force is rather costly compared to a continuous work-life but less costly than incurring the costs of day care. For high levels of education, non-participation is much more expensive than day care, and, at a nine percent discount rate, the present value of the loss in income due to non-participation ($Y_1X_4 - Y_2X_1$) is over $10,000 for post-college education.

---

[19]The present value formula yields an estimate of the value at the present time of all earnings to be received in the future. The need to discount future earnings can be shown by a simple example. If the interest rate stood at 10% and someone offered you $105 one year from today or $100 today, you would take the $100. In this way, you could invest the $100 at 10% and, in one year, it would have increased in value to $110. In this situation, $105 a year from today is worth less than $100 in the present period. In order to determine the present value of future earnings streams, the dollars to be earned in the future must be discounted by an appropriate discount rate which reflects the potential market rate of interest. Table 1 presents calculations of the present value of future lifetime earnings streams for three rates of discount, 6%, 9%, and 12%.

TABLE 1   PRESENT VALUE OF LIFETIME FEMALE EARNINGS FOR VARIOUS
FAMILY-DOMESTIC SITUATIONS

Family-Domestic Situation	Education Level and Discount Rate					
	Eight Years			High School		
	6%	9%	12%	6%	9%	12%
Y_1X_4	9,375	3,061	697	15,918	6,238	2,436
Y_1X_5	4,184	186	— 1,120	10,732	3,365	665
Y_1X_6	— 6.451	— 5,794	— 4,810	354	— 2,483	— 2,998
Y_2X_1	12,365	5,548	2,690	17,569	7,803	3,760
Y_2X_2	9,119	4,093	1,984	14,327	6,350	3,055
Y_2X_3	2,632	1,187	573	7,837	3,442	1,642
Y_3X_1	19,426	10,503	6,291	26,422	13,962	8 215
Y_3X_2	13,544	7,167	4.205	20,574	10,651	6,147
Y_3X_3	1,787	565	55	8,817	3,984	1,977
Y_4X_4	12,117	6,955	3,841	20,298	10,605	6,452
Y_4X_5	6,609	2,597	1,120	14,169	6,762	3,760
Y_4X_6	— 5,923	— 5.331	— 4,444	1,855	— 1,018	— 1,735
Y_5X_1	14,579	8,044	5,146	20,056	10,757	6,719
Y_5X_2	10,284	5,525	3,436	15,872	8,254	5,023
Y_5X_3	1,689	499	34	7,197	3,218	1,606
Y_1X_4	35,826	18,851	11,006	50,252	27,016	16,125
Y_1X_5	30,670	15,865	9,108	45,127	24,000	15,026
Y_1X_6	19,717	9,894	5.314	34,882	17,971	10,293
Y_2X_1	24,657	11,873	6,279	33,729	16,474	8,871
Y_2X_2	21,815	10,477	5,529	30,912	15,053	8,083
Y_2X_3	16,128	7,684	4,029	25,279	12,211	6,507
Y_3X_1	44,940	24,773	15,309	58,807	30,295	16,891
Y_3X_2	39,056	21,285	12,998	53,655	27,563	16,332
Y_3X_3	29,603	14,348	8,410	43,354	22,102	12,217
Y_4X_4	36,802	20,862	13,474	52,680	29,357	16,700
Y_4X_5	31,091	17,281	10,985	47,061	25,043	15,200
Y_4X_6	20.360	10,160	6,041	37,494	20,028	11,033
Y_5X_1	26,285	15,437	10,055	40,072	23,222	12,554
Y_5X_2	23,695	13,085	8,387	36,641	19,137	11,099
Y_5X_3	16,175	8,418	5,085	29,782	16,966	8,693

The Y_4 and Y_5 combinations involve working in the labor force for three years before having children. For the Y_4 combinations, the female puts the children in day care and immediately reenters the labor force; for the Y_5 combinations, the female stays out of the labor force until the children reach school age. The Y_4 combinations with heavy amounts of domestic help (X_6) are very costly to females with low education levels. For females with eight or twelve years of education, the (Y_4X_4) and (Y_5X_1) combinations involve similar costs but the (Y_4X_5) and $Y_4X_6)$ combinations involve considerably greater costs than the comparable (Y_5X_2) and (Y_5X_3) combinations. At high education levels, the Y_5 combinations are more costly than the Y_4 combinations, although the differences narrow considerably at high discount rates and with heavy amounts of domestic help. The differences between the Y_3 and Y_4 combinations decline steadily as

education and the discount rate increases.   At low levels of education, the differences between the Y_3 and Y_5 combinations are rather small, especially at high
rates of discount and with domestic help. On the contrary, for college and post-
college education, the differences between the Y_3 and Y_5 combinations are substantial for all discount rates and domestic help situations.

A convenient summary of the differences between the various combinations
in Table 1 is provided in Table 2. The figures show the present value (9% discount rate) of the loss in income incurred by each of four combinations (Y_1X_4),
(Y_2X_1), (Y_4X_4), and (Y_5X_1) compared to a continuous work-life (Y_3X_1).[20] For females with eight years of education, the least costly method of bearing and rearing
children is to work for several years, drop out of the labor force to have children,
and reenter the labor force after children have reached school age. For females
with a high school education, the results are very similar for the Y_4 and Y_5 situations, and, while it is clear that it is economical to defer having children, it is not
clear whether it is more economical to put children in formal day care or to remain out of the labor force until the children reach school age. For females with
college or post-college education, the most economical approach to family formation is to work for several years, drop out of the labor force to have children, put
the children in day care, and return immediately to the labor force.

TABLE 2   LOSS IN FEMALE EARNINGS DUE TO FAMILY-
DOMESTIC SITUATION
(9% Discount Rate)

Adjustment for Family-Domestic Situation	Eight Years	High School	College-4	College-5+
$Y_3X_1 — Y_1X_4$	$7,442	$7,724	$ 5,922	$ 3,279
$Y_3X_1 — Y_2X_1$	4,955	6,159	12,900	13,821
$Y_3X_1 — Y_4X_4$	4,048	3,357	3,911	758
$Y_3X_1 — Y_5X_1$	2,459	3,205	9,336	7,073

Summary

This paper has attempted to approximate the economic costs incurred by
females as the result of child bearing and rearing. We should recognize that the
estimated costs of the various family-domestic situations are a function of the
underlying assumptions, and a change in these assumptions such as free day care
could alter the conclusions reached in this paper. However, the assumptions are
clearly stated and represent a wide range of family-domestic situations, and the
estimates provide useful approximations of the economic costs borne by females
as the result of family formation.

The results suggest that for many females with low educational attainment it
is most economical to stay at home until children reach school age. Alternatively,

---

[20]The calculations shown in Table 2 were constructed as follows: $(Y_3X_1—Y_1—X_4)$, $(Y_3X_1—Y_2X_1)$,
etc.

the figures suggest that for many females with high educational attainment it is most economical to put children in day care centers and return to the labor force as soon as possible. The estimates suggest that these are generally the most rational procedures from the standpoint of maximizing female earnings. However, there are many factors involved in the decision to participate in market employment that are not reflected in the above calculations. For example, a recent study by Leibowitz (11) suggests that the amount of time spent with children by parents is an important factor in determining differences in the ability of children at the time they enter first grade. Concern for child development, the quality of home-life, and other factors may discourage labor force participation for many females. On the other hand, some females may not feel rewarded by home-life, and they may want the freedom and independence associated with market employment. Many females may base their labor force participation decision on non-economic forces, and the calculations in this paper do not take such factors into account.

REFERENCES

Becker, Gary S.
  1964   *Human Capital: A Theoretical and Empirical Analysis* (New York: Columbia University Press).

Bowen, W. and T. Finegan
  1969   *The Economics of Labor Force Participation* (Princeton: Princeton University Press).

Cain, Glen G.
  1966   *Married Women in the Labor Force: An Economic Analysis* (Chicago: University of Chicago Press).

De Tray, Dennis N.
  1973   "Child Quality and the Demand for Children." *Journal of Political Economy*, March/April.

Gronau, Reuben
  1973   "The Effect of Children on the Housewife's Value of Time." *Journal of Political Economy*, March/April.

  1973   "The Measurement of Output of the Nonmarket Sector: The Evaluation of Housewives' Time", in Milton Moss, ed., *The Measurement of Economic and Social Performance* (New York: National Bureau of Economic Research).

Gwartney, James and Richard Stroup
  1973   "Measurement of Employment Discrimination According to Sex." *Southern Economic Journal* April 1973.

Heckman, James J.
  1974   "Effects of Child-Care Programs on Women's Work-Effort." *Journal of Political Economy*, March/April.

Hines, Fred, Luther Tweeter and Martin Redfern
  1970   "Social and Private Rates of Return to Investment in Schooling, by Race-Sex Groups and Regions." *Journal of Human Resources*, Summer.

Kreps, Juanita
  1971   *Sex in the Marketplace* (Baltimore: Johns Hopkins Press.

Leibowitz, Arleen
   1974   "Home Investments in Children." *Journal of Political Economy*, March/April.

Mattila, J. Peter
   1973   "The Effect of Extending Minimum Wages to Cover Household Maids." *Journal of Human Resources*, Summer.

Mincer, Jacob and Solomon Polachek
   1974   "Family Investments in Human Capital: Earnings of Women." *Journal of Political Economy*, March/April.

Ruderman, F.
   1968   *Child Care and Working Mothers* (New York: Child Welfare League of America).

U.S. Bureau of the Census
   1973   *U.S. Census of Population: 1970. Detailed Characteristics, United States Summary*, Washington.

   1973   *U.S. Census of Population: 1970, Subject Report, Employment Status and Work Experience*, Washington.

U.S. Department of Health, Education and Welfare Children's Bureau
   1973   *Child Care Arrangements*, Washington.

U.S. Department of Health, Education and Welfare Public Health Service
   1972   *Vital Statistics of the United States, 1969*, Washington.

U.S. Department of Labor, Bureau of Labor Statistics
   1973   *Children of Working Mothers*, Washington.

   1973   *Handbook of Labor Statistics.*

U.S. Department of Labor Women's Bureau,
   1973   *Day Care Facts*, Washington.

   1972   *Women Private Household Workers*, Washington.

U.S. Department of the Treasury, Internal Revenue Service
   1972   *Statistics of Income, Individual Income Tax Returns*, 1970, Washington.

Wilkinson, Bruce W.
   1966   "Present Values of Lifetime Earnings for Different Occupations." *Journal of Political Economy*, December.

Some Comments on the Home Roles of Businesswomen in India, Australia and Canada

AILEEN D. ROSS*

This paper discusses one of the main problems faced by married women in assuming top level business positions—that of the conflict entailed in having to deal with the demanding work of a career and still carry on the roles of wife, household manager and possibly mother.[1] For the few available studies show that, whereas on the whole men still play the single role of provider, working wives by and large have retained their home duties while taking over those of work. (Rao, V.N. & Rao, V.V.P., 1973, 174) Single women do not have the problem of looking after husbands and children, but they still have to take care of their homes and perhaps dependents as well as work.[2]

One important factor that has great bearing on this problem is that the married woman's role has changed radically in recent years so that she must contend with many new conditions at home as well as work. One of the most demanding of these is that she now must supervise and administer a very complicated time-budget, for the lives of men, women and children have become more diversified and complex over time, particularly in view of the ever increasing new patterns of consumption. If her husband has a position of importance she may have to handle a time-consuming social schedule as well. In fact, the allocation of her time becomes one of her major problems.

Many questions arise out of this situation: What price is a woman willing to pay to achieve a career? And, equally important, what price will her husband be willing to pay for having his wife work? What happens when the wife forsakes

---

* Professor of Sociology, McGill University, Canada.

[1] Form, W.H., 1968, 252. A career will be defined in this study as Form has defined it to mean "notable achievement in any occupation."

[2] The upsetting effect of this new movement of married women into the labour force on family relations can be surmised from statistics that show that the proportion of married women has increased steadily in all countries as they have become more fully industrialized. By 1970, for example, married women had become the main source of female labour in Australia and helped raise the rate of female participation to about 28% of the total Australian labour force. (Changing Horizons, 1970, 100). In Canada the participation rate of married women rose from 12.6% in in 1961 to 18.6% in 1971. This meant that 20.8% of all married women were employed in 1961, 33.0% in 1971. (Women in the Labour Force, 1971, 18, 19), Similar statistics for married Indian women were not available but in 1964 20% — 25% of the total female population was working, and from 1960—70 the number of employed women increased by 47%. Translated into numbers, 19 million more women entered the labour force in that decade. (Sengupta, P., 1970—71, 93)

her former supporting position, and instead, takes over a similar role to that of her husband? What happens to the wife—or the single woman—who may take over just as demanding a career as a man—without a "wife's" support? What happens to the husband's career and ambitions when he comes into competition with his wife in a field he has been trained to consider uniquely his own? What happens to the children when both parents are dedicated to careers?

The few studies that have been done on this subject have shown that the adjustment of both husbands and wives to their new roles is extremely complex. Each author has attempted to study a few of the many variables concerned. This paper will concentrate on 3 areas in which husband-wife relations are affected, namely in the realm of authority, responsibility and in their personal relations. The remarks will be based on the relevant literature and interviews with businesswomen in India, Australia and Canada and other informants.

Sample

One hundred and eighty-five women were interviewed who had either achieved or seemed anxious to achieve careers in business. Sixty-five of these were interviewed in Sydney, Australia; 55 in Delhi, India, and 65 in Montreal, Canada. The large majority identified themselves as coming from middle, upper middle or upper class families.[3] All illustrations in this paper will refer to women of these classes.

As an attempt was made to analyze changing patterns over time the ages of the interviewees ranged from 20 to over 60 years. Marital status could not be held constant due to the fact that, whereas unmarried older women are a rather common phenomenon is Sydney and Montreal, in Delhi they are rare exceptions. Seventeen Sydney and 14 Montreal respondents were married at the time of the interview, 39 in each city had never married and 9 Sydney and 12 Montreal interviewees were either widows, separated or divorced. In contrast, 9 of the Delhi respondents were single, 42 married, 3 were widows and one separated from her husband.

In view of the larger number of married Indian respondents the emphasis of this paper will be on their experience in handling multiple roles. However, very similar problems and role conflicts were found amongst the married businesswomen in both Sydney and Montreal.

Changing Authority

One of the problems in studying the wife's changing power in relation to her husband has been due to the fact that students have measured different aspects of their power—with contradictory results. (Blood, R.O., Jr., 1963, 291—294) The

---

[3]Ross, A.D., 1961, 301. D'Souza, V. & Sethis, R.M., 1972, 37 — 46. The interviewees in both of these studies had little trouble in placing their families in the usual social class divisions. Forty-one percent of the 185 respondents of this study claimed that their families belonged to the upper or upper middle class, 55% to the middle or lower middle class and 3% to what they referred to as the working class. Sixty-two percent of the Delhi, 40% of the Sydney and 26% of the Montreal respondents came from the upper and upper middle classes.

power to control decisions is usually considered the most important in family relations. Men have typically been considered the "head" of the house, which
infers full power in decision-making, but this title hides the fact that women have
always been able to wield at least some authority in the domestic sphere, although
in other areas Indian women have been expected to give "unquestioned obedience
and unending assistance to their husbands." (Wood, M.R., 1972, 24) (Kapur, P.,
1971, 13). Studies show that the wife's power to make decisions has increased as
countries have become more highly industrialized (Goode, W.J. 1963, 368)
(Christensen, H.T., 1975, 420) (Ross, A.D., 1961, 107, 108)[4]. And additional
power has been achieved by married women who have moved into the labour force
and become at least partly financially independent (Goode, W.J., 1963, 372)
(Wood, M.R., 1972, 11) (Rao, V.N. & Rao, V.V.P., 1973, 173, 175).

This new independence has meant that the husband must accept a lower
position of authority in the home and a corresponding lowering of his self-esteem.
To the extent to which he needs his wife's extra financial support to that extent
will he have to adjust to her new importance. The husband's socialization will be
important in this respect. Indian husbands who have grown up in orthodox
families in which the traditional expectations are more or less still retained, for
example, will find it more difficult to give up power over their wives than husbands who lived in nuclear families.

If a husband finds it difficult to adjust to the fact that his wife is no longer
financially dependent on him it is even more difficult for him to accept her success
at work if it threatens his own position of prestige and power as a provider. The
second threat to a husband's self-esteem, then, comes if and when his wife earns
a higher salary and/or achieves a higher position than he does. This could become
a crucial factor in their relationship.[5] The few wives who earned more money or
were more successful than their husbands in this study recognized the problem
and tried different ways of getting around it. Most played down their accomplish-
ments in front of their husbands. In one case in which the wife was General
Manager of her firm while her husband had remained a clerk in his, and she
earned double his salary, they had made a satisfactory compromise by his being
"definitely" head of the house. However, in another case the wife's success at
work appeared to have been the major reason for their divorce.

---

[4]Ross, A.D., 1961, 105 — 108. In the traditional Hindu family the wife's authority depended in
large part on her husband's position. The wife of the oldest son, for example, might have more
power in household matters than an older sister-in-law. Their respective ages were also important. Straus found that the "mean effective power" score of husbands living in joint housholds
was considerably greater than that of husbands living alone with wives. He believes that one
reason for this reduction in the husband's power is that, isolated from other kin, he is more dependent on his wife for services and companionship. (Straus, M.A., 1975, 140)
Mead, M., 1971, 2. Mead believes that a married woman has the greatest opportunity of exerting
power in her own domestic sphere. Should she move into the labour force she may lose some of
this power and, at the same time, find it difficult or impossible to attain equal authority in the
new field.
[5]Changing Horizons, 1970, 24,25: It is very difficult to obtain data on the salaries of both husbands and wives. A survey of a sample of 459 Sydney couples found that the average earnings
of the husbands was $3,982 and that of the wives $1,514 from 1963 to 1965.

The degree to which a mother's assumption of greater authority effects her relations with her children is an unexplored field. As industrialization proceeds various outside agencies, such as schools, gradually take over some of the socializing functions. The latest agency to introduce outside authority into the home is the mass media, particularly television, and particularly advertising. As these outside influences increase and impinge more heavily on children's lives we would expect the authority of parents to become correspondingly less effective. But we know very little about what this means in terms of parent-child relations.

Changing Responsibility

In simple societies family obligations are clearly defined and strictly alloted. They include responsibility for different facets of the domestic work, for children, old people, dependents and those who are ill. Typically, too, certain family members alloted the different social and religious duties. In India, as change has come more slowly than in many Western countries husbands and wives are still expected to carry out many of the traditional obligations (Ross, A.D., 1961, Ch. 3). However, better education and city life has made middle and upper class women more aware of their own rights as individuals and "less capable of sacrificing their individuality to the interests of the family" (Phadke, S., 1967, 194). So, as with many aspects of social change, husbands and wives are caught in the dilemma of re-forming their conceptions of their rights and duties—to whom they owe assistance or care, and to whom they can go in case of need.

Domestic Duties

One might safely generalize for all industrializing countries that, when married women first move into the labour force they are still expected—and still expect—to carry on their former roles of wife and mother. It is very difficult for an Indian woman, in particular, to neglect her home duties, for she is still socialized for one purpose only—that of becoming a wife and mother. The ability of a wife to cope with 2 or 3 demanding jobs depends on the assistance she receives from her husband, relatives or servants. Adequate domestic help seems to disappear with industrialization. Since World War 2 Western women have found it more and more difficult to obtain adequate household help, and this situation seems to be developing in India. Even the equivalent of the English Nanny, the famous Indian Ayah, seems to be disappearing. Businesswomen who live in joint families can depend to some extent on women relatives to help with domestic affairs. But 27 of the 47 married Delhi respondents lived in nuclear families, and 4 lived alone. Only 13 lived in homes in which there were an assortment of mothers. fathers, brothers, sisters, aunts, etc., living in the same house. The remaining 3 respondents did not mention their living arrangements. So many Indian businesswomen return home from work to do the shopping, cooking and cleaning, just like their Western counterparts. Fifty-five per cent of Haté's 1,534 married interviewees said that their leisure time was spent in household work. As 43.3% of the sample were single it can be assumed that the great majority of the married respondents had little leisure time for social activities or relaxation. A number of the respondents of this study when asked what they did with their leisure time asked *"What* leisure time?" For many the heavy load of work entailed in 2 jobs meant exhaustion, frustration and the irritation of feeling that their homes were not run in the way they would wish (Kapur, P., 1974, 115).

Twenty-one of the Delhi, 8 of the Sydney and 10 of the Montreal respondents said that their home work and responsibilities interfered in one way or another with their work. A few mentioned their great fatigue: "You may find me washing the clothes at 7 a.m. and ironing them at 11 p.m." Some of the respondents put their work first and would not let family problems interfere with it. One or two attempted to solve the problem by moving to smaller houses.

The attitude of husbands to sharing their wives' household responsibilities do not seem to have changed as rapidly as their attitude to their working. Even those who express liberal attitudes may change their views when they are put to the test. An English study found that, although the sample of men interviewed had relatively liberal views of the appropriate home roles of husbands and wives before marriage, after marriage and having children they played their home roles much as their fathers had before them (Fogarty, M.P., 1971, 241, 293, 294). Nor do husbands' attitudes change evenly within one country. Whereas Kapur (1971, 6) found that 86% of a sample of men interviewed in Delhi still considered household tasks to be beneath their dignity, a study of men in Hyderabad suggests that men in that city were beginning to take over some of their working wives' home responsibilities; (Rao, V.N. and Rao, V.V.P., 1973, 175, 176)

An Indian husband's attitude may in part be due to caste training which assigns certain jobs to the lower castes because of their "unclean" nature. Wives too have been socialized into the traditional caste division of labour and may find it equally difficult to take them over when servants are not available. (Phadke, S., 1967, 194) But even if Western husbands are more inclined to assist their wives, they may not be willing to take over women's work which they consider to be disagreeable. Some of the husbands of a sample of over 1,000 graduates of the University of Sydney were willing to help with certain household tasks, such as washing-up, child care or shopping, but they would not iron or mend. (Dawson, M., 1965, 49)

Several of the Indians respondents said that their husbands still came home from work expecting to find everything ready for them as usual, whereas when they arrived home they had no time to themselves or anyone to look after their interests, but had to immediately deal with their husband's wishes and the household and child problems. However, another respondent said that her husband now gets his own tea and occasionally looks after the baby until she arrives home from work. And still another husband had agreed to alternate with his wife in taking over the housekeeping every second day. A Montreal respondent's husband confined his assistance to cooking:

"The groceries are delivered on Saturdays when one of us is home. I make one meal a day at night and on work-ends my husbands takes over. I work Monday to Friday, so on Saturday I change the beds, take everything to the laundry and do the shopping. On Sundays I clean the house, do the ironing and cook for the week. I'd love to have a three-day week-end, then I would have a day off!"

Perhaps the rate at which the husband will finally share his wife's household duties will be determined by the relative importance of his job, whether her additional income is necessary to maintain a satisfactory standard of living and the strength of the wife's ambitions for a career.

Children

A warm affectionate environment has usually been thought essential for the adequate socialization of children. A working mother, and particularly one who is dedicated to a career, thus poses some crucial questions: To what extent will her loyalty and devotion to work interfere with or lessen her loyalty and devotion to her children? And, on the other hand, if she continues to play the traditional mother role, what effect will this have on her work and ambition?

Thirteen of the 39 Delhi, 8 of the 15 Sydney and 9 of the 15 Montreal respondents who had had children said that their care had not interfered with their careers. The remaining married women, 26 from Delhi, 7 from Sydney and 6 from Montreal said they had made their work more difficult.[7] Their care had taken so much time that some had not been able to do overtime assignments, particularly when they lacked adequate domestic help.

The respondents' replies tend to support Kapur's study (1974, 116) in which the employed mothers of her sample were found to have greater problems with their children than non-working mothers. For their work interfered with their ability to give their children adequate health care and help with their social development and education. It also added to the mothers' feelings of guilt as they could not spend what they felt to be the appropriate time with their children. Another Indian study found that employed house-wives found their mother role more difficult to carry out than their working role (Kapur, R., 1969, 59). And the result of an Australian study of University of Sydney graduates showed that 44% of those with children found the double load exhausting. Twenty-four percent of these working mothers said they did not have enough time with their children, 10% found it very difficult to make arrangements for them when they were at work and 20% felt conflict between the 2 responsibilities of work and home. (Dawson, M., 1965, 175)

The great strain of both working and caring for children came out in the interviews. Some of the respondents worried about being their childrens' sole support, some were upset by their illness, or fear of illness. Others found that, at the end of a hard day at the office, it was very difficult to be patient. A Sydney respondent who collected her children at a day-care center on her way home

---

[6]Christensen, H.T.. 1975, 420,421. This author thinks that the American philosophy of progressive education has influenced American parents to such an extent that their attitudes to their children have become more permissive, and this has freed the childrens to some extent from parental control.

[7]If the 5 step-children of one of the Sydney respondents are left out the married Sydney respondents averaged 2.9, the Montreal 2 and the Delhi 1.9 children.

from work said that she always put them to bed in a few hours because by that time she was nearly "up the wall."

The careers of other respondents were hampered by the fact that they put the interest of their children before their work. One, a successful Indian Journalist, who was at the point of her career that demanded the utmost attention, was willing to change to a part-time job because she thought her children needed her at home. Another fairly ambitious Indian businesswoman found her attention divided when her first child was born, although she had adequate domestic help. "I was in anguish leaving my daughter with a nurse. I phoned home 5 or 6 times a day to see if she was alright." Still another Indian respondent who had established a very successful factory felt her growing sons were more important and if she thought her work would prevent giving them adequate attention she would give it up.

Certain variables such as whether a child is handicapped, unhealthy, a personality problem or an unwanted or accidental child will have important bearing on the mother's attitude. Another is the size of her family, for each additional child adds to her home responsibilities and means more demands on her time and energy. Moreover, a large family may affect a working woman's relation with her husband. An Indian and an English study both found that the more the children the more disagreements occurred between husband and wife, for each additional child placed more financial and time pressures on the husband as well as the wife (Kapur, P., 1970, 67) (Fogarty, M.P. et al, 1971, 294). Very little information is available as to whether couples living in nuclear or joint families in India have fewer children than their parents, or, indeed, whether work motivates middle and upper class women to limit their families. This information is difficult or impossible to obtain for all countries.[8]

The problem of older children was only mentioned by one Indian respondent, a widow who was having trouble with her teenage son.

"My oldest son has become very difficult. He won't stay within his allowance but demands more money all the time. He is always rude and defiant. We quarrel a lot because I find it very difficult to be patient. It makes life at home miserable."

The apparent lack of concern for teenage children amongst the respondents is curious as most modern parents seem to be having trouble with the "hippie" age, and although some studies assume that even the great strain of overwork does not affect the woman's maternal role, it is difficult to believe that in our complex society a mother's care is not as important at this age as earlier. (Bell, R.R., 1963, 367, 368) (Kapur, P., 1974, 113)

A few of the Indian respondents had accommodated by taking up the type of work that permitted them to keep close watch over their children during the day, such as setting up their offices at home. Those who could not accommodate in

---

[8]Kapur, P., 1970, 67. Kapur found that 64% of a sample of 300 married, middle and upper class working women, between the ages of 20 and 50 years, had only 1 or 2 children. Slightly over 1% had as many as 5 or 6 children.

some way found their children their main problem. The role conflict seemed greatest for the respondents who felt their children's needs should come ahead of their work.

Family Obligations

In the traditional Indian village the system of obligations and rights worked almost automatically. Parents looked after their children and the sons in turn supported them in their old age, for parents were seldom able to save enough to be financially independent after they stopped working. In this way a person's obligation as an adult became his right as his son reached adulthood. Desai has probably made the most complete study of kinship obligations in India.

"Mutual obligations and rights and privileges limit role expectations and define the relationships of consanguinity and affinities... (People) had rights and obligations on several occasions such as births, marriages, deaths, financial difficulties and other... occasions... they were specified and the expected behaviour on such occasions was institutionalized" (Desai, I.P., 1964, 125).

The problem of dependents becomes more critical as societies urbanize. This is partly due to the movement of families to the more anonymous environment of the cities away from the traditional forms of assistance, the gradual aging of the population, and because each addition to the family increases the strain on the family economy.[9] Moreover, as many urban families are nuclear in structure and family members tend to live geographically apart sons can escape from many family responsibilities and controls and parents are able to avoid some of their former commitments to their children. In highly industrialized countries escape from personal responsibilities is facilitated by business and government pensions and by the geographic disperal of the family members.[10] In other words, both parents and sons tend to become independent of each other and this gradually develops into the desire of parents for social independence—to live apart from married sons and daughters when they are old. As early as 1954 only 1 in every 8 married couples and 1 of every 4 elderly widows lived with their children in Australia (Bower, H.M., 1974, 120). In India the attitudes to and practises of caring for parents in their old age vary. They appear to be changing amongst the more sophisticated, more highly educated urban families, but not amongst the rural, poorer population. Formerly close family networks entailed financial responsibility for relatives even when they did not live in the same house. These traditional responsibilities are changing and widows with children, for example, can no longer count on automatic financial assistances from relatives. In Wood's

---

[9]Narain, D., 1975, 83 — 93. The lowly position of a widow in traditional India may be an indication of the strain caused by an extra dependent person, although she did appear to pay her way by doing a lot of the housework. More recently she seems to have been better treated but may non-the-less be a drag on the family income. Statistics show that widows far out-number widowers in India and are much less likely to be self-supporting.

[10]Goode, W.J., 1963, 369,370. Goode thinks that changing family obligations and controls are due mainly to geographic family mobility. This means decreasing frequency of kin contact, the differential social mobility of sons, that urban agencies take over problems formerly solved by relatives and industrial specialization creates new jobs which make sons less dependent on kinsmen for jobs.

study 6 of the 7 Indian widows had received very little financial assistance for their children from their families (Wood, M.R., 1972, 10). And in this study 4 of the Delhi, 3 of the Sydney and 5 of the Montreal widowed, separated or divorced respondents had to work to fully or partially support their children.

New responsibilities may replace or be added to old ones as times change. In India educated women are beginning to think in terms of assisting their own families as well as their in-laws. This may mean cutting down their former assistance to their husband's family. Such changes involve a fundamental revision in a person's conception of his or her obligations, and may become a crucial problem in the adjustment of husbands and wives. Another recent change in India is the growing expectation that working daughters should contribute to the family income. In extreme cases they may become their family's sole financial support. When the father of one of the respondents died she had to replace him by educating her brothers and sisters and finding them jobs, but she resented the fact that this had prevented her marrying. Her case was almost identical with that of several eldest sons who had had to assume financial responsibility for their families in a Bangalore study of 1961 (Ross, A.D., 1961, 78).

The demands of other traditional responsibilities may be just as great even though they require more time than money. Family illness, for example, may make demands on a businesswoman's time even though the sick person does not live in her house. For it may entail visiting the sick person in his or her home or in a hospital.[11] Another time-consuming duty in India has been that children are expected to visit parents and relatives on many religious and social occasions, such as births, deaths and marriages (Desai, I.P., 1964, 131). As cities increase in size visiting takes more time even within one city.[12] Daily religious rituals too have always occupied much of the time of Indian wives in the past. Studies have shown that many urban Indians have cut down the time they spend on these religious obligations, and on marriage and death rituals, although the time spent has not changed evenly over the whole country (Srinivas, M.N., 1969, 127, 128).

Working wives will find it difficult, if not impossible, to carry out all the traditional family, social and religious duties. They must inevitably reassess them, for lack of domestic help or assistance from relatives in looking after children may cut into the time and energy they should be putting into their careers. The care of elderly and/or sick relatives also may become a burden as well as former social and religious obligations. An additional problem in this regard will lie in the guilt working wives will almost certainly feel in not being able to fulfil some of the obligations towards which they have a deep sense of responsibility.

Changing Husband-Wife Relations

A modern business career is so demanding for those in high positions that

[11]Desai, I.P., 1964, 128. The illness and/or operations of relatives are occasions when visits are expected in all parts of Gujarat. As family members are closely monitored it is difficult to evade these obligations.

[12]Kapur, R., 1969, 50. In this study nurses, social workers and researchers found it difficult to visit parents and relatives as often as they were expected to, and some did not have time to participate in other obligatory social functions.

over time a modus vivendi has been worked out in which, in reality, each important business position has been carried out by two people—a husband and a
supporting wife. The former has the job of producing, managing and administrat-
ing in a world in which he must have international as well as national business
skills. The wife plays the all-important role of looking after a home commen-
surate with his position, raising suitable well-educated children, caring for his
personal needs and entertaining on a scale that will enhance his position. She
also may act as an advertising agent by doing prestigious volunteer work in the
community. When the importance of her supporting role is recognized the
problem of a married woman whose husband does not take over some of the
home duties, or play the same role in relation to her work, becomes clearer. An
Indian respondent emphasized this point :

> "When a man returns home at 6 o'clock his wife looks after him. I may not
> get home until 7, tired out, but it is taken for granted that if my husband
> wants his tea, I get it for him. An Indian man has a *very* strong mother-
> complex and he wants his wife to replace her and give him all her attention.
> He is brought up to think that he only has responsibility for his work. His
> wife is responsible for everything else. So, even when she works he leaves
> all her former duties to her."

Single men and single working women do not have "supporting wives" and we
do not know what problems this may cause, but we do know that the single
woman has the additional problem of being expected to play a feminine role
socially and at home, and that the former becomes increasingly difficult as she
grows older and male escorts disappear.

Very little is known of how the new changes in husband-wife roles affect
their personal relations. Kapur (1974, 114)[13] mentions a number of studies that
agree with her contention that a wife's employment *per se* does not bring about
role conflict, or significantly disturb her marriage happiness. However, perhaps
it is too early to say anything too positive about their personal accommodation
to the new situation as it depends on so many variables, some of which have
not yet been identified. We do know, however, that the personalities of the
husband and wife are of crucial significance in their adjustment and become even
more important in nuclear families whose stability depends on this relationship.
It is not such a pivotal relationship in joint families, for their stability depends on
the larger unity of all members (Ross, A.D., 1961, 177).

Eleven of the Indian respondents had been encouraged to work by their
husbands, or had had understanding and cansiderate husbands. A few of the
respondents, however, still felt guilty in spite of their husbands' cooperative
attitudes because they thought that they could no longer live up to their former
standards as wives and mothers. Some of the husbands had been of practical
assistance, accepting homes that were not meticuously run, introducing their

---

[13]Kapur, P., 1970. 346 — 349. The case histories of this study suggest that it was the conflicting
attitudes of the husbands and wives towards the demands and expectations of each other's roles
that led to marital discord rather than the wives' employment as such.

wives to people who could be of help in their work, or assisting them in the routlne aspects such as looking after accounts, booking orders, acting as liaisons with their clients or handling the red tape connected with exporting their commodities. One husband had looked after the children while his wife took special training for a job.

Not all husbands were helpful, however, and some even tried in subtle ways to make their wives' lot more difficult. In two cases it appeared to be due to their personalities. Both seemed to need to thwart their wives' work by putting obstacles in their way. One of them, for example, invariably exasperated his wife by making her late for the bus that called to take her to work each morning.

A couple's social life is another important area that may be affected by a wife's work. As a person moves up the business scale entertaining and being entertained becomes more demanding. Even a non-working wife may find that a great deal of her time and effort becomes involved in "keeping up with the business Jones" socially. This not only includes entertaining and dressing in a way thought appropriate to the husband's position, but doing a lot of homework so as to be able to join in or contribute to the latest sophisticated conversation and gossip of that social level.[14] Not much is known about the way in which a wife's inability to live up to her husband's position socially affects their relations. But it could be hypothicized that even divorce may be considered by an ambitious man whose wife cannot, or will not, play the correct social game. Not much is known either of how a working wife impinges on a husband's self-image, and consequently on his feelings of identity and inner security in the role he expects to play. Will she have the time, energy and interest to bolster up his difficult move to the top—as well as her own—particularly if she does not get comparable support from him?

It is evident that his attitude and the degree to which he supports her will be of crucial importance to her adjustment, for a husband's attitude often makes the "margin of difference" in whether a wife can stand the double load (Ginzberg, E., 1966, 135).

Summary

One thing that is safe to say about the new division of labour between the sexes is that we know practically nothing about the effect it is having on the men, women and children concerned. So far studies have only been able to test a few of the many variables involved and so over-emphasized the importance of certain factors in the equation.

The degree to which male and female roles are converging has been given some attention (Goode, W.J., 1963, 373), but perhaps the modern superficial sex similarities in behaviour such as long-haired boys, hitch-hiking girls, wrestling

---

[14]She will be expected to know the latest gossip about people and politics as well as threatre, music, art and literature fashions. Indian women may find it difficult to play this social game, particularly if their husbands do not support their efforts. In a Bangalore study only a few of the educated single men interviewed wanted their future wives to share their social life or meet their men friends (Ross, A.D., 1961, 244).

women and dish-washing fathers are somewhat misleading, and middle and upper class mothers still essentially raise their daughters to be "girls," their sons to be "boys." If this is so it may be a long time before women attain many of the coveted top business positions or are liberated from the care of children and dish-washing when they work.

In the meantime, the entrance of married women into the labour force is still so new that tnere are few guide lines, and husbands and wives still must make ad hoc adjustments. The studies mentioned in this paper and the illustrations from interviews show some of the role conflicts and the wide variety of problems the couples face. Some of the working wives had cooperative husbands but no domestic help, some had small children to care for, others had dependents to look after, some did not mind leaving work to look after their homes and children, others could not bear to be confined in that way. The husbands, too, reacted differently to their wives' work. Sometimes they were supporting at other times they thwarted their work in every possible way.

The wife's main problem is to assume an additional demanding role at a time when even the non-working wife is faced with many new time-consuming tasks. Her adjustment is made more complicated by changing world events as well as the reciprocal changes in the roles of her family. "These influences operate concurrently, sometimes working towards the same end, in other cases as diametrically opposed forces" (Occupational Histories, 1959, 61). The constant pressure on her time may lead to many frustrations and even exhaustion, and she may find it difficult to attain much personal satisfaction from either home or work.

A single woman has many advantages in carving out a career. Marriage is no longer as important for status or security and many women are beginning to believe that their lives can be emotionally satisfying without it. For some, the urge to have children can be satisfied without a husband.

A few studies have attempted to assess the effect of a working mother on her children. But not enough has been done to cover all the variables involved and older children have been neglected.

This paper has attempted to give some suggestions about 3 of the areas in which husbands and their working wives must adjust, namely, in the realms of authority, responsibility and in their personal relations. It is hoped that it may be useful to future students of the "quiet" but critical social revolution entailed in the new division of labour of the sexes.

REFERENCES

Bell, Robert R.
    1963   Marriage and Family Interaction. Homewood: The Dorsey Press Inc.

Blood, Robert O. Jr.,
    1963   "The Husband-Wife Relationship." In Nye, F. Ivan & Hoffman, Lois Wladis (eds),
            The Employed Mother in America. Chicago: Rand McNally & Co.

Bower, H.M.
    1974   "Aged Families and Their Problems." In Krupinski. Jerzy & Stoller. Alan (eds),
            The Family in Australia. Sydney: Pergamon Press Australia.

Changing Horizons
  1970   Melbourne: Wamen's Bu eau. Department of Labour & National Service.

Christensen, Harold T.
  1975   "The Changing American Family." In Narain, Dhirendra (ed), Explorations in the
          Family and Other Essays. Bombay: Thacker & Co. Ltd.

Dawson, Madge
  1965   "Graduate and Marriage." Sydney: The Department of Adult Education, University
          of Sydney.

Desai, I. P.
  1964   Some Aspects of Family in Mahuva. New York: Asia Publishing House.

D'Souza, Victor & Sethis, Raj Mohini
  1972   "Social Class and Occupational Prestige in India: A Case Study." Sociological
          Bulletin, Vol. 21, No. 1, March.

Fogarty, Michael P., Allen, A.J., Allen, Isobel & Walters, Patricia
  1971   Women In Top Jobs; Four Studies in Achievement. London: George Unwin &
          Allen

Fogarty, Michael P., Rapoport, Rhona & Rapoport, Robert N.
  1971   Sex, Career and Family. Edinburgh: T. & A. Constable.

Form, William H.
  1968   Occupations and Careers. International Encyclopedia of the Social Sciences.

Goode, William J.
  1963   World Revolution and Family Patterns. London: Collier-Macmillan Ltd.

Hate, Chandrakala
  1969   The Changing Status of Women in Post-Independent India. Bombay: Allied Pub-
          lishers Private Ltd.

Kapur, Promilla
  1970   Marriage and the Working Woman in India. Delhi: Vikas Publications.
  1971   "Roles and Relationships with Special Reference to the Changing Role and Status of
          Women." Paper read at the All India Seminar on the Indian Family in the Change
          and Challenge of the 70's. Delhi, November 28 — December 2.
  1974   The Changing Status of the Working Woman in India. Delhi : Vikas Publishing
          House Pvt Ltd.

Kapur, Rama
  1969   "Role Conflict Among Employed Housewives." Indian Journal of Industrial
          Relations, Vol. 5, No. 1. July.

Mead, Margaret
  1971   "Beyond the Household." The American Review, Vol. 15, No. 2, January.

Narain, Dhirendra
  1975   Explorations in the Family and Other Essays. Bombay: Thacker & Co. Ltd,

Occupational Histories
  1959   Ottawa: Department of Labour.

Phadke, Sindhu
  1967   "Special Problem of the Education of Women." In Gore, M.S., Desai I.P. & Chintis
          Suma (eds) Papers on the Sociology of Education in India. Delhi: National Council
          of Educational Research and Training.

Rao,V. Nandini & Rao, V.V. Prakasa
    1973   "An Analysis of the Employed Mother In India." International Journal of Sociology
            of the Family, Vol. 3, No 2, September.

Ross, Aileen D.
    1961   The Hindu Family in its Urban Setting.   Toronto: University of Toronto Press.

Sengupta, Padmini
    1970—71 "Woman Power: The Neglected Infrastructure." Today, Magazine of the YWCA of
            India, Winter.

Srinivas, M.N.
    1969   Social Change in Modern India.   Berkeley: University of California Press.

Straus, Murray A.
    1975   "Husband-Wife Interaction in Nuclear and Joint Households."   In   Narain,
            Dhirendra (ed), Explorations in the Family and Other Essays. Bombay: Thacker &
            Co. Ltd.

Women in the Labour Force
    1971   Ottawa: Queen's Printer.

Wood, Marjorie R.
    1972   Women in Urban Gujarat.   Paper read at the Canadian Society of Asian Studies.
            Ottawa, May 26.

23 The Demands of Work and the Human Quality of Marriage: An Exploratory Study of Professionals in Two Socialist Societies

MARILYN RUESCHEMEYER*

How do the conditions of work affect personal relations outside of work, especially in marriage? The question is crucial to the quality of living in any modern society. Its importance was recognized early by Karl Marx in his analysis of alienation: alienation at work destroys the human qualities of man and thus the possibility for meaningful personal relationships. A second important condition contributing to a humanly fulfilled relationship between marriage partners is, at least in modern society, a fundamental equality. Here again, Marxists and other social thinkers of the nineteenth century not only recognized the importance of equality in marriage but understood how sexual equality and inequality are rooted in the organization of work and the conditions of production.

In an exploratory study, I looked at these problems in socialist societies to see whether serious attempts to reduce discrimination against women in the world of work and changes in some of the conditions of alienation have resulted in changed personal relations in marriage. I limited my study to professionals, not only to improve comparability and to find respondents for this exploratory effort who reflect more on their lives than many other kinds of people but also because, even in capitalist societies, professionals are said to suffer the least alienation.

The issues of both alienation and equality require more discussion. Marx wrote about the alienation of work in capitalist society as the disassociation of labor from the worker's interest and personality. He viewed the product of man's labor as his life in objectified form and saw the surrender of the control over the worker's labor, the submission of the worker's labor to someone else as the source of his alienation. The alienation of men from each other is seen as a consequence of the alienation experienced in the process of production.

A direct consequence of the alienation of man from the product of his labor, from his life activity and from his species-life, is that *man* is *alienated* from other *men*. When man confronts himself he also confronts *other* men...

Thus in the relationship of alienated labor every man regards other men according to the standards and relationships in which he finds himself placed as a worker. (Marx, 1963 : 129)

*Deptt. of Sociology, Brandeis University, U.S.A.

Since Marx, the term alienation has been used to cover a wide variety of personal and social ills. For the purposes of this paper, I limit the concept of alienation to the ways in which it was used by Marx; however, I shall include, as Blauner has done, the worker's subjective reaction to his condition.

> Alienation is viewed as a quality of personal experience which results from specific kinds of social arrangements. (Blauner, 1964:15)

Blauner distinguishes four components of alienation experienced by workers in industry: powerlessness, meaninglessness, isolation, and self-estrangement (Blauner, 1964). According to these standards, professionals are far less alienated than other workers. They have some role in defining their own problems; they take part in determining how the work will be done and in creating their time schedules; they see work as an important part of their lives and they drive meaning from what they do, rather than view their work as something to be gotten over with as soon as possible; they often participate in decisions concerning the results of their work; they are involved and identify with a professional community—or at least some colleague group—with its shared competence, language, and spirit. Aside from these advantages enjoyed by professionals in both socialist and capitalist societies, socialist societies do not have an owning class separate from those employed. Although one cannot ignore the substantial power of those in managerial positions, the German and Soviet professionals with whom I spoke did not feel they were an insignificant part of a large organization; they believed they made important contributions to the social welfare of their societies even outside their narrow sphere of expertise.

Focusing on subjective reactions in the study of alienation raises the problem of false consciousness. The worker may have so adapted to alienating conditions that they are perceived uncritically as normal. Marx inferred individual alienation from his conceptions of human nature and human fulfilment and from the study of objective conditions of whole classes. The study of individual reactions has the advantage of opening a way of assessing variations in the degree of alienation. That it may be based in part on false consciousness must be borne in mind for the analysis as a whole.

Another important factor influencing the marital relationship is that of equality between husband and wife. According to early socialist theory, the woman cannot participate on an equal basis either in the family or in the society as a whole unless she is part of the world of work.

> ...the peculiar character of the supremacy of the husband over the wife in the modern family, the necessity of creating real social equality between them, and the way to do it, will only be seen in the clear light of day when both possess legally complete equality of rights. Then it will be plain that the first condition for the liberation of the wife is to bring the whole female sex back into public industry, and that this in turn demands the abolition of the monogamous family as the economic unity of society. (Engels, 1942:66)

The ideal socialist family is based on human affection rather than on economic dependence and material interests. Firstly, if the woman works, she is free to marry for love rather than economic necessity. Secondly, both husband and wife participate in work which is non-alienating; their lives together reflect the standards and relationships of their work situation. Erich Fromm is strongly influenced by Marx in his analysis of the effects of the marketing orientation on the personality.

> The superficial character of human relationships leads many to hope that they can find depth and intensity of feeling in individual love. But love for one person and love for one's neighbor are indivisible; in any given culture, love relationships are only a more intense expression of the relatedness to man prevalent in that culture. Hence it is an illusion to expect that the loneliness of man rooted in the marketing orientation can be cured by love. (Fromm, 1962:451)

The research took place in the United States, Israel, and the Federal Republic of Germany, where I talked with Jewish emigrants from the Soviet Union, and in the German Democratic Republic, where I talked with East German citizens. These talks included thirty-three long, intensive, and fairly structured conversations lasting two hours or more, as well as frequent meetings on a more informal basis with both these respondents and others, such as the husbands or wives of people I spoke with more intensely or people I met on another basis.[1]

My main interest was exploratory; I hoped, in this study, to catch a glimpse of the human reality of work and family life rather than to test specific hypotheses.

With few exceptions, I talked only with those Soviet emigrants who had lived at least a year in their new country in order to be able to speak with them in English, Hebrew, or German and in order to allow for time to adjust to their new country and reflect a bit more dispassionately about their lives in the Soviet Union. Because they had made the decision to leave, however, I suspected from the beginning problems of bias and decided to visit East Berlin and try to speak with professional men and women there. My East German respondents, although strongly critical of some aspects of their society, were predominantly favorable towards socialism and found capitalism an inhumane system.

The World of Work

Socialism in the Soviet Union and East Germany has succeeded in reducing certain alienating features of work. While many of the non-alienating aspects

---

[1] I also had talks with several people who worked with the Soviet emigrants in their new countries, such as the Hebrew teacher in a Kibbutz Ulpan (a six-month language program at a collective settlement), an English teacher of Russian professionals in Jerusalem, a German teacher in West Berlin, and some social workers in all three countries. Although the teachers and social workers were concerned with the adjustment of the Soviet emigrants to their new country, rather than with past experiences in the Soviet Union, some of the unfulfilled expectations and problems expressed by Soviet emigrants provided insight into their past. Thus, these peripheral talks were a helpful addition to the main set of conversations.
The ages and professions of the respondents are listed in the appendix. I included both the respondents from the Soviet Union and East Germany in one table; differences in their experiences will be discussed when they are relevant.

of the work of my professional respondents are shared by workers, it is important to keep in mind that professionals have many privileges that workers do not have, such as better wages and opportunities to travel abroad.

Socialist societies provide guarantees of employment, education, medical and old age care, which contribute greatly to a sense of security enjoyed by most workers. There are certain levels below which workers cannot fall provided they do not engage in deviant political activity or outlandish personal behavior.[2] Indeed, these security expectations are so ingrained that their loss generated great tensions with many of the Soviet emigrants I spoke with.

The general atmosphere at work described by both German and Soviet respondents was one of cooperation. For example, several respondents commented on the help they had gotten once they were accepted into a job.

"If you need experience, which you do at the beginning, doctors will help you ...or if you have problems at work, you can take courses. You have your time—you have your job."

(a Soviet dentist)

Professional workers also participate in collective decision-making and have important controls over their work environment. My respondents mentioned committees for grievances and women's rights, election of leadership, and the collective setting of work goals, time schedules, and deadlines.

Job security and a cooperative working atmosphere are complemented by a reduction of competition among workers. There are no great disparities in salaries. Salary raises occur for most professionals at definite time periods and, except for a few privileged people who negotiate separately as individuals, are centrally determined for every worker at a certain level of experience. Although some respondents, for example, engineers in large organizations, mentioned tensions relating to payment of premiums, the relative standardization of salaries contributes to the solidarity among colleagues, according to the men and women I spoke with.

With a non-competitive and helping atmosphere, a relative standardization of salaries and the life-long security of one's position, it is not surprising that the work collective becomes an important friendship group. This is formally encouraged, and, from my conversations, it seems that the work collective does constitute an important part of the professional's life. Husbands and wives are encouraged to participate as much as possible in the work collective together.

"I must have my work collective......We go together to the theatre and on outings."

(a journalist)

"I studied ceramics with my work collective; when they gave it up, I lost interest."

(an engineer)

---

[2] A few Soviet emigrants mentioned political manoeuverings which were related to their Jewish background and which caused considerable insecurity. Some even lost their jobs in the fifties because of purges.

Although it will become evident that involvement in the work collective is not without problems, it is important that the people I spoke with did not feel like isolated workers in an unfair and insecure world; rather, they were absorbed and involved in their working environment.

Finally, my respondents found personal meaning in their work and expressed deep commitment to what they were doing. For some, this commitment stemmed from their sense of participation in building a new society; they believed that what they were doing was important, that they were "making a contribution."

"My work is most difficult because, on the one hand, there is a problem of building a communist society with the special relationship men should have to their work, according to Marx, and, on the other hand, there are pressures to achieve in industry."

"Several years ago, I had an attractive offer in West Germany but I refused. I wanted to bring something beautiful to the people here . . . For me, my work is most important, to make a contribution to society; I couldn't just live a personal life; it would be boring."

Some of the research two scientists worked on was requested by party heads. Although this control and concern may limit certain kinds of research, the professionals I spoke with felt they could sometimes influence policy.

"Our research is very much connected to the party. The regime looks at everything and we work on particular problems."

Even those who no longer believed the system was worth working for had an intense commitment as professionals to what they were doing.

"I worry and sometimes don't sleep at night thinking of my patients . . . The most important thing for me is my work, whether the operation succeeds."

(a Soviet doctor)

On balance, I had the impression that the East European professionals I spoke with suffered less alienation at work than their American counterparts.[3] This seems primarily due to greater job security and less competition, and it is particularly true of those who identify with the political system. I should make it clear at once, though, that my respondents faced a variety of serious personal problems, some of which were clearly, if indirectly, related to their work situation. I will return to these later.

Equality of Women

The hope for creating a new kind of relationship between men and women combined with the need for the participation of women in the labor force led to great changes in the roles of women in Eastern Europe. In both East Germany and the Soviet Union, nearly all women now work outside the home.

[3] I had done some preliminary interviewing with American professionals which is being continued now.

In the Soviet Union 88 per cent of women of working age are gainfully employed, nearly all full-time or students; in East Germany 70 per cent, of whom one third have three-quarter-time jobs. (Mandel, 1975: 322)

Both East German and Soviet women participate fully in professional work although not always in the same professions as men. Table I shows the percentage of women in three professions in several countries, including the German Democratic Republic and the Soviet Union.

TABLE I   PROPORTION OF WOMEN IN SELECTED PROFESSIONS, BY COUNTRY*

Country	Occupation (percentage)		
	Lawyers	Physicians	Dentists
U.S.	3.5	6.5	2.1
U.S.S.R.	36.0	75.0	83.0
U.K.	3.8 (barristers)	16.0	6.9
Japan	3.0	9.3	3.0
Sweden	6.1	15.4	24.4
Germany (Fed. Rep.)	5.5	20.0	14.0
Germany (Dem. Rep.)	30.0	36.0	24.7
Italy	2.8	4.9	—
India	0.7	9.5	3.9
Denmark	—	16.4	70.3
Poland	18.8	36.4	77.0

*Most of the data in this table were brought together by Cynthia F. Epstein from a variety of sources. See her *Woman's Place*, Berkeley: University of California Press. 1971, p. 12. Jutta Menschik and Evelyn Leopold added the data for dentists in East and West Germany and for physicians in East Germany. See *Gretchens Rote Schwestern* (Gretchen's Red Sisters), Frankfurt am Main: Fischer Taschenbuch Verlag, 1974, p. 23. The base population for all percentages is the total number of persons engaged in a profession in a given country.

The primary areas of work of female university graduates (in the German Democratic Republic) are literature and languages, where they account for 55% of those in employment. For female graduates of lower level professional schools, the main fields are culture and education, where they fill 80% of all positions. In all other areas the proportion of women is less than one third. Among the graduates of universities and lower level professional schools under the age of 30, women have a share of more than one third in all fields except engineering, where they still account for 10-20%. (Menschik and Leopold, 1974:88)

In both the Soviet Union and the German Democratic Republic women are under represented in leadership positions.

It is true that [in the German Democratic Republic] 25% of the directors of schools are women, 13% of the mayors of cities, 36% of members of the bar, 44% of union functionaries; however, in industry, only every 11th position is occupied by a woman.   (Menschik and Leopold, 1974:88)

Some of the problems women have in being appointed and elected to leadership positions relate to their traditional roles within the family. Although the problems and prospects of leadership positions for women in socialist countries cannot be fully discussed in this paper, a later section on the integration of work and family life will provide some insight into the difficulties faced by women aspiring to these positions.[4]

Several of the women I spoke with started their professional studies after working in lower level jobs and when they already had families and children. These women were not exceptions; in both the Soviet Union and the G.D.R., there are opportunities for further education, and work positions are available for more qualified people although the decrease in need in some professional fields in the Soviet Union has restricted opportunities (Jacoby, 1971:33-39; Lipset. 1973:359).

In socialist countries, women are given time out from work with full pay for some period before and after the birth of a baby, and they may take a longer period without pay in order to care for the child.   Conditions vary from country to country.   In the G.D.R., the legislation shows evidence of concern for what happens to the woman after she returns to work.   Women get their salaries paid for six weeks' vacation before and twelve weeks after the child is born. They may take a year off to spend with their child after birth while retaining their affiliation with their place of work and must be given a position of similar rank after their return.

Encouragement and support for women to work are part of a system of supports for workers in socialist countries.   Aside from the many opportunities to study and the time allowed out before and after the birth of a child, there are *cribbes* for infants and kindergartens (although not enough and of mixed quality); there are special supports for single women, who in the G.D.R. are among the first to receive new apartments and places for their children in *cribbes;* there are inexpensive laundry services and the canteen or inexpensive restaurant where most workers eat their main meal at noon.

Crucial for the encouragement women receive are the public discussions of their right to work and the importance of the man's contribution to the household chores.   Although there are great problems in practically working these goals out, they were generally viewed as legitimate by the men and women I spoke with. The men thought it normal and important for the woman to participate in the world of work.   In addition to ideological reasons, both men and women agreed that women have problems staying at home.

"A woman can't stay in the house the whole day and not work. It would drive her crazy."

(a male Soviet psychiatrist)

---

[4] For an interesting discussion of these problems in Czechoslovakia, see Scott (1974).

"A woman has to participate, be a part of life—then they both give. She has money of her own; it gives her honor...My family is important but I can't live without my work."

(a female Soviet industrial engineer)

As will become clear, this acceptance of the new woman's role is uneven, and there are serious unsolved problems. More problematic was the actual participation of husbands in household work. My East German respondents, younger and more integrated into the political system of their country, reported fewer problems in this regard than the Jewish emigrants from the Soviet Union, although there was no difference in the high proportion of women working. This suggests there is no automatic connection between the participation of women in the labor force and the equality of their status and power in the family.

I have, for purposes of this discussion, stressed the positive aspects of work conditions, the many structural supports of working men and women and the encouragement given to women to study, to enter and to remain active in the world of work. I did refer to the difficulties of gaining admittance to certain professional schools, the inadequate number of *cribbes* for children, tensions related to premiums and the problems of getting work at all if one is associated with oppositional political activity. The briefness of these references is not an indication that they are to be taken lightly. Political and national or religious difficulties, unsolved daily practical problems and economic hardships are straining and exhausting. Even if we assume, or hope or fantasize for theoretical purposes, that these difficulties will be lightened, the problems of arranging both a professional working life and a satisfactory family life are far from solved for professionals in socialist societies.

The Problems of Integrating Work and Family Life

Intense commitment to work does not mean that men and women can feel free of responsibilities in the household. Even with all the efforts to ease the amount of household work, there is still shopping, which, especially in the Soviet Union, is an exhausting experience according to many of the people I spoke with, child care and help with homework, some food preparation, some household chores. Who is responsible for this after a long working day? In spite of the appreciation of the husbands for the working lives of their wives, the women saw themselves as having the main responsibilites for their families. The Soviet emigrants thought of this traditional role of the woman more as a natural division within the family than the East Germans, but women in both countries, although certainly not all, complained that their husbands were not helping enough. Sociologists I spoke with in East Berlin suggested that, when women marry, they accept the traditional roles but, later on, as they go back to school or get involved in their professions, they demand more equality at home. This observation was certainly confirmed in my talks with Soviet and East German women. The man may react angrily to the new relationship in the house and, if he cannot accept it, the marriage may break up.

"I had been away for a year to the Soviet Union...My wife said that now she wanted to improve her qualifications, that I should do for her what she did for me, It was my hardest year at work. All sorts of commitments came due...Before, we used to go to concerts, the theatre—now I was doing nothing but work. She couldn't get emotional attention from me and turned to someone in her school. We got a divorce..."

(an East German)

My impression was that German professional men, even while retaining some traditional attitudes, accepted the legitimacy of their wives' demands. Soviet men recognized the burdens of their wives but often did not see the solution involving their own participation in household tasks. An East German raised in the Soviet Union made this difference dramatically clear:

"I think that there should be automation for cleaning the windows, etc., but not that the man should do it. In Russia, the men are more conservative, Even if the women has equal work, she's not the same as a man. She's still the mother —that's natural."

The more progressive convictions of most German professional men and women, supported by frequent public discussions of this issue, however, have had and I think will continue to have tremendous impact on the future of equality between men and women in East Germany.

Problems of the new role of women come to a head over the matter of childcare. It is the woman who, in most cases, takes the time out to care for the infants. Where this has not happened and the woman has insisted on the man taking over the care of the child while she pursues her profession, the man has not only found the time he has to put into childcare difficult but has been unable to accept his wife's dropping out to such an extent from the life of the family.

Many women take this period out for the early care of their children with joy. However, they expect their husbands to later share more fully in the household in order for them to establish themselves satisfactorily at work. Yet these interests in further education and work development add new demands on an already strained "time budget" of the couple. As I observed before, the man may have great difficulties accepting the changes of his wife's and his own role.

Despite diminished alienation at work, there are also difficulties flowing over from work affecting personal relationships. Since both men and women now are interested in working, there is not only tension about the division of labor in the household but both are involved in their work. Each may, to begin with a seemingly trivial matter, worry about completing concrete tasks at work in time. This pressure exists even when the deadline is collectively set by the workers, which is often the case according to the people I spoke with.

"There is difficulty when the collective decides on a deadline and you have to make it. The different groups in the collective must work together and if you miss the deadline, everything is messed up and then you're criticized."

(an engineer)

Usually, the demands on professionals go beyond their actual work "duties". It is not that they are "ruled over" by managerial or political elites but, through a long professional and political socialization process, come to feel their work roles as an integral part of their being, although with great variety, of course. A teacher, for example, in both the Soviet Union and the G.D.R. may be doing research, is expected to meet regularly with parents, attend party and union meetings, and take further professional training.

> "I'm already nervous on Sunday before the week begins. My husband complains I flare up easily."

> "If my husband asks me to do something extra in the morning I explode because my work is all planned."

Aside from the strain and the nervousness which both men and women now experience because they have too much to do, their very absorption in work, which is an absorption in a world and with people very much apart from their lives together as husband and wife, may cause difficulties.

> "In Russia, among high level professionals, the problem is absorption in work...often the wives find someone else who isn't such a great professional but will pay more attention to them, with whom they can live.
>
> (a Soviet woman)

> "My wife was a ballerina...It's impossible to be married to a ballerina—that's no kind of life. She had a tight regime...When she finally came home from a performance, she was exhausted. The profession itself interested her. We had no private life."
>
> (a Soviet man)

Although the work collective encourages participation of husbands and wives, often the "outsider" does not feel an integral part of the group. One woman complained that her husband once belonged to a collective which went out drinking several times a week. A few of the women were disappointed their husbands did not care for their colleagues.

A frequent complaint about the modern nuclear family is that, when the man leaves the house to work, he is no longer directly involved with his wife in activities for the common good of the family, even if he does bring home a paycheck. The problem is greatly relieved if the wife also goes out to work; however, the relief, the solutions bring with them their own problems, their own pressures on family life.

I am not only thinking about the normal work day but also the activities the work colleagues participate in together, the union meetings and party obligations which take time and which take husbands and wives away from each other for even longer periods. Because the demands of work are concrete, oftentime determined, because the consequences of not working well are not only disturbing but have practical impact on one's daily living and because people are devoted to their work, both men and women respond to the demands of work, leaving family relationships for energies and hours left over. The respondents cared about both their work and their families but, if the absorptions in work were too great, there were effects on the family many of the respondents found difficult and unwelcome, yet felt unable to change. Among the East Germans I talked to, there was not one couple where one member had not been married before or where the marriage was not now in serious trouble. Among the Soviet Jews, where family life is somewhat more traditional, half of the respondents had been divorced and were now alone or in new marriages. I am not suggesting that work caused all the difficulties; however, many of the men and women indeed felt strong connections between absorption in work and the breaking up of their marriages.[5]

Conclusion

There are several important questions raised by this discussion of alienation at work and the equality of men and women in the G.D.R. and the Soviet Union. On the one hand, according to the conception of alienation developed by Marx, it seems that alienation at work has been diminished; yet, men and women are tense in their relationships and feel overburdened. One important source of these problems can be traced back to the work situation, even if in many respects it is relatively non-alienating. The demands of work do not fully take into account what is happening to people outside. The individual learns that he or she must work within a certain institution and that the demands of that institution may often be at odds with other demands and with his or her own personal concerns.

Should not the reduced alienation of professional men and women allow them to have more fulfilling human relationships? The paradox is that professional work, though relatively non-alienating, tends to be all-embracing and people are inclined to become totally absorbed with what they are doing; the strength and energy for personal relationships is diminished, even if the caring is strong. Men and women are absorbed in different worlds, with different people and sometimes a different "spirit."

Despite the participation of women in the work force and the structural supports encouraging their education and equality, the woman is overloaded. Especially in the Soviet Union, the man does not fully participate in household work. Although among professionals in East Berlin there is a great deal of discussion about equality and more sharing of household work, women still feel they have ultimate responsibility for the house and especially for the children. At the same time, professional women have the same ambitions and work interests as their husbands.

A stable, sharing relationship is of great importance to the men and women I spoke with; marriage and the nuclear family are not mere relics of the past for

---

[5] From comparative interviews in the United States, it is my impression that the problems in American marriages are as intense, though for other reasons which cannot be discussed in this paper; however, the Soviet and East German women have more supports if the marital relationship is broken.

people who grew up in families disrupted by war and imprisonment. The issue is how work can be structured to allow time and energy for personal commitments; this is a problem professionals face in other industrial societies as well (Wilenski, 1963: 107-146; Young and Willmott, 1973).

The consequences of the demands and absorptions in work and the problems of changing family roles result in difficulties which men and women are not really prepared for. They assume as young adults a certain harmony in their work and family lives which is not there. The possibilities of incorporating two such important aspects of one's being, one's working life and one's personal relationships, are limited despite the many supports working men and women are given in socialist societies. These supports are only the beginning of solutions. Reduced working hours for both men and women, increased sharing of tasks and the open and sharp questioning of what is happening and what should happen in the work world of professionals may lead to a lessening of the tension between work and personal life. Dealing with this tension, intellectually and politically, remains an unfinished task.

REFERENCES

Blauner, Robert
    1964   *Alienation and Freedom.* Chicago: University of Chicago Press.

Engels, Frederich
    1942   *The Origin of the Family, Private Property and the State.* Marxist Library, Works of Marxism-Leninism, Vol. XXIII. New York: International Publishers.

Epstein, Cynthia F.
    1971   *Woman's Place.* Berkeley: University of California Press.

Fromm, Erich
    1962   "Personality and the Market Place." *Man, Work and Society*, Sigmund Nosow and William H. Form, eds. New York: Basic Books, Inc.: 446-452.

Jacoby, Susan
    1971   "Towards an Educated Elite: The Soviet Universities." *Change* (November) : 33-39.

Lipset, S.M.
           "Stratification Research and Soviet Scholarship." *Social Stratification and Mobility in the U.S.S.R.*, Murray Yanowich and Wesley A. Fisher, eds. New York: International Arts and Science Press: 355-391.

Mandel, William M.
    1975   *Soviet Women.* New York: Anchor Press/Doubleday.

Marx, Karl
    1963   *Early Writings*, T.B. Bottomore, ed. New York: McGraw Hill.

Menschic, Jutta and Evelyn Leopold
    1974   *Gretchens Rote Schwestern* (Gretchen's Red Sisters). Frankfurt am Main: Fischer Taschenbuch Verlag.

Scott, Hilda
    1974   *Does Socialism Liberate Women?* Boston: Beacon Press.

Wilenski, Harold
    1963   "The Uneven Distribution of Leisure: The Impact of Economic Growth on 'Free Time,' " *Work and Leisure*, Erwin O. Smigel, ed. New Haven, Conn. : College and University Press: 107-146.

Young, Michael and Peter Willmott
    1973   *The Symmetrical Family.* London: Routledge and Kegan Paul, Ltd.

APPENDIX   PROFESSIONS AND AGES OF RESPONDENTS FROM EAST GERMANY AND THE SOVIET UNION

Males		Females	
Profession	Age	Profession	Age
Composer	35	Adult educator	35
Dentist	40	Anthropologist	48
Educator and administrator	45	Editor, publishing house	37
Engineer	61	Fashion designer	58
Engineer	47	High school teacher	37
Industrial engineer	50	High school teacher	36
Technical engineer	50	High school teacher	37
Music teacher and composer	45	Industrial engineer	36
Physician	38	Industrial psychologist	33
Physician	47	Journalist	37
Physicist	46	Physician	47
Pianist	38	(Assistant) professor	35
(Assistant) professor	33	Translator	36
Psychiatrist	28	Graduating university student	30
Psychiatrist	43		
Psychiatrist	62		
Violinist	32		
Violinist	47		
Writer	50		

Occupational Choice Among Female Academicians*—The Israeli Case

RINA SHAPIRA**
EVA ETZIONI-HALEVY**
and
SHIRA CHOPP-TIBON**

In recent years public attention has been focused on the occupational aspirations of women by feminists who claim that women must be liberated so that they can engage in occupations similar to those of men, if they so choose. The question must be raised: is this what women actually choose to do? In other words, what are the occupational role images of women, and are they indeed similar to those of men?

In this analysis we direct this question to female university students and graduates in Israel, a society which (in contrast to many Western societies) has developed an egalitarian ideological bent with regard to the social role of women. The most visible manifestations of this ideology of equality between the sexes have been in the pre-state clandestine military organizations, in the labor movement which has been dominant in the society, in the kibbutz movement, and in the youth movements which inculcate their members with general precepts of equality and with the ideology of the kibbutz. Regardless of whether the precepts of equality between the sexes are realized in the actual social patterns of the kibbutz, they form an essential part of its ideology, and are thus transmitted to a large part of Israeli youth via the youth movements. Since we know that some seventy to eighty percent of all Israeli university students (including female students) have at one time or another been members of youth movements, the question is, to what extent has the egalitarian ideology to which they have been exposed exerted any visible influence on their outlooks?

Research done in Western societies and especially the United States shows that women are socialized toward, and that most women (including academicians) still adhere to a traditional feminine role image, composed of the following tenets: a woman's greatest achievements are in the realm of home and family and it is to these that she should devote most of her time and effort; if engaged in an outside occupation, she should limit the time and effort invested therein, and not aspire to outstanding occupational achievements which might impair her ability to fulfil her feminine role in the home; if intent on working outside her home,

---

*By this term we mean, following a modified Israeli usage, persons with higher education—university students and graduates.
**Tel Aviv University, Israel.

it is appropriate for her to choose an occupation that involves serving and nurturing of others, that is, one which is reminiscent of her role as housewife and
mother. (See for instance Gornich and Moran, 1971; Safilos-Rothschild, 1972
and Freeman, 1974). Do Israeli women academicians, like so many of their
sisters overseas, still lean toward this traditional role image, or have they adopted
occupational role images which are more nearly in line with those of their male
peers, as might have been expected in view of the egalitarian ideology with which
they have been confronted?

   We examined this question at various points in time, thus tracing the development of the women's role images, as compared to those of their male counterparts) throughout the process of their professional socialization at the university
and at the time of their initial entry into the labor market after graduation. It
was our expectation that at the beginning of their studies at the university, the
women's role images would be least "feminine" in the traditional sense of the
term, and most similar to those of male students as a result of their past socialization. Since the educational system is relatively more egalitarian in its treatment of the sexes than is the occupational structure, we expected that as women
approach their initiation into the labor market, they would become more
"realistic" adapting their occupational choices to their actual possibilities in this
market, and that their role images would thus become more traditionally
"feminine". Since ours was a follow-up study, it was particularly suited for the
examination of this expectation.

   To bring out the special qualities of the role images of female academicians—
We compared them with those of their male counterparts in the following three
respects: occupational choice per se; decisiveness of occupational choice; and consistency of occupational choice.

The Study

   The analysis is based on a follow-up of students at Tel-Aviv University (one
of the six academic institutions of higher learning in Israel) from the beginning of
their university studies until they entered the labor market. The study was on a
stratified random sample of students from three faculties (Natural Sciences, Social
Sciences and Humanities) who had begun their studies in 1966/7. A questionnaire
that included items on social background and attitudes was administered to the
students shortly after they enrolled at the university. A similar questionnaire was
administered when they were in their third year at the university.[1] A third questionnaire was administered five years after the respondents had begun their academic studies; this last stage included additional questions regarding the graduates' entrance into the labor market. Of the respondents who participated in all
three stages, this analysis deals with 323 individuals for whom we have full details
on social and academic background. One hundred and seventy-six of the
respondents (53.5%) were men, and 153 were women. The distribution of the

---

[1]In Israel studies toward the B.A. degree last for three years. For details on the first two stages of
the follow-up, see Shapira and Etzioni-Halevy, 1973.

respondents on all socio-economic background variables corresponds to their distribution among the overall student population at that time.

A. Occupational Choice

Can distinctively "feminine" patterns of occupational choice be discerned among Israeli women and how do they develop through the various stages of professional socialization? The pertinent data are presented in Table 1.

TABLE 1 OCCUPATIONAL CHOICE OF MEN AND WOMEN[2]

Occupational field	First Year at University		Third Year at University		Entrance into Labor Market	
	m	w	m	w	m	w
Science	33%	22%	36%	24%	31%	16%
Business	15%	2%	18%	3%	17%	3%
Administration	27%	10%	26%	10%	31%	20%
Technology	3%	2%	8%	5%	12%	10%
Teaching	16%	52%	9%	18%	4%	45%
Services	4%	11%	3%	9%	4%	7%
	98% (n=149)	99% (n=126)	100% (n=147)	99% (n=128)	99% (n=145)	100% (n=138)

There were clear differences in occupational choice between the sexes. Male students tended to choose science, business administration and technology more than did their female counterparts; these fields will therefore be referred to as "masculine". Female students tended to opt for teaching[3] and services

---

[2]The question by which we determined occupational choice was open ended: "What field do you intend to work in when you complete your education?" Occupations were classified (with minor changes) according to the system developed by Roe (1956). The category of "services" included occupations such as clinical psychology, social work, youth guidance and the like.
Not all of the possible academic professions appear on this list since our study included students of only three faculties; we did not include students of medicine, law etc. In addition, the list does not include occupations that were chosen by only a small number of respondents; for this reason, the percentages in the tables do not always add up to 100%.
In this and in the subsequent tables each "n" reflects the number of persons who replied to the particular question at that particular stage. Since there are respondents who replied to a certain question at one stage but not at another stage, "n's" are not identical at all stages. The differences between the first and the third year are usually small. But at the last stage we added a larger number of pertinent (and similar) questions. For this reason, apparently, the number of respondents who replied to each question was smaller.
[3]The tendency for female students to prefer teaching appeared to be related to the fact that they tend, more than men, to go into the humanities—where most of the subjects are particularly relevant for teachers. However, the data indicated that more female than male students go into teaching in each of the faculties—so choice of faculty could not explain occupational choice.

(hereafter referred to as "feminine"[4] occupations),[5] more often than their male counterparts.

The "masculine" fields are characterized by relatively high income or prestige. They may, therefore, be viewed as achievement-oriented occupations. The "feminine" fields are relatively low in prestige and income. They give less emphasis to self-advancement and more to nurturing others. This corresponds to findings of previous studies in the United States (for instance Davis, 1956 and Rosenberg, 1957);[6] however, we stress two additional points:

First, while the data indicate distinctive feminine patterns of occupational choice, they also indicate (Table 1) that a sizable minority does not conform to these patterns. At each stage of socialization there were some female non-conformists who opted for "masculine" occupations such as science. Second, grouping all "masculine" occupations together it may be seen that *the percentage of women who picked such occupations increased as the process of occupational socialization advanced.* During their first year at the University, 36% of the female students opted for "masculine" fields: by their third year, the figure was 42%. At the final stage, approximately half of the women chose masculine fields. We had expected women to become more "realistic" in their choice as they approached entry into the labor market, thus concentrating more heavily in occupations in which they must have perceived they have a better chance. Actually, the opposite occurred.

This being the case, one would think that the differences between "feminine" and "masculine" fields would have become indistinct by the final stage. However, men too, gradually decreased their choice of "feminine" fields—so the gap between the percentages of men and of women who chose "masculine" fields, remained more or less uniform.

As we found that a significant number of women opted for "masculine" occupations, our next question was, what were the special characteristics of this group of women? Since they rejected the well-trodden path of their female compeers, we expected that they would be more hesitant in their commitment, that is, less decisive and less consistent than others in their occupational choice.

---

[4]By "masculine" occupations we mean occupations chosen more frequently by men; by "feminine" occupations we mean occupations more frequently chosen by women. These are simply short hand terms; they are completely value neutral and do *not* imply either approval or disapproval of this pattern.

[5]During all three stages, the differences between the sexes in their choice of either "feminine" or "masculine" fields was significant at the 0.01 level. The statistical levels of significance reported in this article do not relate to the tables, but to the reported differences. The level of significance was determined by the X^2 test.

[6]A comprehensive bibliography on studies relating to these subjects may be found in Astin (1971).

B. Decisiveness of Occupational Choice[7]

Generally speaking, there were no significant differences between men and women with regard to decisiveness of occupational choice. But our interest focused especially on "non-conformist" women. To ascertain whether women who had chosen "masculine" occupations were in fact especially indecisive in their occupational choice, we compared them to men who chose similar occupations, to men who chose "feminine" occupations and to other women. This comparison is presented in Table II.

TABLE II   MEN AND WOMEN DISPLAYING A HIGH DEGREE OF DECISIVENESS IN OCCUPATIONAL CHOICE

	First Year at University		Third Year at University		Entrance into Labor Market	
	M	W	M	W	M	W
Chose "Masculine" Fields	48% (n=115)	42% (n=45)	78% (n=68)	63% (n=49)	62% (n=133)	63% (n=65)
Chose "feminine" Fields	53% (n=34)	70% (n=80)	100% (n=19)	81% (n=70)	100% (n=12)	69% (n=71)

The table indicates two conspicuous tendencies. First, both men and women tended to be more decisive than others of their sex (in all three stages) when choosing the less achievement-oriented "feminine" occupations. It follows that non-conforming men are more decisive than others of their sex, whereas non-conforming women tend to be less decisive. Second, it is characteristic of the non-conforming groups of both sexes (and of them only) that their decisiveness increases as they approach the final stage of occupational choice. For the non-conforming males, the percentage displaying a high degree of decisiveness increased from 53% to 100%; for the non-conforming females, it increased from 42% to 63%.

By combining these two tendencies we learn that, as expected, the women who opted for "masculine" fields were indeed more hesitant than other women—but their decisiveness increased, while the decisiveness of other women showed no

[7]Degree of decisiveness was determined on the basis of the above question on occupational choice. Respondents were divided into the following classifications:
High decisiveness: knew exactly what they wanted to do.
Low decisiveness: considered two alternatives, said "maybe", or indicated a field in general terms without committing themselves to anything in particular.

clear trend.   Thus the differences between the two groups of women almost disappeared at the final stage.[8]

To help visualize women's development of decisiveness, we constructed a model that combines occupational choice with decisiveness.

We distinguished four types of women:

Model A   WOMEN'S OCCUPATIONAL CHOICE

Degree of Decisiveness	"Feminine" Nurturing-oriented Occupations	"Masculine" Achievement-oriented Occupations
High	Type 1	Type 2
Low	Type 3	Type 4

We then broke down the female population into these four categories, as visualized in Model B.

Women's decisiveness increased slightly over the years (types I and II combined increased from 60% at the first stage to 66% at the third stage).

However, the proportion of women belonging to type I decreased (from 45% to 36%) while the proportion belonging to type II increased (from 15% to 30%). In other words, an increasing incidence of females chose achievement-oriented occupations and were determined to realize this choice—although it necessitated greater competition with men. Although this type remained a minority, it became a quite significant one at the final stage.

Since women who opted for "masculine" occupations were initially less decisive than others in their occupational choice but became more so as they went along, we now thought that they would display a similar pattern with regard to consistency of occupational choice.

C. Consistency of Occupational Choice

Consistency of occupational choice was measured by the correspondence between such choice and the most desirable rewards expected from work.   We distinguished between rewards of income and advancement, which are in line

---

[8]During the first and third years at the university, the differences between the non-conforming women and the others were significant at the 0.05 level.   The report on men indicated only tendencies, since the differences between non-conforming men and the others during the first year were not significant.   The differences increased in the following years, but we could not check the significance because one of the squares in each year indicated 0.

Model B : *Typology of Women according to their Occupational Choice and Decisiveness at the Three Stages of Occupational Socialization*

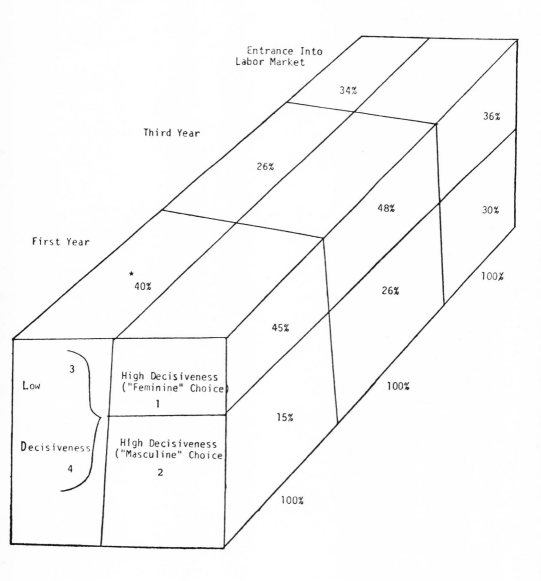

with achievement-oriented occupations, and rewards of security, convenience and leisure, which correspond to less achievement-oriented occupations.[9]

On the whole, the data indicate that (for both men and women) those who chose achievement-oriented occupations showed a greater tendency to expect rewards of advancement, whereas those who chose less achievement-oriented occupations tended more frequently to expect rewards of convenience and leisure. The former pattern of course is more characteristic of men, whereas the latter is more characteristic of women. Table III displays the differences between men and women in this respect.

TABLE III   REWARDS THAT MEN AND WOMEN EXPECT FROM WORK[9]

Rewards Expected	First Year at University		Third Year at University		Entrance into Labor Market	
	M	W	M	W	M	W
"Achievement-oriented" Rewards (advancement, prestige, income)	55%	33%	61%	38%	73%	35%
"Non-achievement-oriented" Rewards (security, convenience, leisure)	45%	67%	39%	62%	27%	65%
	100% (n=165)	100% (n=144)	100% (n=168)	100% (n=144)	100% (n=89)	100% (n=85)

The rewards stressed by members of both sexes at each stage corresponded to the occupations they tended to prefer. Also, the differentiation regarding desired rewards increased; at the first stage, the difference between men and women was 22% — and it increased to 38% at the third stage. This increasing differentiation stemmed from the fact that men increasingly preferred "masculine" rewards, while women were stable in their choice.[10]

[9]The question concerning the most desirable reward was: "Which of the following is most important to you in choosing your occupation?" Six categories were given, which were then collapsed into two reward categories:

A. *Advancement, leadership and material rewards.* ("Work in which you will progress and enjoy social esteem"; "Work which will eventually enable you to be part of the country's leadership and elite"; and "Work in which you will attain good financial income and an appropriate standard of living.")

B. *Security, convenience and leisure:* ("Steady work which ensures future security"; "Convenient and pleasant work which does not involve constant tension"; and "Work which leaves free time to devote to your family").

[10]At each of the three stages, the differences between men and women were significant at the 0.01 level. However, the relationship was strongest at the third stage. The strength of the relationship was measured by the contingency coefficient, and this resulted in the following coefficients:

First year $C=.214$
Third year $C=.225$
Occupational absorption $C=.428$

In general, then, there was a significant and increasing degree of consistency in the role images of both men and women.

We now turn back to the non-conforming groups. As mentioned, the non-conforming women were relatively more hesitant in their occupational choice yet they expressed increasing decisiveness as they approached their first job. Would this be the case with regard to consistency as well? We looked into the consistency shown by non-conforming women compared with that of non-conforming men and that of conforming women. This comparison is presented in Table IV.

TABLE IV   MEN AND WOMEN EXPECTING NON-ACHIEVEMENT-ORIENTED
                         REWARDS FROM THEIR CHOSEN OCCUPATIONS

	First Year at University		Third Year at University		Entrance into Labor Market	
	M	W	M	W	M	W
Chose "Masculine" Fields	41% (n=108)	64% (n=44)	33% (n=124)	48% (n=54)	24% (n=65)	68% (n=38)
Chose "Feminine" Fields	56% (n=32)	70% (n=77)	70% (n=17)	73% (n=70)	25% (n=4)	71% (n=38)

In the initial stages of socialization, the non-conforming men who opted for "feminine" occupations tended to prefer corresponding rewards (convenience and leisure).[11] On the other hand, the non-conforming women who opted for "masculine" occupations often did not prefer the corresponding rewards (advancement, prestige); more often they preferred rewards that are characteristic of feminine choice. The determining factor for women's expected rewards was their sex rather than their chosen occupation. Thus, women who were non-conforming in their occupational choice developed a role image which was less consistent internally than that of non-conforming men, and was also less consistent than that of conforming women.

This becomes even more apparent when we trace expected rewards over the three stages of socialization (see Table IV). An ever-increasing percentage of men who chose "masculine" achievement-oriented occupations also preferred achievement-oriented rewards — but this was not the case for women who opted for "masculine" occupations; they remained more-or-less stable in their tendency to prefer non-achievement-oriented rewards. Thus, the rising percentage of women who chose "masculine" achievement-oriented occupations — and did so with an increasing amount of decisiveness — was not accompanied by a parallel

---

[11]The picture changes at the stage of occupational absorption, but "n" here is so small that we should not attach much significance to the divergence.

rise in the percentage of women willing to sacrifice convenience and leisure for this kind of achievement.   In this sense, the role images adopted by many women who chose achievement-oriented occupations were and remained unbalanced and therefore inconsistent.

Discussions

Israel, as we saw, is a society where an ideology of equality between the sexes has sprouted, and where a major part of academically oriented youth has been exposed to this ideology.   This ideology should have been especially attractive to female academicians who, it may be assumed, comprise a particularly ambitious segment of the Israeli female population, and who, over the years, have received the benefit of training identical to that received by men.   In spite of all this, these women are still inclined to emphasize the feminine role image in rather tradional terms—a role image that advocates of women's liberation are now trying to change.

How can we account for this pattern?   It seems that these images have been shaped by some constraints of social reality which we know to be at work in other contemporary societies and which ideology not withstanding — seem to be at work in Israel as well.   Thus, observers in the United States (for instance Koma-rovsky, 1946; Keniston and Keniston, 1964; Safilos-Rothschild, 1972) have suggested that female academicians are subjected to cross pressures; they are expected (and expect themselves) to prove their ability in the professions for which they have been trained, but they are also expected (and accept the responsibility) to fulfil a feminine, familial role, which demands much time and effort at the expense of their professional role.   While men who invest time and effort in their occupations are usually considered to be *contributing* to their family lives, women who do so are considered to be *depriving* their families (see Coser and Rokoff, 1970-71).

By applying the American analysis to our findings, we may perceive the role images of female Israeli academicians as an attempt to balance such cross pres-sures: they do intend to pursue academic professions, but many of them opt for the kind of professions which are less aehievement-oriented, demand less time and effort and thus will cause the least damage to their feminine roles of house-wives and mothers.   They thus seek a compromise, albeit one which tends to satisfy the demands of the feminine role more than those of the professional role.

Examining the dynamics of role image development, we saw that as women approached the entrance into the labor market they tonded to increase their choice of "masculine" achievement-oriented occupations, and those who chose such occupations became more and more decisive in their choice.   This is rather a surprising finding.   Given the relative lack of differentiation between men and women in the framework of higher education and the relatively greater differen-tiation between the sexes in the labor market the opposite could have been expec-ted.   As women approached the entrance into the sex-differentiated labor market, they should have become more "realistic", adapting themselves to the exigencies of their new situation.

We reasoned that the fact that this is not so, may be attributed to changes in the general ideology prevalent among Israeli women in recent years. Although the women's liberation movement as such has not made much headway in Israel, some of its ideas have recently gained more prevalence amongst Israeli women and the public at large. We reasoned that women's changing role images may have been increasingly influenced by this ideology. If so, it would follow that the new feminist ideology was more potent in influencing women academicians' attitudes than was the traditional Israeli ideology of equality between the sexes to which they have been exposed in the past, and which apparently has not made much of an impact on them.

Since Israel's traditional ideology of equality has been transmitted to a large extent through youth movements, it was easy to test the second part of this interpretation by comparing the majority of students who have been members of such movements with the minority who have not—with regard to occupational choice and decisiveness of occupational choice. As expected, no differences between erstwhile members and other students were found. Possibly, this is due to the fact that the tenets transmitted by youth movements concern mainly the equality between the sexes as manifested in the social or group setting. Since the adolescents attending youth movements are not, as yet, concerned with the exigencies of family life and occupational choice, youth movements devote little or no time to these problems. Hence it makes sense they they should not have left any perceptible traces on their graduates, in these respcets.

The first part of our interpretation was more difficult to test. Our questionnaire included no questions pertaining directly to the new feminist ideology. We did have two questions concerning division of labor within the family and the replies to these showed no significant relationship to women's occupational choice or decisiveness of occupational choice. Indirectly, the lack of relationship would seem to weaken this part of our interpretation.

Nevertheless, we do know that in recent years Israeli women have made more headway into the higher brackets of the occupational structure.[12] This means, that in one way or another women's attitudes and those of the public at large have changed to some extent. This also means that the opportunity structure for women has changed. Possibly it is the interaction between these factors which has wrought the changes in the occupational outlook of our female respondents. However, some further research would be called for to test this interpretation more extensively.[13]

---

[12]Thus, in recent years, the number of women engaged in scientific, professional and technical occupations, has grown dramatically. While the general number of persons engaged in such occupations in Israel has grown considerably, this growth has been especially conspicuous amongst women: Between the years 1960 and 1970 the number of men engaged in such occupations had grown by 70 percent; the number of women on the other hand had grown by 100 percent. [computed from: Central Bureau of Statistics, (1971)].

[13]We have now embarked on a replication of our study on a new, comparable population of students. We have added some pertinent questions to the questionnaire and we hope to be able to test this interpretation in the new phase of the study.

In any case, it must be borne in mind that the women's increasing tendency to choose achievement-oriented occupations was not accompanied by an increasing tendency to seek achievement-oriented rewards in their jobs and to forego the leisure they apparently felt was due to their families. Hence we must reach the conclusion that if the newer feminist ideology in combination with changes in the opportunity structure has made any impact at all on our respondents, this impact is of a rather limited nature.

In this study we paid special attention to the non-conforming-women who chose "masculine" occupations. These women proved to be more hesitant, less balanced and less consistent in their role images: at the initial stages of professional socialization they were less decisive than others in their occupational choice, and although they chose achievement-oriented occupations, most of them did not seek the type of achievement-oriented rewards appropriate to these occupations, but rather the leisure and family-oriented rewards characteristically aspired to by their female colleagues. This may be accounted for by the fact that these nonconformists were less successful than other women in coping with their cross-pressures, hence the greater ambivalence in their role images.[14]

Another possible interpretation for this pattern is that even a traditional, feminine role image does not necessarily involve a specifically "feminine" occupation. Rather, the traditional role image may manifest itself in specifically "feminine" attitudes toward "masculine" occupations. In the United States, for instance, it was found that even women who pursued distinctly "masculine" occupations tended to cut down on their professional involvement in favor of family demands. (See for instance Fuchs-Epstein, 1970 and Poloma, 1972). Evidently, as far as advancement is concerned, these women could not compete with men in similar professions. On the other hand, they managed to combine their professional and feminine roles quite successfully. It is possible that our female academicians who opted for "masculine" occupations but preferred "feminine" rewards chose a similar manner of solving their role conflict: like their American sisters they intended to *work* in masculine professions, but did not intend to make *careers* in them.

Some time ago Parson (1942) claimed that "career women" in the full sense of the term, comprise a small minority of their sex. This was written in regard to American society more than thirty years ago. Surprisingly it still seems to be applicable to female academicians in Israel today. Although these women tended to change their role images toward greater career-orientations, most of them were not prepared to pay the full price required for such careers by adopting job expectations like those of their achievement-oriented male colleagues. Most of them thus stopped short of adopting an entirely career-oriented approach. If this is the case among university students and graduates, we would expect it to be even more so among the general female population. Thus even in a society

---

[14]A discussion on the psychological aspect of this ambivalence may be found in Keniston and Keniston (1964).

with a traditional ideology of equality between the sexes, and one in which the new feminine ideology has made some headway as well, the full-fledged "career-woman" is still the exception.

At the same time, we cannot ignore the fact that the female academicians in our sample did show a significant attitudinal change over a period of five years which, as noted, may well reflect changes in the general climate of opinion among women in Israel. We hope to be able to determine whether this trend is continuing, by carrying out additional follow-ups in the future.

BIBLIOGRAPHY

Adams, M.
    1971   "The Compassion Trap" pp. 555-75 in Gornick, V. and Moran, B.K. *Woman in Sexist Society*. New York: Basic Books.

Astin, H.S.
    1971   *Women—A Bibliography on Their Education and Careers*. Washington, D.C.: Human Service Press.

Central Bureau of Statistics
    1971   *Statistical Abstract of Israel* No. 22, Jerusalem.

Coser, R.L. and Pokoff, G.
    1970-71   "Women in the Occupational World—Social Disruption and Conflict". *Social Problems*. Vol. 18, pp. 535-54.

Davis, J.A.
    1956   *Undergraduate Career Decisions*. Chicago: Aldine Publishing Co.

Freeman, J.
    1974   "The Social Construction of the Second Sex", pp. 201-18 in Skolnick, A. and Skolnick, J·H. *Intimacy, Family and Society*. Boston: Little Brown & Co.

Fuchs-Epstein, C.
    1970   *Woman's Place*, Berkeley: University of California Press.

Cornick, V. and Moran, B.K. (eds.)
    1971   *Woman in Sexist Society*. New York: Basic Books.

Keniston, E. and Kenirson, K.
    1964   "The American Anachronism: The Image of Women and Work". *American Scholar* Vol. 33, No. 3, (Summer) pp. 355-75.

Komarovsky, M.
    1946   "Cultural Contradictions and Sex Roles." *American Journal of Sociology*. Vol. 52, pp. 604-616.

Parsons, T.
    1942   "Age and Sex in the Social Structure of the United States." *American Sociological Review* 7.

Pavalko, R.M.
    1971   *Sociology of Occupations and Professions*. Itasca, III: F.E. Peacock.

Poloma, M.
    1972   "Role Conflict and the Married Professiodal Woman" pp. 187-98 in Safilos-Rothschild, C. (ed.) *Toward a Sociology of Women*. Lexington, Massachusetts, Toronto: Xerox College Publishing.

Roe, A.
1956   *The Psychology of Occupations.* London, J. Wiley.

Rosenberg, M.
1957   *Occupations and Values.* New York: The Free Press.

Rossi, A.S.
1972   "Women in Science: Why So Few?"   pp. 141-53 in Safilos-Rothschild, C. (ed),
         Toward A Sociology of Women.   Lexington, Massachusetts, Toronto: Xerox
         College Publishing.

Safilos-Rothschild, C. (ed.)
1972   *Toward A Sociology of Women.* Lexington. Massachusetts, Toronto: Xerox College
         Publishing.

Shapira, R. and Etzioni-Halevy, E.
1973   *Who is the Israeli Student.* Tel-Aviv, Am Oved.

25   Variations in Women's Roles and Family Life Under the Socialist Regime in China*

WILLIAM T. LIU**
and
ELENA S. H. YU***

Two opposing viewpoints prevail in the literature with respect to the impact of the socialist revolution on family life and fertility patterns in China today. Some authors (Aird, 1972; Parish, 1975; Yu, 1976; 1977a) have argued that little has changed in the basic values and motivational forces underlying fertility behavior.[1] There is a second argument, to wit, that other social forces are potent enough to change the normative size of the family. Given sufficient time lag, such forces will produce a steep decline in the fertility rate of the next generation although it may not seem visible at present (Liu, 1974; Orleans, 1974; Rogers, 1973).[2] These seemingly incongruent viewpoints emerged primarily because the former group of scholars (Aird, 1972; Parish, 1975; Yu, 1976; 1977a) based their arguments on rural women whereas the latter group (Rogers, 1973; and Liu, 1973; 1974); employed samples from the urban scene. Beyond the simple dichotomy of urban and rural China there are other significant factors which could be expected to have an impact on fertility behavior but which have not been adequately or sufficiently

---

*This is a revision of the paper read at the Annual Meeting of the Population Association of America, Seattle, Washington, April 17-19, 1975. The Senior Author is indebted to the Population Council for a grant to visit the People's Republic of China in 1973. The Junior Author is indebted to the Ford Foundation for the research support she received while at the Center for the Study of Man, and to the Sociology Department, University of Victoria, for granting her permission to visit China at the start of the school year in 1976.
**University of Illinois Chicago Circle, U.S.A.
***University of Victoria, Canada

[1] On the basis of newspaper accounts, interviews with former residents of China, and an actual visit to the countryside (Yu, 1976; 1977a), these authors have independently conveyed the recalcitrance of rural women to family planning programs. For instance, Aird (1972) maintained that the traditional value on large family still persists in spite of attempted reforms. Parish (1975) cited the peculiar characteristics of the Chinese welfare system, the rural economy of grain allotment and strict migration laws which keep young adults in the countryside as some of the major impediments to fertility control. Yu (1977a) stressed the significance of Chinese kinship structure and contend in stemming sex-role equality, thereby subverting official fertility goals. Hence, according to both Parish (1975) and Yu (1976; 1977a), the modern social and economic forces in rural China which shape the desire to have a traditional family size may be different from the old forces, but they produce the same end results.

[2] They provide statistics and accounts relevant to the public health delivery system, family planning campaigns, and small group pressures (Orleans, 1974; Rogers, 1973; Liu, 1974) in addition to observations made while in China for a short visit (Liu, 1973; 1974).

analyzed. Some of these factors are: the genuine desire of the Chinese to push for sex-role equality and to equalize opportunities, the possible emergence of a new form of conjugal relations in the family, the reported increase in labor participation of married women, commune organization, and the structure of urban neighborhoods, among others. In this paper, we shall concern ourselves with the ways in which these factors are articulated with the family system, the economic structure, and the socio-political context in China. We wish to examine the economic motivation of women's participation in the labor force and some of the factors that are conducive to women's ascendance to political leadership roles. For this reason, we go beyond the individual as the unit of observation. Instead, we look at the requisites of the kinship structure, housing conditions, co-residence patterns and other factors external to the family and assess their implications on women's roles, fertility behavior and family life in China.

China's Policy on Women's Roles

Officially, party leaders in China have been pushing for sex equality at home — to free women from the traditional bondage, particularly with respect to arranged marriage, filial obedience, and patrilineal servitude. In this regard, dramatic changes have been documented. Moreover, for ideological as well as economic reasons, the Party has also endorsed sex equality in the non-domestic front. Thus, women are not only permitted but are encouraged to take part in economic production.

In reality, however, the policy has not been all that consistent, nor the practice uniform. Variations are discernible across time and space. Along the temporal dimension, for example, Leader (1973) indicated that the Party policy has swayed like a pendulum from militancy to moderation since the establishment of the regime.[3]

In the wake of China's push for self-determination and self-reliance, the aphorism "use two legs to walk" was applied to almost every aspect of Chinese life. It was — and still is — aimed at inspiring the masses to combine whatever means in existence that they could utilize in order to attain the desired goal on

---

[3] Between 1950 and 1953, the initial period of reconstruction, there was a concentrated attack on "feudal marriages," and broad grounds for divorce were granted (Yang, 1959; Leader, 1973), accompained by the promotion of marriage through free choice or marriage for love (Salaff, 1971). For the next three years, women were urged to participate in the labor force, yet from all evidence gathered in the newspapers, it was clear that few jobs were in fact available to potential female workers. In retreat, the Party called for women "to manage family affairs by industry and thrift." However, from 1958 to 1961, with the initiation of the Great Leap Forward, nearly every woman who could be employed was engaged in some form of productive labor. Thus, even though the Great Leap Forward was an economic disaster, it was an unprecedented boost for women's emancipation.

The retreat from the Great Leap Forward in 1961 also signaled the return of women to their traditional housekeeping tasks. But the advent of the Great Proletariat Cultural Revolution (1966-69) brough forth a new wave of campaign slogans aimed at the liberation and politicization of women. Marriage by free choice was redefined very strongly as a fulfilment of Communist revolution rather than blind romanticism. Women were urged to emulate the pioneering spirit of Taching workers and the agricultural achievements of Ta-chai's "Iron Girls."

any job.   In the Chinese woman's case, the combination of productive labor and political work with household tasks represents her ability to walk with both legs. This has been the official policy line of the People's Republic. That this desired role has not yet been fully accepted and practised may be discerned from an article by Ching-ling Soong (1972 : 6-12).

Aside from the temporal variation, there is also a vast regional difference with respect to labor participation, wage scales, and welfare benefits for women workers, compounded by the great disparity between urban and rural life-styles. The most notable difference is that between agricultural labor compared with urban employment.   The former is generally paid on a workpoint basis; the latter on a wage-scale system (Liu and Yu, 1975).

Both (spatial and temporal) dimensions of variations as well as the general social and economic conditions of the locale underscore the influence of state policies on familial roles and women's participation in the labor force. Regional and time series data on wages, workpoints, and women's labor participation offer clues to understanding the impact of the economic and political factors on the family. But they are often inadequate in providing a satisfactory explanation for the individual's motivations.

The Conceptual Frameworks of Sex Role Analysis

Analyses of women's roles have generally been restricted to a description of the domestic role structure in a nuclear family which ranges from a delineation of the housekeeper versus the breadwinner role, the mother-child bond versus the husband-wife dyad, to Parsons and Bales' (1955) and Zelditch's concept (1955) of instrumental versus expressive role constellations.

On a different level, women's roles have also been conceptualized from an economic perspective by assessing the extent of equal participation in the labor force, comparability of wage scales with men and occupational prestige. A cursory examination of existing literature reveals that much of the sociological works on sex role and the family have tended to treat women's roles either in terms of conjugal role structure and network relations (Bott, 1957; Rainwater, 1959; Komarovsky, 1964), *or* exclusively from the standpoint of their work role, and ignoring the family role structure of women (Whyte, 1948; Horsfall and Aresberg, 1949; Lupton, 1973; Cunnison, 1966; O'Neill, 1972).

Published works on women in China have not gone beyond the insular treatment of work and home.[1]   The need to undertake a holistic perspective in understanding the roles of the Chinese woman derives from the fact that temporal and spatial variations aside, there is a wide range of variations in the way Chinese women in the socialist regime perform their sex roles. For the fact remains that

[1] For example, Salaff (1971) treated these topics in different chapters of her dissertation, but the issues of women's employment and the changing family structure were not clearly articulated in a mutually explanatory manner.

not all women in China feel obliged to participate in the labor force, and not all of them work.[5]

In looking over some of the detailed reports obtained by visitors to China in recent years, one is led to believe that the variation in sex role activities is best understood by examining the extent to which familial obligations and economic behavior are integrated with the immediate environment of the family. By and large, we believe that personality variables aside, these choices are shaped by a number of factors over which the family does not always have direct control. It is at this point that the total social, economic and political milieu becomes relevant. The economic system, occupational differentiation, formal education, kinship structure, care of the young and the elderly, housing supplies, the organization of the neighborhoods, the age of women as well as the specific stage of the family life cycle, among others, affect the choice pattern by defining the range of alternative choices a woman may have in the new society. Thus, against the principle of "variation" in both time and space is the principle of "interaction." Under the principle of interaction, women's roles must be analyzed in terms of the degree to which the internal factors of family dynamics are interwoven with external forces of neighborhood organizations, economic contingencies, social realities, and state policies. Conceptually, the dynamics of sex roles stand between the family and the external environment which are *selectively* acting upon the family. Not all factors have equal impact on all families. Selectivity is, in a sense, the process by which individual families adapt their own conditions to the external environment.

Women in Rural Areas

Beginning in the mid-fifties when the collectivization of farm land began, rural families became dependent on collective efforts for grain allotment. However, unlike the kibbutz organization, payment in China is not gauged according to needs but according to the total workpoints accumulated by family members. Since women are perceived as unable to compete with men in work output, their average annual workpoints (which affects their grain allotment) often fall to as little as one-half of the men's workpoints (Schram, 1955; Yu, 1977a).[6] Aside from the basic grain a family receives from taking part in the work team, there is also a need for cash to purchase consumer goods, e.g. cooking oil, soap. In many instances, the cash income has to come from the joint efforts of family members — especially women and children, through the sale of vegetables grown in one's yard, or through sub-contracting handicrafts from light industrial factories or

---

[5] At one extreme, the traditional home-maker's role is played by some Chinese women: they take no part in the external community and there is a strict division of labor in the household. At the other extreme, one finds a family in which the husband and wife may take separate domicile, each pursuing an economic production which contributes to the goals of the collectivity. The children, if there are any, are often taken care of by a third party — usually a grandparent or close relative, or a day-care center nearby. In between these two extremes, one finds innumerable variations. Even focusing on these two extremes alone variations exist depending on the family life cycle.

[6] Consequently each family must maintain for itself its optimal hand/mouth ratio whereby the labor resources of able-bodied males can appreciably increase the accumulated workpoints and augment their grain allotment from the production team.

cottage industries. In southeastern China, the peasants' desire for cash income has escalated to such an extent that some of them are privately raising and selling pigs, ducks, and chickens in the flourishing black markets instead of turning them in to the production team for collective earnings as required (Yu, 1976; 1977b).[7]

The ideological debate on private production notwithstanding, some writers (Burki, 1970: 40; Parish, 1973) have estimated that it accounts for between 25 and 33 percent of the total team income. These figures, however limited and inaccurate, suggest that many rural folk (especially in southeastern China) indeed must choose between participation in collective agricultural work and private production. This problem is particularly salient to women. Since the man must leave the house daily either for collective farm work or for the market, the woman is the one who frequently tends the private plot. The household thus remains a production unit for farm women. The attraction of household production economy in addition to the need for some women to stay home for child care and other supportive activities, have indeed kept a fairly sizable proportion of rural women at home.[8]

Regardless of the attraction of housework for some rural women, they must take part in collective work during the busy season on the farm (cf. Myrdal, 1965: 229-39) or they are vulnerable to mass criticism for lack of collective interest. Thus, the articulation of women's roles in rural China is shaped primarily by economic realities but the social and political milieu are important factors as well.

Social Climbing through Political Participation

Chinese revolutionary leaders have long perceived the significance of mass political participation, especially peasant involvement in their struggle toward a socialist construction.[9] Nevertheless, the difficulty of sustaining the revolutionary fervor through the decades of land reforms and collectivization became apparent when the activists-turned-cadre-peasants tasted the sweetness of material gains and aspired to broaden their economic base. As a result, a large number of them gradually withdrew from political involvement on account of cross-cutting pressures and conflicting demands on their time. Accounts of passivity among

---

[7] The selling of vegetables has also become so lucrative that in some regions of southeastern China, able-bodied males are known to neglect their work in the communal field. This has finally resulted in the stipulation that any peasant who wishes to engage in the commercialization of private production may not receive workpoints in collective farm work. Still, some farmers persist. One middle-aged peasant who used to be a production team leader but resigned to attened to private production explained his rationale as follows: "If I work in the field, I will receive utmost 50 *yuan* (a day), usually just about .40 or .45 *yuan*. But if I go out to sell vegetables, I can make 2.00 *yuan* a day."

[8] Some writers estimated that only about 30 percent of the rural women did agricultural work (Leader, 1973: 64).

[9] In this light, exploited peasants from the previous regime have been encouraged to speak out their "bitterness." Many have achieved key leadership positions.

the new crop of village leaders abound in the Chinese media during the fifties.[10] Obviously, many cadres were caught in a bottleneck squeeze and decided to disengage from politics in order to devote their time to production, theirby enriching themselves and their families. Although subsequent class struggles succeeded in reprimanding and purging a large number of such village leaders, the problem merely transferred hands when some of the poor peasants who filled the vacant positions patterned themselves after the discredited (middle or newly rich) peasants whenever the tension between politics and production became too much to bear. After his visit to China, Liu (1974) concluded that the cycle of rural class conflict among the middle and the poor peasants was probably a major factor in turning rural women to political activities. The more hardship a woman experienced, the more active she and her family became since such attitudes and behavior were (and still are) socially rewarded.[11]

The authors thus take the position that at least in some regions of China during the period of utopian militancy (1958-59), one of the important elements in changing sex-typed work expectations was the call for political leadership and administrative talents among women workers. Commune operations required a new type of managerial skill for which the peasants were ill-prepared. In view of the demand for able-bodied male laborers in the field for collective farming and for maximization of workpoints badly needed by the family (since women earned less workpoints), managerial work and political leadership were left to women-folk. However, Yu's analysis (1977a) strongly indicated that women's monopoly on managerial roles and political posts is thwarted by the requisites of the Chinese patrilineal kinship structure and its ramifications. For instance, patrilocality in single-surname villages is an obstacle to women's rise to leadership position since they are transposed out of their natal kin groups and must cope with a new village environment where their husband's lineage members' loyalities are not assured but must be courted and delicately balanced in the face of intra-familial squabbles. On the other hand, a woman who marries within her village (as happens in multi-surname villages) will have a greater chance for political involvement and will likely be more successful in obtaining mass support because she has an established kinship network (i.e. her kin group), is a familiar person in the neighborhood, and is conversant with the situations in her village. It is, therefore, not surprising that Liu (1973) found women in north-central China

---

[10] Berstein (1968) noted that such dissonance is further exacerbated by the fact that (a) the material reward for village leadership positions was not great enough to allow peasants not to depend on economic production for greater earnings, (b) some villagers harboured resentment at not being promoted to more important positions above the village level and felt devalued, and (c) pressures to produce staggering results mounted as the rural administrative machinery sought to maximize the mobilization of the countryside in an effort to achieve the goals outlined by top party leaders.

[11] Liu's observation is supported by Salaff's earlier analysis (1967) of the changing status of women in China. Moreover, in the much publicized Ta-chai Production Brigade during the mid sixties, unmarried women working the field were called "Ironside Girls." They received special honor for their devotion to collective production and for their political commitment. Girls who later married were ineligible for the ironside status. The situation in Ta-chai has since been widely emulated in other rural communes throughout the country.

(where predominantly single-surname villages are relatively few compared to southeastern China) to be quite active politically, while Yu (1976) indicated that women in southeastern China (where many predominantly single-surname villages are concentrated) are politically passive.

Nevertheless, matrilocality does not guarantee life-time political participation (cf. Myrdal and Kessle, 1970). Neither does it guarantee that the woman will not experience the tension between political activism and other interests (cf. Myrdal and Kessle, 1970:137). Women cadres are torn between political involvement and their household chores, just as men were pressured by the demands of politics and production. Finally, matrilocality in and of itself is not a sufficient reason for women's political involvement either.

The contrast is, therefore, dramatic. Even though the social system of collective farming has changed the rural economy drastically, home-making and private production remain the same today as they were three decades ago prior to the socialist revolution. The intricate process of expressing the woman's new roles in the rural scene is the end result of several intersecting "push" and "pull" forces—political, social and economic (which were different in an earlier regime) and the requisites of the kinship structure (which has remained the same in spite of the Communist Revolution).

Women in Urban Areas

Little has been said about the urban women's roles although there is a mistaken common belief that womens' participation in urban employment is universally accepted. On the contrary, our observations in China and the figures we extracted from Hsu-Balzer et al.'s pictorial (1974) indicate that for those who work, variations in labor participation of men and women are quite discernible. First, there is a non-random assignment of work between heavy and light industries according to gender differences. Women by and large are concentrated in light industrial roles. Heavy industries allegedly require energies and skills which are regarded as not suitable for women.[12] Furthermore, wage scales for light industries are considerably below that of the heavy industries. Second, at least in Peking, women-intensive industries seem to have a much *lower* wage scale than those which are less women-intensive (see table below).[13] By matching the figures for different factories mentioned *et passim* in Hsu-Balzer et al.'s pictorial (1974), we found that the Peking Embroidery and Applique Factory which has 85% women workers, has a salary range of only 30 to 80 *yuan*. The Peking Glassware Factory, which hires 60% women, has a salary range of 30 to 100 *yuan*. In contrast, the Peking Arts and Crafts Factory, a light industry with only 45% of its workers who

---

[12] Hsu-Balzer et al. (1974) reported that as many as 50 percent of light industrial workers in the cities were women, but the proportion of women in heavy industries fell much below that figure.

[13] The reader should bear in mind that these are at best very limited data and may well be grossly inaccurate because of the limited number of cases.

are women, offers a salary of up to 200 *yuan* per month.[14] Third, it appears that the different wage systems are *not* due to the variation in the type of skills that these women have. This is inferred from Hsu-Balzer *et al.* (1974) that about 8,000 housewives are employed by the neighborhood workshops which have contracts with the Peking Arts and Crafts Factory and that the average monthly salary for women in these workshops (who engage in the same type of work as the women at the factory) was estimated at about 30 *yuan*, a figure well below the average monthly wage of those who work in the factory. Piecing together the observations which Hsu-Balzer *et al.* presented, we found that although light industries hire more women than heavy industries, they (the light industries) also seem to provide fewer facilities for women, especially married women. For example, fewer light industries (compared to heavy industries) have day nurseries, a factor which prevents many women from working at the factory site. Unless babysitters are available elsewhere (from extended kin, for instance), some women have to take their work home.

Characteristically, light industries seem to provide fewer fringe benefits and give women an earlier retirement age than men.

Several conclusions on women's participation in urban employment may be drawn. First, industries vary greatly in terms of wage scales and fringe benefits. Heavy industries such as oil refineries and steel companies or tractor factories all have rather comprehensive welfare, education and housing facilities for the employees and their families. Other industries, such as those cited above, do not as a rule provide comparable benefits to take care of the necessities of a single female worker. Second, which is a corollary of the first point, relatives of workers who have jobs in "better" industries (in terms of benefits accrueing to the family) would find it unimportant to choose their job assignment, since they will be able to obtain such benefits through their relatives. Young female workers, single or married, who live apart from their extended kin, would be in a disadvantageous position if the place of work does not provide such benefits as recreation, baby-sitting, nursery schools, or clinics. Yet, the irony of the situation is: younger women with families may need work outside the home, especially when the wage scale between working in the factory and working in the neighborhood workshop on a part-time and piece-rate basis is different.

The wage differential (between a factory and a neighborhood workshop) may, in part, be explained by the ownership of the enterprise. Factories are ordinarily owned by the state, especially after the collapse of the experiments in the urban commune (Salaff, 1967). Workshops, on the other hand, are still controlled by the Street Committee, or the urban commune in some cities where such organizations remained. Along with the higher wages and better benefits for its female

[14] Since no information was given by Hsu-Balzer *et al.* on the relative size of these factories, the observed differences may well be an artifact of (a) the different wage scales between light and heavy industries and/or (b) the uneven distribution of women in the two types of industries, and/ot (c) the factory size and volume of production rather than the proportion of women to men workers. Further investigation and more accurate data are definitely needed before we can make any conclusive statement about the situation.

TABLE 1 · · · A COMPARISON OF THE PERCENTAGE OF WOMEN AND THE WAGE SCALE IN DIFFERENT FACTORIES IN CHINA[a]

	Ivory-Carving[b]	Peking Glassware[c]	Peking Arts & Crafts[d]	Peking Embroidery and Applique[e]
% Women	estimated to be 50%	60%[f]	45%	85% of 700
Apprenticeship required	3 years	3 years	3 years	———[h]
Monthly salary: 1st year apprentice	Yen 22+(Yen 20)[g]	Yen 16+(Yen 32)[g]	Yen 17+(Yen 25)[g]	———[h]
2nd year	Yen 22+(Yen 20)[g]	Yen 19+(Yed 32)[g]	Yen 19+(Yen 25)[g]	———[h]
3rd year	Yen 22+(Yen 20)[g]	Yen 22+(Yen 32)[g]	Yen 22+(Yen 25)[g]	———[h]
Average pay (monthly)	———[h]	Yen 50	Yen 60	Yen 40
Salary range (monthly)	Yen 40 - Yen 172	Yen 30 - Yen 100	up to Yen 200	Yen 30-Yen 80
Persons with highest salary	———[h]	5 persons	3 persons	———[h]
Fringe Benefits	———[h]	free showers, haircuts & movies at the factory	free transportation and barbering	none
Maternity leave	56 paid days after birth	———[h]	———[h]	———[h]
Nursery	———[h]	Yes, for children under 3. Cost: Yen 3 - Yen - 9 monthly	———[h]	Yes, for children under 3 1/2 years old only

a. The data in this table are obtained by piecing together the figures supplied *et passim* in Hsu-Balzer *et al.* (1974).

b. The Ivory-Carving Factory in Canton was organized as a cooperative of 46 members in 1955.

c. The Peking Glassware Factory was organized from 50 independent handicraft units in 1956.

d. The Peking Arts and Crafts Factory (including: ivory carving, cloisonne, jade carving, lacquer ware and Chinese traditional paintings).

e. The Peking Embroidery and Applique Factory has 700 in-factory workers plus 8,000 housewife workers.

f. This is the figure for the entire factory, but within the factory some workshops wherein the main creations are flowers or animals, 100% of the workers are women. Hsu-Balzer *et al.* (1974:10-11) also mentioned that some men workers receive government subsidies in the form of oil and meat.

g. Clothing allowance. From Hsu-Balzer *et al.*'s account, it is not clear if the clothing allowance is a monthly or annual figure. It is more likely to be an annual figure, however, because of the Chinese practice of rationing clothing material.

h. Data is not available because they were not mentioned at all in Hsu-Balzer *et al.* (1974).

workers, state owned factories stipulate retirement for women workers at the age of 50. On the other hand, neighborhood workshops as a rule do not have an age limitation.[15]

In addition, urban women are not necessarily confined to their house. In some instances where the crowded housing situations encourage a number of different families to live in close proximity and share a courtyard, the women may pool their labor resources to help one another. Moreover, Street Revolutionary Committees play a significant role in delivering urban services such as housing, sanitation, health stations, recreational establishments and political sessions in addition to registering births, deaths, marriages and other statistics.[16] Third, if the husband earns sufficient wages, or if the woman has reached the age of 50, a great deal of the neighborhood services can be performed by women at a no-cost basis to the neighborhood which is an indirect form of participation in productive work. In any event, Chinese families in large urban centres do not experience the (Western) urban dweller's sense of alienation and social isolation Wirth (1934) described. The family is extended to include the immediate neighborhood of which the residents are a part. The variation of participation in factories, neighborhood workshops, voluntary work, and the like are largely determined by the family life cycle, household composition, the accumulated wages and income of all working members in the family, as well as the woman's own desire to work outside the home among others.

Living Arrangements

Unlike the rural population who are able to build their houses on a property of their choice (within limits), and in as large a size as they can afford, the urban dwellers are experiencing an acute housing problem, especially in the old industrial cities (Chao, 1966; Salaff, 1967; Howe, 1968). It seems logical to expect that given the limited space, families must learn to "make do" with what housing they have,[17]. The housing shortage in urban China thus affects the lifestyle of women in a number of ways. First, co-residence with relatives provides some basic household services to the young couple since the extended kin can play the role of surrogate parents. The young couple can take part in productive work without having to pay the price of nursery expenses. From the point of view of the municipal government, there is no urgent need to invest large sums of money for day-care centers either. Second, co-residence with relatives, especially with elderly parents and other adult females, provides the children with multiple equivalent bonds which helps to shape the typical domestic role of a housewife as well

---

[15] In a sense, working in a neighborhood workshop represents the half-way point between full-time home-making and full-time industrial work (outside the home) for the woman. But it is not entirely cost-free since a housewife must have a babysitter at home (generally a relative) at near-zero cost in order to make her efforts beneficial to the family.

[16] Such neighborhood self-government gives women a sense of stability and allows housewives to participate in neighborhood political activities. Women can help out at their convenience without having to travel out of the neighborhood.

[17] Consequently, some families will probably try or may be encouraged to accommodate as many of their relatives as possible if they have available space, but others who do not have sufficient rooms would have to turn down the offer of, or desire for co-residence.

as blurr the rigid division of labor in the family, thereby freeing the young wife to perform diversified economic and/or political roles outside the home. The nuclear household that one sees in North America is essentially both a consequence of and the prime reason for the clear division of labor in the industrial societies. Third, the difference between individual earnings and family earnings is quite substantial in China. In this context, the individual earnings of the housewife and her unmarried children and/or relatives represent a significant contribution to the family coffer. The head of household in this case is not the exclusive wage earner in the family.

Aside from the housing shortage, two practices in China militate against a uniform living arrangement pattern. First is the policy of "rustifying" the young people who have had a senior middle school education. This means that not all the young people are always living with their parents. Second is the practice of sending the skilled and rustified young people to wherever they could be of best service to the country. This prolongs the absence of young people from their own family for more than the two-year period required for rustification.[18] Fortunately the age distribution of siblings within a family assures that not all the young person's siblings will be away from the parental home at once.

Thus, the ideal traditional arrangement of "everyone living under one roof" still exists but its indefinite expansion in large metropolitan areas is curtailed by external factors such as the housing conditions, employment situation, stricter enforcement of fertility control programs and late marriage stipulations (than in the rural areas). Yu (1977a) suggested that under these mounting pressures, rigid adherence to patrilocality is not always feasible, and multi-locality (any combination of *consanguineal* co-residence where a unilocal residence prevailed previously) becomes the most adaptive residential pattern.[19]

The consequences of the emergence of multilocality are clear: (a) The previously almost invariable rule of postmarital residence gives way to more flexible alternatives. (b) Since multilocality in China is essentially an adaptation to conditions external to the family, it is able to maintain inter-generational continuity, thereby preventing the intensification of conjugal affectivity at the expense of lineal solidarity. (c) Because co-residence with (lineal) relatives is far more common than isolated, nuclear living arrangements (which tend to break

---

[18] In cases where the young person is married and his wife does not have a skill, she may or may not be able to move with her husband to his place of work. It all depends on the commuting distance, the availability of housing in his place of work, and the comparative advantages of moving. In those cases where both the young man and woman are skilled workers, there is a likelihood for them to live separately if they have, or are assigned to, jobs in different locations. Should they have children, the living arrangement pattern becomes more complicated since the child may be living with either the husband's or the wife's relatives, to mention just two possibilities.

[19] Our independent observations while in China indicate the proliferation of various combinations of consanguineal co-residence, ranging from three-generational extended family, elderly couples with grandchild whose other siblings are living with their own parents, husband and wife establishing separate domicile (duo-locality) to instances of matrilocality occurring in some places along with patrilocality (*ergo*, bilocality).

generational continuity), multilocality undermines the emergence of a strong conjugal ideology rooted in individualism (Yu, 1977a), thereby making nuclearization less indubitable than Goode (1963) predicted. (d) As the rule of postmarital residence becomes less and less invariable, kin affiliations and sentiments are likely to shift as well. With the expansion of network support to non-patrilineal kin, the family will be in a much better position to mobilize their resources to meet shortages of one kind or another.

We suggest, therefore, that an analysis of women's roles and family size must take into consideration the extra-economic and extra-work roles of women. Communist China is an excellent case for studying the fertility implications of women's roles in the larger social context.

Changing Fertility Behavior

Fertility analysts often attribute the decline in fertility rates in developed countries to the contraceptive mentality associated with changing norms on sex roles. Women who adhere to the traditional roles are said to have large families while those that have new role models are said to have small families. The argument is based on the assumption that the traditional role stresses parenthood whereas the new role emphasizes a consumer-career goal in marriage. Children are therefore considered to be expendable items and are carefully budgeted and planned (Hill *et al.* 1971). The social structure of sex roles in developing nations is different from that which has evolved in developed countries where private properties dominate human relations. For the majority of urban and rural Chinese families, cash residues are rarely used for consumer items not considered as essential household items. Without a doubt, the standards of consumption in China are austere and the ranges limited. For most families, home economics and management chores are kept at a spartan level. There is evidence that the fertility rate in China will not be increasing as rapidly as it used to.[20] With the great improvement in the health delivery system and rural health care, peasant women can be expected to be less resistant to contraceptive utilization since the cost of "getting sick from contraceptives" (Yu, 1977a) will be offset by the comparative advantage of a small family size. The emergence of multi-locality as a postmarital residential pattern would also help reduce the need to have male heirs. The elderly can have the security of consanguineal co-residence without requiring the younger generation to adhere strictly to the rule of patrilocality. Women would no longer occupy such a low status on the kinship structure. Consequently, educating women would not be such a "wasted" investment from the peasants' point of view. There will be one reason less for assigning them lower workpoints than men. Once women are also assigned the same workpoints for the same work as men, the comparative advantage of women pursuing higher education would also

---

[20] Field (1969) for example, has compared the statistics released by Chinese officials in the media with Aird's predicted high and low series for China's population growth. Although he cautioned against the accuracy of the Chinese figures and noted the extreme difficulty in estimating China's population, he indicated that the figures released by the Chinese press have been moving closer and closer to Aird's low series.

be greater than it is now. If, in addition to all these, late marriage is enforced so that women come to enjoy some degree of economic productivity and social independence (not to mention political involvement) *before* they get married, then we could reasonably expect that they will have or want fewer children than their parents. Leaders in Peking are now urging women to regard a small family size as part of the revolutionary duty of the average married woman. Moreover, the changing sex role expectations within the family would lighten the woman's household load. As household tasks are gradually being shared by adults of both sexes, housework will become less gender specific (compared to previous times). If and when it becomes truly non-gender specific, home-making will not give the housewife a special sense of achievement. Furthermore, the increasing availability of nurseries and the persistent pattern of co-residence with relatives will shorten the woman's absence from the labor force. In a society characterized by a high level of collective conscience and relatively homogeneous value orientations, the organization of urban neighborhoods in China could further ensure the early return of women to the labor force since neighbors can pool their resources.

There are reasons to believe that the changing sex roles in China goes beyond ideological rhetoric. The policy makers in Peking over the years have established a complex set of institutional support to allow women to take alternative careers or a combination of several careers during the span of the family iife cycle. A principal stance in this paper is that any analysis of women's labor participation in the new regime must take into consideration the kinship structure, neighborhood organizations, housing conditions, household composition, wage systems, and the ratio between employed and unemployed members in a single household. Beyond the threshold of a sudsistence income the family already has, the married woman now has a number of options.

We can thus expect that the interaction between the family system and its external milieu will have a significant effect on changing women's roles, fertility patterns, and family life in China.

REFERENCES

Aird, John
    1972   "Population Policy and Demographic Prospects in People's Republic of China." Paper submitted to the Joint Economic Committee, Congress of the United States, reprinted by HEW.

Berstein, Thomas P.
    1968   "Problems of village leadership after land reform." China Quarterly 36 (October-December): 1-22.

Bott, Elizabeth
    1957   Family and Social Network. New York: Free Press.

Burki, Shalid Javed
    1970   A Study of Chinese Communes, 1965. Cambridge: Harvard East Asian Monograph No. 29.

Chao, Kang
    1966   "Industrialization and urban housing in Communist China." Journal of Asian Studies 25:381-396.

Congressional Research Service, Library of Congress.
   1974   China's Experience in Population Control: The Elusive Model. 93rd Congress,
           Second Session, Committee Print, prepared for the Committee on Foreign Affairs,
           U.S. House of Representatives. Washington, D.C.: U.S. Government Printing
           Office.

Cunnison, S.
   1966   Wages and Work Allocation. London: Tavistock.

Field, Robert M.
   1969   "A note on the population of China." The China Quarterly 38 (April-June): 158-163.

Goode, William J.
   1963   World Revolution and Family Patterns. New York: Free Press.

Horsfall, A. and C. Aresberg
   1949   "Teamwork and productivity in a shoe factory." Human Organization 8:13-25.

Howe, Christopher
   1968   "The supply and administration of urban housing in Mainland China: the case of
           Shanghai." China Quarterly 33:73-97.

Hsu-Balzer, Eileen, Richard J. Balzer and Francis L.K. Hsu
   1974   China Day by Day. New Haven and London: Yale University Press.

Hill, Reuben et al.
   1971   Family Developments in Three Generations. Schenkman.
   Komarovsky, M.
   1964   Blue Collar Marriage. New York: Random House.

Kosa, John, Leo Rachiele and Cyril Schommer
   1960   "Sharing the home with relatives." Marriage and Family Living 22 (May): 129-131.

Leader, Shelah Gilbert
   1973   "The emancipation of Chinese women." World Politics 26 (October): 55-79.

Liu, William T.
   1971   "The myth of nuclear family in urban Philippines." Paper read at the San
           Francisco Southeast Asia Development Consultant Group (revised version read at
           the IX meeting of World Congress of Sociology, Toronto).
   1973   "Journey to Nanchang." Notre Dame Magazine (Fall). University of Notre Dame,
           Indiana.
   1974   "Family changes and family planning in the People's Republic of China." Paper
           given at the Annual Meeting of the Population Association of America. New York
           City, April 18-20.

Lupton, T.
   1963   On the Shop Floor. Oxford: Pergammon.

Myrdal, Jan
   1965   Report from a Chinese Village. New York: Pantheon.

Myrdal, Jan and Gun Dessle
   1970   The Revolution Continued. New York: Pantheon.

O'Neill, W.
   1972   Women at Work. Chicago: Quadrangle.

Orleans, Leo
   1974   See Congressional Research Service.

Parish, William L., Jr.
   1975   "Socialism and the Chinese peasant family." Journal of Asian Studies 34 (May):
           613-630.

Parsons, Talcott and R. Bales
1955   Family, Socialization and Interaction Processes. Glencoe, Illinois: Free Press.

Rainwater, Lee, Richard Coleman and Gerald Handel
1959   Workingman's Wife. New York: Oceana Publications.

Rogers, Everest M.
1973   Communication Strategies for Family Planning. New York: Free Press.

Salaff, Janet
1967   "The urban communes and anti-city experiment in Communist China." China Quarterly 29:83-110.
1971   Youth, Family and Political Control in Communist China. Unpublished Ph. D. Dissertation. University of California, Berkeley.
1973   "The emerging conjugal relationship in the People's Republic of China." Journal of Marriage and the Family 35 (November): 705-717.

Schram, Peter
1955   "The Structure of income in Communist China." Unpublished Ph. D. Dissertation, University of California, Berkeley.

Whyte, W.F.
1948   Human Relations in the Restaurant Industry. New York: McGraw-Hill

Wirth, Louis
1934   "Urbanism as a way of life." American Journal of Sociology.

Yang, C.K.
1959   The Chinese Family in the Communist Revolution. Cambridge: Centre for International Studies, M.I.T.

Yu, Elena S.H.
1976   "Women's roles in the wider social context of a rural community in Southeastern China." Paper read at the Annual Meeting of the National Council on Family Relations. New York, October 19-23.
1977a   "Kinship structure, postmarital residence and sex-role equality in China." Sociological Focus 10 (April).
1977b   "Overseas remittances and social change: Southeastern China." Unpublished.

Zelditch, Morris
1955   "Role differentiation in the nuclear family: a comparative study." In Talcott Parsons and R.F. Bales, Family: Socialization and interaction. New York: Free Press.

26

Women in the Cuban Bureaucracies: 1968-1974*

BENIGNO E. AGUIRRE**

The experience of women during the course of the Cuban revolution is important as one measure of human dignity in the island. It is interesting also because of the parallels which it has with reforms proposed or realized in this country to improve the status of women. The purpose of this paper is to examine the experience of women in achieving positions of authority and responsibility in Cuba, a country ruled by a revolutionary movement that has untiringly declared itself to be the hemisphere's champion of egalitarianism.

The Marxist interpretation of women's liberation during a dictatorship of the proletariat exemplifies what Gusfield (1973: 14-15) called a political utopia. According to it, the emergence of the bourgeois family signaled the final degradation of women into servants and childcarers. Women's liberation is theoretically realized once the society's economic structure is socialized, so that all persons, regardless of sex, stand in the same relation to the means of production. Quite apart from the frequent need to substitute labour for decreasing levels of capital, it is because of this ideological tenet that the incorporation of women into the labor force characterizes periods of socialist domination. It is assumed (Gusfield, 1973: 18) that the society of the past (the thesis) represents a monistic, consistent system, to be contrasted with the antithesis—changes that supposedly have taken place since the revolution.

Indeed, the notion that the triumph of the proletarian revolution erodes all the structural elements that previously had resulted in discrimination against women persists in the imagination of countless persons even against the counsel of their own experience. The continued discrimination against Soviet women (Goldberg, 1973; Holter, 1973; Salaff and Meckle, 1970) is explained by the Stalinist oppression and the present-day rule of the Soviet bureaucrats (Trotsky, 1970), while the experience of discrimination against women in the Kibbutz movement in Israel (Padan-Eisenstark, 1973) which in part was strongly Marxist in its inception, is either ignored or explained away as a temporary aberration.

Such an interpretation of history (Engels, 1972; Marx, 1970), with its emphasis on stages or historical epochs, is reflected in Cuba's official stand on family

*The data presented in this paper was collected during the summer and fall of 1974. I am grateful to George Hart and Angus M. Thuermer who helped me secure some documents, and to Professor Alfred C. Clarke who provided research assistance to me. I am indebted to Professors Laurel Walum and William Petersen for their incisive substantive and editorial comments to earlier drafts of the manuscript, and to Professor Wen L. Li for his comments on the statistical methods used in this paper. Sole responsibility for its final contents rests with the author.
**Department of Sociology, The Ohio State University, Columbus, Ohio 43210

and women (de la Torre, 1965). And yet, the ideology is interpreted selectively. For instance, the Cuban authorities have attempted to strengthen the family by providing contraceptives and abortion services on demand (de Onis, 1967; Perez Tobella, 1967; Chelala, 1971; Stamper, 1971; Boyd, 1974), by encouraging people to marry rather than forming common-law unions (Blutstein *et al.*, 1971: 105-112; Cooney, 1974), by maintaining, despite the well-publicized new family code (Granma, 1975a; 1975b), the pre-1959 legal basis for divorce (le-Riverend, 1966: 536), and, in general by respecting the bonds between parents and their children (JPRS no. 35954)—though the new basis for the formation of families and parent-child relations is supposedly love combined with ideological compatibility (JPRS no. 265256).

Undoubtedly, these measures are a reaction, in part, to the upsurge in family instability that Cuba experienced and, in part, is due to the regime's revolutionary puritanism (Yglesias, 1969). Increasing even prior to 1959, the national divorce rate rose extraordinarily during the 1960's, from 8.3 divorces per 100 marriages in 1958 to 18.1 per 100 marriages in 1968, with peaks in the measure of 20.3 in 1966 and 1967. In the province of La Habana, in fact, the divorce rate reached 30.1 per 100 marriages in 1966 (Roberts and Hamour, 1970: 80). Moreover, most extended families were disrupted by geographical and ideological separations.

Cuba's political myth that women's freedom has been achievd inhibits the development of an independent women's movement. According to Camarano (1971), for instance, the historical experience of women is irrelevant as the foundation for female consciousness in Cuba. The actual consequence of this orthodoxy is to make it more difficult to realize greater equality between the sexes. In practical terms, it keeps women from forming independent social organizations, unable to force the male authorities to recognise the importance and immediacy of their needs (Purcell, 1973).

Of course, the Federation of Cuban Women (FMC), one of the most active and important mass organizattons, is the government's main instrument to mobilize women. As such, it is not an independent organization of women. Rather, after prodding from the highest levels of the government (FCW, Press Office, 1965) it was formed in 1960 from a merger of various Cuban women's associations, among them the Democratic Federation of Cuban women, an organization of the Cuban Communist Party and a member of the International Democratic Federation of Women, with headquarters in the USSR (Randall, 1972: 91; Montes and Avila, 1970: 367). More important, the Federation (FMC) has not maintained a critical stand on the issues affecting women's freedoms. Its draft program dealt exclusively with problems arising from the incorporation of women into the labor force and other revolutionary efforts in health, education, and welfare, to involve women in the construction of the new society (Book Institute, 1967: 83-90). Nowhere does its draft program mention the re-education of the Cuban male, inequalities in authority at home or work, the redefinition of sex-linked household and family tasks and obligations, discrimination in hiring and pay, and the many other concerns of a vigorous and autonomous women's movement (Reports, 1962). This limited orientation has remained unchanged throughout the years (JPRS, 1964; Espin, 1969; JPRS, 1969: Granma Weekly Review, 1971).

The political myth of women's freedom, in fact, co-exists with traditional attitudes and practices (Berman, 1970; Gordon, 1970 ; Purcell, 1973) in a culture known for its strong emphasis on male supremacy (Lawrenson, 1973; Rodriguez, 1962), and with no offical organized efforts to combat them. Instead, women are encouraged to participate in the life of the country that retains a culture of continuing male supremacy. Not surprisingly, it was possible to incorporate them into the labor force only through extensive pressure and official recruitment (JPRS, 1969), including finally a virtually gratis child-care program operation throughout the island (Leiner, 1973; Garrity, 1971).[1]

In spite of widespread resistance, however, women's participation in the labor force has risen since the late 1950's (Mesa Lago, 1972: 41; Perera, 1962; Acevedo, 1961). The available data on the range of this participation can clarify the degree to which women are discriminated against in positions of authority and responsibility.

Sample and Method

The information used in this paper was collected from the six editions of the *Directory of Personalities of the Cuban Government, Official Organizations and Mass Organizations.* In these directories the U.S. Central Intelligence Agency has compiled the names of all persons that appeared in the Cuban mass media occupying administrative bureaucratic offices in the Cuban government and official organizations.[2] These represent mainly high status positions due to a cultural tendency in the Cuban mass media to give preferential coverage to important appointative announcements.

Conceivably, the CIA may have purposefully distorted[3] the sexual make-up

---

[1] The program, however, perhaps as a result of the lack of an independent and critical women's organization, perpetuates the traditional division of labor between the sexes which have been in the past associated with male exploitative behavior. There are no male workers in the child centers (Leiner, 1973: 18-19; Garrity, 1971: 61). Thus, in this as well as in a number of other instances (Valdes Perez, 1964; Bohemia, 1964), sex-specific occupational practices continue in a setting considered by the Cubans as being the first step in the revolutionary education of the new generation (Rodriguez, 1966).

[2] I do not know the exact criteria used to include or exclude names from the six editions of the Directory. Mr. A.M. Thuermer, an official of the Central Intelligence Agency, informed me that the directories were compiled by an independent research organization which is now disbanded. According to Mr. Thuermer, "the goal of the independent research organization, however, was to compile a *comprehensive* administrative directory of the Cuban government and official organizations using available Cuban mass media. Every bureaucratic position mentioned in the Cuban media was considered for the directory and the position was included unless the information was not sufficient to warrant inclusion. Every effort was made to obtain additional information so that the position could be included in future editions of the directory," (Emphasis in the original, personal communication with Mr. Angus MacLean Thuermer, Assistant to the Director, Central Intelligence Agency, November 14, 1974). Clearly then, although plausible, the adequacy and representativeness of the information in these documents are not proven.

[3] For a discussion of the use of archival material see David C. Pritt, *Using Historical Sources in Anthropology and Sociology.* New York: Holt, Rinehart and Winton, Inc., 1972, especially Chapter 4.

of the subpopulation included in the directories so as to minimize the participation of women in the administration of the Cuban bureaucracies. However, the avowed intention of the Agency in publishing the directory was to provide background material on Cuban officials to various United States Government agencies. Thus, it is likely that the CIA would include all known Cuban officials, regardless of their sex, in order to provide accurate information to the intended government users of the directories. A more likely cause of the distortion is that the Cuban mass media which served as the sources for the names listed, following their ideological public relations (Fagen, 1972), may have overreported the appointments of women to administrative positions if compared to its coverage of males in similar posts.[4] Such a sampling error insures a greater reliability to any criticism of women's labor-force participation.

The same regulations were applied throughout the six editions of the directory so that they are comparable.[5] For each edition the total number of persons and the number of administrative positions in each bureaucracy occupied by both sexes were counted. The total sample consists of 25,704 persons, of whom 25,274 could be identified by their sex.[6] To calculate the relative importance of women's participation in each of the bureaucracies included in the directories, the percentage of positions that women occupied in them was calculated for every year for which data were available.

A standardization index was used to determine the relative female participation in each of the bureaucracies during specified years:

$$\left[\frac{\Sigma W_i}{\Sigma W_y} \times \frac{\Sigma N_y}{\Sigma N_i} \right] \times 100$$

where

ΣW_i = total number of women–occupied administrative offices in a given ministry.

ΣW_y = total number of women–occupied administrative offices in a given year.

ΣN_y = total number of sex-identifiable (both sexes) administrative offices in a given year.

ΣN_i = total number of sex-identifiable (both sexes) administrative offices in a given ministry.

---

[4]As one support of this assumption Premier Fidel Castro announced recently (*Granma*, August 4, 1974, p. 4) the results of the elections to the popular assembly of the province of Matanzas (Mesa, 1974; Cooney, 1974b). Only five of the 151 persons elected were women. Prior to Castro's announcement, however, *Granma* (June 30, 1974, p. 4) had given extensive coverage to the candidacy of a young high school girl. The very fact that so very few women were elected, according to Castro's own estimates, as contrasted to the emphasis which *Granma* placed in covering the nomination of one female suggests that this type of distortion is a constant characteristic of mass media coverage in Cuba.

[5]Personal communication with Mr. Angus MacLean Thuermer, August 9, 1974.

[6]I could not identify the sex of persons who were mentioned by their last names only, or whose first names could not be clearly classified, or who were mentioned by nicknames with no clear sexual referent.

the index ranges from 0 to more than 100 for above-average female representation with 100 as the statistical norm.

To measure longitudinally the extent of women's segregation in the bureaucracies, a dispersion index proposed by Gibbs and Martin (1969: 312-315) and initially modified by Li (1971) was used. The index of female diffuseness varies between 0 and 1, in which 0 represents equal number of females in all the categories (bureaucracies) and 1 stands for the segregation of all the women in one category.

The construction of this index involves three steps. We first calculated unadjusted coefficients using the formula,

$$\frac{\left(\Sigma X^2\right) \div \left(\frac{\Sigma X}{\Sigma N}\right)^2}{\Sigma N}$$

where

ΣX = the total number of women-occupied administrative offices in each ministry.

ΣN = the total number of ministries and organizations for which comparable data are available in a given period.

The range of the unadjusted coefficients using this formula is 1 to N, whenever N is smaller than X. The coefficients, which stand to each other in the same proportion as the Ns on which they are based, were made comparable to each other.

The third stage in the index was to convert the adjusted coefficients to a scale of 0 to 1 so as to make them more easily comparable. We first subtracted 1 from the adjusted coefficients so as to create a common lower limit of zero. Then, the proportion which 1 is of the N-1 for which adjusted coefficients had been calculated was noted, and this constant was then multiplied by each of the adjusted coefficients so as to convert them to a zero to one scale. Due to the longitudinal constraints imposed by the calculation of this adjusted coefficient, the bureaucracies were divided into four groups, reflecting degrees of shared completeness of the data. Group A bureaucracies are those for which we have complete information for the 1968-1974 period, group B includes bureaucracies for which information was available for the 1969-1973 period, Group C includes those with information during the 1971-1974 period, and Group D bureaucracies could not be meaningfully grouped due to the poor longitudinal data available.

Findings and Discussion

The increase in female participation in the national labor force during 1968-1974, although not known with any precision, is nevertheless large. Taking the pre-revolutionary 1956-1957 national survey estimates as the base, women's participation increased by roughly a third by 1969. The increase continued in 1970 and 1971, so that by 1972 close to a half million women were in the labor force (Randall, 1972: 80-91) and since that date the government's sharpened demand

TABLE 1*   THE CUBAN LABOR FORCE BY SEX, SPECIFIED DATES

	1943a	1953a	1956-1957b	1969c	1970c	1971c
Male	1,363,841	1,706,477	1,890,000	1,460,673	1,573,603	1,604,259
	(89.7%)	(82.9%)	(85.7%)	(77.1%)	(76.2%)	(77.1%)
Female	157,010	353,182	314,000	434,671	490,360	475,341
	(10.3%)	(17.1%)	(14.3%)	(22.9%)	(23.8%)	(22.9%)
Total	1,520,851	2,059,659	2,204,000	1,895,344	2,063,963	2,079,600
	(100%)	(100%)	(100%)	(100%)	(100%)	(100%)

SOURCES : aCarmelo Mesa-Lago, *The Labor Force, Employment, Unemployment and Underemployment in Cuba* : *1899-1970,* pp. 16, 22; bCuban Economic Research Project, *A Study in Cuba,* p. 431, Table 293; cJunta Central de Planification, *Boletin Estadistico 1971,* Cuba, Direccion General de Estadistica. pp. 48-49.

*The figures in this table are not strictly comparable for they were estimated by different methods: (A) National Census 1943, 1953; (B) National Survey 1956-1957; (C) Population Estimates 1969-1971. Thus, for instance, the apparent drop in female participation during 1953-1957 is probably a methodological artifact; for a number of reasons the latter figure is probably more accurate.

The quality of the population estimates made in Cuba after 1959 is not known, although they are probably the best available (Nelson, 1970: 398-399). The total labor force estimates for 1969-1971 include only persons working in the public civil sector, which causes the drop in the total labor force figures after 1957. According to Carmelo Mesa-Lago (personal communication with the author, January 15, 1975; see also his *The Labor Force Employment, Unemployment and Underemployment in Cuba*: *1899-1970,* Beverly Hills: Sage Professional Paper, 1972), owners of farms and their employees, persons in the armed forces and internal security forces, and self-employed workers, were excluded from the total labor force of these years (1969-1971). Since women probably do not work in any appreciable numbers in these categories, the available official estimates of female participation in the labor force may exaggerate their real participation.

that women work has probably had some success. At the administrative levels of the Cuban bureaucracies, however, the participation of women, as reflected by the mass-media coverage has remained quite stable during 1968-1974, fluctuating around 9 percent.

TABLE 2   PARTICIPATION IN THE CUBAN BUREAUCRACY : BY SEX AND
                                              SPECIFIED YEARS

	1968	1969	1970	1971	1973	1974
Male	2897	3812	3940	4445	5564	2239
Female	290(9.1%)	379(9%)	387(8.9%)	467(9.5%)	641(10%)	213(8.7%)
Subtotal	3187	4191	4327	4912	6205	2452
Unidentifiable Names	59(1.8%)	82(1.9%)	97(2.2%)	105(2.1%)	45(0.7%)	42(1.7%)
Total	3246	4273	4424	5017	6250	2494

The expansion of female participation in the labor force has not been associated with a proportionate increase in female employment at administrative and decision-making levels of the bureaucracies. Indeed, Randall (1972: 80-81) estimates that in 1972, 29 percent of all employed women worked in production, 38 percent in service occupations, 8.5 percent in administrative positions, 21 percent in technical occupations, and only 3.5 percent in leadership positions. Castro (Oui, 1975) puts the participation of women in the leadership of the Cuban Communist Party at 5 percent, while Boyd (1974: 991) mentions that although half Cuba's medical doctors are female, administrators in almost all cases are male.

Contrary to the stylized heroic image of a new Cuban woman breaking with traditions and engaging in large numbers in all types of work, Cuban women in administrative and leadership positions are found most often in traditional female lines of work, although even in many of these they are under-represented.

TABLE 3   PERCENTAGE OF SEX-OCCUPIED BUREAUCRATIC OFFICES : BY
                           BUREAUCRACY AND SPECIFIED YEARS

	1968-1974	1968	1969	1970	1971	1973	1974
Group A							
Communist Party of Cuba							
Index*	59.1	61.5	59.7	50.1	67.9	57.1	67.2
Percentage Women		3.8	3.6	3.0	4.6	4.2	3.5
Subtotal**		728	501	498	548	632	677
Presidency of the Republic							
Index	258.5	328.3	365.0	365.3	326.5	188.7	148.2
Percentage Women		20.5	22.0	22.0	22.0	14.1	7.8
Subtotal		39	41	41	41	85	64
Ministry of Revolutionary Armed Force							
Index	22.4	0	54.2	44.2	8.4	7.4	18.0
Percentage Women		0	3.3	2.7	0.6	0.6	.09
Subtotal		95	184	188	176	181	211
Ministry of Interior (Minit)							
Index	26.6	103.7	31.9	29.4	7.8	11.6	22.8
Percentage Women		6.5	2.0	1.8	0.5	0.9	1.2
Subtotal		108	158	171	194	232	255

(Contd.)

*The standardization index figures in this table do not include the number of persons listed as working in the Cuban Federation of Women (FMC). This was done so as to eliminate the downward distortion which otherwise it would have occasioned in the index. There were no men listed as working in the Federation (FMC). The total number of women listed in it for each of the six years studied was 76, 154, 171, 182, 173 and 83. They accounted, respectively, for 26, 35, 38, 34, 25 and 37 percents of the total number of women annually listed in the directories. In overall terms, 2637 women were listed in the directories, of which 839 or 31.8 percent were listed in the Federation (FMC).

**The figures appearing under this rubric represent names which were identified by their sex (see footnote 6).

Table 3 *(Contd.)*

	1968-1974	1968	1969	1970	1971	1973	1974
National Institute of Agrarian Reform (INRA)							
Index	46.7	31.4	57.6	57.1	47.2	40.2	33.9
Percentage Women		2.0	3.5	3.4	3.2	3.0	1.8
Subtotal		153	231	233	252	299	56
Ministry of Public Health (MINISAP)							
Index	93.6	100.0	115.5	92.4	102.6	66.3	130.8
Percentage Women		7.9	7.0	5.6	6.9	5.0	6.9
Subtotal		144	187	216	232	282	29
Civil Aeronautics Institute (IAC)							
Index	91.6	157.4	138.5	134.2	0	0	146.0
Percentage Women		9.8	8.0	8.0	0	0	7.7
Subtotal		61	60	62	47	44	13
Ministry of Construction (MINCONS)							
Index	63.4	54.9	59.2	70.5	212.5	58.9	62.6
Percentage Women		3.4	3.6	4.2	14.3	4.4	3.4
Subtotal		204	281	283	21	272	61
Ministry of Education (MINED)							
Index	269.6	336.5	309.4	303.7	221.7	253.0	184.2
Percentage Women		21.0	18.6	17.5	15.0	18.9	10.7
Subtotal		214	387	400	557	444	103
National Commission of the Cuban Academy of Sciences (ACC)							
Index	32.8	24.2	20.8	41.0	17.3	53.4	0
Percentage Women		1.5	1.2	2.5	1.2	4.0	0
Subtotal		66	80	81	86	100	11
Book Institute (I.L.)							
Index	114.0	0	0	0	185.9	162.0	0
Percentage Women		0	0	0	12.5	12.1	0
Subtotal		6	11	14	24	33	7
Cuban Institute of the Motion Picture Arts and Industry (ICAIC)							
Index	82.1	47.0	121.6	121.8	103.7	31.1	0
Percentage Women		2.9	7.3	7.3	7.0	2.3	0
Subtotal		34	41	41	43	43	5
Cuban Broadcasting Institute (ICR)							
Index	90.0	84.2	118.8	110.9	76.2	81.8	0
Percentage Women		5.3	7.1	6.7	5.1	6.1	0
Subtotal		19	28	30	39	49	7
Central Planning Board (JUCEPLAN)							
Index	95.5	80.0	69.3	66.5	90.1	130.4	100.0
Percentage Women		5.0	4.2	4.0	6.0	9.7	5.3
Subtotal		20	24	25	33	41	19

(Contd.)

Table 3 *(Contd.)*

	1968-1974	1968	1969	1970	1971	1973	1974
Ministry of Labor (MINTRAB)							
Index	226.5	114.3	262.5	277.4	253.6	201.8	0
Percentage Women		7.1	15.8	16.7	17.0	15.1	0
Subtotal		28	57	60	88	106	16
Ministry of Foreign Trade (MINCEX)							
Index	62.5	22.8	45.6	44.3	91.3	93.8	0
Percentage Women		1.4	2.7	2.7	6.1	7.0	0
Subtotal		70	73	75	114	114	49
Ministry of Justice (MINJUS)							
Index	98.9	81.4	105.2	64.8	117.0	120.3	0
Percentage Women		5.0	6.3	3.9	7.9	9.0	0
Subtotal		59	79	77	89	100	18
National Fishing Institute (INP)							
Index	60.3	25.4	79.1	79.2	67.0	49.9	0
Percentage Women		1.6	4.8	4.8	4.5	3.7	0
Subtotal		63	105	105	111	134	20
Ministry of Foreign Relations (MINREX)							
Index	202.1	194.4	242.1	215.2	192.4	195.2	204.6
Percentage Women		12.2	14.6	13.0	13.0	14.6	10.8
Subtotal		107	103	116	116	137	102
Cuban Institute of Friendship with Peoples (ICAP)							
Index	276.2	170.7	232.8	242.4	269.5	313.7	474.4
Percentage Women		10.7	14.0	14.6	18.0	23.4	25.0
Subtotal		75	100	103	138	179	32
Ministry of Basic Industry (MINBAS)							
Index	45.3	94.1	50.9	64.0	41.3	20.5	0
Percentage Women		5.9	3.1	3.8	2.8	1.5	0
Subtotal		51	98	104	108	130	21
Ministry of Mines and Metallurgy (MMM)							
Index	45.3	0	34.0	67.9	26.1	60.8	0
Percentage Women		0	2.5	4.0	1.8	4.5	0
Subtotal		13	40	49	57	66	14
National Coordination of Local Administration							
Index	36.3	50.0	31.3	30.2	21.5	33.4	210.9
Percentage Women		3.1	2.0	1.8	1.4	2.5	11.1
Subtotal		32	53	55	69	80	9
Union of Young Communists (UMC)							
Index	108.2	171.1	112.2	99.7	99.7	78.9	123.4
Percentage Women		10.7	6.7	6.0	6.7	5.9	6.5
Subtotal		318	326	334	358	542	123

(Contd.)

Table 3 *(Contd.)*

	1968-1974	1968	1969	1970	1971	1973	1974
Federation of Cuban Women (FMC)							
Index							
Percentage Women		100.0	100.0	100.0	100.0	100.0	100.0
Subtotal		76	154	171	182	173	83
Committee for the Defense of the Revolution (CDR)							
Index	103.3	231.9	128.9	119.7	89.2	69.3	90.4
Percentage Women		14.5	7.8	7.2	6.0	5.2	4.8
Subtotal		69	129	139	150	270	126
Confederation of Cuban Workers (CTC)							
Index	73.4	61.6	57.5	81.5	87.8	56.0	144.9
Percentage Women		3.8	3.5	4.9	5.9	4.2	7.6
Subtotal		156	289	286	305	454	131
Ministry of the Sugar Industry (MINAZ)							
Index	64.3	47.8	103.9	96.7	101.4	12.0	0
Percentage Women		3.0	6.2	5.8	6.8	0.9	0
Subtotal		67	80	86	88	111	25
Ministry of Domestic Trade (MINCIN)							
Index	52.1	78.0	51.7	54.6	20.9	63.6	111.6
Percentage Women		4.9	3.1	3.3	1.4	4.7	5.9
Subtotal		41	289	61	71	84	17
Ministry of Food Industry (MINAL)							
Index	54.0	0	56.4	56.4	72.0	58.7	0
Percentage Women		0	3.4	3.4	4.8	4.4	0
Subtotal		28	59	59	62	91	16
Ministry of Light Industry (MINIL)							
Index	64.2	57.2	0	0	29.1	121.6	223.2
Percentage Women		3.6	0	0	2.0	9.0	11.8
Subtotal		28	45	47	51	77	17
National Institute of the Tourist Industry (INIT)							
Index	7.6	0	0	0	0	0	146.0
Percentage Women		0	0	0	0	0	7.7
Subtotal		30	37	40	39	44	13
Ministry of Communications (MINCOM)							
Index	69.3	71.7	83.1	81.8	91.8	41.3	0
Percentage Women		4.4	5.0	4.9	6.2	3.0	0
Subtotal		45	60	61	81	97	13
Ministry of Transportation (MITRANS)							
Index	33.3	62.4	29.4	29.2	35.0	25.9	0
Percentage Women		3.9	2.0	1.8	2.4	1.9	0
Subtotal		77	113	114	85	103	18

(Contd.)

Table 3 *(Contd.)*

	1968-1974	1968	1969	1970	1971	1973	1974
National Association of Small Farmers (ANAP)							
Index	34.7	15.8	33.4	31.8	30.0	52.0	0
Percentage Women		1.0	2.0	1.9	2.0	3.9	0
Subtotal		101	149	157	149	180	0
Union of Cuban Newspapermen (UPEC)							
Index	340.7	160.0	461.0	293.7	343.3	297.1	517.6
Percentage Women		10.0	28.0	17.6	23.0	22.2	27.3
Subtotal		10	18	17	26	36	11
Union of Cuban Writers and Artists (UNEAC)							
Index	78.9	123.1	110.9	110.9	70.8	53.4	0
Percentage Women		7.7	6.7	6.7	4.5	4.0	0
Subtotal		13	15	15	22	25	9
Group B							
Cuban Tobacco Enterprise (CUBATABACO)							
Index		106.7	79.2	104.0	40.2	0	
Percentage Women		6.7	4.8	6.0	2.7	0	
Subtotal		15	21	32	37	44	
National Forestry Institute (INDAF)							
Index		0	72.3	66.5	139.4	81.8	
Percentage Women		0	4.3	4.0	9.4	6.1	
Subtotal		11	23	25	32	49	
Cuban Chamber of Commerce							
Index			138.5	138.6	0	222.8	
Percentage Women			8.3	8.3	0	16.7	
Subtotal			12	12	15	18	
Center for Automotive Technical Services (CESETA)							
Index			53.6	0	41.3	29.7	0
Percentage Women			3.2	0	2.8	2.2	0
Subtotal			31	24	36	45	7
National Institute of Veterinary Medicine (INMV)							
Index			83.1	75.6	43.8	34.2	271.1
Percentage Women			5.0	4.5	2.9	2.5	14.3
Subtotal			20	22	34	39	7
Centennial Youth Column (CJC)							
Index			48.9	53.7	114.4	133.7	
Percentage Women			3.0	3.0	7.7	10.0	
Subtotal			34	31	39	50	
Group C							
National Bank of Cuba (BNC)							
Index		0		55.5	41.3	68.6	0
Percentage Women		0		3.0	2.8	5.1	0
Subtotal		21		30	36	39	18

(Contd.)

Table 3 *(contd.)*

	1968-1974	1968	1969	1970	1971	1973	1974
Ministry of Merchant Marine and Ports (MMM & P)							
Index					0	0	0
Percentage Women					0	0	0
Subtotal					50	77	17
Cuban Petroleum Institute (ICP)							
Index					87.5	116.2	0
Percentage Women					5.9	8.7	0
Subtotal					17	23	6
Mid-Level Students Federation (FEEM)							
Index					274.0	334.3	189.8
Percentage Women					18.4	25.0	10.0
Subtotal					38	60	10
Union of Cuban Pioneers (UPC)							
Index					343.3	262.6	669.8
Percentage Women					23.0	19.6	35.3
Subtotal					13	56	17
Prensa Latina News Agency (PL or PRELA)							
Index					168.2	133.7	191.5
Percentage Women					11.3	10.0	10.1
Subtotal					115	150	218
Group D***							
Percentage Women		3.4	4.5	4.4	4.9	22.5	21.0
Subtotal		58	88	90	183	301	76
TOTALS							
Number of Women	1798	215	288	283	358	512	142
Subtotal of Occupied positions (both men and women)	27,807	3441	4789	4710	5326	6846	2695
Number of Occupied positions, by gender, including unidentifiables, and FMC							
Men	26,009	3226	4501	4427	4968	6334	2553
Women	2637	291(8.3)	442(8.9)	454(9.3)	540(9.8)	685(9.8)	225(8.1)
Subtotal	28,646	3517	4943	4881	5508	7019	2778
Unidentifiable	370	29	72	58	92	92	27
Total	29,016	3546	5015	4939	5600	7111	2805

***The specific bureaucracies in this group are listed in Appendix A. They are not included in this table due to the incompleteness of the information found in them. Thus, no standardization index was computed for this group, nor are they analyzed in terms of the segregation patterns of women in them (see Table 4).

Females in administrative offices during 1968-1974 consistently comprised over 10 percent only in the following bureaucracies: Presidency of the Republic, Ministry of Education, Book Institute, Cuban Institute of Friendship with Peoples, Federation of Cuban Women, Union of Cuban Newspapermen, Mid-Level Student Federation, Unions of Cuban Pioneers, Prensa Latina News Agency, and (not shown in Table 3) the Children's Institute and the National Council of Culture. Moreover, their presence in the Presidency of the Republic declined during 1968-1974, from 20.5 percent to 7.8 percent.

Apart from the overall low representation of women compared to men most of these bureaucracies show high coefficients (>100) using the average female representation of the standardization index (Table 3). We need only to add the Ministry of Justice, Union of Young Communists, and the Committee for the Defense of the Revolution to complete the list of bureaucracies with average female representation in terms of the very low female presence predominating.

It is quite obvious from Table 3 that generally, women are most under-represented in sectors in which they have not traditionally worked, which tend to be those of greatest import and prestige. Thus, though they are well represented at this level in the Ministry of Education, they are almost totally absent from the National Commission of the Cuban Academy of Sciences. Nor are they equally represented as members of the Communist Party, or in the internal security and armed forces; or in the ministries of construction, planning, foreign trade, basic industries, mines and metallurgy, sugar, domestic trade, food, light industry, communication, transportation; or in the institutes of Agrarian Reform (INRA), Fishing, Forestry, Veterinary Medicine; or in the Confederation of Cuban workers, National Administration, National Association of Small Farmers, and in the National Bank of Cuba.

Indeed, this list suggests how enduring cultural practices (Cooney, 1975) affect women's achievement of high occupational status in a socialist administration.

Quite apart from the problem of their adequate representation in it, women's segregation in a bureaucratic structure is important, since it also reflects ingrained social attitudes and values. It is in this respect that the situation gives greatest basis for optimism.

TABLE 4   INDEX OF FEMALE DIFFUSENESS, BY YEAR AND GROUP OF
                                              BUREAUCRACIES

	1968	1969	1970	1971	1973	1974
Group A*	0.1016	0.1436	0.1641	0.1524	0.1124	0.2127
Without Cuban Federation of Women	0.0782	0.0699	0.0745	0.0777	0.0594	0.0825
Group B*	—	0.1774	0.1774	0.2291	0.2513	—
Group C*	—	—	—	0.2925	0.3799	0.5100

*See Table 3 for the bureaucracies included in each of the three groups.

The relative importance of the Federation of Cuban Women (FMC) in terms of the overall bureaucratic structure, as the focus of female concentration at this level of employment, has steadily increased during 1968-1974. However, once its influence is eliminated, it becomes quite clear that female employees are not segregated in any one sector of the labor force. While women continue to be under-represented in most of the bureaucracies, they nevertheless participate throughout the labor force; their problem is not total exclusion, but under-participation.

Premier Castro has recognized the cultural roots of women's low status (Granma, 1974). Yet his attempts to solve the problem by providing childcare centers and cafeterias (Jenness, 1970; Castro, 1969: 205; 1960) ignores the fact that the liberation of women depends not simply on the development of social capital, but also on changing the stereotypes about the appropriate behavior of the two sexes. If for instance, household tasks and occupations traditionally performed by women are to be shared by both sexes, the prerequisite is as much to re-educate males and females as to develop the necessary facilities so that women can work (Castro, 1966: 266-267). Significantly, elsewhere (Jenness, 1970: 8) Castro states that women's most important function is the procreation of new generations and they are not allowed to perform certain jobs which are seen as unsuited to their weaker nature. Moreover, perhaps in response to the ideological orthodoxy, it is only rarely in Cuba and then briefly, that an awareness is evinced of how cultural stereotypes of the relation between the sexes affect the life experience of Cuban women (Ramos, 1971: 72). In fact, it has been until recently, and most visibly during the II Congress of the Federation of Cuban Women, in the last week of November, 1974, that Fidel Castro, as well as other officials, have recognized the existence of discrimination and prejudice against women in the island. The Cuban premier, in his most important speech on the subject so far (Granma, December 8, 1974), lashed against the cultural roots of women's oppression and promised to the Congress to make its future resolution one of the most important goals of the revolutionary government. A new family code has been discussed at all levels of the government and mass organizations. It stipulates that housework is the joint responsibility of both married spouses. This laudable legislation is unenforceable in practice and could very well be substituted by a vigorous national affirmative action program.

The discussions in the Congress mark the first time that adequate emphasis is given to the cultural roots of women's oppression and may, indeed, be the turning point in revolutionary policies and programs (Chertov, 1970)[7]. But judging from past performances on past promises, the outlook for the future is uncertain. The lack of an independent and active women's movement and the consequent absence of autonomous women leaders, considerably lessens the

---

[7]Since then, Vilma Espin's address to the participants to the Women's World Conference in Mexico (Espin, 1975), Raul Castro's speech on the occasion of the XV Anniversary of the Federation of Cuban Women (FMC) (Castro, 1975), Fidel Castro's speech to the First Congress of the Cuban Communist Party (Castro, 1976), and the resolution adopted by the first congress (Granma, 1976), have strongly underscored the need to eliminate discrimination and prejudice against women and represent significant advances.

pressure on the Cuban male leadership to act decisively on the woman question and augurs unauspiciously for the progress of women in this area of employment.

APPENDIX A

The following bureaucracies constitute Group D (see Footnote***, Table 3):

Children's Institute (I.I.); Foreign Organizations Section; National Commission on Economic, Scientific and Technical Collaboration (CNCECT); Consumer Goods and Domestic Trades Industries Sector; Institute of Domestic Needs (IDI); Transportation and Communications Sector; National Institute of Hydraulic Resources (INRH); Energy Research Institute; The Construction Sector; Council of the Soil, Fertilizer and Cattle Technological Education Plan; Directorate for the National Development of Agriculture and Cattle (DAP); Development of Social and Livestock Agricultural Construction (DESA); Ministry of Economy; Education, Culture and Science Sector; Basic Industries Sector; Cuban Institute for Normalization, Metrology, and Quality Control; National Institute of Sports, Physical Education and Recreation (INDER); Institute of Animal Science (ICA); Transportation Equipment Import Enterprise (TRANSIMPORT); Cuban Construction Machinery and Equipment Import Enterprise (CONSTRUIMPORT); Cuban Red Cross; House of the Americas (CA); National Council of Culture (CNC).

Among these bureaucracies, only the Children's Institute and the National Council of Culture had sizable numbers of women, respectively, 54 and 18 women for the years 1973 and 1974. The author will, upon request, furnish information on this group of bureaucracies.

REFERENCES

Acevedo, Arturo
    1961   "La Mujer de hoy en nuestros campos." INRA (April): 54, 59.

Baldes Perez, Enrique
             "Nurses Aides: New Steps in the Development of Public Health Plans," JPRS 26041, Translations on Cuba, No. 171.

Berman, Joan
    1970   "Women in Cuba." Women, A Journal of Liberation (Summer): 10-14.

Blutstein, Howard I., L.C. Anderson, E.C. Betters, D. Lane. J.C. Leonhard, C. Townsend.
    1971   Area Handbook of Cuba. Washington, D.C.: U.S. Government Printing Office, 75-610124, DA PAM 550-752.

Bohemia
    1964   Translations on Cuba. JPRS 26136, No. 172.

Book Institute
    1967   Cuba '67: Image of a Country. Havana.

Boyd, Edmond
    1974   "Castro Remodels the System." CMA Journal 3 (November): 991-1002.

Camarano, Chris
    1971   "On Cuban Women." Science and Society (Spring): 48-58.

Castro, Fidel
    1960   "Agui no solo luchan los Hombres. Agui, como los Hombres, luchan las Mujeres." Obra Revolucionaria 25: 9-15.

Castro, Fidel
    1966   "Discurso pronounciado en el acto de clausura de la V Plenaria Nacional de la Federacion de Mujeres Cubanas." Politica Internacional 16: 263-280.

Castro, Fidel
1969   "Communism Cannot be Built in One Country in the Midst of an Underdeveloped
            World." pp. 200-219 in Martin Kenner and James Petras (eds.), Fidel Castro
            Speaks. New York: Grove Press, Inc.

Castro, Fidel
1976   "Informe Central de Fidel al Primer Congreso." Granma Resumen Semanal (4 de
            Enero): 6.

Castro, Raul
1975   "Raul en el XV Aniversario de la Federacion de Mujeres Cubanas." Granma
            Resumen Semanal (1 de Septiembre): 4.

Chelala, Jose
1971   "Contraception and Abortion in Cuba." IPPF Medical Bulletin 5 (October): 3-4.
–   "Fertility of Women in Cuba. Abortion and Contraceptive Methods." Unpubli-
            shed manuscript.

Chertov, Eva
1970   "Women in Revolutionary Cuba." The Militant (September 18): 9.

Cooney, John E.
1975   "Even After 15 Years, Life in Cuba Pivots on 'The Revolution'." Wall Street
            Journal (January 15).

1974a   "Popular Power." Wall Street Journal (December 4)

1974b   "Best Things in Life Are. . .? Well, Nuptials are in Cuba, Anyway." Wall Street
            Journal (December 5).

de la Torre, Silvio
1965   Mujer y Sociedad. Santa Clara: Editorial Universitaria.

de Onis, Juan
1967   "Cuba Now Trying to Reduce Births." New York Times (March 22): 4.

Engels, F.
1972   The Origins of the Family, Private Property and the State. New York: Pathfinders
            Press, Inc.

Espin, Vilma
            "Speech on FMC 9th Anniversary." JPRS 48855, Translations on Latin America,
            No. 231.

Espin, Vilma
1975   "Discurso de Vilma Espin en la Conferencia Mundial del Ano Internacional de la
            Mujer, Celebrada en Mexico." Granma Resumen Semanal (6 de Julio): 10.

Fagen, Richard
1972   "Mass Mobilization in Cuba: The Symbolism of Struggle." pp. 201-224 in Rolando
            E. Bonachea and N.P. Valdes (eds.) Cuba in Revolution. New York: Anchor
            Books.

FCW Press Office
1965   "The Federation of Cuban Women is Five Years Old." Women of the Whole
            World 12: 18-21.

Garrity, Nancy J.
1971   Cuba as a Case Study: The Role Played by Education in the Socialization of the
            New Man. MA Thesis, Tufts University.

Gibbs, Jack P. and Walter T. Martin
1969   "Urbanization, Technology and the Division of Labor: International Patterns."
            pp. 309-321, in Gerald Breese (ed.). The City in Newly Developing Countries:
            Reading on Urbanism and Urbanization. New Jersey: Prentice-Hall, Inc.

Gordon, Linda
1970   "On Women's Liberation in Cuba." Women, A Journal of Liberation (Summer): 14.

Granma
1974   "Fidel el 26 de Julio en Matanzas." (Agosto 4): 3.

Granma Weekly Review
1971   "The Federation of Cuban Women: A Decisive Force of Our Revolution." (August 29): 3.

Granma Resumen Semanal
1975a   "Comenzara a regir el proximo 8 de marzo, Dia Internacional de la Mujer, el Codigo de la Familia, segun hey 1289 recien dictada por el Consejo de Ministros." (Marzo 2): 5.
1975b   "Codigo de Familia." (Marzo 16): 7-9 (full text of the new family code).
1976   "Resoluciones del Primer Congreso del Partido Comunista de Cuba." (1 de Febrero): 9.

Goldberg, Marilyn Powell
1973   Women in the Soviet Economy. A Warner Modular, Reprint 42: 1-15.

Gusfield, Joseph R.
1973   Utopian Myths and Movements in Modern Societies. New Jersey: General Learning Press.

Jenness, Linda (ed.)
1970   Women in The Cuban Revolution. Speeches by Fidel Castro, New York: Pathfinder Press, Inc.

Jenness, Linda (ed.)
1972   Feminism and,Socialism, New York: Pathfinder Press, Inc.

JPRS 26526
1964   "Marriage to a non-Revolutionary Frown Upon." Translations on Cuba, No. 186, 20055.

JPRS 26526
1964   "Fourth Anniversary of the Federation of Cuban Women." Translations on Cuba, No. 186, 20055.

JPRS 48855
1969   "Labor Minister Addresses FMC on 9th Anniversary." Translations on Latin America, No. 231.

Lawrenson, Helen
1973   "Latins Are,Lousy Lovers." Esquire (October): 266.

Leiner, Marvin
1973   Major Developments in Cuban Education. A Warner Modular, Reprint 264: 1-21.

Li, Wen L.
1971   "Status Integration and Suicide: A Methodological Critique." Issues in Criminology 6 (Summer): 85-93.

Le-Riverend, Eduardo
1966   "El Divorcio: Derechos Cubano y Puertorriqueno." Revista Juridica: 535-634.

Marx, Karl
1970   Das Kapital. Chicago: Henry Regnery Co.

Mesa, Enrique
1975   "Crondogia de la creacion e inicio del funcionamiento de los democraticos organos del Poder Popular en Matanzas." Granma, (January 12): 7.

Mesa, Lago, Carmelo
1972   The Labor Force, Employment, Unemployment and Underemployment in Cuba, 1899-1970. Beverly Hills: Sage Publications.

Montes, Jorge G. and Antonio Alonso Avila
1970   Historia del partido comunista de Cuba. Miami: Rema Press.

Morgan, Ted
1974   "Cuba." The New York Time Magazine (December 1): 27.

Nelson, Lowry
1970   "Cuban Population Estimates, 1953-1970." Journal of Inter-American Studies and World Affairs 12 (July): 392-400.

Oui
1975   "Exclusive Interview with Fidel Castro." (January): 160.

Padan-Eisenstark, Dorit D.
1973   Are Israeli Women Really Equal? Trends and Patterns of Israeli Women's Labor Force Participation: A Comparative Analysis," Journal of Marriage and The Family 35 (August): 538-545.

Perera, Hilda
1962   "Women in a New Social Context in Cuba." International Journal of Adult and Youth Education 3: 144-149.

Perez Tobella, Sonia
1967   "On The Use of Contraceptives." Granma Weekly Review (July 9).

Purcell, Susan K.
1973   "Modernizing Women for a Modern Society: The Cuban Case." pp. 257-272 in Ann Pescatello, (ed.) Female and Male in Latin America, Pittsburgh: University of Pittsburgh Press.

Ramos, Ana
1971   "La Mujer y la revolucion en Cuba." Casa de las Americas 11: 56-72.

Randall, Margaret
1972   La Mujer Cubana Ahora. La Habana: Instituto Cubano del Libro

Reed, Evelyn
1972   Problems of Women's Liberation. New York: Pathfinder Press, Inc.

Joint Publications Research Service
1962   Reports on Cuban Women's Federation. (December): Item No. 15930, catalogue No. 23764.

Roberts, Paul C. and Mukhtar Hamour (eds.)
1970   Cuba 1968: Supplement to the Statistical Abstract of Latin America. Los Angeles: University of California Latin American Center.

Rodrigues, Anibal C.
1962   "Sobre La Familia Cubana." Havana (May-June): 7-29

Rodriguez, Javier
1966   "Education in Day Care Centers." JPRS 35406, Translations on Cuba, no. 416.

Salaff, Janet W. and J. Merkle
1970   "Women and Revolution: The Lesson of The Soviet Union and China." Socialist Revolution 1 (November-December).

Stamper, B. Maxwell
1971   "Some Demographic Consequences of the Cuban Revolution." Concerned Demography 2 (March): 19-25.

Trotsky, Leon
1970   Women and the Family. New York: Pathfinder Press, Inc.

Waters, Mary A.
1972   Feminism and the Marxist Movement. New York: Pathfinder Press, Inc.

Yglesias, Jose
1969   "Cuban Report: Their Hippies, Their Squares." New York Time Magazine (January 12): 25.

27

Career Constraints Among Women Graduate Students In A Developing Society: West Pakistan*

A Study in the Changing Status of Women

J. HENRY KORSON*

Throughout the history of Islam the status of women in Muslim societies has been low. The tradition of *purdah,* or the seclusion of women, has dictated their subordinate position and only within the last two generations have any of the Muslim societies taken positive steps to reduce the discrimination against women in such areas as education and occupational opportunity outside of marriage. Pakistan might be considered one of the more conservative of the Muslim societies because *purdah* is still very much in evidence and a significant proportion of Pakistani women still adhere to its norms. Inevitably such a practice results in a subordinate role for the women of a society.[1]

This subordinate role is further demonstrated by the practice of arranged marriages, usually with little or no voice in such decisions by the principals, and limited educational and occupational opportunities for the women. Historically Muslim societies have been patrilineal, patrilocal and patriarchal for centuries, but political changes in this century in some of these nations have also brought changes in the other social institutions of these societies.

---

*J. Henry Korson, Ph.D., is Professor of Sociology, Department of Sociology, University of Massachusetts, Amherst, Mass., U.S.A.

This paper is a revision of one prepared for the Family Research Section of the VIIth World Congress of Sociology, sponsored by the International Sociological Association, Varna, Bulgaria, September, 1970.

*The author is indebted to the University of Massachusetts Research Council for the financial support of this project; to Drs. Anwar Syed, Hanna Papanek and Albert Chevan for their helpful suggestions; to Professors M. Fayyaz and H. Zoberi for their administrative assistance; and to Laila Hussain, Azra Bashir and Timm Thorsen for their technical assistance.

[1]The literal interpretation of the term *purdah* is the seclusion of women. In West Pakistan the term refers largely to the minority of women who wear the *burqa,* or veil, in public. In the broader sense, it might be thought of as a whole syndrome of the segregation of women from men who are not their relatives, and the maintenance of modesty in dress and manner. Regardless of costume or style, women are fully covered from neck to ankle; segregated seating is found in public buses in Karachi as well as in trains, and women are expected to have as little contact as possible with men who are not relatives.

A developing nation usually has limited resources at its command to achieve its proclaimed goals of modernization, and it is inevitable that a system of priorities must be established as an integral aspect of its short and long term planning. Since the allocation of its manpower and other resources is, inevitably, a basic ingredient in any formula the government of a developing nation must consider, no less important must be its concern with the education and training of its population. In a society where the illiteracy rate today is approximately 80 percent,[2] allocation of scarce resources in the field of education in Pakistan is made after very serious consideration of a variety of alternatives. And since females make up approximately 47.4 percent of the nation's population, their total role in the economy must be given serious consideration.[3]

Among developing nations universal literacy inevitably becomes a goal to be achieved at the earliest possible time, and every government confronted with a high illiteracy rate finds it politically expedient to do so. In striving for universal literacy, what some western nations accomplished in three or four centuries the developing nations are trying to accomplish in a generation or less, usually with a series of Five Year, or similar, plans. The impatience such governments manifest in such matters is to be commended. Since efforts call for long range as well as short range planning, and since political leaders must make choices among several alterantives in the allocation of economic resources for education, national pride will almost always dictate that universal literacy receive first priority.

Schools in Pakistan are coeducational through the primary grades, but thereafter the sexes are segregated through the intermediate, secondary and college years, but at the university level, where largely graduate programs are offered, coeducation is the practice.

Because of Pakistan's limited resources and its great need for trained professional and technical manpower, the question arises concerning how its trained men and especially its women are absorbed into the economy of the country. All the universities in Pakistan are government supported, and are open to all who qualify — subject only to space limitations. To this writer's knowledge, no discrimination is practiced against women, and they are free to elect their own programs.

---

[2]Estimated, 1968. According to the last census taken in 1961, 19.2 percent of the population 5 years of age and over was literate. See, Government of Pakistan Ministry of Home Affairs, *Population Census of 1961*, Census Bulletin No. 4, Karachi, 1962, p. vii. Also, there was a great disparity between the sexes: in West Pakistan males had a literacy rate of 23.9 percent and females 7.4 percent. Because the annual net population increase is approximately 3.0 percent, and the government support of education has been totally inadequate, there has been little significant improvement in the literacy rate since 1961. The Government of Pakistan has been spending increasing sums on education, although much of the emphasis appears to be on the lower levels, with little increase at the upper levels, such as graduate education.

[3]*Population Census of 1961, Census Bulletin*, No. 3 (3). Even though schooling is open to all, in 1961-62 girls made up only 25 percent of the student body in the primary grades, and only half that percentage in the middle and secondary schools. See, Muhammad S. Huq, *Education and Development Strategy in South and Southeast Asia*, Honolulu, 1965, p. 218.

In attempting to assess social change in a traditional society, it is useful to explore the participants' roles in the processes of social change. Since opportunities for advanced training in specialized fields are available to young women in Pakistan today whose mothers rarely had such an opportunity in pre-Partition India, an effort was made to assess the employment experience of women students since completion of their master's degree work, and to determine to what extent these women had availed themselves of employment opportunities.

The following hypotheses are suggested:

Hypothesis I: It is highly likely that women graduate students, exposed to the rational and logical systems of the natural and social sciences and the intellectual challenge of the humanities, are motivated to serve as initiators of and participants in social change from the traditional norms.

Although the respondents come almost entirely from middle and upper class families, the level of educational achievement of their mothers is very low, while that of their fathers is quite high.   The whole syndrome of *purdah* calls not only for seclusion from males who are not relatives, but also a minimum of participation in community affairs.   Traditionally, the woman's prescribed role is that of serving her husband's and family's needs, and is not concerned with the problems of the larger world outside the home.   Women are more likely to be concerned with matters of the "women's world," and with the continuity of the traditional values of the society to which they have been socialized than they are with the initiation and implementation of social change.

Hypothesis II: Since Karachi is a much more cosmopolitan city than Lahore, students from the University of Karachi are more likely to participate in the labor force after graduation and serve as initiators of social change than are students from the University of the Punjab at Lahore.

Karachi, which has the largest sea- and airport of the nation, has experienced very rapid population growth based almost entirely on the very important expansion and growth of industrial and commercial enterprises, while Lahore has experienced far less growth.   This very rapid economic growth has provided more employment opportunities for entrance into the labor market in Karachi than in Lahore.

Hypothesis III: Because of the tradition of *purdah,* it is permissible for middle and upper class women to accept segregated employment as teachers, or other professionals, but under no circumstances "in offices where men are employed."

Muslim women in Pakistan have made their own adjustments to the constraints of *purdah*.   Women usually prefer to be attended by women doctors, will normally accept employment where the sexes are segregated, or have the least possible contact with men.

For this reason, "ladies' banks" have been opened as branches of larger banks, where only women are employed, and where female customers can conduct their business without the embarrassment of having to talk to strange men. This new development has also opened new employment opportunities for women university graduates. Although a few women have chosen to challenge the norms by accepting employment as hostesses for Pakistan International Airlines, this particular job has been singled out by many respondents as one their families would not permit them to take because close contact with strange men is considered "improper," if not "indecent." Or, as one respondent expressed it, "My parents will permit me to teach in a girls' school or college, but I am strictly forbidden to work anywhere in the company of men." In fact, the same respondent had difficulty obtaining her father's permission to attend her undergraduate college because two of her teachers were men.

Hypothesis IV: In a developing society, employment opportunities are most readily available for graduates in the Natural Sciences (including the applied fields), the Social Sciences, and the Humanities, in that order. Although this statement might also be applicable to the more developed nations, the needs of the developing societies are far more acute and they have a smaller pool of trained scientists to draw upon. There is the further problem of the so-called "brain-drain" with which almost all developing nations are confronted.

METHODOLOGY

In 1968 stratified samples were taken of 50 percent of the women graduate students at the University of Karachi and 25 percent from the University of the Punjab in Lahore who had completed their work for the M.A. or M.Sc. degrees in the various Arts and Sciences departments in June, 1966. Although the interviews were conducted by female interviewers in 1968, the class of 1966 was chosen in order to permit those students who were so interested to actively seek employment. The interviewers were themselves members of the class of 1966, so that the problems of rapport with the respondents were reduced to a minimum. Both samples were made up of women who were never married at the time they completed their academic programs. Two years after that time, however, 18, or 12.7 percent of the Karachi sample, and 12, or 12.0 percent of the Lahore sample, had married. The median age of the students in both samples was 24.0 years at the time of interview, hence, their median age at the completion of their studies was 22.0 years.

From Table 1 it is seen that there is quite a significant disparity in enrollment in the various fields of study between the two institutions. Although enrollment at the University of Karachi appears to show a fair balance among the Natural Sciences (39.4 percent), Social Sciences (34.5 percent), and the Humanities (26.1 percent), the sample from the University of the Punjab at Lahore was skewed toward the Humanities with a 66.0 percent representation; 25.0 percent in the Social Sciences, and only 9.0 percent in the Natural Sciences.

TABLE 1

STUDENTS MAJOR AREAS OF STUDY

(Percentage)

	Karachi N=142	Lahore N=100a
Natural Sciences	39.4	9.0
Social Sciences	34.5	25.0
Humanities	26.1	66.0
Total	100.00	100.0

a—Since the N for Karachi is 142 and 100 for Lahore, these will not be repeated in the balance of the tables. The percentage totals in all tables are rounded.

PARENTS' EDUCATIONAL ACHIEVEMENT

In a developing society manifesting rapid social change, perhaps one of the most revealing indicators of intergenerational change is a comparison of educational achievement of the generations, assuming, of course, that educational facilities were, and are, fairly readily available. For middle and upper class women of Pakistan this is not too much of a problem today. Although there were limited educational opportunities for the students' fathers a generation ago, such opportunities for their mothers in pre-Partition India were exceedingly limited, depending on the community in which they resided. Although many people, especially women, have never formally attended a school, an important segment of the population does, indeed, informally learn to read. This is especially true of the middle and upper class women whose families arrange private tutoring in order to conform to the constraints of *purdah*. For this reason, the category "no formal schooling" was used, as it was felt to be more accurate in describing educational achievement rather than literacy *per se*.

From Table 2 it is seen that the educational achievement of the Karachi fathers is considerably higher than that of their counterparts in Lahore, with a weighted mean of 5.8 versus 4.9, while the achievement of the Lahore mothers (1.5) is somewhat higher than that of the Karachi mothers (1.2). The greatest disparity, however, is that found between the mothers and fathers in both samples. What is perhaps most significant is that only 1.4 percent of the Karachi fathers and 4.0 percent of the Lahore fathers claimed no formal schooling, while 63.4 percent of the Karachi mothers and 45.0 percent of the Lahore mothers fell in this category. Not only have the graduates far outstripped their mothers in educational achievement, creating a gulf that is difficult to comprehend, but even surpassed, on the average, the educational achievements of their fathers.

TABLE 2

PARENTS' EDUCATIONAL ACHIEVEMENT

Percentage

		Karachi		Lahore	
		Fathers	*Mothers*	*Fathers*	*Mothers*
(7)	Post graduate or professional training	25.4	0.7	25.0	1.0
(6)	College graduate (B.A., B.Sc.)	36.6	2.1	15.0	0.0
(5)	Intermediate, or post-secondary school diploma (F.A. or F.Sc.)	10.6	4.2	13.0	2.0
(4)	Passed matriculation exam for secondary school	19.7	11.3	34.0	14.0
(3)	Some secondary, but did not pass matriculation examination	3.5	5.6	2.0	1.0
(2)	Middle school	2.8	7.7	7.0	34.0
(1)	Primary school	0.0	4.9	0.0	3.0
(0)	No formal schooling	1.4	63.4	4.0	45.0
	Total	100.0	100.00	100.0	100.0
	Weighted mean:	5.8	1.2	4.9	1.5

FATHERS' OCCUPATIONS

One of the survivals from the days of Britain's colonial rule of the sub-continent is the high prestige of the civil and military services. It is said that "400 or 500 CSP [Civil Service of Pakistan] people run the country," and such comments are meant not only in reference to the bureaucracy that controls the reins of many governments, but in Pakistan there is the further implication of an elite group that holds great social prestige. The Civil Service of Pakistan is a national service. Each wing (West and East Pakistan) has its own Provincial service known as the Pakistan Civil Service or PCS. Both the CSP and the PCS are said to attract the elite among public officials, with the former holding greater prestige than the latter. Officers in the military service of the country hold prestige positions that are considered roughly the equivalent to the CSP and the PCS. Both the civil and military services form elite groups whose social status is unchallenged. Table 3 shows that 38.0 percent of the Karachi students' fathers are represented in this highest category, compared to only 6.0 percent of the Lahore students' fathers. One of the reasons for this difference is that even though the central government undertook, in 1959, the building of a new national capital at Islamabad, outside the city of Rawalpindi, not all of the central government offices have moved from Karachi. Many government officials still reside there, waiting the completion of the building program in Islamabad. On the other hand, Lahore shows a higher representation of professionals.

TABLE 3

FATHERS' OCCUPATION

Percentage

	Karachi	Lahore
CSP, PCS, or some other position of authority in a government service (including armed forces)	38.0	6.0
Medicine, law, engineering, scientist, college or university teaching	16.9	23.0
Owner, executive, business manager, property or land owner	22.5	25.0
Teacher: primary, middle, secondary	1.4	1.0
Shopkeeper, salesman, assistant or clerical worker in business or government service	19.7	45.0
Skilled worker, artisan	1.4	0.0
Total	100.0	100.0

The second occupational group is made up of professionals, and here the Karachi fathers are less well represented, with 16.9 percent of the total in this group, compared with 23.0 percent of the Lahore fathers. The third occupational group, largely made up of businessmen and management, including property and land owners, is represented by 22.5 percent of the Karachi fathers and 25.0 percent of the Lahore fathers. These three occupational groups make up more than three-fourths, or 77.4 percent of the Karachi sample and more than one-half, or 54.0 percent of the Lahore sample, or the bulk of the fathers in both samples.

In prestige terms, the teachers at various sub-college levels rank next in order, but have an exceedingly low representation in the two samples under consideration. Only 1.4 percent of the Karachi and 1.0 percent of the Lahore fathers fell in this category. One of the reasons for this low representation is the low salaries paid teachers at the lower levels, making it difficult, if not impossible, to support children who aspire to higher education in Pakistan.

Although the next category of "shopkeeper, salesman, assistant or clerical worker in business or government service" was well represented in the Karachi sample, with 19.7 percent, the Lahore sample totaled 45.0 percent, which would indicate that an important percentage of the Lahore fathers were representative of the lower middle or middle class. As expected, the "skilled worker or artisan" had a very low representation among the fathers: only 1.4 percent among the Karachi fathers, and none in Lahore.

FATHERS' MONTHLY INCOME

Table 4 shows that the higher income of the Karachi fathers is a reflection of their higher occupational status. Almost 60 percent of the Karachi fathers' incomes falls in the two highest income categories, compared to only 30 percent of the Lahore fathers' incomes. The median incomes further demonstrate the great disparity between the two samples.

TABLE 4

FATHERS' MONTHLY INCOME

Percentage

	Karachi	Lahore
Rs 1,000 or more	43.7	22.0
Rs 750-999	16.2	8.0
Rs 500-749	14.1	29.0
Rs 300-499	13.4	24.0
Rs 0-299	4.9	15.0
No information (deceased or retired)	7.7	2.0
Total	100.0	100.0
Median	Rs 785	Rs 586

MOTHERS' EMPLOYMENT STATUS

If one were to test the validity of the hypothesis "economic independence breeds social independence"[4] (as it applies to married women), one means of doing so would be to examine the employment pattern of the respondents' mothers outside the home. In this study, the Karachi sample showed only two mothers employed outside the home, and both were school teachers, while the Lahore sample showed only one mother employed, and she was a physician. These cases, although rare, present a picture of "enlightened" or "modern" families in a traditional and relatively closed society. Their life style could easily parallel the activities of many upper middle class families in the west. For unmarried women, the kind of freedom in decision making that employed western women know is practically unknown to employed unmarried Pakistani women. The latter are expected to continue to live with their parents, or other relatives, until the time of marriage, and to contribute their earnings to the family exchequer.

STUDENTS' EMPLOYMENT STATUS

In a society that is as religiously conservative as is Pakistan, women have historically been assigned a very subordinate role. The tradition of *purdah* has insured the continuance of the status of women students as economic dependents so that they are usually neither expected nor permitted to take employment before they have completed their studies.

In an effort to determine the total employment experience of the women graduate students since the completion of their master's degree work,

---

[4]J. Henry Korson, "The Roles of Dower and Dowry as Indicators of Social Change in Pakistan," *Journal of Marriage and the Family*, 30, 4, November, 1968, p. 705.

questions were asked which focused on their employment history and their present position in the labor force. From Table 5 it is evident that the Karachi graduates are far more active in the labor force, with a total of 64.1 percent of the sample employed at the time of the study. Of the total sample, 38.0 percent were employed as teachers at various levels; 14.1 percent held positions as research assistants; only 0.7 percent were employed in social work, while 11.3 percent held positions in government agencies or in business organizations. This compares with 21.0 percent of the Lahore women employed in teaching positions; 6.0 percent employed as research assistants; 3.0 percent as social workers; and 3.0 percent in administrative or business positions. These results validate Hypothesis II.

TABLE 5

GRADUATE STUDENTS' EMPLOYMENT STATUS

	Karachi	*Lahore*
	percentage	
A. *In Labor Force*		
Employed		
1. Teaching	38.0	21.0
2. Research	14.1	6.0
3. Social Work	0.7	3.0
4. Administrative, business	11.3	3.0
	64.1	33.0
Unemployed:		
1. Was temporarily employed, now unemployed, but seeking employment	4.9	1.0
2. Never employed, but seeking employment	10.6	31.0
	15.5	32.0
B. *Not In Labor Force*		
1. Continuing education	5.6	10.0
2. Formerly employed, now married and not seeking employment	2.1	0.0
3. Married, never employed, and not seeking employment	5.6	0.0
4. Unmarried, never employed, and not seeking employment	7.0	25.0
	20.3	35.0
Total	100.0	100.0

Also included in the labor force were those who had been employed, but were unemployed at the time of the study and were seeking work. These made up 4.9 percent of the Karachi sample and 1.0 percent of the Lahore sample. Those who had never been employed but were seeking employment at the time of the study made up 10.6 percent of the Karachi sample and 31.0 percent of the Lahore sample, almost three times that of their Karachi peers. Women graduates not in the labor force were made up of those who were continuing their education for advanced degrees: Karachi, 5.6 percent and Lahore 10.0 percent; those formerly employed, but now married and not seeking employment: Karachi, 2.1 percent and none in Lahore; those married, never employed, and not seeking employment: Karachi, 5.6 percent, Lahore none; and those who were unmarried, were never employed, and not seeking employment: Karachi, 7.0 percent and Lahore 25.0 percent.

The contrast between the two major cities in labor force activity is significant in many respects. Although one hears many generalizations and analogies from the residents of the two cities,[5] two possible explanations can be offered. Since Karachi is the major commercial and industrial city of the nation and has experienced enormous growth since partition of Pakistan from India in 1947,[6] far more opportunities for employment are available in the rapidly expanding economy of the city, while fewer opportunities are available in the more conservative and traditional city of Lahore, which has experienced far less population growth.

Furthermore, since the bulk of the population increase is made up of immigrants from India, many of whom were entrepreneurs and have continued and expanded their business activities in Karachi, there appears to be a different social climate in the latter city — one based on the rapidly expanding business and industrial community, rather than the relatively quiet social climate that one finds in Lahore.[7] The latter has traditionally been considered the cultural center of the nation, with a century-old university, and many famous mosques and other attractions, such as the Shalimar Gardens.

The marked difference in labor force participation between the two samples can also be interpreted as reflecting the social conservatism of the Lahore women with the more "progressive" approach of the Karachi women. Lack of employment opportunities may, indeed, explain the very considerable differential between the employed women in Karachi and Lahore (64.1 and 33.0 percent, respectively), as well as those who are unemployed, but seeking employment (15.5 and 32.0 percent, respectively),

---

[5]Karachi has often been referred to as the "New York City" of Pakistan, while Lahore has been termed the "Boston" of the nation.

[6] The censuses of 1941, 1951, and 1961 gave the following populations for Karachi: 387,000; 1,068,000; and 2,032,000 respectively. The figure of 3,200,000 is an estimate of the city's population in 1968 as published in the local press. This estimate is not supported by an official government statement. See, Sultan S. Hashmi, *The People of Karachi, Demographic Characteristics*, Monographs in the Economics of Development, No. 13, Karachi: Pakistan Institute of Development Economics, 1965, p. 12.

[7]In 1959, only 17 percent of the population of Karachi was native to the city. Source: Sultan S. Hashmi, *The People of Karachi, op. cit.*, p. 34. The earlier immigration from India following partition has been replaced by migration to the city from rural areas. It is generally assumed that one of the results of the large-scale migration to Karachi in the post-partition period has been the weakening of many traditional constraints on the behavior of women, while Lahore, which has experienced far less growth in the same period has seen much less change in the normative behavior of its women.

but when those not in the labor force, who are unmarried, were never employed, and are not seeking employment, are found to be more than three times as great in Lahore as in Karachi (25.0 percent compared with 7.0 percent for Karachi), then the thought suggests itself that the families of the Lahore women are far more conservative and closer to the constraints of *purdah* than are the Karachi families and their women. It is also suggested that more Lahore families either do not encourage their daughters to seek employment, or even actively discourage them from doing so.

In assessing students' employment in terms of their major field of study, from Table 6 it is seen that those students who had majored in the Natural Sciences had the best employment record. In both the Karachi and the Lahore samples more than three times as many Natural Science majors were employed as unemployed. In Karachi the employed Social Science graduates outnumbered the unemployed by a three to two margin, which was reversed in the Lahore sample. Among the Humanities majors the Karachi graduates were almost evenly divided between employed and unemployed, while in Lahore somewhat less than a quarter were employed. These results appear to validate Hypothesis IV and offer additional support to the statements made above concerning the difference in employment opportunities to be found in the two cities, as well as the more liberal attitudes toward the employment of women in Karachi.

TABLE 6
GRADUATE STUDENTS' EMPLOYMENT BY FIELD OF STUDY
Percentage

	Karachi			Lahore		
	Empl.	Unempl.		Empl.	Unempl.	
Natural Science	76.0	23.2	100.0	77.7	22.3	100.0
Social Science	59.2	40.8	100.0	40.0	60.0	100.0
Humanities	51.3	48.7	100.0	24.2	75.8	100.0
All Fields	64.1	35.9	100.0	33.0	67.0	100.0

In one of the few studies done on the urban labor force in Karachi, in 1959 Hashmi demonstrated that women made up only 2.6 percent of the labor force in the city. As is seen in Table 7, his data show that the top three categories of professional and technical, administrative and management, and clerical and sales make up 22.8 percent of the total, or only 0.59 percent of the city's labor force. Skilled workers, who are employed in factories make up 9.9 percent of the total, while two-thirds, or 67.3 percent of the women are classified as semi- and unskilled workers, or servants. Although the 2.6 percent figure has probably changed, it is doubtful that there has been a significant change in female participation in the labor force since 1959.[8]

---

[8] *Op. cit.*, p. 26.

TABLE 7

FEMALE WORKERS, BY OCCUPATIONAL GROUP

KARACHI, 1959a

(Percentage)

Professional and technical	16.5
Administrative and management	2.7
Clerical and sales	3.6
Skilled workers	9.9
Semi- and unskilled workers	14.5
Servants and related occupations	52.8
Total	100.0

aSource: Sultan S. Hashmi, M. R. Khan and K. J. Krotki, *The People of Karachi, Data From a Survey*, Statistical Paper No. 2, Karachi, Pakistan Institute of Development Economics, 1964, p. 26.

GRADUATE STUDENTS' EMPLOYERS

Of all the Karachi graduates who were employed at the time of the study 65.5 percent were working as teachers. From Table 8 it is seen that 31.6 percent of the employed graduates teach in primary or secondary schools, 25.3 percent in colleges, and 8.9 percent at the university level. Of the 33.0 percent of the Lahore graduates who were employed at the time of the study, 63.5 percent were employed as teachers: 36.3 percent at the primary or secondary level, 24.2 percent at the college level,and 3.0 percent at the university level. Further analysis reveals that almost two-thirds of the employed group in both samples are engaged in teaching. This would appear to validate Hypothesis III, viz., that women graduates are largely limited to teaching and other professional careers where *purdah* conditions of employment apply.

TABLE 8

GRADUATE STUDENTS' EMPLOYERS

Percentage

	Karachi	Lahore
School	31.6	36.3
College	25.3	24.3
University	8.9	3.0
Government Agency	18.6	30.3
Private Organization	15.5	6.0
Total	100.0	100.0

Employment by a government agency is claimed by 18.7 percent of the Karachi and 30.3 percent of the Lahore employed graduates, while private organizations offer employment to 15.5 percent and 6.0 percent of the Karachi and Lahore employed graduates, respectively.

GRADUATE STUDENTS' MONTHLY EARNINGS

One would hardly expect students, especially women, entering the labor market for the first time, to command very high salaries. Table 9 demonstrates that only 6.5 percent of the Karachi sample and 5.7 percent of the Lahore sample were earning Ro500 or more per month at the time of the study. The mode for both samples fell in the Rs300-499 range, while the median monthly earnings for the Karachi graduates were Rs340, and for the Lahore graduates Rs362.

TABLE 9

GRADUATE STUDENTS' MONTHLY EARNINGS

Percentage

In Rupees	Karachi	Lahore
Rs 500-999	6.5	5.7
Rs 300-499	54.3	68.6
Rs 0-299	39.1	25.7
Total	100.0	100.0
Median	Rs 340	Rs 362

FAMILY ATTITUDES TOWARD DAUGHTERS' EMPLOYMENT

Basic to any long range career goals the individual student might have would be the socialization experience, and the form this socialization takes would certainly have a strong influence on the decision making process. Not only are adolescents fully aware of the societal norms which tend to limit their decisions, but they are also sufficiently perceptive of their family's attitudes in regard to the role that daughters are expected to play. As in all societies, the norms at any given time might be thought of as the mode, and responses to the norms can be scaled in relation to the ideal that is verbalized.

Within the context of middle and upper class Pakistani society, employment outside the home for adult women presupposes higher education and/or training in a specialized field. The enormous differential in educational achievement between the mothers and their daughters is readily apparent, and it is evident that few of the mothers have achieved sufficient education to hold the positions in the labor market their daughters do today.

In examining Table 10 it is seen that 11.3 percent of the Karachi parents and 25.0 percent of the Lahore parents either "do not want or will not permit their daughter to work." Two major reasons are offered for this position: 1) some middle class families feel quite defensive about a daughter working outside the home for money. They are fearful that friends and relatives will believe the family needs the financial assistance of the daughter, and that, in the long run, this will damage her marriage pros-

406 WOMEN IN THE ECONOMY

pects; and 2) although they are willing to have the daughter achieve higher education while she waits for the propitious time for marriage, the family is either bound by the constraints of *purdah,* or otherwise considers it improper for a female member of the family to enter the labor market. This attitude is supported by the second option the students chose, viz., that their families would only permit them to work under *purdah* conditions, such as at girls' schools or colleges. This response was chosen by 52.0 percent or more than one-half of the Karachi students and two-thirds or 67.0 percent of the Lahore students. These attitudes would appear to reflect the "heavy influence of the *purdah* mentality," as some have put it. A few parents, 1.4 percent of the Karachi sample and 2.0 percent of the Lahore sample, had other objections, which were not specified. These results offer further evidence in support of Hypothesis III.

TABLE 10

FAMILY'S ATTITUDE TOWARD DAUGHTER'S EMPLOYMENT

Percentage

	Karachi	Lahore
Do not want or permit her to work	11.3	25.0
Will permit her to work only under *purdah* conditions, such as teaching at a girls' school or college	52.0	67.0
Parents have other objections	1.4	2.0
Parents do not object to any kind of work	35.2	6.0
Total	100.0	100.0

At the "liberal" end of the scale are those parents who "do not object to any kind of work" the daughters might decide to undertake. Here it is seen that 35.2 percent of the Karachi students but only 6.0 percent of the Lahore students responded positively to this option. An examination of all the options would indicate that far more Karachi students came of liberally inclined families, and that the freedom of action in the matter of career choice was far greater than that of their Lahore peers. The evidence from this table offers further support that the middle and upper class families in Karachi generally take a more liberal stance in regard to the behavior of their women and that the evidence supports Hypothesis II.

To test Hypothesis IV, it is seen in Table 11 that of those Karachi graduates *employed* at the time of interview, 53.5 percent of those in the Natural Sciences, 55.1 percent of those in the Social Sciences and 79.0 percent of those in the Humanities were employed as teachers, while the Lahore sample showed 43.0 percent of those in the Natural Sciences, 40.0 percent of those in the Social Sciences and 87.5 percent of those in the Humanities were engaged in teaching. It is very evident that the Humanities graduates found greater occupational opportunity in teaching than in other fields of endeavor.

TABLE 11
EMPLOYED GRADUATE STUDENTS' FIELD OF STUDY AND EMPLOYMENT EXPERIENCE

Percentage

Employment Experience	Karachi *Field of Study*				Lahore *Field of Study*			
	Natural Science N=43	Social Science N=29	Humanities N=19	Total N=91	Natural Science N=7	Social Science N=10	Humanities N=16	Total N=33
Teaching	53.5	55.1	79.0	59.3	43.0	40.0	87.5	63.6
Research	37.2	13.8	0.0	22.0	57.0	20.0	0.0	18.2
Social and Administrative Work, Business	9.1	31.0	21.0	18.5	0.0	40.0	12.5	18.2
Total	100.0	100.0	100.0	100.0	100.0	100.0	100.0	100.0

As might be expected, Natural Science graduates were more heavily represented in research positions, with 37.2 percent of the Karachi and 57.0 percent of the Lahore employed graduates thus engaged. Social Science graduates were represented by 13.8 percent of the Karachi and 20.0 percent of the Lahore employed graduates, and no Humanities graduates from either institution.

Social work, administrative and business employment attracted 9.1 percent of the Karachi employed Natural Science graduates, but none from Lahore. Social Science graduates from both institutions were the most successful in gaining employment in these fields, with 31.0 percent of the Karachi and 40.0 percent of the Lahore employed graduates while 21.0 percent of the employed Karachi Humanities graduates and 12.5 percent of the Lahore graduates were working in these fields.

From the above analysis it appears that Hypothesis III has been largely validated. With 81.3 percent of the Karachi and 81.8 percent of the Lahore employed graduates working in the fields of teaching or research (assuming the latter are in laboratories where men and women work in relatively separated situations), it would be difficult to deny the very strong preference for employment in these two fields. Even in "social and administrative work and business" which attracted 18.5 percent of the employed Karachi students and 18.2 percent of those from Lahore, it must be kept in mind that many of the appointments are in government agencies or offices where only women are employed. In summary, then, even though it cannot be stated categorically that *no* unmarried women are employed where they are placed in close association with men, it would appear that few, if any, indeed, are so employed.

As for Hypothesis I, it has been demonstrated that a majority of the graduates in the two samples have entered the labor force, although a minority of the total were actually employed at the time of the interview. Since such employment opportunities as the girls find themselves in today did not in large measure exist for their mothers, the evidence suggests that the economic and social roles the graduates are playing, and will continue to play, will have cumulative effects in the modernization of their nation.

Open-end questions revealed several reasons for families to invest in higher education for their daughters. Among the non-economic ones are: 1. Although not all women students who embark on graduate education complete their degree work requirements, it is a "good thing for a girl to do while she waits for her family to arrange her marriage." This position was also supported by non-respondents in reference to those women who have received their degrees, but who "do not want to work," or whose "families will not permit them to work." 2. The prestige of a higher degree for an "educated" girl evidently carries considerable weight in the negotiating process when representatives of the two families are arranging a marriage. Some economic reasons offered are: 1. Some young men view with favor the idea that an employed spouse can contribute to a higher level of living, both before the arrival of children and after they have grown. 2. In case of divorce or widowhood the woman will always have the training to enter the labor market and be relatively self-sufficient. It would appear that the egalitarianism of the west is beginning to make itself felt.

CONCLUSION

As Myrdal has stated, "From a development point of view, the purpose of education must be to rationalize attitudes as well as to impart knowledge and skills."[9] Certainly the majority of women graduate students who have completed their master's degree work at the two major institutions in West Pakistan can be assumed to perceive their role as young adults in a traditional Muslim society quite differently from that of their mothers. Whatever the motivation for their pursuit of higher education, the women students' level of educational achievement not only surpasses that of their fathers, but far outstrips that of their mothers and must create an almost insurmountable gulf between mothers and daughters.

Although there are no data on the employment history of the students' mothers as young adults, the fact that their educational achievement is so low almost precludes a very high level of participation in the labor force. Since 79.6 percent of the Karachi graduates are in the labor force (64.1 percent employed and another 15.5 percent unemployed but seeking work), and since 65.0 percent of the Lahore graduates are in the labor force (33.0 percent employed and 32.0 unemployed but seeking work), it can be assumed that very important segments of the middle and upper class young women in Pakistan who have completed their master's degree programs have manifested attitudinal changes toward their roles that are in sharp contrast to those of their mothers a generation ago.

The fact that at age 24 roughly 88 percent of the two samples were unmarried would indicate that at the very least higher education has had the effect of delaying marriage well beyond the norm for middle and upper class girls in West Pakistan. For example, the median age at first marriage for middle and upper class girls in Karachi for the period 1961-64 was 18.4 and 19.9 years. Although there is no comparable data available for Lahore, there seems little reason to assume the pattern is very different from that of Karachi.[10] Certainly the economic independence of the employed graduates is something their mothers had no opportunity to experience, and this will undoubtedly have its effect on their relationships with their future husbands and other members of their families.

In Table 10 it was shown that more than a third, or 35.2 percent of the Karachi graduates' parents did "not object to any kind of work" the girls

[9]Gunnar Myrdal, *Asian Drama*, Vol. III, New York, 1968, p. 1621.

[10]J. Henry Korson, "Age and Social Status at Marriage: Karachi, 1961-64," *Pakistan Development Review*, V, No. 4, p. 590.

might undertake. Although the Lahore graduates' parents' response was far smaller, with only 6.0 percent subscribing to this view, the very liberal attitude of such an important segment of the Karachi parents indicates a significant change not only in attitude on the part of the parents, but in the role behavior of their daughters. It can be assumed that the lag between the two cities will, in time, inevitably be overcome or at least narrowed.

Although different criteria were used in this study, perhaps a modification of Lerner's typology is in order here.[11] Since the mothers of the respondents in this study show a very low level of educational achievement and participate in the labor force hardly at all, they might, indeed, be termed "traditional." Those students who completed their graduate training, but whose families do not want or permit them to work might be termed "transitionals," because they have broken out of the tradition of *purdah* to the extent that they have sought higher education and training and have maximized or at least taken advantage of the opportunity to satisfy their intellectual curiosity. (It is also claimed that a highly educated girl can hope to make a better marriage, and, therefore, it is felt to be a good "investment.") Those students who have not only taken advantage of the opportunity of higher education but have sought and found employment in the labor market have also established a degree of economic independence which their unemployed peers lack. These girls might indeed be classed as "moderns," — willing, with the moral support of their families, to challenge the traditional norms of their society.

In a developing nation where the social norms limit the participation of women in its labor force, the question arises whether it is economically sound for the government to subsidize the higher education of women when the norms largely deny them the opportunity to put their knowledge and abilities to use in helping advance the economic and social development of their nation.[12] (In the last few years, women have made up approximately 50 percent of the graduate student enrollment at the University of Karachi, and about 25 percent at the University of the Punjab at Lahore.)

Although much has been written in recent years about the "brain-drain," or the loss of highly trained professionals from one nation to another which offers greater financial and other attractions, little has been said about the economic loss caused by the voluntary withdrawal of such manpower from the labor force within the nation. The unemployed respondents in this study who are not in the labor force because of personal

---

[11]Daniel Lerner, *The Passing of Traditional Society,* Glencoe, Ill., 1958, Chapter III.

[12]The whole question of the extent to which economic growth in developing nations is directly dependent upon investment in education at various levels has been widely discussed. McClelland has concluded that, other things being equal, those ". . . countries investing more heavily in education have tended to develop more rapidly . . ." See, David C. McClelland, "Does Education Accelerate Economic Growth?" *Economic Development and Cultural Change,* XIV, 3, April 1966, p. 278.

preference or social constraints represent a loss to the economy and welfare of the nation just as surely as though they had left the country and were contributing their knowledge and skills abroad. That the new government is concerned with the problem of the "educated unemployed" is evident from a recently issued statement in which it is proposed that a National Literacy Corps be organized so that employment opportunities would be made available to college and university graduates, and at the same time a major effect to reduce illiteracy would be launched.[13] An important question to be raised at this point is, should higher education be offered only to those students, men and women, who will make a commitment to enter the labor force either in the private or public sector for a stated period after graduation?

Unquestionably, those respondents who have entered the labor force not only have made a sharp break with the norms of the previous generation but the syndrome of the attitudes inherent in their new status will inevitably affect the social processes of their interpersonal relations with their parents' generation and with the males of their own generation. Islamic ideology calls for all Muslims to marry, and the norm in Pakistan calls for all marriages to be arranged by the families of the principals. Young women who have achieved higher education and a degree of economic independence that usually results from their participation in the labor force are hardly likely to emulate the behavior patterns of their mothers in decision making. The latter have had relatively little formal education and almost no opportunity to achieve a degree of economic (and social) independence that their employed daughters have. It is suggested that the greater the degree of participation in the labor force as wage earners, the greater the degree of economic and social independence the women graduates will achieve. The drift toward the egalitarianism between the sexes, so widespread in the west will be slow, but it is difficult to see how the process, now well under way, will be reversed.

---

[13]Government of Pakistan, Ministry of Education and Research, *Proposals for a New Educational Policy*, Islamabad, July, 1969, p. 6.

28 Minority Within a Minority—On Being South Asian and Female in Canada

RATNA GHOSH

Women are a numerical majority, yet in terms of access to power, status and privilege they constitute a minority in the sociological sense. The identifying factor in a "minority group" is discrimination and the defining characteristics include both objective and subjective criteria: that is, the fact of discrimination and the awareness of the same (Hacker, 1951:60). It has been pointed out by Hacker that, while women share the objective factors of a minority group by being denied full participation in societal opportunities generally open to all, they do not always have a minority group consciousness, either because they are not aware of being discriminated against or because they accept the differential treatment. Nevertheless, as a group they do possess a sex-identification and may be said to occupy a minority group status.

There is a need for consciousness-raising of women as well as of men, towards a transformation of their social role affecting both public and private lives. The separation of roles into "public" and "private" spheres has generally meant asymmetrical roles and differential participation of males and females in the two structurally opposed spheres of activity (Lewis, 1977:342; Rosaldo, 1974:17-42). Dorothy Smith points out that "it is the constitution of public vs. private spheres of action, and the relegation of the domestic to that sphere which is outside history—*this* is the contemporarily relevant transformation and the contemporary form of oppression" (1977:19). While women have historically been placed only in the private, domestic sphere, the public sphere has generally been the sphere of male activity. When the public sphere of power and authority excludes women on the basis of sex it is sexism, and when it excludes other groups for reasons of race and ethnicity it is racism. It is when minority groups try to penetrate the public sphere (e.g. the job market) that conflicts arise.

The Minority Within

Literature on female subordination focuses almost exclusively on theoretical implications of sexism. Cross-cultural models have studied differences in women's strategies, motives, and influence on power and authority. Studies on the effects of additional ascriptive dimensions which affect minority women are extremely limited. Concepts such as double-jeopardy (Beal, 1971) and the multiple negative (Epstein, 1973) have analyzed the effects of racism and sexism on black women in the United States. The analysis of problems of other minority group women in North America who do not share the black woman's awareness of civil rights nor her historical experience of racial and sexual oppression have been largely ignored.

Women in Canada experience conflicts and disadvantages because Canada is still geared in its laws, values and attitudes to the male. It is a society in which values and attitudes are shaped largely by the dominant white middle class Anglophone or Francophone groups, so multiple problems exist for certain groups of women because of their sex, race, ethnicity and class.

One such group is composed of a relatively small number of South Asian women[1] who may face multiple barriers at some time or other. To the extent that they suffer from the disadvantages or repressions according to race, ethnicity, class and sex, they are victims of what has been called the multiple negative and therefore face both vertical and horizontal oppression. "Cumulative disadvantage" explains the compounded negative effects on persons having several negatively evaluated statuses (Epstein, 1973:912).

According to Merton's conceptualization of the dynamics of the status sets, the dominant statuses determine the other statuses which a person acquires (Merton, 1957:368-84). The status set which includes being black and being a woman (two negatively evaluated statuses) has been found to be one of the most cumulatively limiting (Epstein, 1973:913). So, the effects of the two dominant ascribed sex status of female and race status of non-white have at least two dimensions: they impose limits on the individual's capacities (1) by restricting the range of options and (2) by decreasing possibilities of influencing others' attitudes and behaviors towards them.

This paper attempts to explain the situation of South Asian women in a complex society, women who experience negative and sometimes positive effects of the principle of the multiple repression.

Not all South Asian women face the same problems and many may not perceive any particular problems in their lives. Some have positive experiences as well, and some others do not perceive any particular problems of adaptation at all. The attempt in this study has been to deal with the combination of difficulties particularly faced by South Asian women, whether perceived as problems or not, at the occupational level. Some of these problems are shared with South Asian men, some others with women in general, some with immigrant women in particular. Several are specific to them and combine together to make their situation very complex.

Information has been gathered through interviews and personal observations, but largely through case studies taken from social service agencies in Montreal which deal with South Asian women, such as the CLSC (Local

---

[1] It is estimated that there are 250,000 South Asians in Canada (Buchignani, 1977).

Community Service Centre), and the Women's Information and Referral Centre which has a program specifically designed to meet the needs of South Asian women.

Immigration Policy and the Status of South Asian Women in Canada

The first immigrants who came from India in the early 1900s were virtually all male. They were Sikhs who had served in the British Army in the Far East and had come to the west coast of Canada (British Columbia) without their families. Canadian immigration regulations denied entry to South Asian women and they could not join their husbands until 1919. The population remained rather imbalanced for several years (Buchignani, 1979:50). A general ban on South Asian immigration between 1909 and 1947 was relaxed after the Second World War and by 1967 the regulations were liberalized and formally disregarded race, ethnicity and nationality in the selection of immigrants. During 1967-74 South Asians responded in large numbers to Canada's need for professionals in the fields of medicine, engineering and higher education. The 1976 Act focussed on the need to take in blue collar workers, and though South Asian immigration has become more restricted it has seen a shift from professionals to skilled workers. So, besides being racist, Canadian immigration regulations have discriminated against South Asian women in particular.

Analysing the status of the immigrant woman in Canada, Monica Boyd (1977:228) points out that "they bear a double burden with respect to their status in Canadian society". This is so, first because they are subject to a sexist immigration coding which largely classifies women as dependents even when the wife is sometimes better qualified than the husband. The dependent status also means that if a husband faces deportation his wife may (subject to appeal) be deported along with him (Royal Commission on the Status of Women, 1970:301). Moreover, an immigrant woman on her own cannot go on welfare because for that she might be deported (Women and the Law in Quebec, 1975:27). Secondly, compared to immigrant males, women occupy the lower-paying "female" jobs, and even when compared to Canadian-born women they occupy the lower strata jobs. Not only have immigrant women been a neglected subject of research[2], but immigration policies disregard the work pattern of female immigrants in spite of government data indicating their high rates of participation in and contribution to the Canadian economy. Besides the "psychological stigma" (Boyd, 1977) related to dependency, a more concrete effect is that they are assumed to be uninterested, unavailable or unable to take up jobs—or more responsible jobs—particularly if married. Further, Boyd points out, not only does gender have an extremely important effect on the allocation of occupational roles but the entry statuses of male

[2]There is very little data on the employment of South Asian women in Canada.

and female immigrants in Canada have the impact of depressing their representation in the intended categories of work. In addition, Department of
Manpower and Immigration statistics under-report married women's labor
force participation (because they are categorized as dependent), whereas
marital status does not influence immigrant men's occupational data (Boyd,
1977:233). Most South Asian women go to Canada because their husbands
are going. So, even those who are highly qualified have dependent status.
South Asian immigrants have legal equality but discrimination[3] exists and is
most frequently encountered in the job market. The dependent status and
several additional dimensions of the overall status of non-professional South
Asian women make it difficult for them to gain entry in anything other than
low-paying, mechanical jobs, and then eventually it becomes difficult to
survive and succeed in the employment world.

Economic Environment

The principle of the multiple repression indicates the significance of the
relationship and function of the negative statuses—in this case, of race,
culture, gender and class.

South Asian women in Canada have moved from a developing society to
an industrially advanced society, and this often necessitates changes in
their economic roles. In South Asia as well, industrialization and urbanization
have led to a period of transition resulting in changes in the economic roles
and personal status of women. The conflict between the traditional role of
the housewife and the uncertainty of the roles involved in being a working
wife subject women to ambiguity and conflicts both in their working world
and in their personal lives. In Canada, additional factors such as difference
in status in terms of race, culture and dependence, absence of close kinship
ties, extreme weather conditions—all inter-relate to make their situation
complex. And these experiences are in turn subject to differences according
to class.

The need for economic security and high priority on economic advancement leads South Asians to adapt quickly to the Canadian economic structure.
In a study done in the Vancouver area, Buchignani (1977) found that South
Asians secure at least minimally satisfactory jobs soon after they arrive and
many are able to buy houses within five years of their arrival (Buchignani,
1979:57). Wives very often contribute significantly to the family income.
More than 60 percent of the South Asian Fijian wives in the metropolitan Vancouver area were found to be working (Buchignani, 1977). A small survey of
South Asian women in Montreal indicated that 60 percent of the women surveyed had jobs outside the home (Ghosh, 1980).

[3]Discrimination, even overt forms, has not been eliminated as reported in Ubale, 1977; Pitman,
1977; Richmond, 1974; Berry, 1977; Frideres, 1978.

Employment

With the exception of the number of South Asian women professionals, the large proportion of South Asian women, like other immigrant women, are concentrated in service and production occupations. Within the broader immigrant population, a higher percentage of foreign-born males were found to occupy managerial or professional occupations as compared to Canada-born males, but the reverse was observed for foreign-born females who were in less-skilled occupations as compared to Canada-born females and foreign-born males (Boyd, 1977:242).

Gender

It is generally assumed that most women are housewives, and even those who work outside the home continue to be so. Yet data exclude the economic contributions of the housewife.

The housewife's role is central but the housework performed is not recognized as being sufficiently useful in social terms. Smith (77:19) points out that it is not the nature of domestic activity but its relation to the social spheres of action that makes it insignificant. Yet, the position of the employed housewife is not particularly liberating when it becomes a double workload because for the woman the role of the employee is not separated from that of the housewife.

The problems in the labor of women in paid jobs and at home are dependent largely on how the workload is shared. Even when the South Asian woman works it is she who almost entirely responds to the various demands of household and children. The consequences of severe mental and physical stress resulting from workload are magnified, more often than not, because household and child-rearing chores do not fit the values of the South Asian man's conception of suitable work for himself. This is especially true in the middle class. Whereas in South Asia, neither the middle class men nor women did housework and reared the children, when they moved to Canada, the women tended to take on the greater responsibilities of home and parenthood generally. Much of this kind of work is shared in South Asia by outside help and by older family members because even urban nuclear families in traditional societies maintain kinship ties which are normative and obligatory. Lack of knowledge of child-rearing and housework in a Canadian setting and the inability to obtain outside help result in stress for the woman. However, evidence shows that more and more middle-class men share their work. A very small number of professional women have hired help.

In the case of working class families, men quite often help out with babysitting and other chores, particularly if they are working on shifts. But the women nevertheless work extremely hard and have very little leisure time.

The present labor market situation does not provide a very hospitable environment for anyone, much less for women, and even less for a visible minority of women. As skilled/non-skilled professionals or workers, South Asian women have first to overcome the common barriers such as sex-segregation and low pay. Discrimination in employment is difficult to prove, but South Asian women often find the more desirable positions closed to them; they are often underemployed. Non-professional women are also exploited by way of long hours of work and lack of fringe benefits, and on the whole they have a marginal status in the economic structure. In the case of middle-class educated South Asian women, many are expected to forego desires for career. Some take part-time jobs or take the consequences of career interruptions. Some professionally qualified women work in non-professional jobs and sometimes take short training courses for skilled work. A good percentage of professional women find suitable jobs and are perceived as successful, however.

Race and Ethnicity

Evidence indicates that prejudice and discrimination have considerable effect on job allocations (Martin, 1972:349). The problems of women in an ethnic minority group are in addition to the common conflicts and psychic consequences of perceived discrimination suffered by males and females of the group alike. Regarding the visibility of the South Asians in Canada, Buchignani (1979:66) points out that "Canadians are sensitive to what they see as racial difference (Berry, 1977:95-99) but the markers of race for Canadians are often cultural rather than biological". Cultural differences are related to dress and personal grooming, but also to attitudes and values which influence sex-specific behavior resulting in social distance in personal interactions between the sexes. In addition differentiation in areas of concern and sex-segregation, all affect the South Asian woman's job opportunities. Racist attitudes are exhibited by both males and females in the dominant culture (Brown, 1976:295) and Canadian and immigrant women continue to view each other in stereotypical ways (Alberro, 1976:147).

Racist discrimination in employment is complex and subtle and therefore extremely difficult to prove. Often the last to be hired, non-white working class women are the first to be fired. Franklin and Resnick (1973:20) point out that employers, particularly those trying to minimize labor turnover costs, are likely to fire those employees who for reasons of racial discrimination are not likely to get permanent jobs elsewhere. Many non-professionals register with Canada Manpower Centres where counsellors who are responsible for giving information on suitable jobs or training placement have been reported to be discriminatory towards people from Third World countries. "A woman with a Ph.D. degree was told by a counsellor that the only job she could hope for would be as a cleaner" (Ubale, 1977:110). Professionals encounter a general suspicion and ignorance of educational qualifications obtained in South Asia, which result in unfair evaluation of qualifications and make the initial entry into appropriate employment difficult. For professional South Asian women, recertification, writing qualifying exams and upgrading qualifications are often secondary to the similar needs of the husband, more so because the process is often unclear and lengthy. The requirement of Canadian experience is a convenient method of discriminating against non-whites in general without violating the formal provisions in the Human Rights Code (Ubale, 1977:119). This is particularly detrimental to South Asian women who are less likely than their husbands to have overseas degrees and training.

Social Class

In social interaction, factors affecting social distance or ranking are not only racial/ethnic background but also socio-economic, educational and occupational levels (of husbands in particular). Within their own groups the situation of South Asian women is further complicated because the greatest differences in stratified societies like South Asia are in the lifestyles between the elite and the masses. While certain basic values cut across class lines and women of all classes face problems in distinctive ways, the situation among the middle and working class imiigrants differs in a number of ways even though class lines are blurred and the gap is narrower when they emigrate.

South Asians who went to Canada in the 1960's were mostly professionals with a middle-class background. All of them were highly educated but came from different strata of the middle class. The women generally had a fair amount of education, several of them had graduate and professional degrees. A distinction should be made, however, between their modernized and tra-ditional backgrounds because the extent of modernization influences the degree of adaptation to the Canadian environment. Factors such as mobility, training in social etiquette, social interactions with a wide range of people and facility in English (occasionally in French as well) are a definite asset. In addition, the economic advantages of the professional class make the quality of life of the professionals different from that of the working class women. Nevertheless, in places where class position is not apparent they face the same problems as the others.

The majority of cases from the social service agencies deal with the problems of the working class. Differentiation must be made between the working class members in South Asia who can emigrate to North America, and those whose economic and social conditions are such that emigration is not even a remote possibility. Though economically handicapped and not highly trained, skilled workers of South Asian background started emigrating to Canada around 1972. Many of them went by way of England and East Africa. It is the working class South Asian who is more visible and who faces the more overt forms of prejudice and discrimination. Because the economic factor is an important impetus for emigrating, and the economic need is accentuated for new immigrants, many working class women go to work. A common problem for them is that of language. Speaking neither English nor French they are linguistically isolated. Although many of them do not recognize it as such, lack of knowledge of the main language is largely responsible for their marginal status in the work force. It prevents further training in skills and accounts for their lack of participation in work activities. Like many other immigrant women, working class women from South Asia are largely unskilled and are employed in labor-intensive industries. They are employed in small businesses, are very isolated and earn the minimum wage. In the factory situation in Montreal they are grouped by ethnic origin. They do not need to speak English or French in their routine and mechanical jobs and do not come in contact with other groups—male or female. They are totally distant from union activity and their special problems are ignored by the unions. They are very exploited but unwilling to register their complaints even when urged by the service organizations because they would rather not jeopardize their position in the country. There is often a lack of consciousness about oppressive situations. They are usually ignorant of their rights and unfamiliar with the law.

Positive Effects

South Asian women in Canada face yet another dilemma. They are very often characterized as persons with an unusual combination of features— non-white, female, passive, exotic, mysterious, working woman/professional and so on. But they are never sure how they are being appraised, i.e. they are affected by what Robert Merton (1972) calls "the haunting presence of functionally irrelevant statuses". This could, on occasion, work to their advantage. First, focusing on one of the negatively valued statuses could result in cancelling the other negative effects (Epstein, 1973:914). Because of differences in personal appearance and generally reserved behavior they appear "distant" and may therefore be perceived as less threatening (e.g. they may not be seen as competing in the marriage market). Secondly, gender, race and culture often combine to create a new status which is often viewed as "unique" and have the result, for example, of being viewed not as women but as more serious workers or professionals (Epstein, 1973:914,917). Thirdly, this uniqueness puts them outside the normal opportunity structures (Epstein, 1973:914) and as outsiders they are not seen as potentially powerful and can, therefore, compete professionally.

In addition, Canadian perceptions of the South Asian women among professionals are often positive. A study done in Ontario (Naidoo, 1978) revealed examples of liked characteristics as pertaining to the South Asian woman's beauty, grace, intelligence, femininity, mystique and self-control (p. 244). Whereas such perceptions may have positive effects in personal interactions, references to the career/professional woman as charming and exotic are likely to reduce perceptions of her professionalism. The point is that the positive or negative attitudes may be responses to characteristics irrelevant or inappropriate to a particular situation.

In order to illustrate the conditions surrounding employment in the lives of working South Asian women in Canada we would like to consider the case studies of two women: one of an unskilled worker in a factory in Montreal, the other of a university professor and writer.

C is in her forties, a factory worker and lives with her two teenage children. She went to Canada in 1975 from a city in India. She had been married very early at the age of twelve but being independent by nature, she decided to begin her own education when her youngest son started school. She finished high school within a very short time and went on to college and obtained a B.A. When she went to Canada the greatest problem was the language—"They were just sounds"; she could not understand anything in spite of having been exposed to some English (no French) in India.

Although more secure and settled now, C went through a very unstable employment period. She has never been through an interview. She was once required to show her passport and has also been asked if she was pregnant. C wears only Western outfits because of negative comments about her ability to work in a long skirt one day, after which she decided not to wear a saree to work. In the beginning she encountered questions and comments regarding her jewelry and personal appearance.

Her first job was as a baby sitter at $15 per week and that lasted one month. She got to know a few people from India, and one man who worked in a wood factory was able to get her a job painting furniture at minimum wage ($3.47 per hour). It was very hard work, and the odor of paints was nauseating. After 12 days she was laid off because she wasn't "qualified" for the job. Unaware of available services and unable to go looking for jobs on her own, she became increasingly depressed during the next two months. Another Indian woman offered to show her how to approach factory management for work, and one day they went knocking on doors in one area of the city to no avail. More confident, she went on her own the next day starting at one end of the street and working her way along. A textile factory gave her a job for minimum wage for doing things such as packing textiles, mending clothes, and putting on buttons. At the end of eight months she, being one of the newer employees, was laid off. The same day she got a job for one month as a leave replacement in a leather factory, where she glued purses for minimum wage.

Discouraged by job-hunting, she applied for unemployment insurance which she obtained for eight months. During that time she tried to improve her English. At the end of that period C spent eight days job-hunting and got a job in a knitting factory which makes socks. She was asked to work on the knitting machine and she was given training, but after some time she preferred to do something else. She pairs socks for minimum wage and feels secure about her job now that she has been there three years. While at this job she became a Canadian citizen.

She works in a small factory which employs 25 women who work in one large room. There is no union. Many workers are senior citizens and the majority are Greeks and speak neither English nor French fluently. She has been given a Western name. Communication is difficult but she feels at home now. In the beginning she was always observed and made great effort to work hard so that she would not be laid off. Lunch time is for half an hour and there is a 10-minute coffee break at 3 p.m. The workers take their own packed lunches and coffee to work with them. On occasion they send out for pizzas or Chinese food collectively. Overtime does not bring a higher hourly wage, so she avoids working extra hours. Because the workers are paid by the hour, being five minutes late means a 15-minute pay cut. They are paid in cash every week. Deductions for Canada pension plan, unemployment and health insurance are made at source.

C leaves the house at 7 a.m., takes the metro then a bus. She works from 8 a.m. to 6 p.m. She is taking English classes, so twice a week she goes straight to her evening class and gets home around 10 p.m. C feels she works too hard. There is no opportunity for promotion. She has very little leisure time and would like to have another kind of job. She makes money enough to have visited India once and has been able to buy property there. She feels unsure about her future and old age in Canada.

M is in her late thirties, a university professor and writer, and lives with her husband and children. She came to North America in the early 1960's as a student and entered her present position after having held one-year positions at two universities simultaneously where she felt administrators went out of their way to cooperate and arrange teaching loads feasible to her as the mother of a very young child. After completion of graduate studies, she applied to two Canadian universities, was offered jobs at both and her final acceptance was determined by the reputation of the university and the advice of her academic supervisors.

M is highly qualified. Having come from an upper-class family in India, she had all her schooling and undergraduate training in elite institutions there. She obtained her Ph.D. from a prestigious American university. A tenured professor with several years of teaching experience now, M is ambitious for her career and highly motivated. She has been invited to teach in prestigious universities and accepted the positions even though they meant separation from the family.

M has no complaints in terms of initial hiring practices and felt that she has been equitably treated in terms of renewals, promotions, fellowships and grants. She has had difficulties regarding space allocation and class schedules which she felt were generated by clashes in personality and administrative styles between the chairman and herself. The initial clash, however, revolved around a feminist issue when her holding an administrative position was questioned because her husband's being in the same profession was considered a conflict of interest.

The university has had sexist policies with regard to benefits such as insurance claims and maternity leaves. During the birth of her second child neither the department nor the university had any policy regarding maternity leave. The benefits handbook in the mid-1960's specified a one-day leave for new fathers but did not mention leave for teaching mothers, the possible assumption being that female faculty were not likely to be pregnant! Her child was born the first day of Christmas break and she did not take a single day off for childbirth.

Faculty club privileges have been very sexist and even when women faculty were permitted to become its members they were for a long time denied access to the main floor lounge and the reading and billiards rooms. Once, unwittingly, in the mid-1960's, M transgressed the access rule and was asked to leave the lounge where she had joined her male colleagues. She still finds the older male faculty members looking anxious and violated when she enters the reading room.

There is no faculty union. She was slow to join the faculty association and has shown little interest in its activities. She has felt a discrepancy in salary and sought the association's support to investigate salary policy but did not find their help very productive.

With regard to interpersonal relationships with students and professional acquaintances (not colleagues), particularly women, she is regarded as "mysterious", "cold", "hard to figure out". She began wearing sarees less frequently, suspecting that dress might have something to do with this image. M regards this phenomenon—"of converting me into a mysterious subject which then must be prodded and forced to react— as a form of racism".

In terms of deportment, she has always entertained the anxiety that the university administration is not likely to take seriously a faculty member who does not fulfil the sexual, social profile of the institution which is that of the white male wearing tweeds. And while overt forms of discrimination are absent the significant fact is that she has felt that "the climate in which one operates appears to sustain the anxiety".

Regarding profession-related activities outside the university she has encountered what she considers strong racist and sexist tendencies. Besides being "hassled" in the subway by teenagers, she has encountered discourteousness from airlines functionaries when traveling alone for job-related activities. And on one occasion at a Toronto hotel, when she entered the lobby ahead of her husband after a university party, the hotel detective questioned her to determine that she was not a lady of questionable repute. He did not question other unaccompanied women who entered shortly after. Other examples she cited were the lack of invitations to read at academic institutions in spite of the heavy federal government subsidies, and lack of invitations to read and assess manuscripts even though she is well known by literary editors. She was initially excluded from the list of founding members of a professional organization although she had just been widely acclaimed in reputable newspaper and periodical reviews and compared with several well-known authors. Apologies on this matter included excuses such as the assumption that an invitation issued to her husband would take care of the wife (ironically, given by a woman writer), and ridiculous explanation-cum-apologies such as they did not know how to spell her name. In fact, a review of one of her books seemed to question the validity of reviewing a book about feminism, "colonialism" (their words, it was a story on an immigrant woman), in a Canadian magazine "just because the writer lives in Canada". She was a Canadian citizen by then.

A successful writer, she is one of the youngest persons to be promoted to full professorship at her university.

Conclusion

South Asian women in Canada are a relatively new and small minority who have been subjected to a sexist and racist immigration policy and in addition face multiple repressions according to their social class and in terms of differences in race, culture, attitudes and behaviors. Given the fact that the majority of them work outside the home in addition to, rather than instead of, being housewives in a new and complex environment, the issue of their economic adaptation becomes acute. In general, South Asian women exhibit great endurance to face the many difficult situations they encounter daily in their working and personal lives. As a mode of adjustment they indicate an ability to vary their behavior according to the definition of the situation. Even within the limits imposed by the present social structure due to their unique combination of characteristics, many South Asian women survive in the economic environment, but it is only those who are intellectually gifted, have attractive personalities and are extraordinarily motivated who can succeed.

REFERENCES

Alberro, A. and G. Montero
   1976   "The immigrant woman". In G. Matheson (ed.), Women in the Canadian Mosaic. Toronto: Peter Martin Associates.

Beal, F. M.
   1971   "Double jeopardy: to be black and female". In Liberation Now! Writings from the Women's Liberation Movement. New York: Dell Publishing Co.: 185-196.

Berry, John et al.
   1974   Multiculturalism and Ethnic Attitudes in Canada. Ottawa: Minister of Supply and Services.

Boyd, M.
   1977   "The status of immigrant women in Canada". In M. Stephenson (ed.), Women in Canada. Don Mills, Ontario: General Publishing Co. Ltd.

Brown, R.
   1976   "A new kind of power". In G. Matheson (ed.), Women in the Canadian Mosiac. Toronto: Peter Martin Associates.

Buchignani, N. L.
   1977   "South Asian Canadians and the ethnic mosaic". Canadian Ethnic Studies 11: 1, 48-67.

Epstein, C. F.
1973   "Positive effects of the multiple negative: explaining the success of black professional women". American Journal of Sociology 78: 4, 912–935.

Franklin, R. and S. Resnick
1973   The Political Economy of Racism. New York: Holt, Rinehart and Winston.

Frideres, J.
1978   "British Canadian attitudes toward minority ethnic groups in Canada". Ethnicity 5: 20–32.

Ghosh, Ratna
1980   "Social and economic integration of South Asian women in Montreal, Canada". In George Kurian and Ratna Ghosh (eds.), Comparative View of Women in Family and the Economy. Westport, Conn.: Greenwood Press.

Hacker, H. M.
1951   "Women as a minority group". Social Forces 30: 60–69.

Lewis, D. K.
1977   "A response to inequality: black women, racism, and sexism". Signs, Journal of Women in Culture and Society 3, 2: 339–361.

Martin, W. T. and D. L. Poston
1972   "The occupational composition of white females in sexism, racism and occupational differentiation." Social Forces 50: 349-355.

Merton, R. K.
1972   Columbia University Lectures. New York: Columbia University Press.

1957   Social Theory and Social Structure. Glencoe, Ill.: The Free Press.

Naidoo, J.
1978   New perspectives on South Asian women in Canada. 18th Interdisciplinary Seminar. Waterloo: Presentation.

Pitman, W.
1977   Now It Is Not Too Late. Toronto: Metro Toronto.

Richmond, A.
1974   Aspects of the Absorption and Adaptation of Immigrants. Ottawa: Department of Manpower and Immigration.

Rosaldo, M. Z. and L. Lamphere
1974   Woman, Culture and Society. Stanford, Calif.: Stanford University Press.

1970   Ottawa: Information Canada, Queen's Press.

Smith, D.
    1977 "Women, the family and corporate capitalism." In M. Stephenson (ed.),
          Women in Canada. Don Mills, Ontario: General Publishing Co. Ltd.

Ubale, B.
    1977 Equal Opportunity and Public Policy. A Report Submitted to the Attorney
          General of Ontario by the South Asian Canadian Community, Ottawa.

    1975 Women and the Law in Quebec. Montreal: YWCA Women's Centre.

Bibliographic Essay

One of the salient issues of the present time is that of integrating the large and growing constituency of women into the paid labor market while ensuring at the same time a satisfactory family set up. In spite of social policies for equal pay and equal opportunity, their implementation leaves much to be desired. Within the family, employed women still face multiple problems, structural and psychological, even where egalitarian ideologies have led to a sexual revolution. These issues are, of course, more than "women's issues". Their roots lie in the present structure of society. The problems that women face are society's problems and they cannot be taken in isolation from societyal hierarchy, theories of stratification, issues of the changing needs of men and women, indeed, their changing roles in the labor market, marriage and family interaction.

This essay attempts to bring to the reader's attention major publications relevant to the topic of women in their familial and employment roles. The list is far from comprehensive; the idea is to confine the references to works published more or less during the last decade. Journal articles, although very important in contributing to knowledge, have with a very few exceptions, been largely omitted. A few reference sources for journal articles have, therefore, been included. The articles in this volume individually have lists of references. The following works mentioned are in addition to them.

BOOKS

General Works: A few publications which go several years back are basic reading and recommended here for a general understanding and theoretical background on the subject: Friedrick Engels, *The Origin of the Family, Private Property and the State* (New York: International Publishers, 1972); V. I. Lenin, *The Emancipation of Women* (New York: International Publishers, 1972); John Stuart Mill, *The Subjection of Women* (Cambridge, Mass.: M.I.T. Press, 1970); Emile Durkheim, *The Division of Labour in Society* (translated by George Simpson, 1964, originally published in French in 1911); Simone De Beauvoir, *The Second Sex* (New York, 1953, originally published in French in 1949). More recent general books for background reading are: J. Freeman (ed.), *Women: A Feminist Perspective* (Palo Alto: May-field, 1975); Vivian Gornick and Barbara K. Moran (eds.), *Women in Sexist Society: Studies in Power and Powerlessness* (New York, London: Basic Books, 1971), which includes a discussion on the paradox of the happy marriage; Joan Huber (ed.), *Changing Women in a Changing Society* (Chicago: University of Chicago Press, 1973), about men, women and their changing work situations; Raphael Patai, *Women in the Modern World* New York: The Free Press, 1967); M. Z. Rosaldo and L. Lamphere (eds.), *Women, Culture and Society* (Stanford: Stanford University Press, 1976); C. Safilios-Rothschild (ed.), *Toward a Sociology of Women* (Lexington, Mass.: Xerox College Publishers, 1972), in which some articles deal with the married professional woman and role conflict; E. Sullerot, *Women, Society and Change* (New York: McGraw-Hill, 1971); L. B. Tanner (ed.), *Voices from Women's Liberation* (New York: New American Library, 1971), with a dis-cussion on the politics of housework. There are a number of excellent comparative studies: Janet Giele and Audrey Smock (eds.), *Women: Roles and Status in Eight Countries* (New York: John Wiley & Sons, 1977), is a systematic analysis of categories which include women and the family, and women and work, in Western, non-Western and socialist countries; Lynne Iglitzin's *Women in the World, A Comparative Study* (Santa Barbara, American Bibliographical Center: Clio Press, Inc., 1967) has articles on North American, European and Third World women; Carolyn J. Matthais-son's *Many Sisters: Women in Cross-Cultural Perspective* (New York: The Free Press, 1974) and Ruby Rohrlich-Leavitt's *Women Cross-Culturally: Change and Challenge* (The Hague: Mouton, 1975) deal with the life and work of women across cultures. The following are a few major works under-taken in specific areas of the world: Donald R. Brown (ed.), *The Role and Status of Women in the Soviet Union* (New York: Teacher's College Press, Columbia University, 1968); Anne Pescatello (ed.), *Male and Female in Latin America* (Pittsburgh: University of Pittsburgh Press, 1973); Yonina Talmon, *Family and Community in the Kibbutz* (Cambridge, Mass.: Har-vard University Press, 1972); Marjory Wolf, *Women in the Family in Rural Taiwan* (Stanford, Cal.: Stanford University Press, 1972); Marjory Wolf and Roxane Witke, *Women in Chinese Society* (Stanford, Cal.: Stan-ford University Press, 1975).

Working Women in the Family: The above books deal with the general theme of women in the family and society. There are, of course, at least two dimensions of women's work. All women do housework whether they are employed in the labor market or not. Helena Z. Lopata in *Occupation: Housewife* (New York: Oxford University Press, 1971), analyzes the situation of woman as housewife. A very interesting discussion on this topic has been carried by *The New Left Review*. The original article by Wally Seccombe "The housewife and her labour under Capitalism" (83:3-24, 1974) induced a critique by Margaret Coulson, Branka Magas and Hilary Wainwright, "The housewife and her labour under Capitalism—A Critique" (89:59-71, 1975). The same volume contains another article by Jean Gardiner on "Women's domestic labour". Peggy Morton's "Women's work is never done" published in *Leviathan* (May 1970) is a much referred to work.

Several other works focus on the effects of the employment of women on the family in general, husbands and children in particular: Michael Fogarty, Rhona and Robert Rapoport in *Sex, Career and Family* (London: George Allen & Unwin, Ltd., 1971), concludes that while it requires considerable skill to do so, it is possible for women to combine a successful career with a happy family life with no particular detrimental effects on husband and children; André Michel (ed.), *Family Issues of Employed Women in Europe and America* (Leiden: E. J. Brill, 1971); F. I. Nye and L. W. Hoffman (eds.), *The Employed Mother in America* (Chicago: Rand McNally, 1963), and their more recent book, *Working Mothers: An Evaluative Review of the Consequences for Wife, Husband and Child* (San Francisco: Jossey-Bass, 1974). A couple of articles relevant to this issue are R. O. Blook and R. L. Hamblin, "The Effect of the Wife's Employment on the Family Power Structure", *Social Forces* (36: 347-352, 1958); M. M. Poloma and F. N. Garland, "The Married Professional Woman: A Study in the Tolerance of Domestication", *Journal of Marriage and the Family* (33: 531-540, 1971). Lynda Lytle Holstrom in *The Two-Career Family* (Cambridge, Mass.: Schenkman, 1972) and Rhona and Robert Rapoport in *Dual Career Families* (Hamdsworth, England: Penguin Books, 1971), look at the situation in families where both husband and wife have careers. Attitudes towards the working mother are changing as more women become permanent members of the work force: R. Helson, "The Changing Image of Career Woman", *Journal of Social Issues*, (28:2: 34-46, 1972); M. M. Kaley, "Attitudes toward the Dual Role of the Married Professional Woman", *American Psychologist* (26: 301-306, 1971). A major work is Margaret Benston's "The Political Economy of Women's Liberation", *Monthly Review* (Sept. 1969). L. E. Davis and A. B. Cherns (eds.) look at *The Quality of Working Life* (New York: The Free Press/Macmillan, 1975). H. S. Astin looks at a small minority of highly educated women, *The Woman Doctorate in America: Origins, Career, and Family* (New York: Russell Sage Foundation, 1969).

Women and Work: While there are several good books on women in specific areas of employment, a few recent publications treat the topic in general terms. Women in management if one field where considerable research has been undertaken. D. C. Basil's, *Women in Management: Promotion and Prejudice* (New York: Cambridge University Press, 1971), treats the problem of discrimination broadly. Some books dealing with women in the labor market are: Edmund Dahlstrom (ed.), *The Changing Roles of Men and Women* (Boston: Beacon Press, 1967); Department of Labour, Canada,

Women at Work in Canada: A Fact Book on the Female Labour Force, 1965;
Norton Dodge, *Women in the Soviet Economy* (Baltimore: Johns Hop-
kins Press, 1966); C. F. Epstein, *Woman's Place: Options and Limits in
Professional Careers* (Berkeley: University of California Press, 1971); M.
Galenson, *Women and Work: An International Comparison* (Ithaca, N.Y.:
Cornell University, 1973); Viola Klein, *Employing Married Women* (London:
Institute of Personnel Management, 1961); Robert W. Smuts, *Women and
Work in America* (New York: Schocken Books, 1971). The argument that
the first step towards equality is involvement in productive labor is made in
M. Kay Martin and Barbara Voorhies, *Female of the Species* (New York:
Columbia University Press, 1975) and Robin Morgan (ed.), *Sisterhood Is
Powerful* (New York: Random House, 1970). Yet paid employment for
women leads to the other problem of work overload which is very per-
ceptively analyzed by Alva Myrdal and Viola Klein in *Women's Two Roles,
Home and Work* (London: Routledge & Kegan Paul, 1956). Changing
societal needs and structures which put women in the labor force has been a
topic of much discussion. A well-known work on this topic is Valerie K.
Oppenheimer's, *The Labor Force in the United States: Demographic and
Economic Factors Governing its Growth and Changing Composition* (Berkeley: Institute of International Studies, University of California, 1970). A
response to the subjective conditions women face in their increasing involvement in the labor force has been government social policy ensuring them
certain rights. A very recent volume on this subject is Ronnie Steinberg
Ratner (ed.), *Equal Employment Policy for Women: Strategies for Implementation in the United States, Canada and Western Europe* (Philadelphia,
Pennsylvania: Temple University Press, 1979). It contains articles with up-to-
date statistics on enforcement of laws against sex discrimination, strategies
such as collective bargaining for improving the economic situation of women,
issues for implementing equal pay and equal opportunity legislation, and the
impact of organizational structure, among others. Yet all women do not
face the same kinds of problems. P. L. Stewart and M. G. Cantor have
edited a volume which deals with the *Varieties of Work Experience: The
Social Control of Occupational Groups and Roles* (Cambridge, Mass.:
Schenkman Publishing Co., 1974). A crucial dimension in the situations
faced by women is social class, because while all women may face disadvantages compared with men of their class, women of the working class are
more handicapped. Illustrative of this face are N. Seifer's *Absent from the
Majority: Working Class Women in America* (New York: National Project
on Ethnic America of the American Jewish Committee, 1973), and A.
Theodore's *The Professional Woman* (Cambridge, Mass.: Schenkman Publishing Co., 1971). Ethnic minorities also suffer compounded disadvantages:
Kathleen Jamieson, *Indian Women and the Law in Canada: Citizen Minus*
(Ottawa, Ministry of Supply & Services, 1978), discusses Canadian policy

and the position of native women historically; Joyce A. Ladner, *Tomorrow's Tomorrow: The Black Woman* (Anchor Books, Doubleday, 1971); S. Chisholm, "Sexism and Racism: One Battle to Fight", *Personnel and Guidance Journal* (51:2 123-125, 1972); Harish Jain and Peter Sloane, "Race, Sex and Minority Discrimination in North America and Britain", *Industrial Relations' Journal* (38-55 Summer 1978). While minority women are more prone than others to be used as a marginal labor force, a general treatment of women in temporary work situations in Patricia Connelly's *Last Hired, First Fired: Women and the Canadian Work Force* (Toronto: The Women's Press, 1978). With an introduction by Margaret Benston, this volume is an analysis from a feminist Marxist perspective. The structural and institutional factors in a capitalist society which create economic conditions and labor needs impelling women to respond to those needs are analyzed in chapters on preconditions and conditions of reserve labor in a capitalist system, the demand and supply, and active and inactive dimensions of female reserve labor. Another important but earlier work along the same lines is Maria-rosa Della Costa's *Women in the Subversion of the Community* (Bristol, England: Falling Wall Press, 1973), which shows that women are not only by-passed in the capitalist economic structure but that their labor contribution to the family is viewed as obligatory and sacred. The most obvious fact of women in paid employment is sex-segregation and some recent studies focus on this not so recent phenomenon: Pat and Hugh Armstrong's, *The Double Ghetto: Canadian Women and Their Segregated Work* (Toronto: McClelland and Stewart, 1978), is a book about structural factors in the labor market and the home which limit women's alternatives and includes a comprehensive reference bibliography. *Women and the Workplace: The Implications of Occupational Segregation* (University of Chicago Press, 1976), edited by Martha Blaxall and Barbara Reagan, includes discussions of differential wages and a comparative analysis of American and Soviet patterns of public policy regarding segregations. Other works are B. Chiplin and P. J. Sloane, *Sex Discrimination in the Labour Market* (London: McMillan, 1976) and J. M. Kreps, *Sex in the Market Place: American Women at Work* (Baltimore: Johns Hopkins Press, 1971). R. J. Schonberger, "Inflexible Working Conditions Keep Women Unliberated", *Personnel Journal* (50: 834-37, 1971). Some solutions are suggested by A. S. Ross, "Job Discrimination and What Women Can Do About It", *Atlantic Monthly* (99-102, March, 1970). Labour March, 1970). A not so obvious distressing burden working women face is discussed by Leah Cohan and Connie Backhouse in *The Secret Oppression: The Sexual Harassment of Working Women* (Toronto: MacMillan, 1979). The roots of the handicaps women bring with them to the labor market are in their sexist socialization and education. While much has been written about differential treatment of boys and girls in all levels of their education and in their sex-role socialization only three works are mentioned here: Eleanor Maccoby (ed.), *The Development of Sex Differences* (Stanford, California: Stanford University Press, 1966), is a well known and often referred to collection of excellent articles on sex differences in intellectual functioning, behavior, cognitive development and the effects of cultural institutions on sex differences. It has an annotated bibliography. Maccoby's more recent work with Carol N. Jacklin is *The Psychology of Sex Differences* (Stanford, Cal.: Stanford University Press, 1974). S. S. Fangi and L. W. Hoffman have edited *Women and Achievement: Social and Motivational Analyses* (Washington, D.C.: Hemisphere, 1975), which focuses on the crucial need for achievement motivation and the social and psychological barriers which impede the development of high aspirations in women.

Women and Development: While articles in this volume contain cross-cultural studies, some carried out in developing countries, a separate issue is that of woman's economic role in development in Third World countries. Because this theme is not dealt with specifically in this collection, only a few major works will be mentioned. Ester Boserup in *Woman's Role in Economic Development* (New York: St. Martin's Press, 1970) argues that the change from traditional to modern economic systems in Africa, Asia and Latin America hinders rather than helps women's participation in the labor force. The gap between levels of knowledge and training is widened by modernization so that man's prestige is enhanced at the expense of women's. In *Women, Bread and Babies: Directing Aid to Fifth World Farmers* (Boulder: University of Colorado, 1975), Elise Boulding examines the "fifth world" which she defines as a set of spaces in every society where women carry out their productive roles. In examining the work situation in *Women in China* (New York: Pathfinder Press, 1975), Katie Curtin points to the inequality that still exists in job discrimination for women in the form of unequal wages and work points. Three other books deserve mention: Denise Paulme (ed.), *Women of Tropical Africa* (Berkeley: University of California Press, 1963); Nadia H. Yousef, *Women and Work in Developing Societies* (Berkeley: Institute of International Studies, University of California Press, 1973), which has an excellent analysis of women's work situation in developing Muslim societies as compared to Latin America; *Women in the Struggle for Liberation* (World Student Christian Federation Book Series, 1973), is a collection of articles by women around the world focusing on certain themes, one of which is the relationship of housework and women's family role to the structures of production.

INTERNATIONAL CONFERENCES AND GOVERNMENT DOCUMENTS

International Women's Year (IWY) focused attention on women and their problems. A great deal of data was published, studies undertaken and conferences sponsored by international organizations, individual governments, women's organizations and research institutes in and around 1975. The United Nations *Report of the World Conference of the International Women's Year, Mexico City, 19 June-2 July, 1975, 1976* is a comprehensive report. Publications based on specific topics were published such as Irene Tinker and Michele Bo Bramsen's (eds.), *Women and World Development* (Washington, D.C.: Overseas Development Council, 1976), which contains papers from a seminar on women in development held at The International Women's Year Conference in Mexico City, 1975. The Government of India's *Towards Equality: Report of the Committee on the Status of Women in India* (New Delhi, Ministry of Education and Social Welfare, 1974), is a very comprehensive and perceptive document and is one of several government studies undertaken in various parts of the world for IWY. Some conference reports worth mentioning are: C. H. Dandiya's *Women in Rajasthan* (Jaipur; University of Rajasthan, 1975) is based on the Seminar on "Women: The Untapped Potential of Rajasthan"; *Proceedings of the Afro-Arab Inter-Parliamentary Women's Conference*, Cairo, May 1974; *Symposium on Race, Sex and Policy Studies* (D. C. Heath, 1979, also published in *Policy Studies Journal* 7:2, 1978); *Women and the Workplace: The Implications of Occupational Segregation* (The University of Chicago Press, 1976 mentioned earlier), based on a conference on occupational segregation held at Wellesley College in 1975; *International Labour Conference*, 60th Session, 1975, Report VIII, *Equality of Opportunity and Treatment for Women Workers*, Geneva, ILO; *U.N. Seminar on Women's Integration in Development and the Elimination of Sex Discrimination*, Ottawa, Canada, 1974; J. J. Mattfeld and O. Van Aken (eds.), *Women and the Scientific Professions* (Cambridge, Mass.: M.I.T. Press, 1965), based on an earlier M.I.T. Symposium on American Women in Science and Engineering. The U.N., ILO, UNESCO and OECD have several reports on women, their status, education and employment. Of particular interest is the OECD publication *The Role of Women in the Economy*, Paris, 1975, which is a summary of ten National Reports from industrialized countries. It gives background information and makes international comparisons on the status of women in the economy referring to aspects such as increasing labor force participation of women, especially married women, their range of occupations and problems of family responsibilities. Among the several U.S. government sponsored studies are: Margaret Mead and Frances Kaplan (eds.), *American Women, Report of the President's Commission* (New York: Charles Scribner's Sons, 1965); U.S. Civil Service Commission Statistics Section, *Study of Employment of Women in the Federal Government*, 1967 (Washington, D.C.: U.S. Government Printing Office, 1968); President of the United States, *A Matter of Simple Justice: The Report of the President's Task Force on Women's Rights and Responsibilities*, 1970; Jerolyn R. Lyle, *Affirmative Action Programs for Women: A Survey of Innovative Programs*, sponsored by the Equal Employment Opportunities Commission, 1973 which includes an annotated bibliography relating to women's employment in the United States. The British Government's *Discrimination Against Women* (London: The Labour Party, 1972) and the Canadian Government's *Report of the Royal Commission on the Status of Women in Canada* (Ottawa: Information Canada, 1970) are important documents. Of particular interest to this volume is Françoise D. Lacasse's *Women at Home: The Cost to the Canadian Economy of the Withdrawal from the Labour Force of a Major Proportion of the Female Population*, which is study no. 2 of the Royal Commission Report on the Status of Women, in Canada (Ottawa: Information Canada, 1971). A recent study by the Canadian Advisory Council on the Status of Women, *Women in the Public Service: Barriers to Equal Opportunity* (Jan. 1979), concludes that the present government structure and policy perpetuates the historical imbalance in women's employment opportunities in Canada.

In historical terms, it is only recently that equality has been interpreted to include equality for the sexes. Egalitarian aspirations throughout the world prompted the United Nations to take the initiative for its Declaration of Human Rights which has had a catalytic effect on the evolution of legislation in countries around the world to reaffirm their belief in justice, equality and individual dignity. The Universal Declaration, adopted and proclaimed by the General Assembly on December 10, 1948 asserts in the preamble, faith in the "dignity and worth of the human person and in the equal rights of men and women". Of particular importance to this essay are: *Convention (No. 100) Concerning Equal Remuneration for Men and Women Workers for Work of Equal Value, June 1951; Convention (No. 111) Concerning Discrimination in Respect to Employment and Occupation,* June 1958 where "discrimination" refers to any distinction, exclusion or preference made on seven counts including sex; *Declaration on the Elimination of Discrimination Against Women* (resolution XXII) Nov. 1967. Documents have originated from Human Rights Commissions in countries which have ratified the UN Declarations and Conventions. A few examples are: Canadian Human Rights Commission, *Equal Pay for Work of Equal Value: Report of the Task Force,* Mar. 1978; *Equal Wage Guidelines* of the Canadian Human Rights Act, 1978. Similar employment policy guidelines are *Title VII of Civil Rights Act* (1964) as amended by the *Equal Employment Opportunities Act of 1972* in the United States, and the *Equal Pay Act, 1970* amended by the *Sex Discrimination Act of 1975* in the United Kingdom.

JOURNALS

There are several good journals which publish articles on women in the society and family, and at work. A few of them are exclusively women's studies journals and some others in addition to having articles on women in regular issues have devoted special issues to women. *African Urban Notes,* published from Michigan State University, special issues Spring 1976 and Fall/Winter 1976/77 which focus on urban working women in North, East and West Africa, *American Journal of Sociology* (Special Issue on Women, Jan. 1973); *Atlantis: A Women's Studies Journal; The Changing Role of S.E. Asian Women* jointly issued by *Southeast Asia Chronicle* (No. 66, Jan./Feb. 1979) and *Pacific Research* (9:5-6, 1978) on women's work in Southeast Asia; *International Journal of Sociology of the Family* (special issue Winter 1975-76); *Journal of Comparative Family Studies* where several articles in this collection were first published; *Journal of Concerned Asian Scholars* (special issue on Asian Women, 7: 1, Jan.-Mar. 1975); *Journal of Marriage and the Family* (special issue 33:3, Aug. 1971); *Manushi: A Journal About Women and Society* which deals with conditions of women in India and elsewhere; *Psychology of Women Quarterly* (Special Issue on Dual-Career Couples, 3:1, Fall 1978); *Resources for Feminist Research,* formerly *Canadian Newsletter for Research on Women,* which contains articles, bibliographies and listings of current research; *Signs: Journal of Women in Culture and Society,* a reputable women's studies journal with a cross-cultural perspective; *Urban and Social Change Review* (special issue on women and work, 11:1-2, 1978); *Women at Work,* a bulletin reporting facts and figures relating to Canadian Women in the labor force; *Women's Studies International Quarterly* (special issue on Education relating to sexism 1:4, 1978). Among international organization bulletins, *Women at Work: An ILO News Bulletin* gives up-to-date statistics on women's employment and status across the globe, and the *U.N. Newsletter on the Status of Women* reports on the organization's activities.

REFERENCE SOURCES

As this bibliographic essay is far from exhaustive, a few reference sources on women—in their family and work roles—are suggested. The *Social Sciences Index* and *Sociological Abstracts* are two common sources. The *Women's Studies Abstracts* is a quarterly service which selectively abstracts relevant journal articles and book reviews and has an author/subject index and some critical articles. Among bibliographies. Mayra Buvinic's (et al.) *Women and World Development: An Annotated Bibliography,* Washington, D.C.: Overseas Development Council, 1976 focuses on socio-economic development and the effects of these changes on women. Kalpana Dasgupta's (ed.), *Women on the Indian Scene: An Annotated Bibliography* (New Delhi: Abhinav Publications, 1977) is an extensive listing of 822 titles covering English language publications up to 1975 and includes aspects such as women in the economy. Genevieve Frank's *Women at Work in Society: A Selected Bibliography, 1970-75* (Geneva, International Institute of Labour Studies, 1975) was prepared for the Research Symposium during International Women's Year. The work by Sue-Ellen Jacobs, *Women in Perspective: A Guide for Cross-Cultural Studies* Urbana, Ill.: The University of Illinois Press, 1974), is a comprehensive international bibliography covering numerous topics including women in family and employment. Another bibliography which is international in scope is Suzanne Nicolas' *Bibliography on Women Workers* (Geneva: International Labour Office, Central Library and Documentation Branch, 1970) which lists books and articles dealing with women workers published between mid-1800 and 1965. Also with international coverage reporting research in progress, innovative projects and discussions is *Women's Work and Women's Studies.*

Data on the division of labor by sex is available for many societies in G. P. Murdock's *Ethnographic Atlas* (Pittsburgh: University of Pittsburgh Press, 1967) and in Blumberg's article on "Cross-cultural Examination of Sex Division of Labor and Sex Status" in Alice Sargent (ed.), *Beyond Sea Roles* (St. Paul, Minn.: West Publishing, 1974).

Author Index

Subject Index

Alienation: of work in capitalist society (Marx), 331; professionals vs. workers, 332

Arabs: honour, modesty code, 117; Islam, 117; Muslim society, 117; role of religion, 117

Arab society: opposition to married women working, 119; status and role of women, 117

Attempts to reduce discrimination against working women, 331

Attitudes: similarity to community (Kerala, India), 132; women's role by sex (Lebanon), 123

Attitudes of: rural women (Kerala, India), 131; rural women to cummunity influences, 131-32

Attitudes to: employment of mother and role reversal, 260; household duties of husbands, 321; of males to equal opportunity, 193-97

Attitude towards: contraceptive knowledge of women (Barbados), 289; equal opportunity for men and women, 192; female professionals, 143, females in labor force, 190-91, 193; household duties of husbands, 321; sex role ideology; women, 181

Attitude towards women: Canada, 143, 180; with children and work (Lebanon), 125; household work (Lebanon), 123

Birth order: meaninglessness, demographic characteristics, 97-99; meaninglessness, socio-economic status, 100; normlessness, 92-94 powerlessness, 87-90; powerless by sons, economic status, 103

Black family: early socialization, 273; family size, 273; female parents, 273; ghetto-dwelling parents, 273; income, 281; income and material aspiration for offspring, 282; material for offspring, 281

Black mothers: early socialization, 273; educational aspirations, 275; educational attainments, 279; family size and aspiration, 277; indigent, 273; job preferences, 275; material aspiration for daughters, 279; professional occupation desires, 280

Canada: Anglophone-Francophone difference about women's issues, 151; attitudes, rights of women, 147-49; choice of friends of wife, 259; employment status of female respondents, 156; equality of opportunity, 145; feminist demand for social change and financial security, 156; feminist scale, 155; feminists and minority group demands, 157; ideological management, 163; implications for conjugal power, 256; kin, friends and community involvement, 257-59; male dominance, 147; male-female differences on women's issues, 150; measuring decision making, 257; the Ottawa Valley Family Cohort Study, 260-61; relative importance of feminist concerns, 160-61; socio-demographic correlates, 153, 157; traditional and gender roles, 146; women's issues and Canadian Indian issues, 157, 180; women's issues and marital status, 156; young Canadians on women's issues, 153-54

Canadian: attitude towards women, 143, 180; labor force data, 248; public opinion towards native people, 144; sex role ideology, attitude towards women, 181

Changing authority, home, 319-20

Changing role of women (India), 131

China: annual work points, 362, attack on feudal marriages, 360; changing fertility behavior, 370; family and fertility, 359; kin affiliations, 370; labour participation of women, 360-61; peasants' needs, cash income and private enterprise, 363; policy on women's roles, 360; women in rural areas, 365-66, 368; rustifying young people, 369; sexual equality, 360; sexual role equality, 360; sharing housework, 371; urban housing shortage, 368-69

Child training practices and social class, 92

Children: college training needs, 274; economic value (Iran) 298; teenage troubles, 323

Community: influences, attitude of rural women (Kerala, India), 131-32; social systems, formation, 4

Conflict, between tradition and change, 338, 339

Conjugal power, 10; implications (Canada) 256; labor force participation, 245, 246

Contraceptive knowledge, of women (Barbados), 289, 290

Cuba, expansion of female labor force, 382

Culture change, 10; importance of women in bureaucracies, 379; new attempts to strengthen family, 376

Cultural attributes, as a source of power, 9-10

Cultural and social barriers, women, 4

Decision, marital, roles, 218

Decision making: cross-national family

218; employed and unemployed women, 223-24, 226; marital, 218; multiple classification analysis, 14; power, 319; shared, 13; by wife, 13; within the family, 11; within the household, 12

Domestic organization, rural Ladino (Guatemala), 29

Dowry: form of dowry payment (Kerala, India) 133; India, 18, women's power, 11, 18

Education, Lebanese adults, 121

Educated women, desire for wealth and comfort, 25

Effect of religious affiliation: boys' responses (Lebanon), 123-25; girls responses (Lebanon), 125-26

Egalitarian: ideologies, xiii, marriages, 248

Egalitarianism: 11; advocacy of action, 173-74

Employed females, percentage of unstable marriages, 267

Employed mothers, children's socialization, 322

Employment of wife (India), 21

Equality of opportunity: Canada, 145; education and feminist scale, 153-55

External decision-making scale, 12

Family: Brazilian, modernization of women, 219; decision-making, cross-national, 218; earning difference, individual and family, 369; female-headed, 3; female-headed, Negroes, 197; income and feminist scale, 155; ideal socialist, 332; Negroes, 198; patriarchal, 17; size and child care problems, 323; theory, 10; traditional obligations and rights (India) 323-24; upsurge in stability (Cuba) 376; urban extended (China) 368; West Indies, 198

Family law (Lebanon), 120.

Family life: integrating work, 338-39; social revolution and fertility, 359

Family power, predicators, 10

Family size: powerlessness, 90; striving, 99

About The Editors

GEORGE KURIAN is Professor of Sociology at the University of Calgary, Alberta, Canada, and Editor of the *Journal of Comparative Family Studies*. His earlier works include *The Indian Family in Transition* and *Cross-Cultural Perspectives in Mate-Selection and Marriage* (Greenwood Press, 1979).

RATNA GHOSH is Associate Professor and Director of Graduate Studies and Research in the Faculty of Education at McGill University in Montreal. Her articles have appeared in the *Journal of Cross Cultural Psychology, Management and Labor Studies, Social Science Journal,* and other publications.